Three Pavilions by Sérgio Bernardes
Contribution to the Brazilian Modern Architectural Avant-Garde in the Mid-20th Century

Fausto Sombra

Latin America: Thoughts

Romano Guerra Editora
Nhamerica Platform

Management Coordination
Abilio Guerra
Fernando Luiz Lara
Silvana Romano Santos

Translation
Irene Sinnecker

Translation Review
Noemi Zein Telles
Irene Nagashima

Three Pavilions by Sérgio Bernardes
Contribution to the Brazilian Modern
Architectural Avant-Garde in the
Mid-20th Century

Fausto Sombra

Brasil 9
Editor
Abilio Guerra
Silvana Romano Santos

Graphic Design and Formatting
Dárkon V Roque

To Roberta Muccia and Beatriz
Sombra, for the family inspiration,
and João Claudio Parucher da Silva
(*in memoriam*), for the institutional
support.

Cultural Support

BERNARDES ARQUITETURA

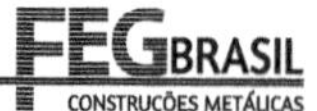

Three Pavilions by Sérgio Bernardes

Contribution to the Brazilian Modern Architectural Avant-Garde in the Mid-20th Century

Fausto Sombra

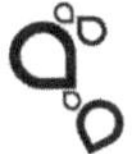

Romano Guerra Editora
Nhamerica Platform

São Paulo, Austin, 2023
1st edition

Summary

Foreword
Text and Context, Theory and Practice
Abilio Guerra

Supervising a postgraduate research, whether a master thesis
or a PhD dissertation, is a unique opportunity to establish
a stimulating relation between supervisor and advisee. To
the experience of the elder, or more experienced, is added
the enthusiasm and perspicacity of the younger, as a rule
more open to new perspectives for old problems (and, when
the problems are new, it is usually up to him to introduce
them into the shared conversation). At times, the mutual
improvement has consolidated more durable relations
based on respect and solidarity. In my specific case, some
masters supervisions developed in the Graduate Program
in Architecture and Urbanism at Mackenzie Presbyterian
University have unfolded into PhD supervisions.[1] And, for my
greater pleasure, two books have resulted from them: The
first, about the work of João Filgueiras Lima, Lelé, derived
from André Marques' masters research;[2] the second, a
synthesis of Fernanda Critelli's scientific initiation, masters
and PhD researches, all on the relation between Richard
Neutra and Latin America, especially Brazil.[3]

A double supervision is the case of researcher Fausto
Sombra. His master's degree, started in 2013, addressed the
work of the paulista architect Luís Saia, including his participation, alongside Eduardo Kneese de Mello, in the design of
the ephemeral pavilion of the 1st São Paulo Art Biennial in
1951, erected on Paulista Avenue,[4] and his long militancy in
the field of historical heritage, as a career professional at the
Service of National Historical and Artistic Heritage – Sphan.
During the research, the focus gradually shifted to interventions in Sítio Santo Antônio, a paradigmatic 17th century
São Paulo colonial complex, a decision consecrated after the
preliminary examination.[5]

As a disciple of Mário de Andrade – the last owner of
Sítio Santo Antônio, currently under the tutelage of the
Institute of National Historical and Artistic Heritage – Iphan
– and his successor as Technical Assistant to Sphan from
July 1938 onwards, Luís Saia was responsible for cataloging,

recovering and preserving an expressive number of colonial historical monuments, and occupied the head position of the 4th District of Sphan for a long time.[6] The foundation of the service, as a fruit of Mário's draft, took place in 1937, already under the Estado Novo regime. Subordinated to the Ministry of Education and Health created by Getúlio Vargas, and already under the responsibility of Minister Gustavo Capanema, the service was directed by Rodrigo Melo Franco de Andrade for two decades, a period that counted on the collaboration of leading figures in the Brazilian arts and culture, such as "Manuel Bandeira, Carlos Leão, Heloísa Alberto Torres, Francisco Marques dos Santos, Gilberto Freyre, Afonso Arinos de Melo Franco, Edgard Roquette Pinto, Carlos Drummond de Andrade, Sérgio Buarque de Holanda, Joaquim Cardoso, Vinicius de Moraes , Celso Cunha and Gustavo Barroso".[7]

The pleiad is formidable, but it was the backstage, especially the well-preserved internal documentation, that excited Fausto Sombra. I would venture saying that it was the handling of the primary material – in particular the correspondence exchanged between Luís Saia and Lúcio Costa,[8] Director of the Division of Studies and Listing for many years, and the documents referring to the Biennial Pavilion, under the tutelage of Wanda Svevo archive of the Biennial Foundation of São Paulo – that turned him into an attentive and astute researcher. By understanding the documents within a social and sociability context, attentive to dates and circumstances, assuming the existence of the expressed and implied content, that is, by discovering how the historian's work is carried out, Sombra wrote a beautiful master's thesis,[9] while preparing for the greater challenge that would follow.

His seemingly drastic shift of interest from the subject of the masters to the one of the PhD has, in my opinion, two explanations. The first, of a theoretical nature, came from the Brazilian peculiarity in which the themes of the preservation of colonial architecture and the defense of modern architecture converged on the same protagonists, an issue faced by his thesis. The second, of a practical nature, is the teaching internship – an activity in which the graduate student helps a professor, almost always his supervisor, in an undergraduate discipline[10] –, which the researcher completed in two different moments, both in the discipline Architecture in Brasil 2 – AB2, with me as tutor: Throughout the school year of 2013; and in the first half of 2017, on that occasion with the participation of Professor Felipe Contier. The syllabus of the discipline[11] covered the evolution of Brazilian architecture from the 1920s to the present, where the work of Sérgio Bernardes appeared within the discussion of the architecture of the second post-war, when Brazilian architects, particularly those from São Paulo, looked more closely at the North American modern architecture, especially its "Wrightian" aspect, more particularly the work of Richard Neutra.[12]

The cultural, social and economic background of the second half of the 1940s and 1950s, which covered the multiple relations between Brazil and the United States, was also part of the content of the AB2 discipline. During the war, in addition to the Department of State, which had a section dedicated to the region, Democratic President Franklin Delano Roosevelt created the Office for Coordination of Commercial and Cultural Relations between the American Republics, which operated from 1940 to 1946. Roosevelt appointed Republican Nelson Rockefeller to the head position of the institution, which had its name reduced to Office of the Coordinator of Inter-American Affairs in 1941. During his entire period as director of the Office – when he also held the position of president of the Museum of Modern Art – MoMA in New York –, Rockefeller became a constant presence in Brazil, with appearances at festivities alongside President Vargas, on coffee plantations in Paraná, in the cultural and artistic scenes of Rio de Janeiro and São Paulo...[13]

Rockefeller's action in the artistic field was significant as he cultivated philanthropy and the appreciation of modern art as an expression of the free forces of capitalism. In Rio de Janeiro, capital of the country at that time, the North American magnate supported the foundation of the Museum of Modern Art of Rio de Janeiro – MAM-RJ in 1948; Raymundo Ottoni de Castro Maya was its first president and received the spectacular headquarters building designed by Affonso Eduardo Reidy. His presence was even more expressive in São Paulo, where the North American policy towards Latin America, and the project of the local elites to build a solid institutional framework in the area of the arts were articulated. Thus, the foundation of important museums in São Paulo – São Paulo Museum of Art – MASP, in 1947, and Museum of Modern Art of São Paulo – MAM-SP, in 1948 –, the emergence of the Art Biennials from 1951, promoted by MAM-SP, the creation of Ibirapuera Park, opened to the public in 1954 during the celebrations of the 4th Centenary of São Paulo City, counted on symbolic figures such as Nelson Rockefeller, on the North American side, and Assis Chateaubriand and Francisco Matarazzo Sobrinho, "Ciccillo", on the Brazilian side.

If the politician Nelson Rockefeller had offered diplomatic facilities for the viability of various economic and cultural cooperations, as philanthropist, he donated fourteen works of modern art to MAM-SP in 1946. As fruits of artists linked to different modern directions – among them, Alexander Calder, Georg Grosz, Fernand Léger and Marc Chagall, Max Ernst –, the works expressed the "multiplicity and breadth of the American cultural pioneerism",[14] that is, they reiterated in a sophisticated and cult manner the American way of life founded on the benefits of capital. Upon arriving in Brazil,

> "On November 28, 1946, the donated works were officially delivered to the citizens of São Paulo by Eduardo Kneese de Mello, president of the Institute of Architects

of Brazil – IAB. They were supposed to help materialize the foundation of the first museum of modern art in Brazil. In the words of Rockefeller's attaché, Carleton Sprague Smith, this collection was the "injection of spirit" that was needed to unleash the old modern dream, already deeply discussed by the generation of the 1922 Modern Art Week. When the Museum of Modern Art was inaugurated in 1948, Rockefeller's donation became part of MAM's initial collection, and was ultimately transferred to the Museum of Contemporary Art of the University of São Paulo – MAC in 1963, where it has remained to this day."[15]

As part of the second generation of modern architects from Rio de Janeiro – at least one decade separated him from the first group of modern architects acting in Rio, such as Lúcio Costa (1902-1998), Jorge Machado Moreira (1904-1992), Oscar Niemeyer (1907-2012) and Affonso Eduardo Reidy (1909-1964) –, Sérgio Bernardes (1919-2002) was a son of the new times. Graduated in 1948 at the National School of Architecture of the University of Brazil, currently the Federal University of Rio de Janeiro, his work began to consolidate precisely in the post-war period, when the North American culture was imposed as the greatest reference in the Brazilian context, leaving the European influence – and the French, as its greatest expression in the country[16] – in the background.

The presence of Le Corbusier, so decisive in the works of older colleagues, lost prominence in Bernardes' thinking, and this vacuum was occupied – according to Fausto Sombra – by the "works of North American architects or those based in the United States: The Case Study House n. 8, (1945), by Charles and Ray Eames; the Coocon House in Siesta Key, Florida, (1948), by Paul Rudolph; the Dorton Arena in Raleigh, North Carolina, (1952), by Polish-born architect Matthew Nowicki; the geodesics developed by Richard Buckminster

Fuller, mainly from the 1960s onwards." Therefore, it was not surprising that the work of the architect from Rio de Janeiro had two special moments in the lands of São Paulo: in 1955, with the success of the Volta Redonda Pavilion (1954-1955), promoted by the Companhia Siderúrgica Nacional – CSN (National Steelworks Company) for the 1st São Paulo International Fair, and built at the recently inaugurated Ibirapuera Park; and in 1963, when his work was exhibited in a special room at the 7th Art Biennial, also at Ibirapuera Park.

Fausto Sombra's research is based on some academic texts that converge in the affirmation of the greater affinity of Bernardes' work with the cultural and technological experience underway in the United States; Yves Bruand's suggestion about the proximity of Sérgio Bernardes' thinking and work to the North American context – he stated that the São Cristóvão Pavilion (1957-1960), built in Rio de Janeiro, was inspired by a work from 1953-1954, built in Raleigh, North Carolina, by Nowicki, Severud and Deitrick[17] – was developed by other authors, notably Ana Luiza Nobre and Alexandre Bahia Vanderlei.[18] However, the initial work concerns, which focused on Bernardes' interest in America, were gradually concentrated on three projects in particular, whose shared nature allowed for experimentalism: The aforementioned Volta Redonda Pavilion, São Cristóvão Pavilion, and the Brazil Pavilion for the Brussels International Exhibition (1957-1958). The temporal covering of the three projects – designed and built in a short period, from 1954 to 1960 – allowed placing them in the same context of architectural culture. Thus, unlike the master's thesis, the preliminary examination of the PhD dissertation occurred with the final theme already established.[19]

Also in 2017, during the period of mandatory credits, Fausto Sombra and Abilio Guerra established the criteria for the model of the CSN Pavilion in Ibirapuera (1954-1955), the first of a series of three models to be executed by the company Practica Maquetes. At this initial moment of the research, it was not yet known how this one and the other models would be used in the work, but their relevance was supported by the didactic experience of AB2 discipline, which had in the models made by students one of its main pedagogical tools. The final thematic decision had not been made, and at that moment, there was still the expectation of including one of the two versions for Hotel Tropical de Manaus, a non-built project. The first version, from 1963, envisaged a geodesic inspired by Richard Buckminster Fuller, with 300 meters in diameter, and a cylindrical tower with 26 meters in diameter, where the suites of the undertaking would be located on the higher levels. In the second version, from 1970, an equivalent tower would serve as a mast for a huge tent that would cover an immense area of forest, a solution that bore some resemblance to the Khan Shatyr Shopping and Entertainment Center (2006-2010), built in Astana, Kazakhstan, designed by British architect Norman Foster (the anticipation seen here was not exclusive; it was surprising how his Brussels pavilion anticipated, by at least one decade, the experiments with tensile structures carried out by German architect Frei Otto). Hotel Tropical Tambaú[20] was also considered as a design to be studied, and was even visited by the researcher, but it was discarded when the selection closed around the three pavilions.

A peculiar aspect of Fausto Sombra's work was its ostensible dissemination during the research development period, with the publication of articles, presentations in classrooms, presence in seminars, tables, congresses and exhibitions. In 2018, after the construction of the second model conceived by the advisee and supervisor – the Brazil Pavilion at the Brussels Universal Exhibition (1957-1958) –, Sombra presented a communication about the project at the 5th Enanparq, held in Salvador in 2018.[21] The centenary of Sérgio Bernardes' birth in 2019 had increased interest in the research in progress, opening the possibility for several participations: Publication of articles in the magazine *Monolito* and journal *Cadernos Proarq*;[22] participation, alongside Guilherme Wisnik, in the debate on the feature-length documentary *Bernardes*, shortly after its exhibition at São Paulo's headquarter of the Institute of Architects of Brazil – IAB-SP;[23] participation in the seminar *SB.100 – Sérgio Bernardes*, held at the School of Architecture and Urbanism of the Federal University of Rio de Janeiro – FAU UFRJ, when he presented, in a synthesized way, some of the ideas present in this book;[24] and collaboration on the *Sérgio Bernardes 100 anos* exhibition,[25] with the loan of the model built for the Pavilion of the International Trade and Industry Fair in São Cristóvão (1957-1960), the third model conceived for the research and built in 2019.

The dissemination strategy for the dissertation in progress culminated in the exhibition *Três Pavilhões de Sérgio Bernardes* held at the Mackenzie Historic and Cultural Center in the second half of 2019.[26] In addition to the three models made during the research, it exhibited pieces machined to the scale 1:1, panels with drawings and photos of the works, notebooks with sheets of the three projects, documents and a slide show synthesizing the making of process for the three pavilions, from conception to construction. In order to establish the historical context and the evolutionary meaning, the three designs by Sérgio Bernardes were arranged in a timeline composed of a select group of Brazilian pavilions:

> "Brazil Pavilion at the New York World's Fair, 1939 (Lúcio Costa and Oscar Niemeyer); Riposatevi Pavilion at the XIII Milan Biennale, 1964 (Lúcio Costa); Brazil Pavilion at Expo'70 Osaka, 1970 (Paulo Mendes da Rocha), Brazil Pavilion at Expo Seville, 1992 (Alvaro Puntoni, Angelo Bucci and João Oswaldo Villela, not built), Santa Sé Pavilion at the Venice Biennale, 2018 (Carla Juaçaba); and Brazil Pavilion, Expo Dubai 2020 (José Paulo Gouveia, Marta Moreira, Milton Braga and Martin Benavidez, not yet built)."[27]

After the exhibition at Mackenzie was dismantled, the three models and the machined pieces were loaned to the re-edition of the *Sérgio Bernardes 100 anos* exhibition, now at National Museum of Fine Arts in Rio de Janeiro, opened in the late 2019.[28] The exhibition was part of the official calendar of Rio World Capital of Architecture, and one of the preparatory events for the 27th World Congress of Architects – UIA 2020 Rio – to be held in Rio de Janeiro in July 2020, later postponed due to the Covid-19 pandemic.

After so many facts and ephemerides, on February 28, 2020, in the videoconference room of the School of Architecture and Urbanism of the Mackenzie Presbyterian University, in the morning, Fausto Sombra defended his PhD dissertation on the three experimental works by Sérgio Bernardes, all of them non-existent today, as a result of history and fate – and understand the omission of the reasons as an extra incentive to read what follows. The examination panel formed by Abilio Guerra (supervisor, FAU Mackenzie), Lauro Cavalcanti (Casa Roberto Marinho), Antonio Carlos Barossi (FAU USP), Helena Ayoub (FAU USP) and Rafael Perrone (FAU Mackenzie), after argumentation, questions and answers, declared that the dissertation[29] had been "approved with praise and distinction."[30] In the supplementary minutes, the opinion of the examining panel has stated the following:

> The panel has highlighted the excellence of the documental research, as well as the reconstitution of the three projects analyzed by the dissertation as a form of research, through redrawings (3D modeling), models and objects in 1:1 scale. It also understands that the text has inserted architect Sérgio Bernardes and his production in the general context of Brazilian modern architecture, revealing its quality. Faced with such predicates, the panel has indicated the dissertation for publication.[31]

The indication of the panel has been accomplished by the present book.

Notes

1. André Marques, Fernanda Critelli and Ana Carolina Brugnera carried out the following masters and PhD researches: André Felipe Rocha Marques, "A obra de João Filgueiras Lima, Lelé: projeto, técnica e racionalização"; André Felipe Rocha Marques, "Aldary Toledo: entre arte e arquitetura"; Fernanda Critelli, "Richard Neutra e o Brasil"; Fernanda Critelli, "Richard Neutra: conexões latino-americanas"; Ana Carolina Brugnera, "Meio ambiente cultural da Amazônia brasileira: dos modos de vida à moradia do caboclo ribeirinho"; Ana Carolina Brugnera, "Rumo às comunidades criativas: as articulações entre natureza e cultura na gestão sustentável das paisagens culturais do Peruaçu, Brasil".
2. André Marques, *Lelé: dialogues with Neutra and Prouvé*.
3. Fernanda Critelli, *Richard Neutra and Brasil*.
4. Secondary theme in the masters thesis, the pavilion theme is better developed in a later article: Fausto Sombra, "O pavilhão da I Bienal do MAM SP: fatos, relatos, historiografia e correlações com o Masp e o antigo Belvedere Trianon".
5. The panel, which took place on February 27, 2014, had the valuable participation of Cecília Rodrigues dos Santos (FAU Mackenzie) and Maria Lúcia Bressan Pinheiro (FAU USP).
6. Luís Saia became a mythological character within the structure of Iphan; among the curious stories told and retold by its employees, the one about the utility vehicle donated by England to the Brazilian government after the Second World War stands out. See: Mauro Bondi, "Se o nosso Land Rover falasse: os primeiros automóveis que trabalharam na preservação do patrimônio em São Paulo".
7. Teresinha Marinho, "Notícia biográfica," 19. See: Cêça Guimaraens, "Rodrigo Melo Franco de Andrade e a paisagem hiperreal do patrimônio".
8. The epistolary relationship between Costa and Saia was explored in an article at the beginning of his master's research: Fausto Sombra, "Luís Saia e Lúcio Costa: a parceria no Sítio Santo Antônio".
9. Fausto Sombra, "Luís Saia e o restauro do sítio Santo Antônio: diálogos modernos na conformação arquitetônica paulista".
10. In addition to other advisees, Fernanda Critelli, André Marques and Ana Carolina Brugnera, who did their master's and PhD studies with me, have also shared the same experience, when, in addition to helping in the classes, they had the opportunity of presenting their research in the form of a class.

11. The discipline "Architecture in Brazil 2" disappeared with the reform of the pedagogical structure in the School of Architecture and Urbanism at Mackenzie Presbyterian University, which became effective in early 2018. Its content was taken over by a new discipline, Theory and History of Architecture and Urbanism 1 – THAU 1.

12. In addition to Fernanda Critelli's scientific initiation, masters and PhD research, master's student Sabrina Pereira tread the same field: Sabrina Souza Bom Pereira, "Rodolpho Ortenblad Filho: estudo sobre as residências".

13. Two books and an article, by the same author, cover this theme in its most varied aspects: Antonio Pedro Tota, *O imperialismo sedutor: a americanização do Brasil na época da Segunda Guerra*; Antonio Pedro Tota, *O amigo americano: Nelson Rockefeller e o Brasil*; Antonio Pedro Tota, "Como um Rockefeller sonhou em modernizar o Brasil".

14. Carolina Rossetti de Toledo, "A doação Nelson Rockefeller de 1946 no Acervo do Museu de Arte Contemporânea da USP", 150.

15. Ibid., 150-151

16. Coincidentally, Lúcio Costa, Affonso Eduardo Reidy and Jorge Machado Moreira were born in France, and mastering the language of their native country was certainly one of the elements that facilitated the group's approach to Le Corbusier and his ideas.

17. Yves Bruand, *Arquitetura contemporânea no Brasil*, 259.

18. Ana Luiza Nobre, "Fios cortantes: projeto e produto, arquitetura e design no Rio de Janeiro (1950-70)"; Alexandre Bahia Vanderlei, "Sérgio Bernardes: el desafio de la técnica".

19. The preliminary examination of the research "Os Pavilhões de Sérgio Bernardes: Volta Redonda, Bruxelas e São Cristóvão: contribuição à vanguarda arquitetônica moderna brasileira em meados do século 20", by Fausto Sombra, took place on March 8, 2019, with the participation of Rafael Perrone (Mackenzie) and Helena Ayoub (USP).

20. Unlike the project for Manaus, the Tropical Hotel in João Pessoa was built and inaugurated in 1971. Germana Rocha, Nelci Tinem, and Marcio Cotrim, "Hotel Tambaú, de Sérgio Bernardes: diálogo entre poética construtiva e estrutura formal".

21. Fausto Sombra, "Sérgio
     Bernardes e o pavilhão brasileiro
     na Exposição Universal e
     Internacional de Bruxelas, 1958:
     industrialização, inventividade
     e experimentação" (annals).
     The article was published the
     following year in the academ-
     ic-scientific journal: *Arquitextos*:
     Fausto Sombra, "Sérgio
     Bernardes e o pavilhão brasileiro
     na Exposição Universal e
     Internacional de Bruxelas, 1958:
     industrialização, inventividade e
     experimentação".
22. Fausto Sombra, "Um breve
     olhar sobre a obra da família
     Bernardes"; Fausto Sombra, "Os
     pavilhões de Sérgio Bernardes:
     Volta Redonda, Bruxelas e
     São Cristóvão. Contribuição
     à vanguarda arquitetônica
     moderna brasileira em meados
     do século 20". The second
     publication was dedicated to
     architect Sérgio Bernardes and
     compiled by the editor-in-chief
     Ethel Pinheiro Santana.
23. The debate, which took place on
     Jul. 16, 2019, was mediated by
     architect Guido D'Elia Otero.

24. The seminar *SB.100 – Sérgio
     Bernardes*, promoted by Proarq
     and organized by Professor Ana
     Amora, took place on Aug. 20,
     2019.
25. Exhibition *Sérgio Bernardes
     100 anos*, curated by Kykah
     Bernardes and Adriana Caúla,
     Centro Carioca de Design, Rio
     de Janeiro, from Apr. 17 to Jun.
     1, 2019. At the exhibition, on
     May 7, Fausto Sombra presented
     part of the research during the
     debate on the work of Sérgio
     Bernardes mediated by Professor
     Ana Amora, from FAU UFRJ.
26. Exhibition *Três Pavilhões de
     Sérgio Bernardes*, curated
     by Abilio Guerra and Fausto
     Sombra, Mackenzie Historic and
     Cultural Center, São Paulo, from
     Sep. 19 to Nov. 14, 2019.
27. According to the curatorial text
     of the exhibition: Abilio Guerra,
     Fausto Sombra, *Três pavilhões
     de Sérgio Bernardes*, exhibition
     at the Mackenzie Historic and
     Cultural Center. *Expo Dubai
     2020* in the United Arab
     Emirates was originally sched-
     uled to take place from 20 Oct.
     2020 to 10 Apr. 2021, but due to
     the Covid-19 pandemic, it was
     rescheduled to the period from
     1 Oct. 2021 to Mar. 31, 2022. The
     Brazil Pavilion was dismantled
     after the event.

28.   Exhibition *Sérgio Bernardes
        100 anos*, curated by Kykah
        Bernardes and Adriana Caúla,
        Museu Nacional de Belas Artes,
        Rio de Janeiro, 17 Dec. 2019 to
        14 Mar. 2020.
29.   Fausto Sombra, "Três pavil-
        hões de Sérgio Bernardes:
        Volta Redonda, Bruxelas e
        São Cristóvão. Contribuição
        à vanguarda arquitetônica
        moderna brasileira em meados
        do século 20".
30.   The final panel took place on
        Feb. 28, 2020, in the videocon-
        ference room of the Faculty
        of Architecture and Urbanism,
        Mackenzie Presbyterian
        University, at 9:30 am, with
        the presence of the following
        members: Abilio Guerra (super-
        visor), Lauro Cavalcanti (Casa
        Roberto Marinho, virtually),
        Antonio Carlos Barossi (FAU
        USP), Helena Ayoub (FAU
        USP) and Rafael Perrone (FAU
        Mackenzie). The thesis was
        approved with praise and
        distinction, with indication for
        publication.
31.   Supplementary text "Avaliação
        da tese de doutorado", Feb.
        28, 2020, signed by the five
        members of the panel.

In today's world, man is continually besieged by the reflections of the environment in which he moves. He is never properly "alone", claimed an Italian thinker. His sensibility is tormented by the anxieties of modern existence. The exterior, with its anonymous influences, dominates him. Imperceptibly, he sympathizes with the movements of contemporary civilization. For this reason, his attitude towards realities cannot be that of an Arcadia, abandoning itself in sentimental manifestations, in a meek world.

The vision that modern man forms of things is merged with dynamic values. The incredible achievements of technique keep preparing a new world for his senses. Therefore, the perceptions accumulated incessantly in these experiences, are translated into intuitive and autonomous forms, without subjection to classical molds, in attempts to explain "his thinking".

Raul Bopp, *Movimentos modernistas no Brasil* (1922-1928), 9.

The human power
of creation
is inexhaustible,
and develops
by the sum of knowledge,
in a fantastic progression,
generating
a technological world.
This development
is so strong that
at times,
supplants man himself.
It is the privilege
of an architect
to establish,
through his sensibility,
the balance
between technology
and man.
Sérgio Bernardes, Special Room Sérgio Bernardes[1]

Introduction
Notes on Critique and Method

Critical Overview

The present publication seeks to be inserted into the critical panorama of the relevant work bequeathed by Sérgio Bernardes. Still restricted because it is under construction, the critique and history of the architect's work has already relied on important research and analysis, developed by researchers over the last few years. Twenty years after the death of the carioca architect Sérgio Wladimir Bernardes, there are only four books dedicated exclusively to his work, all published after 1999: "Expo 58: the Brasil Pavilion of Sérgio Bernardes," authored by Paul Meurs, Mil De Kooning and Rony De Meyer, an agile publication that marked the participation of the Department of Architecture and Urban Planning of the University of Ghent in the 4th International Biennial of Architecture of São Paulo, held from November 19, 1999 to January 25, 2000;[2] *Sérgio Bernardes: herói de uma tragédia moderna*, by Lauro Cavalcanti, published in 2004,[3] a small biographical book in which the author sought, from the first pages, to emphasize and present the "multifaceted and plural nature"[4] of a character who practiced skills ranging from "architect of buildings to race pilot";[5] *Sérgio Bernardes: doutrina de uma civilização tropical*, authored by Sérgio's stepson, Felipe Guanaes, a book from 2016,[6] relating his memories of coexisting with the architect at the Laboratório de Investigações Conceituais – LIC (Laboratory of Conceptual Investigations).

The fourth and last book – *Sérgio Bernardes*, from 2010,[7] compiled by Kykah Bernardes[8] and Lauro Cavalcanti – is divided into two parts. The first presents a selection of essays by ten researchers – Lauro Cavalcanti, Ana Luiza Nobre, Farès el Dahdah, Murillo Boabaid, João Pedro Bachheuser, André Correa do Lago, Monica Paciello Vieira, Rafael Cardoso, Guilherme Wisnik and Alfredo Britto – who had already pored over and reflected on the work of the carioca architect. And the second contains nine selected texts, authored by the architect himself, mostly dealing with themes related to urbanism and large-scale regional planning; and the initial text, entitled "Considerações de base", opening this second part, was extracted from *Cidade: a sobrevivência do poder,*[9] the only book published by Bernardes throughout his career.

Four books cannot be taken as an inexpressive bibliography – even more so in a country where the preliminary survey of the work of several relevant architects is still in progress –, but they do not seem to correspond to the expectations created by the character's trajectory, since Sérgio Bernardes, at a certain point in his career, had obtained prestige similar to that enjoyed by his professional colleague and friend Oscar Niemeyer. This statement was confirmed by the words of Roberto Segre, who equated Bernardes not only with the name of Oscar Niemeyer, but also with that of Lúcio Costa:

> "On Saturday, June 15, architect Sérgio Bernardes passed away in Rio de Janeiro, aged 83. Despite the two decades of age that distanced him from Lúcio Costa and one from Oscar Niemeyer, with both, he formed the trilogy of the "great" modern carioca professionals [...]. For students at the FAU in Buenos Aires, who graduated in the early 1960s, the mandatory pilgrimage to Brazil had three main objectives: knowing the recently founded Brasília by Lúcio Costa; touring the Pampulha complex by Niemeyer in Belo Horizonte, the cradle of Brazilian "modernism"; and visiting Sérgio Bernardes' houses in and around Rio de Janeiro."[10]

During the 1950s to the 1970s, the name Sérgio Bernardes gained great prominence in the architectural world – at the 7th Biennial held at Ibirapuera Park, in 1963, his work was exhibited in a special room – and appeared frequently in specialized publications, such as *Acrópole, Módulo, Arquitetura e Engenharia* etc. His fame began to transcend the specific field of his area of activity, gaining notoriety in the social and cultural milieu, deserving articles in popular magazines of wide circulation. It stood out in particular in the weekly *Manchete*, a vehicle in which the architect's name had a prominent and constant presence.[11] His first appearance in the magazine dates from December 6, 1952 – when he was aligned with other important architects from the carioca school – in the cover story entitled "Brasil potência arquitetônica."

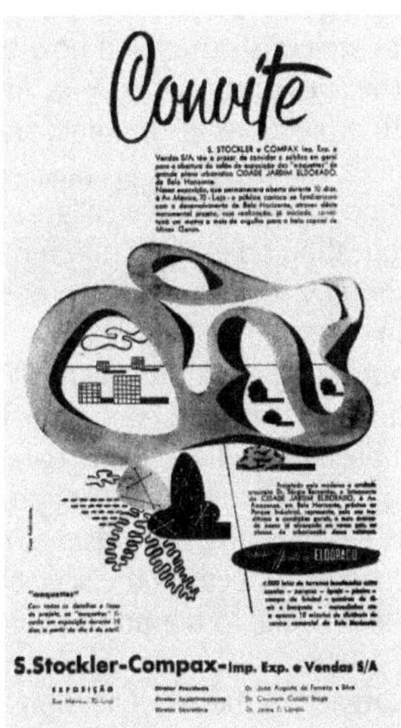

Advertisement for a housing development in Belo Horizonte, highlighting the "modern and bold architect Dr. Sérgio Bernardes" as the author of the project, published in the Rio de Janeiro newspaper *Correio da Manhã*, on April 4, 1954. Hemeroteca Digital Brasileira / Fundação Biblioteca Nacional.

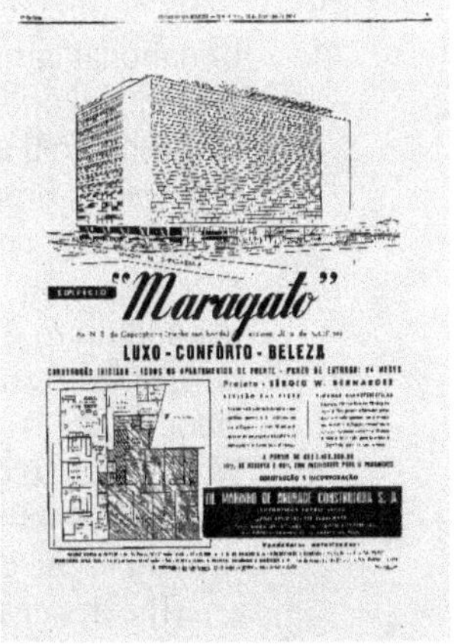

Advertisement for the Maragato residential building in Rio de Janeiro, highlighting Sérgio Bernardes as the author of the project, published in the Rio de Janeiro newspaper *Correio da Manhã*, on February 13, 1952. Hemeroteca Digital Brasileira / Fundação Biblioteca Nacional.

The *Manchete* magazine no. 678, of April 1965, brought a large draft of "Rio do futuro" illustrated by the designs and ideas of Sérgio Bernardes' office, with proposals for mega-structures in line with the proposals of international avant-garde names, such as the English group Archigram. This "foresight of the wonderful city in the electronics century" revealed the growing role played by urbanism and urban planning in the architect's thinking.[12]

Bernardes' book – *Cidade: a sobrevivência do poder* – was released during the period of celebrity and public recognition. Published in 1975 by Guavira Editores, the text reflects on the way our cities are constituted and how this model influences directly the lives of its inhabitants. After analyzing the country's growth projections at the time, and the territory's natural resources, the tiny book proposes the creation of national lattices and their respective cells applied on an orthogonal grid, suggesting an entirely different format from the disordered and improvised occupation process commonly observed in Brazilian cities. At the same time, it takes into account "the need for hiring workforce responsible for the execution of housing, industrial and commercial units,"[13] in addition to the "housing need and other parallel social necessities, resulting from the very mobilization of these labor flows."[14] From then onwards, the presence of Bernardes' work began to gradually disappear in the specialized press and in the mainstream media, to the point of almost disappearing in the early 1980s.

The designs addressed in these publications – a relatively small number compared to the total developed throughout his life – are structured as the well-known work of Sérgio Bernardes, being the ones that will be revisited by scholars in the future, but leaving behind a significant production, which will remain hidden under the fog, unreachable by the eyes of scholars and the general public. Thus, the real dimension of the work conceived by the architect is buried, consequently creating an obstacle for the formation of a critique

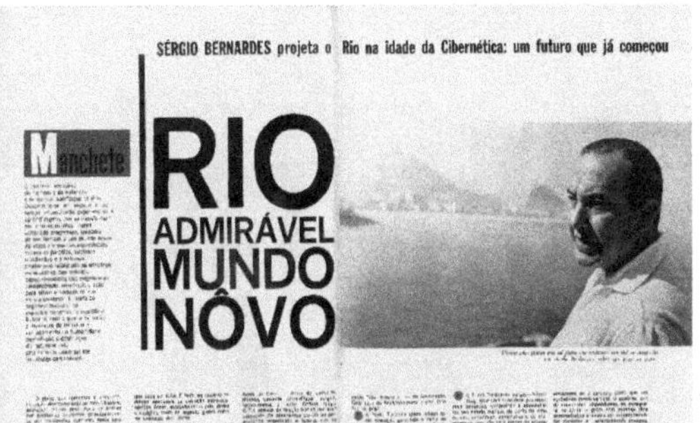

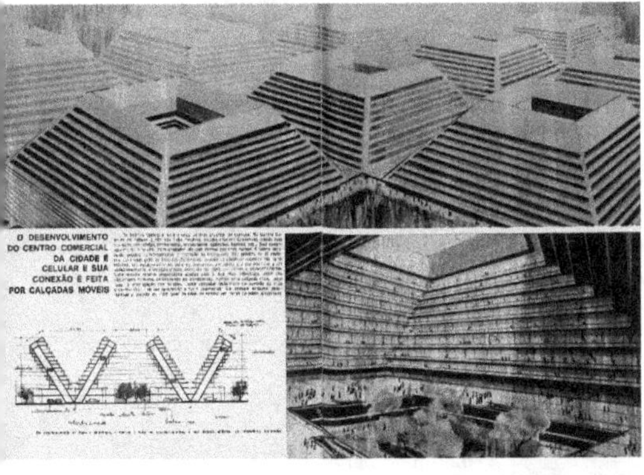

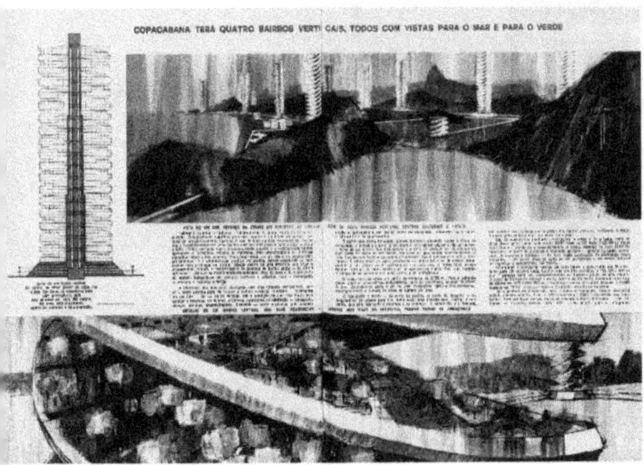

Article by Sérgio Bernardes, "Rio, Admirable New World," published in *Manchete* magazine, no. 678 (special edition Future Rio), April 17, 1965. Fausto Sombra Collection

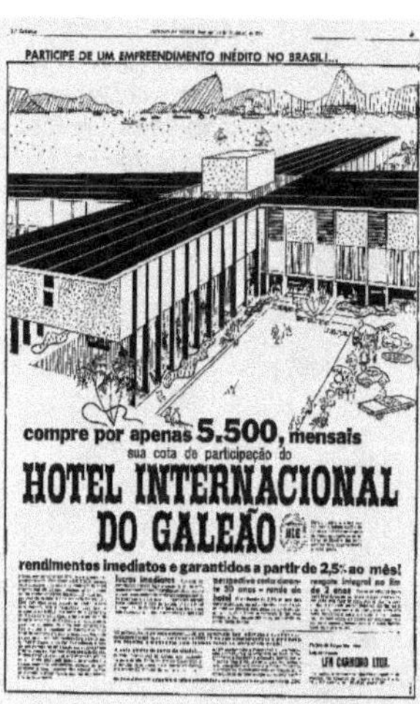

Advertisement for the Internacional Hotel at Galeão in Rio de Janeiro, highlighting Sérgio Bernardes as the author of the project, published in the Rio de Janeiro newspaper *Correio da Manhã*, on November 10, 1963. Hemeroteca Digital Brasileira / Fundação Biblioteca Nacional.

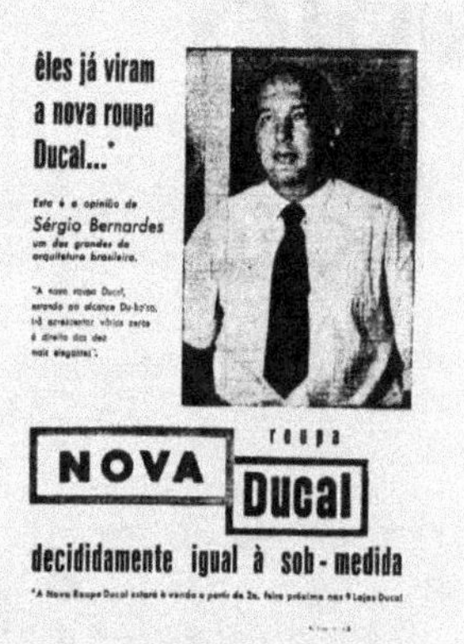

Sérgio Bernardes featured in an advertisement for clothing by the now-defunct brand Ducal, published in the Rio de Janeiro newspaper *Tribuna da Imprensa*, on April 27, 1956. Hemeroteca Digital Brasileira / Fundação Biblioteca Nacional.

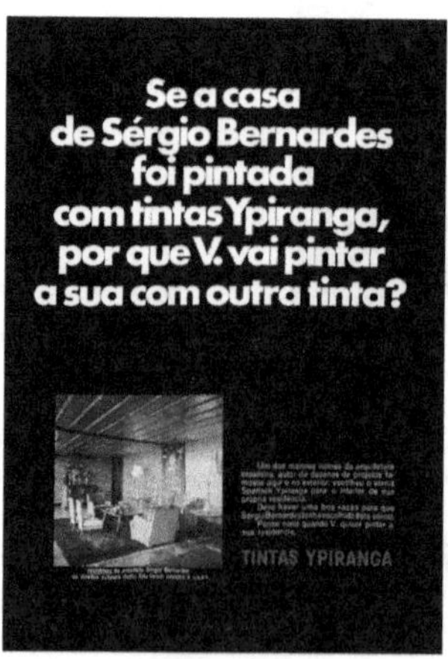

Advertisement for the Ypiranga paint company, using as its theme the house of the architect Sérgio Bernardes, published in the Rio de Janeiro magazine *Jóia*, no. 177, in May 1968. Hemeroteca Digital Brasileira / Fundação Biblioteca Nacional.

that could match the carat of his work. In order to clarify the disconnection between the visibility and the relevance of the architect's work, it is necessary to highlight that the Sérgio Bernardes collection has more than thirty thousand documents, divided into more than 22 thousand plans, sketches, letters and various documents, in addition to an approximate total of 8,500 photographs. This material, enough to occupy around three hundred boxes,[15] was transferred from the collection of the Oscar Niemeyer Foundation, an institution that had kept this vast material for thirteen years, between 1997 and 2010,[16] to the Núcleo de Pesquisa e Documentação – NPD (Research and Documentation Nucleus) at FAU UFRJ, where it currently is.

The evident mismatch between the documental dimension and the critical scarcity of the aforementioned work is due, among other issues, to the gradual process of ostracism suffered by Sérgio Bernardes' work from the 1980s onwards. Considering his constant search for protagonism, fueled by his sanguine temperament, it is likely that the explanation given by Kykah Bernardes and some of the architect's closest collaborators could be the most determining: they attribute the forgetfulness to the negligence with which the architect himself treated the advertising and dissemination of his architectural production. It is even much more likely that the change in mood about his work, especially among the architects, was directly related to the service he rendered to commissions presented by the civil-military government during the dictatorial regime.

Perhaps the most controversial of them, due to its high symbolic content, was the design for the National Pavilion Monument, inaugurated in November 1972.[17] Formed by a set of 24 steel rods, arranged in a circular manner, hoisted in parts and structured on top of each other, the 100-meter high mast was responsible for holding the largest flag raised in Brazil. Built at the back of the Three Powers Plaza and in contrast to the white color of the buildings that compose the

plaza, the monument caused embarrassment to his colleague
and friend, Oscar Niemeyer, who remained in exile abroad for
more than a decade, from 1966 to 1980.

Another iconic building by Sérgio Bernardes, designed
for the military, was the Castelo Branco Mausoleum in
Fortaleza. A monument inaugurated on the July 18 of the
same year of 1972, next to the Abolition Palace, then seat
of the Ceará government. With an evident influence of
the so-called modern Californian architecture, the palace
was inaugurated in 1970, but its design and beginning of
construction predate the military coup of 1964.[18]

Ultimately, in line with the plans for the occupation of
the Amazon, carried out by the military regime during the
1970s, Bernardes had developed architectural and urban
designs for the region, which were not accomplished. His
approach to the military government was not well regarded
by an expressive part of his colleagues, among whom, there
was a hegemony of left-wing thinking at the time. These
episodes have become, in a way, the most plausible explanation for the gradual departure of his name from the specialized media, from events in the area and, as a result, from the
important training centers for architects in the country from
the late 1970s. Thus, in the early 1980s, only a few spoke
about the architect and his work, with the exception of Hugo
Gouthier, former Brazilian ambassador to Brussels, who dedicated some pages of his 1982 book *Presença: memórias*[19] to
the memory of his experiences with Sérgio Bernardes during
the conception and construction of the Brazil Pavilion in
Brussels.

The first attempt to reverse the situation – somehow
a frustrated experience since it was an isolated event in
the period – has occured with two related events in 1983:
a retrospective exhibition on the work of Sérgio Bernardes
in Rio de Janeiro, by the Museum of Modern Art of Rio
de Janeiro – MAM-RJ, aided by Olínio Coelho and Lauro
Cavalcanti; and a special issue of *Módulo* magazine, from

October-November 1983, publishing a synthesis of significant works conceived by the architect throughout his career,
corresponding in practice, to the exhibition catalogue.[20] At
that moment, while being converted into an urban planner
concerned with the future of cities, the architect himself no
longer showed any interest in his remarkable architectural
designs, even by creating obstacles to their presence in the
exhibition.[21]

More than a decade after the exhibition at MAM and
publication in the *Módulo* magazine, precisely in 1997, architect and researcher João Pedro Backheuser developed the
first academic research on the work of Sérgio Bernardes.[22]
As a specialization course monograph – therefore, without
the obligation to delve into its considerations –, the work
has great value, as it has presented, in a context of oblivion,
some of the most expressive works by the carioca architect,
and has gathered statements by Bernardes produced exclusively for the research. These are the first cornerstones to

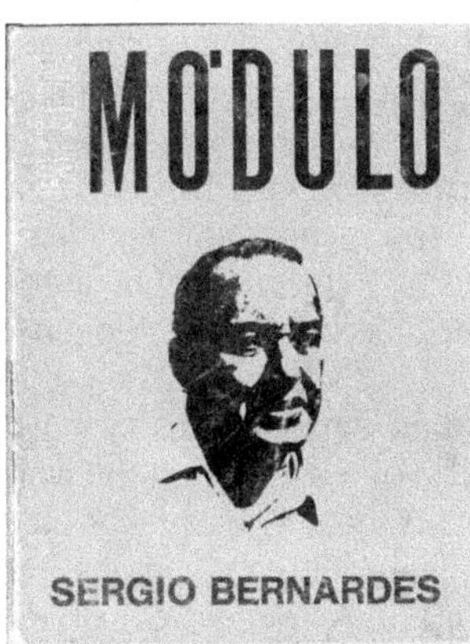
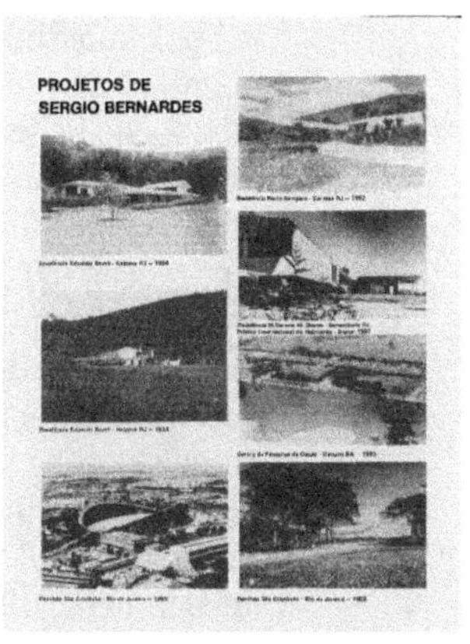

Cover with a photo of Sérgio
Bernardes and an article about the
Eduardo Baouth residence, Itaipava
RJ, 1934, published in the magazine
Módulo, special edition about the
architect, October and November of
1983. Sérgio Bernardes Collection
– Memory Project / Bernardes
Architecture Office

build, in the future, a broader understanding of the architect's life and work.

A few years later, in 2001, engineer Jayme Mason released his memoir book *Humanismo, ciência, engenharia: perspectivas, depoimentos, testemunhos*, commenting on his coexistence with Bernardes for more than half a century, highlighting his great qualities as a human and professional being, contributing to the gradual resumption of interest in the carioca architect.

After Sérgio Bernardes passed away, on June 15, 2002, some memorial articles were immediately published, most of them on the Vitruvius portal, the material was used as main source for the architect's biography, authored by Lauro Cavalcanti and released in 2004.[23] Soon after, in a virtuous interaction involving an expressive group of researchers, there was a slow, but rather continuous growth of academic research and other productions on the architect's work, with dissemination in the form of scientific articles,[24] Master's theses,[25] PhD dissertations,[26] references in exhibitions,[27] and a book published abroad.[28] As well as a film, the 2014 documentary *Bernardes*, directed by Gustavo Gama Rodrigues and Paulo de Barros,[29] was awarded a prize by the São Paulo Association of Art Critics – APCA, 2014.[30] The film presents facts and testimonies by friends, family members, colleagues and researchers, seeking to reconstruct Sérgio Bernardes' image in his multiple facets: architect, pilot, inventor, father, husband, grandfather, public figure, etc.

The centenary of Sérgio Bernardes' birth was another impulse to the process of rediscovering the work of the architect and urban planner. The event was the theme for a special issue of the digital journal *Cadernos Proarq* no. 32, of October 2019, featuring eleven articles on the architect's work,[31] as well as four important exhibitions.

The first – held at the Carioca Design Center – CCD, in Rio de Janeiro, between April and May 2019, entitled *Sérgio Bernardes – 100 anos*,[32] curated by Adriana Caúla and Kykah

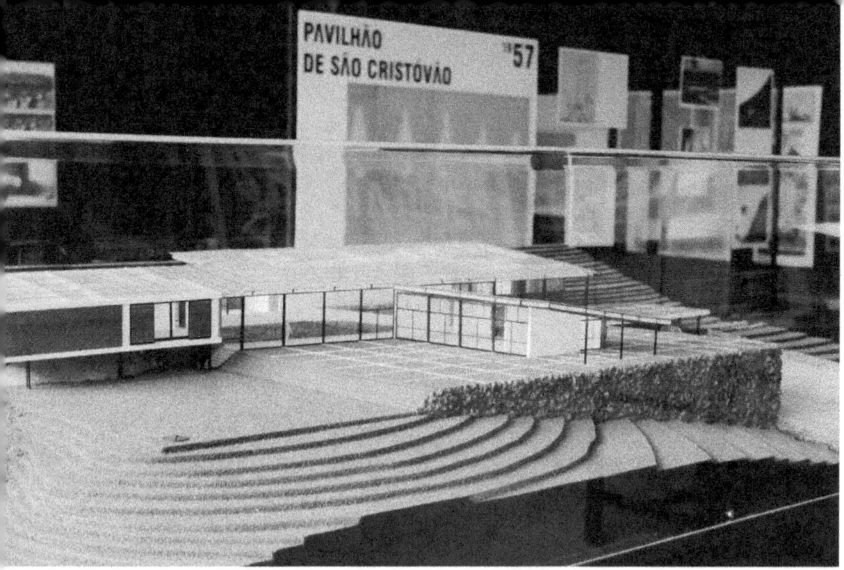

Exhibition SB-100, curated by Ana Amora, Claudio Brandão, and Thaysa Malaquias. FAU UFRJ, Rio de Janeiro, from August 19, 2019, to June 20, 2019. Promotional photo by CAU/RJ

Exhibition "Three Pavilions by Sérgio Bernardes," curated by Abilio Guerra and Fausto Sombra. Mackenzie Historic and Cultural Center, São Paulo, from September 18 to November 14, 2019. Photo by Abilio Guerra

Exhibition "Sérgio Bernardes 100 Years." Curated by Kykah Bernardes and Adriana Caula. Carioca Design Center, Rio de Janeiro, from April 17 to June 1, 2019. Photo by Fausto Sombra

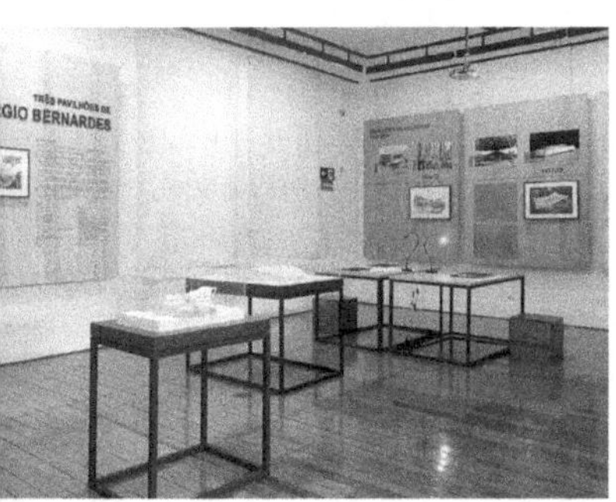

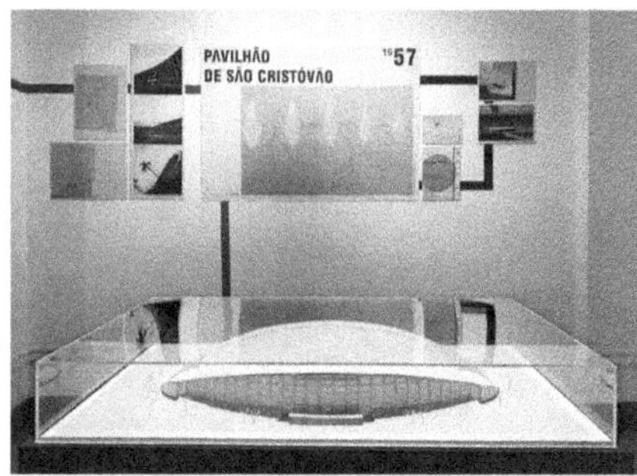

Bernardes – exhibited the architect's designs built in the city of Rio de Janeiro that were nominated to be listed by the Institute Rio Patrimony of Humanity in 2019. The second one – held on the mezzanine floor of FAU UFRJ, in August 2019, entitled *SB-100* – is a small exhibition together with a seminar organized by Professor Ana Amora.[33] The third was held at the Mackenzie Historic and Cultural Center, between September and November 2019, entitled *Três Pavilhões de Sérgio Bernardes*, curated by Abilio Guerra and Fausto Sombra.[34] This exhibition aroused so much interest in the public that it was extended twice and received two reviews, one by Rodrigo Queiroz, professor at FAU USP, and another by Adalberto Retto Jr., professor at FAAC Unesp, both published in October 2019.[35] The fourth exhibition, again entitled *Sérgio Bernardes – 100 anos*, was held at the National Museum of Fine Arts in Rio de Janeiro, from December 17, 2019, an event then linked to the programs of the International Union of Architects – UIA 2020, remaining open until March 14, 2020.[36]

Slowly and gradually, the ostracism scenario has been reversed, as attested by the numbers presented by the survey carried out by the Núcleo de Pesquisa e Documentação – NPD (Research and Documentation Nucleus), an agency linked to FAU UFRJ, and currently responsible for cataloging and conservation of the collection of important names in Brazilian architecture, such as Sérgio Bernardes. According to João Claudio Parucher da Silva,[37] archivist responsible for the research, during the interval between February 2013 and August 2019, consultations carried out on the collection of architect Sérgio Bernardes corresponded to 39% of the total accesses made at this institution.[38] This number is more than double of the consultations on the work of the Roberto Brothers, with 17%; and three times the consultations on the work of Jorge Machado Moreira, with 13%. Other important names complete the list of consultations: Affonso Eduardo Reidy and Severiano Porto, 9%; Carmen Portinho, engineer and urban planner, 6%; Carlos Leão, 4%; and, finally, Paulo Santos, 3%.

As a figure that was "captivating and irresistible for everyone who knew him,"[39] and beholder of a vast work, Sérgio Bernardes has been, little by little, the object of renewed interest, appearing in academic researches, publications and exhibitions, which seek to understand – under the most diverse perspectives – the carioca architect and his work – developed over his nearly seventy years of intense dedication and professional experience –, since what would become his first design, the Eduardo Baouth residence, in 1934, when he was only fifteen years old, until his last works, such as the proposed reconstruction, in 1999-2000, of the old Volta Redonda Pavilion.

It is an ongoing process, with its limitations. The great draft of "Rio do futuro", published in *Manchete* magazine in 1965, is the only and brief mention of Sérgio Bernardes' work present in the book-catalogue of the exhibition *Latin American in Construction: 1955-1980*,[40] a large exhibition held at the Museum of Modern Art – MoMA in New York, in 2015, curated by Berry Bergdoll, Carlos Eduardo Comas, José Francisco Liernur and Patricio del Real. In this aspect, there is a long path to be followed before Sérgio Bernardes is able to regain his position alongside Lúcio Costa and Oscar Niemeyer in the history of Brazilian modern architecture. Perhaps a complete recovery is historically unfeasible, but little by little, gradually, the architect shall occupy a position more consistent with his trajectory in the constellation of great Brazilian architects.

Methodological Issues

Seeking to demonstrate the experimental character that has distinguished the extensive and polyphonic work by Sérgio Bernardes – his dedication and growing appeal to the improvement of technique and the search for a certain industrialization and architectural inventiveness – and based, among other methods, on the analysis of primary sources and the understanding of "evidence knowledge" – a term coined by historian Carlo Ginzburg in his 1989 book *Mitos, emblemas e sinais*[41] –, the following chapters about the three pavilions, in vogue here, have three intertwined approaches that clarify the adopted reasoning for the research:

Historical and contextual analysis: based on information extracted from primary sources and a vast bibliography, seeking to place the reader in the socio-cultural and economic environment in which these buildings were conceived and built.

Descriptive analysis and redrawing: addresses issues related to the effective development of the design, from the studies to the built project. For this, drawings that represent the object in different dimensions are mainly used, as well as their comparative analysis with the images that arrive from the buildings, since, in many cases, differences were identified between the designed object and the built one. In parallel, the process of redrawing the object was carried out according to the reading and interpretation of the plans and images mentioned above. This exercise, developed through digital models in three dimensions, allows the elaboration of models, and the deepening of knowledge on technical issues and composition of the set. Finally, together with the physical models, three machined pieces on a 1:1 scale were created, corresponding to a small and representative section of each of the three pavilions. This work made it possible to materialize symbolically each of the three pavilions, bringing to the fore a constant theme in the architect's work: its materiality or the "truth of materials".

Analysis of technical and ideological scope: the third and final approach takes place through the crossing of information established in the two initial stages and through the crossing between interpretations of the different pavilions and/or other designs, both authored by the architect Sérgio

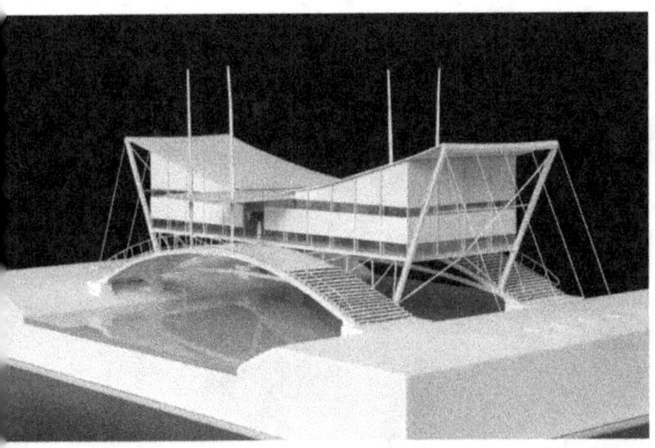

Volta Redonda Pavilion, model developed for Fausto Sombra's doctoral thesis, Ibirapuera Park, São Paulo SP, 1954-1955. Photo by André Nazareth

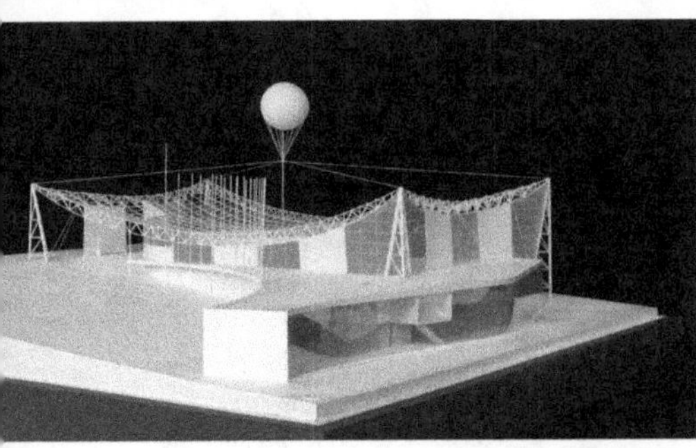

Brazil Pavilion at the Expo Brussels 1958, model developed for Fausto Sombra's doctoral thesis, Brussels, Belgium, 1957-1958. Photo by André Nazareth

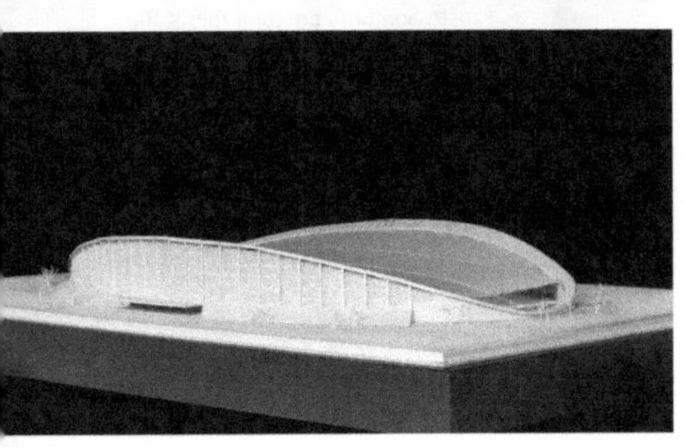

São Cristóvão Pavilion, model developed for Fausto Sombra's doctoral thesis, Rio de Janeiro RJ, 1957-1960. Photo by André Nazareth

37

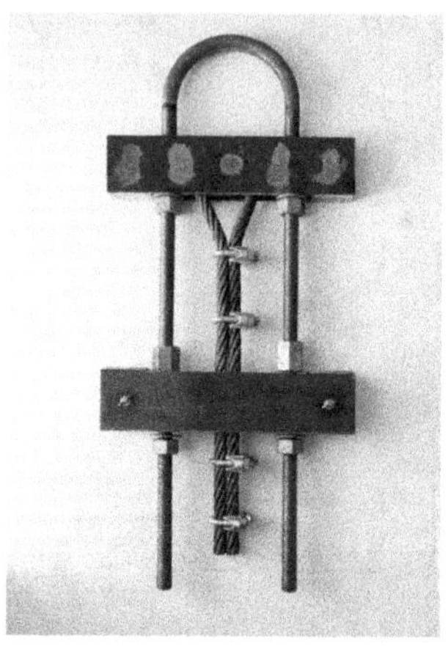

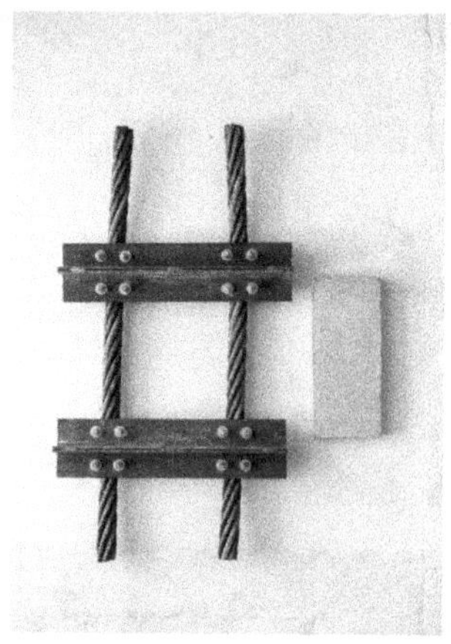

Volta Redonda Pavilion, 1:1 scale steel cable tensioner produced for Fausto Sombra's doctoral thesis, Ibirapuera Park, São Paulo SP, 1954-1955. Photo by André Nazareth

Brazil Pavilion at the Expo Brussels 1958, section of the roof with steel cables and tile, in 1:1 scale produced for Fausto Sombra's doctoral thesis, Brussels, Belgium, 1957-1958. Photo by André Nazareth

São Cristóvão Pavilion, 1:1 scale steel cable tensioner produced for Fausto Sombra's doctoral thesis, Rio de Janeiro RJ, 1957-1960. Photo by André Nazareth

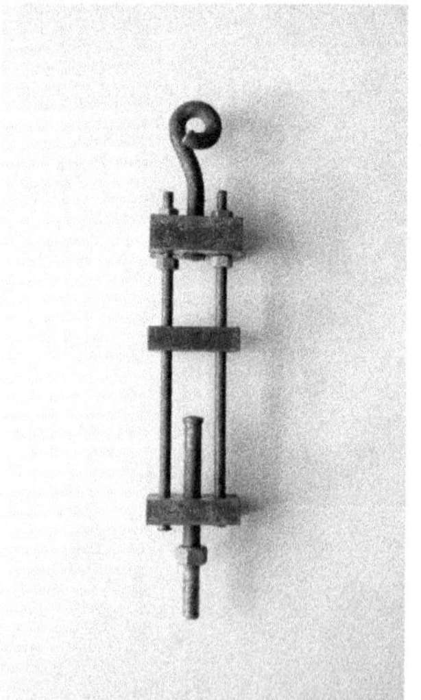

Bernardes and his contemporary peers or from later periods. This stage allows one to have a broader understanding of the objects in focus and, consequently, to develop the final conclusions.

It is noteworthy that these approaches are based on recognized works that touch the same area of knowledge and, sometimes, of research. Among them, the method used by sociologist Maria Arminda do Nascimento Arruda, present in her book *Metrópole e cultura: São Paulo no meio século 20*, 2001.[42] In it, immersed in the ideal of progress and modernity – from the middle of the last century, in the midst of the industrialization process in São Paulo and Brazil – and through the analysis of the production of the cultural avant-garde of the period, the author seeks to organize and describe a chain of "systems" and relevant facts that allow approaching the complex process of metropolization of the city of São Paulo.

Concurrently with the contextual understanding of the period, as a second aspect of a more pragmatic method, the work is based on the procedures of descriptive and documental analysis carried out by architects Ignasi de Solà-Morales, Cristian Cirici and Fernando Ramos, more precisely the process of reconstruction of the German Pavilion by Mies van der Rohe, as recorded in the book *Mies van der Rohe. El Pabellón de Barcelona*, 1993.[43] With this method, we seek to demonstrate that both the research process through primary documentation – photos, newspapers, letters, official letters, plans, projects, prospections, etc. –, and the process of interpretation and redrawing of the building and physical model, as highlighted above, are effective procedures that allow a better understanding of the object of study, even by counter arguing issues raised by other researchers. Here, for example, is a highlighted excerpt from the description of the Volta Redonda Pavilion, prepared by researcher Alexandre Bahia Vanderlei, in which the author states that the tie rods connected directly to the arches at the base of the building

– non-existent in the executive project – may not have been necessary:

> "Through the scarce photos of the Pavilion, one can see that the cables anchored to the bases were replaced by tie rods directly connected to the arches. From the arched shape shown in these photos, it is clear that there is no traction applied to these pieces that are made to work under tension, which denounces that perhaps the tie rods were not even necessary due to the lightness of the building."[44]

This understanding differs from the preliminary analysis carried out with the help of Professor Dr. Yopanan Conrado Pereira Rebello, engineer and renowned calculator, who defended, despite the lack of more in-depth calculations, the need to brace the structure at its critical points. He observed that the pair of arched "pieces" under the bridges, which do not exist in the executive project, made to work under traction, were probably "I" profiles executed with counter-locks to precisely withstand the large horizontal tension stress present there. It is possible, in this case, to admit that the thin vertical lines, observed in the photos, corresponded to rods of different lengths working under traction and preventing the bases of the pair of arched profiles – positioned below the arches that properly formed the bridges – from opening, or that is, to move in opposite directions, culminating in structural collapse.[45]

Beyond this point, the precision in understanding the design has allowed us to defend adequately the technical vanguard of the pavilions, synthesized, among other points, by the boldness of the drawing, structural slenderness and expressive form, solutions that can be observed in the connection and locking points of the metallic pieces that compose these exemplars.

Finally, adopting a third and final reference as method of analysis, the research focuses on the propositions made by Professor Josep Quetglas in his book *El horror cristalizado: imágenes del Pabellón de Alemania de Mies van der Rohe*, 2001.[46] In it, the author draws on his knowledge as a historian and architectural critic to correlate the constitution of the Barcelona Pavilion with a synthesis of the precepts of modernity desired by Germany in the first post-World War, defining it as the representation of the "German house" ideal. Far from the idea evoked by the image of coal, dirty and generally linked to the evils of the Industrial Revolution in the 19th century, among other actions, Quetglas reinforces the role attributed to light and analyzes the effects caused by it when reflected in the "austere" materials present in the building: stone, glass, water, metal and the white stucco of the ceiling. This also reinforces the ephemeral character experienced by its users and the feeling of emptiness provided by the materials, characteristics that will pave the way, in the 20th century, to "a new sensibility", according to the author's own words.

With a similar exercise, we have sought to understand the critical role behind the constitution of Sérgio Bernardes' three pavilions on the national and international scene in the mid-20th century, and how their materiality and form were related at this point.[47] Which forces and ideologies are present and which actors are affiliated with these patterns. The answers to these questions demonstrate Bernardes' effort attributed to the use of steel in the context of national industrialization, seeking to reveal and confront the building's austerity through its materiality – steel and glass, in the case of the Volta Redonda Pavilion; concrete, steel, glass and masonry, in the case of the Brussels and São Cristóvão Pavilions – in contrast to their morphological characteristics and the subtlety of the phenomenological experience arising from the use of water as an active element in the three exemplars. In a specific context, this method points out the

conceptual horizons adopted by the architect and the idea of
a new national representativeness assumed by his patrons:
Companhia Siderúrgica Nacional, Itamaraty and Joaquim
Rolla, in contrast to the architectural pattern commonly
found in the carioca school, usually symbolized by the figures
of Lucio Costa and Oscar Niemeyer.

In this sense, the meaning and importance of understanding the Volta Redonda Pavilion – in a period of great
growth and transformations in the capital of São Paulo –,
and the relevance of this design in the professional career
of Sérgio Bernardes – who a few years later would design
its peers with conceptual principles clearly coming from its
predecessor – is a key piece to establish this inflection point
in the architect's production, as well as in the moment and
place in which he is inserted in the national architectural
historiography.

Notes

1. This text by Sérgio Bernardes opens the article in the journal *Acrópole*, no. 301, December 1963, on the architect's participation in the 7th Biennial of São Paulo, which took place in the same year.
2. Paul Meurs, Mil De Kooning, and Rony De Meyer. "Expo 58: the Brasil Pavilion of Sérgio Bernardes".
3. Lauro Cavalcanti, *Sérgio Bernardes: herói de uma tragédia moderna.*
4. Ibid., 12.
5. Ibid., 12.
6. Felipe Guanaes, *Sérgio Bernardes: doutrina de uma civilização tropical.*
7. Kykah Bernardes and Lauro Cavalcanti, eds., *Sérgio Bernardes.*
8. Journalist Kykah Bernardes, Sérgio Bernardes' last wife, was a fundamental character in the research that resulted in this book. In addition to two formal testimonies in Rio, numerous other contacts took place, especially throughout 2019, when exhibitions, seminars and roundtables about the work of Sérgio Bernardes were held.
9. Sérgio Bernardes, *Cidade: a sobrevivência do poder.*
10. Roberto Segre, "Sérgio Bernardes (1919-2002): entre o regionalismo e o high tech".
11. According to a survey carried out at Hemeroteca Digital about the *Manchete* magazine collection, there are more than eighty reports, of the most diverse genres, related to the architect.
12. See *Manchete*, no. 678 (special edition Rio do Futuro), Rio de Janeiro, 17 Apr. 1965 <https://bit.ly/3KQTORt>.
13. Bernardes, *Cidade*, 145.
14. Bernardes, *Cidade*, 145.
15. According to testimony by Kykah Bernardes.
16. Cf. Kykah Bernardes, testimony to Fausto Sombra through electronic message, São Paulo, Apr. 15, 2022.
17. See Marcelo Augusto Felicetti, "Sérgio Bernardes e o Monumento ao Pavilhão Nacional, Brasília, 1972".
18. See descriptive synthesis of the design in articles published on the occasion of the monument's inauguration: Murilo Mello Filho, "Onde está o castelismo?", 22-23; Redação, "Ceará guarda as cinzas de Castelo," 5; Redação, "O monumento-mausoléu," 5.
19. Hugo Gouthier, *Presença: memórias*, 152-158.
20. *Módulo* (official catalogue for the exhibition Sérgio Bernardes), Rio de Janeiro, Oct./Nov.1983 <https://bit.ly/3OfLHER>.

21. Cavalcanti, *Sérgio Bernardes*, 13.

22. João Pedro Backhauser, "A obra de Sérgio Bernardes".

23. Cavalcanti, *Sérgio Bernardes*, 123-124. For his Sérgio Bernardes's biography, Cavalcanti has surveyed seven articles published in specialized journals after the architect's passing; five of them were published on the Vitruvius portal: Antonio Claudio Pinto da Fonseca, "Um breve olhar sobre o arquiteto Sérgio Bernardes"; Renato da Gama-Rosa Costa et al., "O sanatório de Curicica: uma obra pouco conhecida de Sérgio Bernardes"; Ana Luiza Nobre, "Sérgio Bernardes: a subversão do possível"; Ana Paula Pontes, "Sérgio Bernardes e Eduardo de Almeida: arquitetura que ensina"; Segre, "Sérgio Bernardes (1919-2002)". The sixth, mistakenly attributed to the journal *Arquitextos*, has the following correct reference: João Pedro Backheuser, "Sérgio Bernardes: sob o signo da aventura e do humanism". Finally, the seventh: Alfredo Britto, "Sérgio Bernardes e a invenção do espaço urbano". A little earlier, the Vitruvius portal had published an important article originally from Belgium: Paul Meurs, "O pavilhão brasileiro na Expo de Bruxelas, 1958: arquiteto Sérgio Bernardes".

24. Costa et al., "O sanatório de Curicica"; Ana Luiza Nobre, "Flor rara e banalíssima: Residência Lota de Macedo Soares, por Sérgio Bernardes" (originally published in the extinct digital journal *Arquitetura.Crítica*); Rocha, Tinem, and Cotrim, "Hotel Tambaú, de Sérgio Bernardes"; Monica Paciello Vieira, "A provocação sensorial na arquitetura de Sérgio Bernardes"; Lauro Cavalcanti, "A importância de Sér(gio) Bernardes"; Maria Cristina Cabral, "A multivalência de Sérgio Bernardes: da atualidade da obra de um raro arquiteto, um grande humanista"; Felicetti, "Sérgio Bernardes e o Monumento ao Pavilhão Nacional, Brasília, 1972"; Kykah Bernardes, "Memória da arquitetura moderna brasileira: sobre a conservação dos acervos de Sérgio Bernardes e outros arquitetos cariocas".

25. Mônica Paciello Vieira, "Sérgio Bernardes: arquitetura como experimentação"; Marcel Alessandro Claro, "Transcrição e reconstrução digital: utopias possíveis de Sérgio Bernardes"; Thaysa Malaquias, "A contribuição do arquiteto Sérgio Bernardes para a moderna arquitetura de saúde".

26. Nobre, "Fios cortantes"; Germana Costa Rocha, "O caráter tectônico do moderno brasileiro: Bernardes e Campello na Paraíba (1970-1980)"; Vanderlei, "Sérgio Bernardes".

27. The CSN Pavilion and Hotel Tambaú were presented at an exhibition in Tomie Ohtake Institute in São Paulo, from Jun. 15 to Aug. 1, 2010, and in Palácio das Artes in Belo Horizonte, from Apr. 8 to May 8, 2011. See catalogue: Abilio Guerra, "Arquitetura brasileira: viver na floresta". A model of the São Cristóvão Pavilion was presented at the exhibition *Infinito vão: 90 anos de arquitetura brasileira*, assembled in Matosinhos, Portugal, and in São Paulo, Brasil: Fernando Serapião, Guilherme Wisnik (Cur.), exhibition *Infinito vão: 90 anos de arquitetura brasileira*, Matosinhos, Centro Português de Arquitetura, Sep. 2018/ Apr. 2019; Fernando Serapião, Guilherme Wisnik (Cur.), exhibition *Infinito* vão: 90 anos de arquitetura brasileira, São Paulo, Sesc 24 de Maio, 25 Nov. 2020/27 Jun. 2021. See catalogue: Fernando Serapião, Guilherme Wisnik, eds., *Infinito vão: 90 anos de arquitetura brasileira*. Also see Marcelo Ferraz, "Arquitetura em vão?: sobre exposição da arquitetura brasileira em Matosinhos, Portugal".

28. The São Cristóvão Pavilion is one of the designs highlighted in the book: Renato Anelli, *Architettura contemporanea: Brasile*, 22-23.

29. *Bernardes*, feature-length documentary, 1h31', Rio de Janeiro, 2014. Directed by Gustavo Gama Rodrigues and Paulo de Barros. Story line by Thiago Bernardes. 6D Films and Rhino Productions. GNT co-production.

30. Abilio Guerra, "Prêmio APCA 2014: Documentário Bernardes, direção de Gustavo Gama Rodrigues e Paulo de Barros. Categoria Difusão, modalidade Arquitetura e Urbanismo".

31. Ana Amora, "Apresentação: muito além da arquitetura e urbanismo"; Nobre, "Flor rara e banalíssima"; Romulo Augusto Pinto Guina, "A casa de campo de Lota de Macedo Soares: por uma cronografia do ícone moderno projetado por Sérgio Bernardes"; João Claudio Parucher da Silva, "Arquivo Sérgio Bernardes: a análise do seu significado cultural como justificativa para a sua preservação"; Thaysa Malaquias, "Sérgio Bernardes e o Sanatório de Curicica: herança da formação na FNA"; Sombra, "Os pavilhões de Sérgio Bernardes"; Alexandre Bahia Vanderlei, "Pabellón de Brasil – 1958: ampliación del desafío y perfeccionamiento del manifiesto"; Philipe Cunha Costa, Diego Nogueira Dias, "Uma vida em sistemas: rastros de uma escritura cibernética em Sérgio Bernardes"; Silvia Maciel Savio Chataignier, "A imaginação arquitetônica em Sérgio Bernardes: projetos como esquemas"; Adriana Caúla, "Sérgio Bernardes e a utopia como plano de pensamento sobre a cidade"; Monica Paciello Vieira, "O Parc La Villette na concepção de Sérgio Bernardes"; Marcelo Augusto Felicetti, "Sérgio Bernardes e a biblioteca dos sentidos".

32. Bernardes, Caúla (Cur.), *Sérgio Bernardes 100 anos* (Centro Carioca de Design, Apr./May 2019).

33. Ana Amora, Claudio Brandão, and Thaysa Malaquias (Cur.), exhibition *SB-100*, Rio de Janeiro, FAU UFRJ, 19 Aug./20 Jun. 2019. Also see Redação, "Seminário e exposição SB100 – Sérgio Bernardes na FAU-UFRJ".

34. Guerra, Sombra (Cur.), *Três pavilhões de Sérgio Bernardes* (Mackenzie Historic and Cultural Center, São Paulo, from Sep. 18 to Nov. 14, 2019).

35. Rodrigo Queiroz, "Três pavilhões de Sérgio Bernardes: a geometria da tensão"; Adalberto Retto Jr., "Entre arquitetura e política: a mostra Três pavilhões de Sérgio Bernardes".

36. Bernardes, Caúla (Cur.), *Sérgio Bernardes 100 anos* (Museu Nacional Belas Artes, 17 Dec. 2019/14 Mar. 2020).

37. João Claudio Parucher da Silva, to whom this book is dedicated, passed away on May16, 2021, victim of Covid-19, at the age of 48.

38. About the Bernardes' collection at NPD, see Silva, "Arquivo Sérgio Bernardes".

39. Cavalcanti, *Sérgio Bernardes*, 12.

40. Berry Bergdoll et al., *Latin American in Construction: 1955-1980*, 86.

41. Carlo Ginzburg, *Mitos, emblemas e sinais: morfologia e história*.

42. Maria Arminda do Nascimento Arruda, *Metrópole e cultura: São Paulo no meio século XX*.

43. Ignasi Solà-Morales, Cristian Cirici, and Fernando Ramos. *Mies van der Rohe: el Pabellon de Barcelona*.

44. Alexandre Bahia Vanderlei, "Pavilhão da CSN 1954: recorrência técnica e manifesto da modernidade".

45. Cf. Yopanan Conrado Pereira Rebello, Testimony to Fausto Sombra at the engineer's office, São Paulo, Aug. 20, 2018.

46. Josep Quetglas, *El horror cristalizado: imágenes del Pabellón de Alemania de Mies van der Rohe*.

47. See Sombra, "Os pavilhões de Sérgio Bernardes".

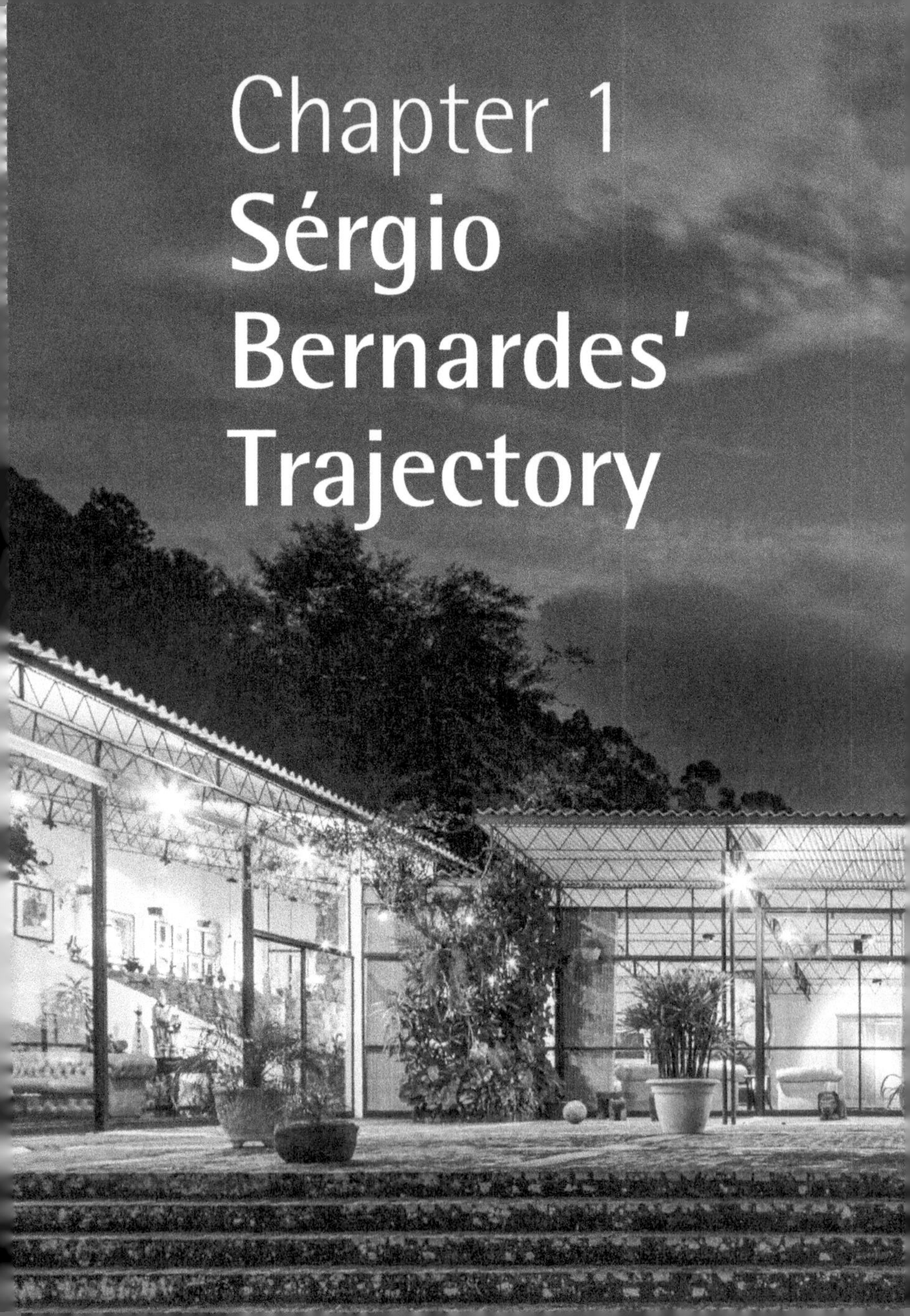
Chapter 1
Sérgio Bernardes' Trajectory

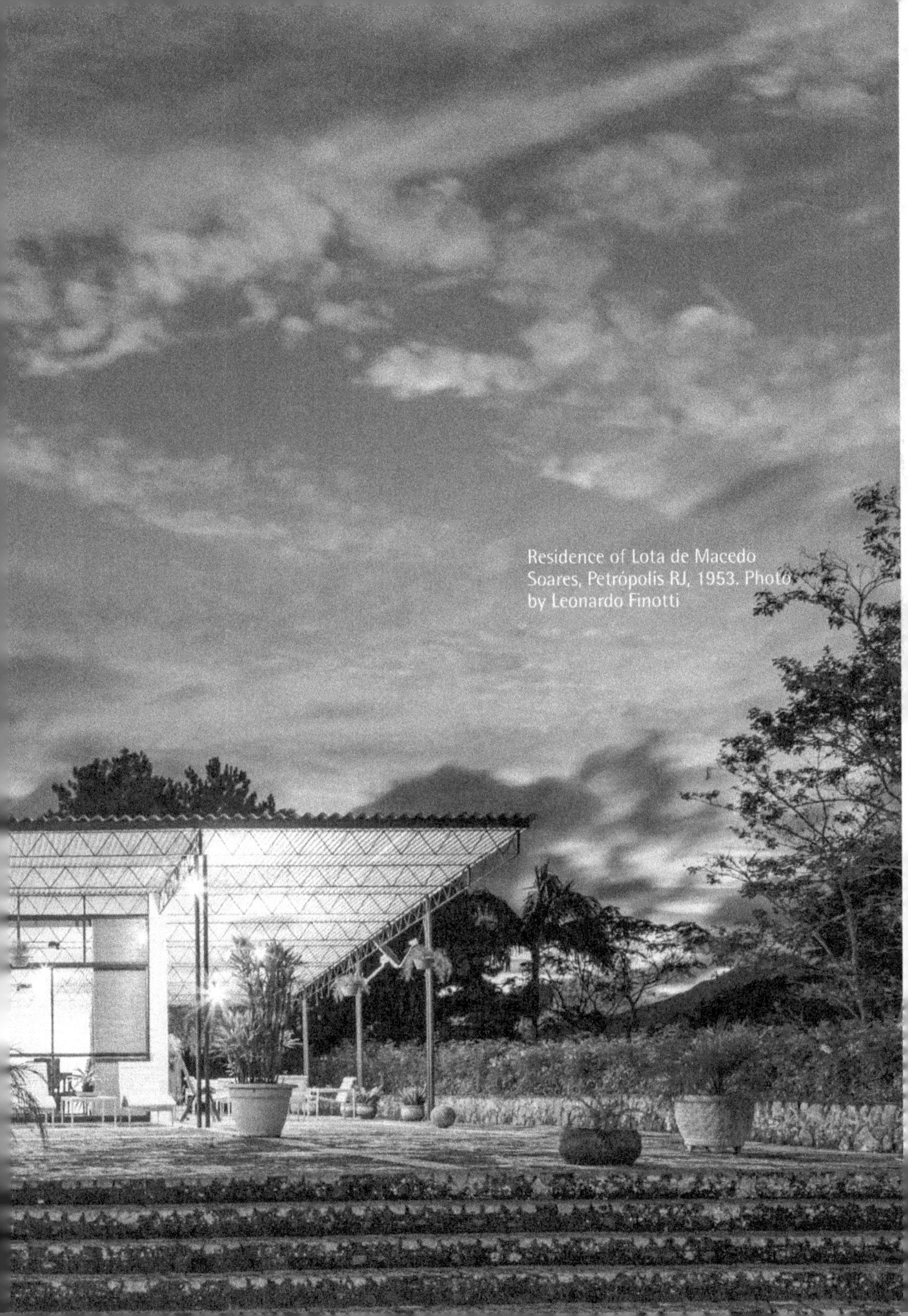

Residence of Lota de Macedo Soares, Petrópolis RJ, 1953. Photo by Leonardo Finotti

Between Modernists and Moderns

Brazilian modern architecture is recognized by many theorists and critics as one of the most important national artistic manifestations of the 20th century, with effects and developments not only restricted to Brazilian culture and customs, but also occasionally reverberating in many other nations. The phenomenon was not an isolated and independent event, but a process triggered by a variety of favorable political and socioeconomic events, leveraged by adjustments and advances in other central cultural nuclei – such as literature, visual arts, music, theater, dance and other aesthetic-cultural manifestations – in a process that, according to many, was triggered by *Exposição de Pintura Moderna* by the Italian-Brazilian artist Anita Malfatti, opened to the public on December 12, 1917.

The questionings suggested and pointed out by literature and the visual arts in Brazil precede by at least half a decade – with the 1922 Modern Art Week – the first concrete simulations of the adoption of the modern architectural style in the country. The episode began with the design of the house on Santa Cruz Street, in 1927-1928, by the Ukrainian-born architect Gregori Warchavchik. This townhouse with straight lines, devoid of adornments[1] and built on a generous lot in the Vila Mariana neighborhood, in São Paulo, is immersed in a garden full of cacti and other native Brazilian autochthonous species, designed by his wife and landscaper Mina Klabin. The house inaugurated what would become, years later, the important dialogue established between Brazilian modern architecture and the surroundings in which it was inserted. It was not, however, as already discussed by Abilio Guerra – through the words of Ana Rosa de Oliveira – a simple subordination of the garden "to nature, architecture, site, tradition,"[2] but the search for an identity that could coexist in balance with the environment. Defined as "mesological conviction", which "assumes

an intimate relationship between human culture and the
natural environment,"[3] this ideal, according to the researcher,
was already present in the work of writer Graça Aranha
since his famous novel *Canaã*, published in 1902. The theme
"pervades the Brazilian artistic intellectual production,"[4] also
and fundamentally in the works of the participants of the
1922 Modern Art Week, that is, in the "desire for harmony
and correspondence between tropical nature and the man
who seeks to nestle in its breast."[5]

Aracy Amaral, in her book *Artes Plásticas na Semana de
1922*, recalled that the conception of modernist architecture – presented during the paradigmatic and referred to art
week – through two architects of foreign origin – the Polish
Georg Przyrembel and, in particular, the Spanish Antonio
Garcia Moya – featured illustrations of exemplars that
bordered more on hybrid models, keeping a deep distance
from the avant-garde prescriptions already advocated by the
then young Le Corbusier, since the mid-1910s. Moya, called
by Menotti del Picchia "the poet of stone"[6] and considered
"the architect of the Week by the modernists,"[7] participated
with sketches of houses, however unbuilt and distant – in
the expression of Professor Silvio Colin – "before the 'trace
of machinist poetics."[8] However, "Moya was, undoubtedly,
the destructive element in the Architecture section, with his
projects full of atmosphere, revolutionary as a conception
for their character of breaking with convention,"[9] adopting a
compositional style of "pre-Columbian inspiration, especially
as decorative element."[10] It was a transitional period in which
"'the aim was to give a modern trend, to re-establish the
Brazilian colonial.'"[11]

During the following years, Brazilian modern architecture, in the midst of a period of dispute with its main
competing style, the neo-colonial[12] – in a process that took
shape with the first visit of Le Corbusier to Brazil, in 1929
– began to emerge through the design for the Ministry of
Education and Health – MES building (1935-1945). Built

in Rio de Janeiro, it was the first skyscraper in the world to be designed with the five points defended by the French-Swiss master: free plan, free facade, horizontal windows, roof garden and pilotis. This process, which began in the first phase of the Getúlio Vargas government, but already close to the implementation of the Estado Novo regime, had the initial traces of Le Corbusier in his second stay in Brazil, now at the invitation of the team of architects in charge of the conception of this emblematic building, then led by Lúcio Costa: Affonso Eduardo Reidy, Carlos Leão, Ernani Vasconcellos, Jorge Machado Moreira and Oscar Niemeyer.[13]

Other subsequent buildings include Santos Dumont Airport (1937-1944), designed by the Roberto brothers – defined by Henry-Russell Hitchcock Jr. as being "probably the most attractive airport in the world"[14] –; as well as the Brazil Pavilion, designed by Lúcio Costa and Oscar Niemeyer for the 1939 New York World's Fair. The MES building, an example of great refinement and undeniable aesthetic and artistic nature, became the focal point of the recognition that Brazilian modern architecture began to enjoy in the mid-1940s, as could be seen in the double edition of the French magazine *L'Architecture d'Aujourd'hui* of September 1947. Entitled *Brésil*,[15] this issue was dedicated to the relevant architectural achievements and the advanced technical-construction capacity with the use of concrete in the tropical country, in a period of strong stagnation and economic retraction for many European nations, in the process of economic reconstruction and facing a large housing deficit as reflections of the Second World War over the years 1939-1945.

For the Brazilian scenario, which remained oblivious to the conflict at the outset – until it began to be intensely enticed by the US government with substantial financial support and other cooperation agreements –, the result would be culturally and economically positive, as the actions of propaganda by the US government regarding the diversity and success of Brazilian architectural production, through recognized institutions, would be of paramount importance in the dissemination of those newly built *tupiniquins*.[16] Mainly after the exhibition organized by American architect Philip Lippincott Goodwin, a detailed work that included photographs by the critic George Everard Kidder Smith. Entitled *Brazil Builds: Architecture New and Old, 1652-1942*, held by MoMA in 1943, the exhibition had a great impact on the cultural milieu, having its reach expanded by the publication and dissemination of the respective book-catalogue. For many years, Henrique Mindlin's catalog and book, *Modern Architecture in Brazil*, published in 1956, were one of the few means that sought to systematize part of the relevant and growing production of Brazilian modern architecture in the middle of the last century.

On the occasion of *Brazil Builds*, Mário de Andrade, in an article of the same name published in the newspaper *Folha da Manhã*, celebrated the importance of the North American recognition, ultimately highlighting and praising our miscegenation:

> "The Ministry of Education and never the Ministry of War; the Esther building and never the Law School; a dwelling by Artigas and never a neo-colonial residence.
>
> The first manifestation of modern architecture in Brazil, like the other arts, also took place in São Paulo. It was a house by architect Warchavchik, much commented on by our magazines at the time. But the modern in architecture had to give way here. The first school, which could legitimately be called a "school" of modern architecture in Brazil, was that of Rio, led by Lúcio Costa, and still unparalleled to this day. [...]
>
> Also admirable is the collection of photographs Brazil Builds, which the Museum of Modern Art in New York has just published, with excellent comments by architect Philip L. Goodwin in general. I believe that

this is one of the most fruitful gestures of humanity that the United States has ever made towards us Brazilians. Because it will, it already did, regenerate our confidence in us, and reduce the disastrous inferiority complex of mestizos that has harmed us so much. I have already heard many Brazilians, not only amazed, but also enthralled by this book that has proved we have a modern architecture as good as the most advanced countries in the world."[17]

At that time, in São Paulo – in addition to the pioneer houses by Warchavchik; the cluster of houses by Flávio de Carvalho, from 1936, built in Lorena Lane, in the Jardins neighborhood; among other modern exemplars after the publication of Rino Levi's article: "A arquitetura e a estética das cidades", October 1925[18] –, modern architecture was still seeking space with a few, but growing exemplars conceived under the new dogmas. Among them, the outstanding Esther building, from 1934-1938, designed by the duo Álvaro Vital Brazil and Adhemar Marinho, built in front of Praça da República Square; Instituto Sedes Sapientiae, by Rino Levi, from 1940-1942 – both incorporated into Goodwin's selection –; as well as the Wrightian-style houses designed by João Vilanova Artigas in the early 1940s, however, they were not included in the curatorial selection by *Brazil Builds*.
Other buildings considered of greater relevance on the Rio-São Paulo axis are part of the MoMA exhibition catalogue, such as the Seaplane Station in Rio, 1937-1938, by Attilio Corrêa Lima; and again the duo Álvaro Vital Brazil and Adhemar Marinho, with Vital Brazil Institute in Niterói, 1942 – occasion of the famous photo of the aforementioned building with straight lines, still under construction, in contrast to the carriage parked in front of it.[19] A few outstanding examples located in other states complete the selection of MoMA's works, such as the Caixa d'Água (water tower) in Olinda, 1937, by the carioca architect Luís Carlos

Nunes de Souza; and the first three exemplars, commissioned by the then mayor Juscelino Kubitschek, already built at the time as part of the Pampulha Modern Ensemble: the Casino, the Ballroom House and the Yatch Club, all from 1942. These buildings, alongside the São Francisco de Assis Church, concluded a year later, in 1943, conceived in partnership with Candido Portinari and Roberto Burle Marx, provided great notoriety and recognition to the then young Oscar Niemeyer.

This succinct introduction, incorporating a brief list of professionals who composed the first and exceptional group of Brazilian modern architects, could be considered as defining the so-called carioca school. A group that used to adopt reinforced concrete as a design structuring element in a rational and often plastic way, under the concept of form and function, raising the building from the ground when possible and convenient – as brilliantly accomplished years later by Affonso Eduardo Reidy in the design for the Museum of Modern Art in Rio de Janeiro – MAM-RJ, 1953; and by Lina Bo Bardi, at the São Paulo Museum of Art – MASP, 1957. Such operation allowed the creation of spaces for permanence and conviviality protected from the intense tropical heat, as well as unobstructing the view at ground level. Allied to these characteristics, there was a rereading and incorporation of elements celebrated by Brazilian colonial architecture, a process carried out through the assimilation and reinterpretation of modern codes imported from the European continent in the late 1920s, as proposed and defended by Lúcio Costa in many of his texts, such as "Razões da nova arquitetura", 1936, and "Documentação necessária",1937,[20] concepts already crystallized in the Vila Monlevade design competition, from 1934, authored by the same professional.

Keeping the wide spectrum of relatively distinct solutions, often developed through a close dialogue with the nature that surrounded them, such traits and notions could be understood as the basic characteristics of the modern architecture developed in the country until the mid-1940s.

In this panorama, it is still necessary to highlight the participation of the State as public patron responsible for promoting and consolidating the modern style in the country, a factor that, added to the control of historical heritage, the theories for popular housing, and the "government's desire to seek a new face for the federal capital"[21] – as Lauro Cavalcanti reminds us –, would be a preponderant issue for Brazilian modern architecture to emerge in the middle of the last century compared to other nations that enjoyed a similar sociocultural trajectory to that found in Brazil.

It was in this dynamic universe that the vast work conceived by the carioca architect Sérgio Wladimir Bernardes would develop and emerge. As a professional belonging to the second generation of Brazilian modern architects, Sérgio Bernardes adhered to and confronted the values, techniques and concepts adopted and established by the carioca school until then, but established new alternatives for dialogue and developments. Roberto Segre has very well detected Bernardes' propensity to risk the new, when he states, in comparison to Lúcio Costa and Oscar Niemeyer, that "without a doubt, from the three masters of the 'carioca school', [Bernardes] was the most controversial and versatile, exerting a strong influence on architecture students, in search of alternative paths to the sterile formalism of our time."[22] If this is a constant search and one of the architect's individuality marks, he never put himself in the position of denying his link with the Brazilian modern tradition; on the contrary, he defended and incorporated the mechanisms already embedded in the fundamental works of our architecture. In the article entitled "Brasil potência arquitetônica", published by the *Manchete* magazine in 1952, Sérgio Bernardes embraced Lúcio Costa's ideas and defended the possibility of incorporating traditional architectural elements

into modern constructions, an issue that would prove to be
relevant in the work itself:

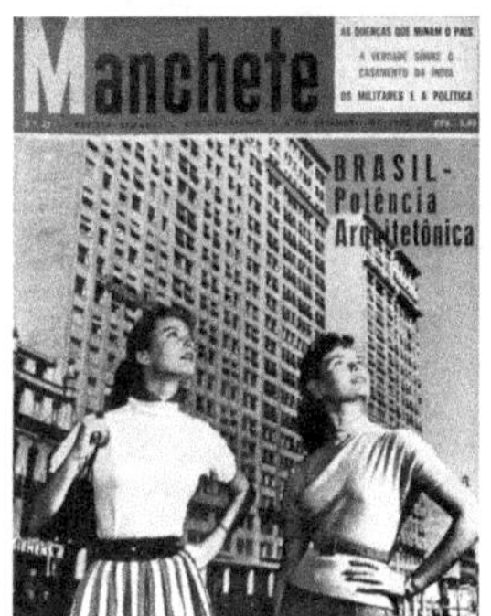

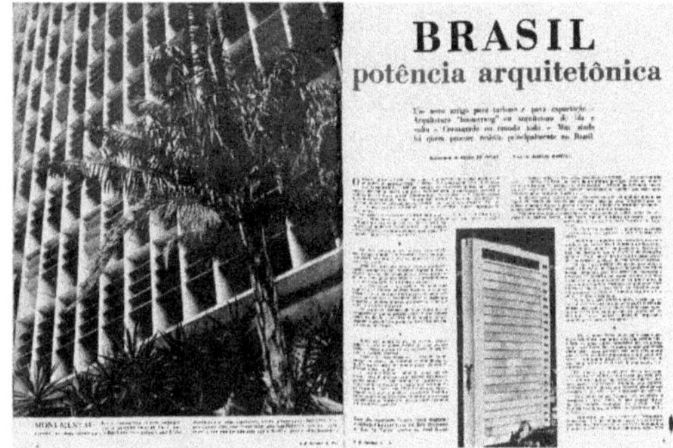

Cover and article "Brazil Architectural
Power," report by Lydio de Souza and
photos by Aymore Marella, published
in Manchete magazine, no. 33, on
December 6, 1952. Fausto Sombra
Collection

"With freedom of form and style, all the details of
ancient architecture could be used in modern constructions, naturally within a specific technique and aesthetic.
The use of such details, however, does not signify a
nostalgic inspiration or tendency, but a contribution of
whatever was beautiful and necessary for the function
of a residence. And that could never be surpassed."[23]

The Volta Redonda Pavilion, a small bridge-building
constructed in Ibirapuera Park, between the late 1954 and
early 1955; the Brazil Pavilion at the Brussels Universal and
International Exhibition, 1958; and the Pavilion for the
International Trade and Industry Fair – a building designed
and built in Rio de Janeiro between 1957 and the late
1960, also known as the São Cristóvão Pavilion – are the
main objects of analysis of the present book. They incorporated relevant technical-constructive issues present in
the international architecture speculations about the use

of new materials and technologies, such as steel, but also
incorporated the practices and elements of the Brazilian
modern tradition – the continuous space and incorporation
of traditional elements resulting in integration with nature –,
an ambivalence that expressed the rich internal political and
socioeconomic context after the Second World War.

Conceived in a short period of time, between 1954 and
1958 – after the first decade of the architect's training in
1948, at the National School of Architecture of the University
of Brazil, currently UFRJ –, it is possible to note, even today,
an incipient critical universe about the valuable plans
and other documents referring to the constitution of the

Volta Redonda Pavilion, remaining
bridge, Ibirapuera Park, São Paulo,
1954-1955. Photo by Fausto Sombra

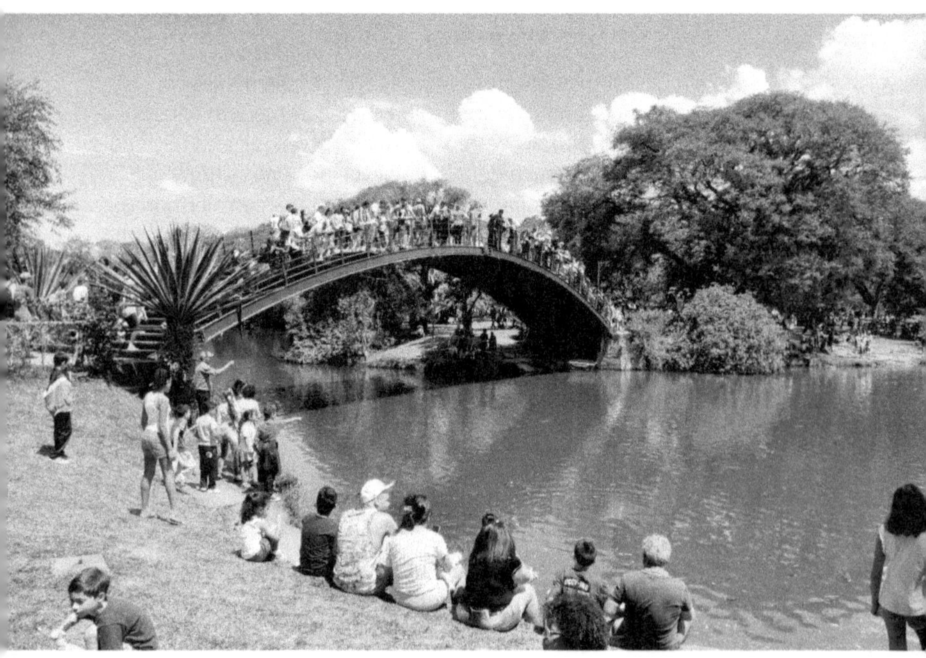

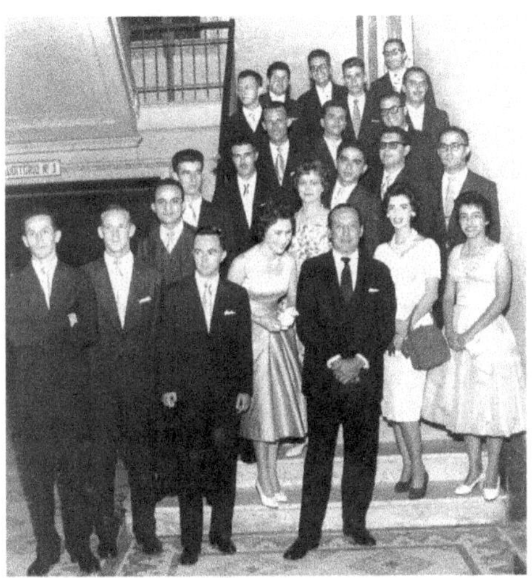

Sérgio Bernardes and classmates, graduation ceremony, Rio de Janeiro RJ, 1948. Collection NPD FAU UFRJ / Sérgio Bernardes Fund

respective exemplars. Some studies, however, deserve to be highlighted, such as the analyzes and interpretations developed by two researchers: Ana Luiza Nobre, in her PhD dissertation "Fios cortantes: projeto e produto, arquitetura e design no Rio de Janeiro (1950-70)", 2008, moment in which the author approached the pavilions in one of her subchapters – "Malhas, redes, cabos e triângulos" – dedicated to architect Sérgio Bernardes; and, more recently, the PhD dissertation "Sérgio Bernardes: el desafio de la técnica", defended by Alexandre Bahia Vanderlei at the Universitat Politècnica de Catalunya, UPC, in 2016, moment in which the researcher adopted two of the three pavilions as object of study: Volta Redonda and Brussels.[24] Other publications touch on the theme of this design triad, with emphasis on two books: *Sérgio Bernardes*, 2010, compiled by Kykah Bernardes and Lauro Cavalcanti,[25] in which architect Murillo Boabaid, a former partner of Bernardes in Rio de Janeiro, described, through a brief statement, the constitution process of the three buildings;[26] and *Arquitetura contemporânea no Brasil*,[27] a famous work by French paleontologist Yves Bruand, the result of a PhD originally published in 1981.

Bruand, in agreement with part of the understanding of this research, mentions in passing the affiliation of Bernardes' designs to the North American architectural production of the time. The link would be defended by other scholars – as is the case of Ana Luiza Nobre and Alexandre Bahia Vanderlei –, when they sought to establish a greater formal proximity between Bernardes and the works of North American or US-based architects: the Case Study House no. 8, 1945, by Charles and Ray Eames; the Coocon House on Siesta Key, Florida by Paul Rudolph,1948; the Dorton Arena in Raleigh, North Carolina by Polish-born architect Matthew Nowicki,1952; the geodesics developed by Richard Buckminster Fuller, mainly from the 1960s onwards. Of these, two are directly related to the pavilions studied here: the Coocon House, with a catenary roof similar to the Volta Redonda pavilion, and the Dorton Arena, with a structure and form similar to the São Cristóvão Pavilion, but on a considerably smaller scale.

In brief analyzes of the three pavilions, Yves Bruand condemned Sérgio Bernardes' large design developed for the São Cristóvão Pavilion, comparing it to Dorton Arena by his North American predecessor, which obtained a positive result and would not be repeated in the experience carried out by the carioca architect:

> "Sérgio Bernardes, an inventive spirit, interested in the most diverse problems of today, lost all sense of measure here; he let himself be seduced by pride: he wanted to break a world record, that of the largest covered area, free of any support (28,000 square meters, the dimensions of the ellipse being respectively 250 and 150 meters in length and width), but one may wonder if he risked simultaneously breaking the world record for ugliness in this type of work."[28]

The intemperate tone observed in this analysis of the São Cristóvão Pavilion would be considerably altered when referring to the predecessor pavilions, starting with the Brussels Pavilion:

"The Brazil Pavilion was of a very different class, receiving the first prize for architecture at the Brussels International Exhibition in 1958. As it was a temporary construction, Sérgio Bernardes did not try to give it an extraordinary emphasis. His efforts focused on two essential points: to use economic solutions that did not bring special problems to assemble and dismantle, and to make the most of the location characterized by quite accentuated differences in levels. [...]
The judicious use of modern materials, both practical and inexpensive, combined with the efficient exploration of difficult terrain, led to a high-quality structural and spatial conception, perfectly adapted to the special requirements of this type of program, being very convenient for the architect."[29]

Bruand's positive discourse expanded in the analysis of the Volta Redonda Pavilion, highlighting the design's qualities and the inventive spirit of its idealizer:

"In fact, he had already been brilliant in the same genre for his inventive spirit, when he was in charge of building the pavilion for the Volta Redonda steelworks on the Exhibition of the 4th Centenary of São Paulo City, organized at Ibirapuera Park in 1954. The idea of transforming this pavilion into a bridge, launched over the small stream that flows on the site, allowed him to multiply the pavilion's advertising effectiveness, an essential objective of the company that had commissioned it: he was not content only to emphasize the possibilities of metallic construction in Brazil – he highlighted its plasticity; ultimately, attributing a utilitarian role to the work and placing it at an almost obligatory point of passage, he took the audience through the installation where a chosen documentation insisted on the importance of the achievements of this national society, considered as a symbol of the country's development."[30]

Loaded with symbolism, the respective pavilions were made with the participation of renowned figures, such as Portuguese artist Eduardo Anahory, landscaper Roberto Burle Marx, and among others, the outstanding engineer from Recife, Paulo Rodrigues Fragoso, one of the pioneers in metallic structure calculation in Brazil. These personalities helped Sérgio Bernardes to build "one of the most beautiful exemplars of Brazilian modern architecture,"[31] expanding the reach and international recognition of the avant-garde production that the architect and his team developed in the mid-20th century.

Closing this brief Introduction here, it is opportune to clarify the most appropriate sense of the term "avant-garde", used above and present in the title of this publication, since, according to the proper cultural sense to us, it refers to innovative and experimental artists and works. From precisely the point of view of architecture, this definition becomes linked to the movements of "European iconoclasts who – in the early 20th century – forged a new architecture more suitable to the age of machines than the values, institutions and wars of bourgeois styles of traditional art and architecture."[32]

These characteristics are present in groups that precede the First World War, the Futurists, and immediately after the war, the Constructivists. Years later, in the second post-World War period, the term was revised and defined as neo-vanguard, becoming commonly associated with the English group Archigram, from 1961 onwards, and then with the Japanese group Metabolists. It is in this context, and preceding the high-tech movement, inaugurated by the Reliance Controls Factory in 1967, designed by Team 4, and definitely by the Pompidou Center in 1977 – designed by Renzo Piano and Richard Rogers[33] – that the term avant-garde seems to be properly applied to the pavilions analyzed here, both because the referred exemplars represent a certain rupture with the defining molds of the carioca school, and because they approach the cutting-edge architecture developed by new and prominent names in world architecture.

This process even preceded the experiences promoted by German architect and engineer Frei Otto, being a reference for many other distinguished professionals, such as Paulo Mendes da Rocha, a figure who would reveal[34] to have used the technical solutions present in the Brazil Pavilion in Brussels as inspiration to conceive the award-winning project for the Atlético Paulistano Club Gymnasium, also from 1958, a work developed in partnership with João Eduardo de Gennaro.

North American Proximity and Constitution of the Pavilions

The dropping of two atomic bombs, on Hiroshima and Nagasaki, respectively on August 6 and 9, 1945, by the government of the then newly sworn in US President Harry Truman, is a moment considered decisive for the outcome of one of the darkest facets of our recent history. The victory of the Allies against the Axis defined the division of most countries into two ideological blocs, capitalists and socialists, led by the United States and the former Soviet Union. Directly involved in the Korean War, between June 1950 and July 1952, the two great potencies competed for world political and economic influence, defining the beginning of the Cold War from that moment on. The long conflict was characterized by the nuclear arms race and the aerospace race, disputes that would intensify the changes triggered by the

Second World War in several areas of knowledge and society in general, including the architectural environment.

A little back in time, in Brazil, from the Revolution of 1930, when the then president Washington Luís was deposed, preventing the inauguration of the already elected president Júlio Prestes, the era of Getúlio Vargas began, a troubled period at the end of the Old Republic, an internal political-social unfolding parallel to the rise of fascism in the world:

> "The Oligarchic Republic faced its deepest crisis at the end of the 1920s, when internal and external factors combined. In a climate of collapse of the current model of liberal or competitive capitalism, coinciding with the impasses of an ill-balanced presidential succession, another military uprising broke out, now led by superior officers who, taking advantage of the disagreements between regional oligarchies, managed to depose the president in 1930.
>
> A president elected by the paulista lordship, Washington Luís, was now forced, with his *coterie*, to lose power to a group that represented the nationalist bureaucratic patriciate. And, worse, outside the Rio-São Paulo hegemonic axis until then.
>
> According to Darcy Ribeiro, it was a new patriciate – nationalist, but also paternalistic –, with openings for the rural lordship and for urban workers. 'In the years of the rise of fascism in the world, Getúlio came into fashion, further weakening the liberal political patriciate and strengthening the civil and military bureaucratic one.'"[35]

Vargas' sympathy for Italian fascism led by Benito Mussolini was blatant and expressed in facts such as the frustrated invitation to architect Marcello Piacentini to design the University City of Rio de Janeiro in 1935, or the proclamation of the Consolidation of Labor Laws in 1943, with some regulations based on the Italian Charter of Labor. The sympathy and ideological identification of the Brazilian dictator with the totalitarian regimes of Benito Mussolini and Adolf Hitler ended up giving way to North American pressure. Brazil started to support the Allies on January 28, 1942, by breaking diplomatic relations with the Axis countries and, months later, on August 21 of the same year, with the definitive declaration of war.[36]

This alliance, on the Brazilian side, led to the permission for the stationing of US troops in bases in the Northeast and the supply of raw materials and strategic products to them. On the North American side, it took the form of re-equipment and modernization for the Brazilian Armed Forces and significant financial contributions. Brazil – at that time, in the initial process of economic and industrial growth, because of the accumulation of capital from the cultivation of coffee and other crops during previous years – could invest, thanks to the North American economic aid, in consumer goods and heavy infrastructure, processes that lead the country to constitute, in 1941, and to inaugurate, in 1946, in the city of Volta Redonda in Rio de Janeiro, the National Steelworks Company – CSN, the first large Brazilian steel company.

To this relevant chapter that illustrated part of the socio-political events in the country in the middle of the last century, one must also include the political-cultural influence developed by the North Americans, mainly through figures such as Republican magnate Nelson Rockefeller, a personality either defined as a "*brilliant* businessman, as a *missionary*, or as one of the maximum symbols of Yankee imperialism."[37]

Such proximity was materialized in different periods, since the mid-1910s, through coordinated actions mainly in the field of health by the Rockefeller Foundation[38] and, years later, under the leadership of Nelson Rockefeller himself, between 1940-1946, by the US agency Office of

Inter-American Affairs.[39] This process was extended for almost two more decades between 1946-1961, through the private philanthropic agency, the American International Association for Economic and Social Development.[40] In the field of arts, the alliance is also present through a set of important actions: the creation of the character Zé Carioca, by Walt Disney, in 1942; the aforementioned exhibition *Brazil Builds*, held at MoMA in 1943; support and partnership in the constitution of MAM-SP, in 1948, also by MoMA; support for the organization of the 1st Biennial by MAM-SP, in 1951, among many others. The exhibition, which remained open to the public for only two months, paved the way for the inauguration, two years later, of one of the most recognized urban facilities in São Paulo, the Ibirapuera Park and, with it, the 2nd Biennial by MAM-SP.

From this point on, the specific narrative of this book begins: the search for a broader understanding of the constitution of Sérgio Bernardes' three pavilions. Not by chance, these buildings appear in a period of great changes and transformations in the country that would create conditions for the still young Bernardes to dedicate himself to technical research focused on industrialization and experimentation. In this sense, it was a sequence of events that began during the celebrations of the 4th Centenary of São Paulo City, and the commission made to the architect by CSN, to idealize the design of its promotional stand at the 1st International Fair of São Paulo, during the years 1954 and 1955, resulting in the Volta Redonda Pavilion. During this period, Bernardes was awarded two important prizes: in January 1954, for designing the Lota de Macedo Soares residence, with the Young Brazilian Architect award, granted at the 2nd International Architecture Exhibition – EIA, during the 2nd Biennial; and months later, with the prize at the Venice Triennale,[41] for designing the Hélio Cabal house.

The 2nd Biennial also awarded the North American architect Paul Rudolph, as the young foreign architect, and

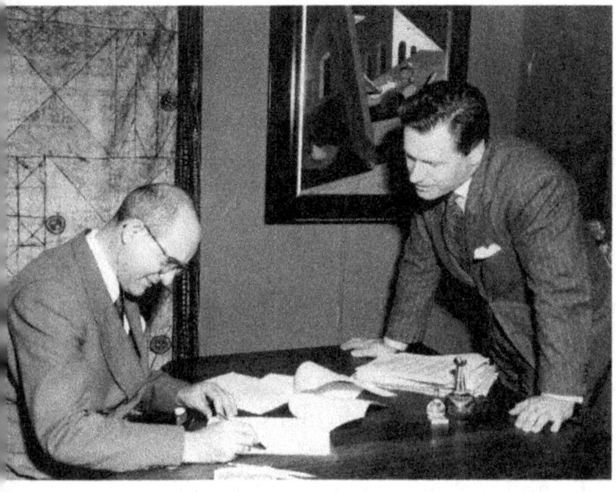

Francisco Matarazzo Sobrinho ("Ciccillo Matarazzo") and Nelson Rockefeller sign an agreement between MAM-SP (São Paulo Museum of Modern Art) and the MoMA (Museum of Modern Art) of New York, 1951. Photo by Leo Trachtenberg / Trayton Studios. Wanda Svevo Historical Archive / São Paulo Biennial Foundation

Walter Gropius, with the São Paulo Prize, a special tribute for his body of work. At that moment, on a visit to Brazil and forming part of the group of professionals who made up the jury of the international architecture show – among them Alvar Aalto, Josep Lluís Sert and Ernesto Rogers –, the experienced German architect stated, in a lecture given in the capital of São Paulo, that "modern architecture is a consequence of scientific and industrial evolution,"[42] a speech perfectly aligned with the precepts Bernardes applied in the design of the pavilion at Ibirapuera.

Basically, composed of profiles and other metallic elements, this ephemeral building carried not only the inventiveness and technical-ideological concepts present in the architect's rich production, but also elements related to the constitution and consolidation of the capital of São Paulo, a city that, at the time, sought modernization through the development of its industrial park, and the intense process of sociocultural effervescence it enjoyed.

The success of the beautiful and delicate forms of this exemplar, alongside its great inventiveness, contributed for Sérgio Bernardes to be invited to idealize the Pavilion for the International Trade and Industry Fair in Campo de São

Cristóvão, in Rio de Janeiro, around 1956.[43] Now, however, through the invitation of businessman Joaquim Rolla from Minas Gerais, active in the tourism sector – and also in refined casinos, at that moment already extinct by the Gaspar Dutra government. The process that resulted in the pavilion also had the direct involvement of the then president Juscelino Kubitschek.

At the same time, still in the first half of 1957, Sérgio Bernardes was also invited by the Ministry of Foreign Affairs, Itamaraty and the Ministry of Labor to develop the building that would become the award-winning Brazil Pavilion at the Brussels Universal and International Exhibition in 1958. Internationally, the grandiose event would be marked by the celebration of scientific and technological advances and the fierce dispute between the North Americans and the Soviets. Internally, due to the moment of vigorous development underway in Brazil, with the growth of the Gross Domestic Product – GDP,[44] driven by the Plano de Metas program – "fifty years in five" was the motto of the time – and by the planning and construction of Brasília, with subsequent transfer of the Brazilian capital from Rio to the Brazilian Plateau. For national pride, it was up to the country's pavilion to disclose to the world Brazil's achievements.

The Universe of Sérgio Bernardes: an Overflight on his Life and Work

Architect of Souls. *For Sérgio Bernardes, man is not an abstraction within a concrete structure. Concrete must serve man and contribute to the humanization of the world we live in. Sérgio is able to display many titles and awards. The greatest, however, is to feel architecture philosophically and deeply, psychologically and humanely. This admirable professional is, above all, devoted to happiness, safety, peace of the human being. He is an architect of souls, an architect of people.*

*Concrete always comes later. An architect who knows
how to calculate everything except the incalculable:
how many friends he has... without knowing.*
Pedro Bloch, "A humanização da arquitetura"[45]

Sérgio Wladimir Bernardes was born at 10 am on a
Wednesday, April 9, 1919, in a townhouse at 177 Voluntários
da Pátria Street, in the neighborhood of Botafogo, a traditional carioca stronghold, close to some of the main postcards sites of the capital of Rio de Janeiro. His parents, Mrs.
Maria de Camargo de Almeida Bernardes and journalist
Wladimir Loureiro Bernardes – an influential figure who
owned the newspaper *Gazeta de* Notícias[46] during the 1920s
and 1930s – had, in addition to Sérgio, one more daughter:
Regina Bittencourt,[47] wife of ambassador Aloísio Régis
Bittencourt. His paternal grandparents, as attested in his
certificate, were Alfredo Bernardes da Silva and Rita Loureiro
Bernardes, while his maternal grandparents were Carlos
Ferreira de Almeida and Helena de Camargo e Almeida.

From a very young age, Sérgio's artistic vocation was
already present, when he "created his own toys and spent
hours fantasizing cities and adventures at the roots of a
large almond tree in his backyard".[48] His growing skill with
carpentry and good treatment with materials allowed him,
at the age of thirteen, to open his model workshop. Sérgio's
father,[49] in an article published in *Manchete* magazine,
revealed some stories about his son's taste:

"'I always dreamed that, after growing up, Sérgio would
be my professional companion, namely, a journalist.'
Wladimir Bernardes, father of architect Sérgio Bernardes,
said that, despite being a very naughty child, his son
always showed a very intense inner life: 'At the same
time that he participated in the pranks of his peers, he
also enjoyed being alone, as if he were thinking about
something serious.' Wladimir said that only later, did he

realize it was not a simple subjective impression. Little Sérgio was really imagining things. [...] Later, when his son came of age, Wladimir founded the newspaper *Gazeta de Notícias* and thought about taking his son

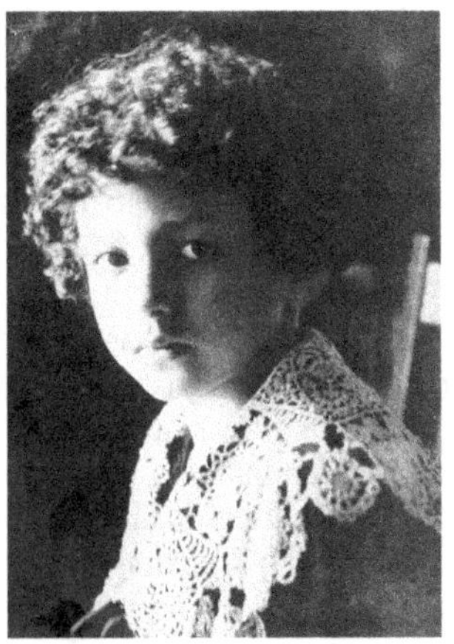

Sérgio Bernardes at the age of six. Sérgio Bernardes Collection – Memory Project / Bernardes Architecture Office

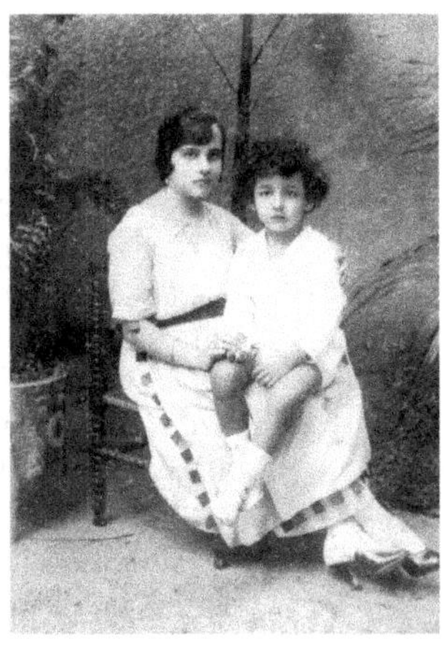

Sérgio Bernardes and his paternal aunt, Beatriz Bernardes. Undated photo. Sérgio Bernardes Collection – Memory Project / Bernardes Architecture Office

Article "If it were up to his father, Sérgio Bernardes would be a journalist today," with a photo of the architect with his father Wladimir Bernardes, published in *Manchete* magazine, no. 1,583, on August 21, 1982. Fausto Sombra Collection

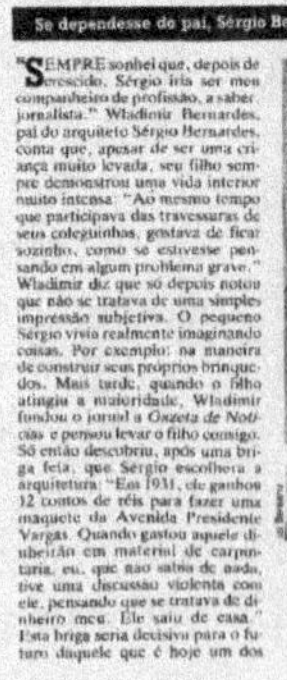

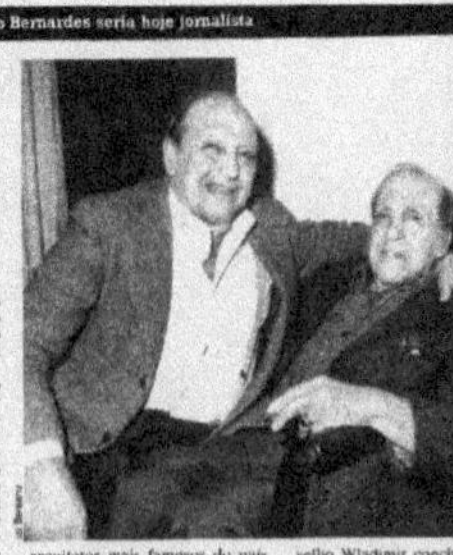

"SEMPRE sonhei que, depois de crescido, Sérgio iria ser meu companheiro de profissão, a saber jornalista." Wladimir Bernardes, pai do arquiteto Sérgio Bernardes, conta que, apesar de ser uma criança muito levada, seu filho sempre demonstrou uma vida interior muito intensa: "Ao mesmo tempo que participava das travessuras de seus coleguinhos, gostava de ficar sozinho, como se estivesse pensando em algum problema grave." Wladimir diz que só depois notou que não se tratava de uma simples impressão subjetiva. O pequeno Sérgio vivia realmente imaginando coisas. Por exemplo: na maneira de construir seus próprios brinquedos. Mais tarde, quando o filho atingiu a maioridade, Wladimir fundou o jornal a *Gazeta de Notícias* e pensou levar o filho consigo. Só então descobriu, após uma briga feia, que Sérgio escolhera a arquitetura: "Em 1931, ele ganhou 12 contos de réis para fazer uma maquete da Avenida Presidente Vargas. Quando gastou aquele dinheirão em material de carpintaria, eu, que não sabia de nada, tive uma discussão violenta com ele, pensando que se tratava de dinheiro meu. Ele saiu de casa." Esta briga seria decisiva para o futuro daquele que é hoje um dos arquitetos mais famosos do país. Porque Sérgio se dedicou então de corpo e alma aos estudos e logo se fez notar entre os colegas e professores. Mais tarde fez as pazes com o pai e voltou para casa, de onde só saiu aos 22 anos, para se casar. E o velho Wladimir concluiu: "Apesar de ele não [ter] respondido ao meu [sonho de fazer] dele um grande jornalista, [sinto-me] ao de me sentir orgulh[oso] em meu filho o g[rande arquiteto] em que se transform[ou]."

with him. Only then, he discovered, after an ugly fight, that Sérgio had chosen architecture: 'In 1931, he earned 12 *contos de réis*[50] to make a model of Presidente Vargas Avenue. When he spent that much money on carpentry supplies, I, who knew nothing, had a violent argument with him, thinking it was my money. He left home! This fight would be decisive for the future of whom is now one of the most famous architects in the country. Because Sérgio then, devoted wholeheartedly to his studies and was soon outstanding among his colleagues and professors. Later, he made peace with his father and returned home, and only left at 22, to get married. And old Wladimir proudly concluded: 'Although he did not live up to my dream of making him a great journalist, I cannot help but feel proud to see my son as the great architect he has become."'[51]

In an interview with journalist Pedro Bloch, almost two decades earlier, Sérgio Bernardes exposed his interest in "carpentry, joinery", and even "car engine".[52] Pedro Bloch, on Sérgio's recognized passion for cars, summarized at the beginning of that text: "A 13-year-old boy, Sérgio Bernardes once ran away from home to be a farmer in Teresópolis. Then he gained fame as a driving ace."[53] Following the interview, this skill and Sérgio's pleasure with cars were described as follows by the architect himself:

"I fulfilled myself in the automobile because I was not convinced that I had found myself. In the automobile, I felt a total fulfilment. Maybe self-destruction. In the first circuit I participated in, I believe in 37, Rio-Vassouras, I was coming first. Almost at the finish line, the shock absorber caught the steering bar of that adapted car. Then I bought a Ferrari. I raced and won the Maracanã Circuit two years in a row. I won the Interlagos race, I think in 53. In 54, I left for

the Lisbon and Porto Circuit, but I did not race either
one. Accident. When I received two million lire, as a
prize at the Venice Triennale, with the house I did for
Hélio Cabal (1954), I bought a new Ferrari and raced
in the *escudérie Guastaglia*, in Pescara, Monza and
Siracusa. In the Thousand Miles of Italy, I took the
13th place among more than two hundred cars."[54]

Still in continuing his account, a relevant fact, initially
mentioned by Kykah Bernardes, was proved; Sérgio
Bernardes' contact with his maternal uncle, the distinguished
architect Paulo de Camargo e Almeida,[55] in some way, had
corroborated with Bernardes' decision to follow the same
career as his uncle: "I started, still as a student, to design, to
idealize things. At the age of fifteen, I was already working in
the office of Paulo Camargo de Almeida."[56]
It was precisely at that age, in 1934, that Sérgio
Bernardes conceived his first design, the house for Mr.
Eduardo Baouth: a townhouse with certain Wrightian traces
and composition, with wide eaves, built in the midst of a
generous garden on land located in the district of Itaipava, in
Rio de Janeiro.
Shortly afterwards, around 1937, Sérgio Bernardes
entered the National School of Architecture at the University
of Brazil, where he "studied architecture until the third year
and then dropped out."[57] The following year, in October 1941,
he married Clarice Ramos Leal, a friend of his sister Regina,
having three children with her:[58] Cristiana, Sérgio and the
youngest Claudio Bernardes, born in 1949 after Sérgio
Bernardes had returned to college to complete his studies
and to graduate in architecture in 1948, at the age of 29. His
wife Clarice commented on this period:

"Sérgio had such a capacity for creation and work that it
took him a long time to graduate. I almost made him do
it. And although my big dream was to see him graduate,

I could not be there. It was just that my son was due to be born at any moment. We got married very young."[59]

Engineer and friend Jayme Mason confirmed the relevance of Clarice's support to the conclusion of studies by the "rebel" Sérgio, and reported:

"Sérgio graduated in architecture at the School of Architecture, after much struggle to dominate his indiscipline and rebellion against systematic studies.
Since he was a boy, so his mother Mrs. Maria Bernardes told me, Sérgio designed and made models.
Great credit should go to his first wife and mother of his children, Mrs. Clarice, in the arduous task of helping Sérgio obtain the diploma as architect. She told me that she often took Sérgio to school and picked him up, thus imposing a minimum of systematic on his rebellious spirit."[60]

It was at that moment, and probably helped by the uncertain time of internship with his uncle, that Sérgio Bernardes, even before graduating, began to ascend in his professional area through major designs, such as the Country Club of Petrópolis, in Rio de Janeiro, in 1947, a non-built project, but published in a special issue of the magazine *L'Architecture d'Aujourd'hui* that same year.[61]
Two years later, having recently graduated, Sérgio Bernardes developed one of his important designs: the Curicica Sanatorium, in Jacarepaguá, also in Rio de Janeiro. This process took place "during his leadership in the Architecture Sector of the National Campaign against Tuberculosis – CNCT, a position he held in the two years following his graduation, 1949-1950."[62] The typology of the pavilion, elaborated by means of a well-defined structural mesh in reinforced concrete, connected by linear covered walkways, however open, structured by slender metal pillars

in the form of a "V", facing airy patios, allowed the adoption of landscaped areas, some with the presence of small gutters, in the open air, to capture and conduct rainwater. This solution illustrates the relevance of the treatment Sérgio Bernardes gave to water in his designs, and it was more intensely explored in many other of his future works, including the design of the three pavilions portrayed here. The construction started in May 1949 and was inaugurated on January 25, 1951, the event was attended by the then president Gaspar Dutra, who praised the "high concept in which the Brazilian modern architectural school is [or was] held."[63]

Among other projects from the early 1950s – including two multi-family residential buildings: Barão de Gravatá (1952) and Justos Wallerstein (1953) – Sérgio Bernardes has developed the houses for Lota de Macedo Soares and Hélio Cabal, both conceived in 1951 and awarded in 1954. In 1952, Sérgio Bernardes won the competition to design the São Domingos Church, in São Paulo, non-built, but later awarded the International Prize for Sacred Art in Darmstadt, Germany, in 1956.

The two award-winning residences, Lota and Cabal, here represent a much larger cluster of bourgeois buildings executed by the architect in his first professional phase, which includes, among others, the two-story Staub summer house, built in Petrópolis in 1950. On that occasion, Bernardes proposed to use pillars formed by a mesh of thin metallic profiles arranged in the form of lattice towers, similar to those used later in the four peripheral pyramidal pillars of the Brazil Pavilion in Brussels, but working directly under compression.

Also from the same period, two more houses stood out. The Sampaio Vidal house, published in 1954, built in Petrópolis and defined by a single floor, but composed of two distinct blocks, whose main body, the social one, is defined by a large roof with generous eaves structured by thin

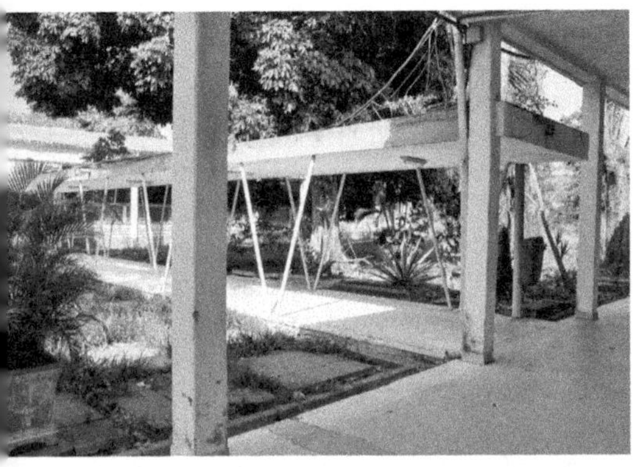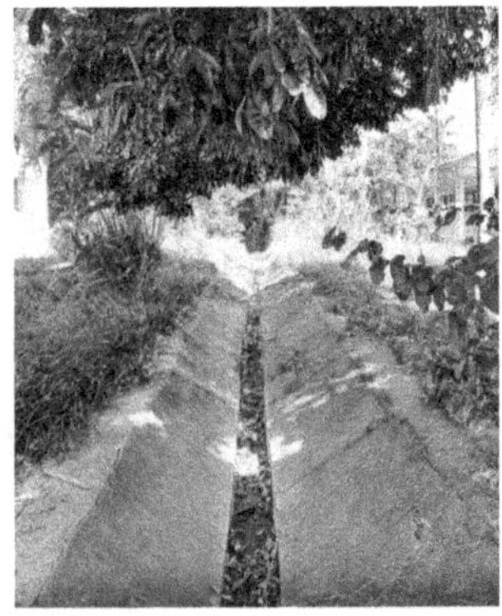

Sanatorium of Curicica, covered walkway and gutters for rainwater drainage, Jacarepaguá, Rio de Janeiro RJ, 1949-1951. Photos by Fausto Sombra

circular metallic pillars and whose closures that make up the internal environments take place independently. As well as, and mainly, the architect's own house, a three-story building of great repercussion in the architectural field in Brazil and abroad, even by receiving a visit from Le Corbusier.

Conceived in the second half of the 1950s and probably completed in 1961, Bernardes' own house was built on rocky terrain by the sea on Niemeyer Avenue, next to a cluster of eight row houses also of his authorship. It was built especially to accommodate his family and host friends, also to house the architect's office, a phase that preceded the office on Sernambetiba Avenue, in Barra da Tijuca. Made up of simple elements celebrated by Brazilian traditional architecture, such as ceramic floors, stone foundations and hollow bricks as dividing walls, but combined with inventive and innovative solutions, such as the use of fiber cement pipes cut in half, adapted as tiles that managed to cover more generous spans with a lower slope, in this project, Sérgio Bernardes also incorporated one-meter-long gargoyles. Composed of the same roof pipes, they launched towards the sea and were positioned precisely on the axes of the bedroom windows. Once again, Sérgio valued water as an active and phenomenological element in his designs, for on rainy days, small waterfalls were created on these openings due to the capture of water from the uncovered terraces located just above. This beautiful solution, probably inspired by the experiences of the water use in his three pavilions, is a relevant design concern in the architect's work, as already pointed out, and, it will appear with greater or lesser intensity in different ways.

The solution given to the roof of his own house would be widely used by the architect from then on, as could be seen in the 1960 residence of the Passarinhos, at 281 Avaré Street, Pacaembu, in São Paulo.[64] Also in the house that currently houses the French consul, at 199 Prudente Correia Street, Jardim Europa, in São Paulo, originally conceived for Mr. Jayme Souza Dantas Filho.

Journalist Pedro Bloch, still in his article, sought to emphasize the architectural relevance of Bernardes' own house through a brief descriptive synthesis, at which point he highlighted the presence of the architect's office in the same location.

> "His house overlooking the sea is extremely personal.
> (Le Corbusier, when visiting, said: 'This house deserves
> a book!'). A glass wall where a door turns into a table.
> Walls of material created and adapted by him. A study
> of reflections that allows having the distant city in the
> glass of the door. Panels appear and disappear according
> to the light they receive. But what amazes me most is
> to see, while crossing the courtyard, a huge building,
> with drawing boards, models and projects. An office,
> right on Niemeyer Avenue? Yes, it is Sérgio Bernardes'
> Architecture office, where fourteen people work."[65]

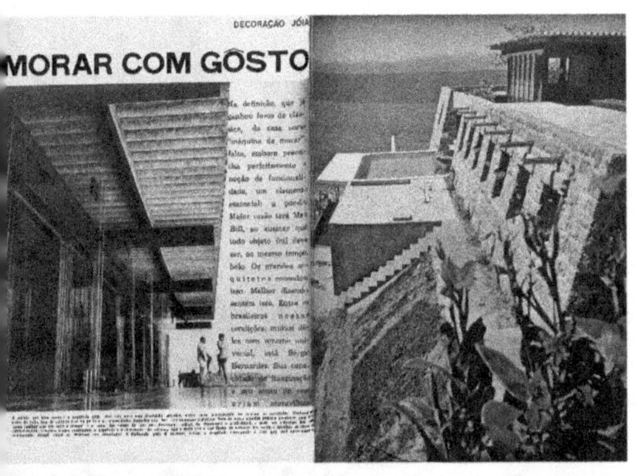

Architect's house, Niemeyer Avenue, Rio de Janeiro RJ, 1955-1961. Published in the article "Living with taste," in the Rio de Janeiro magazine *Jóia*, no. 107, on October 16, 1962. Hemeroteca Digital Brasileira / Fundação Biblioteca Nacional

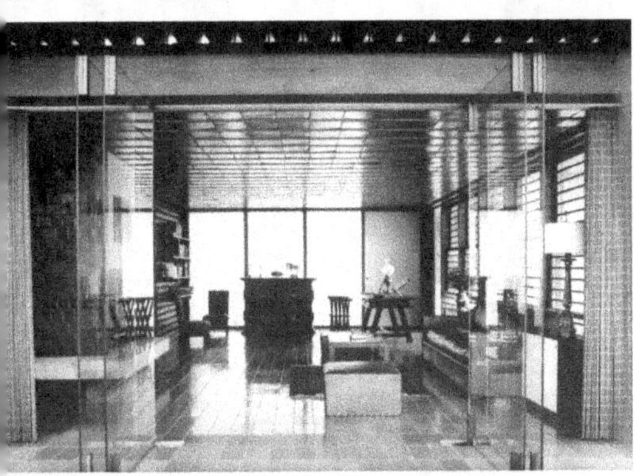

Architect's house, living room on the access floor, Niemeyer Avenue, Rio de Janeiro, 1955-1961. Sérgio Bernardes Collection – Memory Project / Bernardes Architecture Office

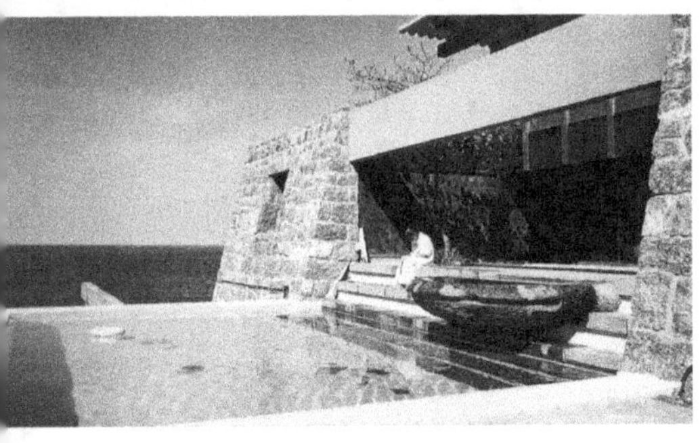

Architect's house, swimming pool with deck under construction on the lower floor, Niemeyer Avenue, Rio de Janeiro RJ, 1955-1961. Sérgio Bernardes Collection – Memory Project / Bernardes Architecture Office

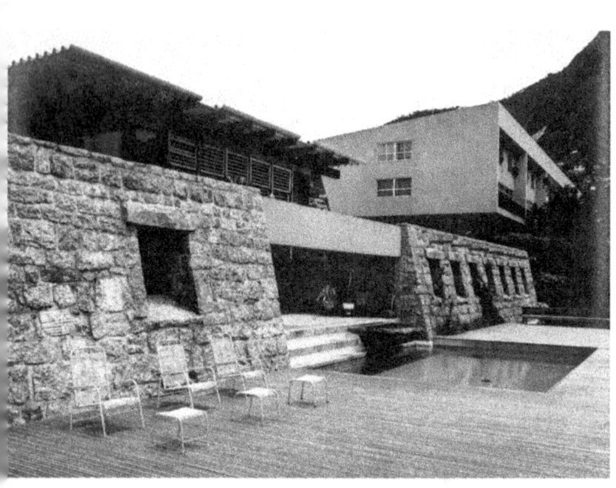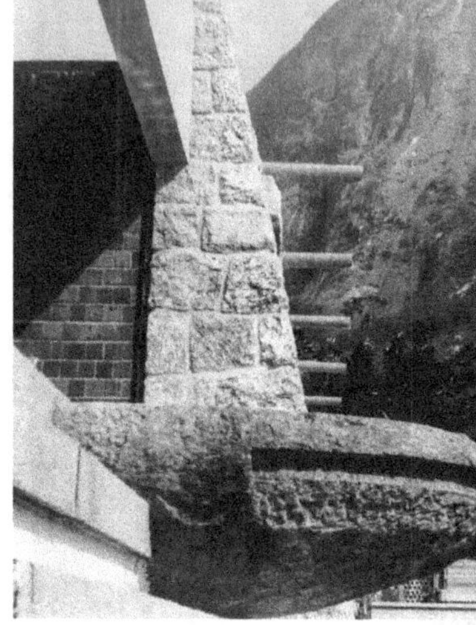

Architect's house, gargoyles over
the bedroom windows, pool deck,
and the stone cradle supporting it,
Niemeyer Avenue, Rio de Janeiro

RJ, 1955-1961. Sérgio Bernardes
Collection – Memory Project /
Bernardes Architecture Office

Jayme Mason also described his perceptions of Bernardes' office when it was located alongside the architect's residence:

"He had an office on Niemeyer Avenue, alongside his famous house on the rocky headland, which overlooks all of Leblon and Ipanema. A house that appeared in international architectural magazines.

Sérgio's office and house were open to all friends and strangers who came to him, to whom he gave precious attention even at the cost of his time.

Fixed on the wall, there was a large map of Brazil, where Sérgio pictorially noted the distribution of mineral resources, means of communication, economic potentialities, which he studied carefully, and about which he had his own theories.

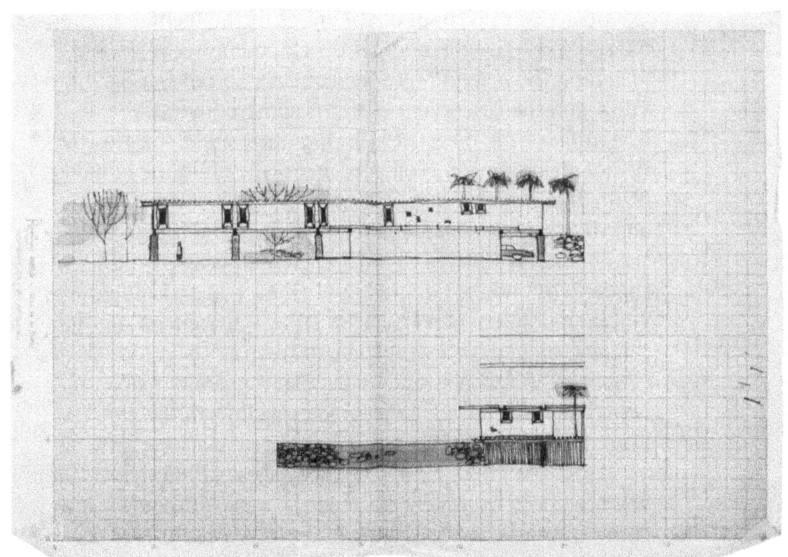

Jayme Souza Dantas Residence, facade sketch, Jardim Europa, São Paulo, 1960s. Collection NPD FAU UFRJ / Sérgio Bernardes Fund

Many years later, elsewhere, the map of Brazil was replaced by a 'world map' and Sérgio began to worry about geopolitical, astronomical and cosmological problems."[66]

It was precisely in this phase of intense and promising production, of great experimentation, already with a certain degree of professional maturity, and the particular vision of the possibilities and applicability of steel – in an environment in which reinforced concrete was, and still is, the majority in relation to to the other construction systems adopted in Brazilian civil construction –, that Sérgio Bernardes would be invited to develop the design of the three Pavilions revisited here. Idealized and built between 1954 and 1960, they are exemplars conceived on the premises of the technical potential of steel, at a time of great development in the country; including the beginning of the construction of Brasília, from 1957, and the essential use of this constructive system in the execution of the ministries, among other buildings. However, the logic adopted by Niemeyer and his team in the buildings of the monumental axis was completely opposite to that adopted by his colleague Sérgio, for since the design of the Lota house, in 1951, with its long latticed beams on display – similarly to the one adopted by Niemeyer, in an isolated way, in Edmundo Caravelas House, in 1954 –, Bernardes kept his thinking guided by the principle of truth of the materials and construction techniques employed in them, a principle that would gain strength and become explicit from the conception of the Volta Redonda Pavilion.

From the 1960s, and with the success of his architectural achievements, especially in the latest years, despite the late completion of the São Cristóvão Pavilion after numerous setbacks and technical adjustments, Sérgio Bernardes – one of the few outstanding architects who did not prepare a study for the new capital Brasília – presented his proposal for the airport of the new Brazilian capital, still in the form of "basic ideas", through *Módulo* magazine no. 19, in August 1960. In fact, and as usual, his proposals for this urban facility were far beyond an aesthetically well-resolved design. In it, Sérgio Bernardes proposed an innovative airport model that was "modern and functional, capable of adjusting existing airport facilities on the ground to the technological innovations introduced in the aircraft construction industry."[67] Named Intercontinental Airport South America-Brasilia, the principle was based on the centralization of the infrastructure in a common core, transferring a good part of the program to three underground levels positioned precisely below, allowing "economy of scale, at the same time increasing aircraft turnover and airport efficiency, reducing operating costs, which will enable the complex to function as an industrial unit."[68]

With an already advanced design sketch, presented in the aforementioned magazine through plans, sections, schemes and a siting of the airport in relation to Lúcio Costa's Brasilia Pilot Plan, 20 kilometers away from the Three Powers Plaza, it was possible to understand the increase in scale and complexity of the designs on which Bernardes and his team would start working from the late 1950s onwards. It is interesting to realize that, due to the greatness of the proposal, and possibly because it aroused the interest of the general public, one month before the publication in *Módulo* magazine, *Manchete* magazine took the lead and had dedicated a three-page article on the subject, presenting it to its readers as the "Airport of the century", and summarizing it on its initial page:

> "The design for the world's first intercontinental airport is ready. It will be built in Brasilia, and this is equivalent to saying that it will be operational within a short time. [...]
>
> – It will even have platforms for future interplanetary aircraft launches!
>
> For the conception of his work, Bernardes started from the principle that an aircraft carrier works within a very limited area and that does not mean that its planes are less efficient. He calls this the 'vertical system', which also encompasses the need for land services to be centralized. Using the "T" ruler as an airport and turning his right hand into a powerful jet, he explains:
>
> – I have modified the horizontal airport construction system because, the way things are going, the day will come when passengers will have to walk more than half an hour to reach the station building."[69]

It is worth realizing that a part of Sérgio Bernardes' premonitions regarding the problems of an airport in the 21st century was correct, especially regarding the dimensions that large airports have reached, making it one of the great obstacles to the implementation and expansion of airports worldwide. On the other hand, as so many other avant-garde designs that Sérgio would dare to propose and sometimes even develop, a good part of them would end up being shelved – as the innovative airport – and, among others, the Manaus Tropical Hotel.

Conceived as a commission of Companhia Tropical de Hotéis, a group by Varig Company, it would be sited in the middle of the Amazon rainforest, ten kilometers from Manaus, "on the banks of the Negro River and with access only by boat."[70] At least two versions were developed in greater depth.[71] The first, in 1963, would be composed of a large geodesic dome in the form of the structures designed by the North American Richard Buckminster Fuller, but with a diameter of 300 meters, four times larger than the one executed by him in the United States pavilion at Expo 67 in Montreal.[72] The entire program of the hotel would be distributed within the large dome, with a large cylindrical tower 26 meters in diameter at its center where the suites of the undertaking would be located in its highest section.

The calculation of the dome structure was in charge of engineer Paulo Fragoso, the same professional responsible for the structure of the Brussels and São Cristóvão Pavilions, as well as engineer Jayme Mason. Mason would be "responsible for the final version of the dome's structure, which consisted of a double latticed cap, obtained through the juxtaposition of flat lattice beams, three meters long and one meter high and, therefore, reasonably different from the tetrahedral mesh of the Fuller geodesics."[73] The engineer has addressed his participation in the design by describing:

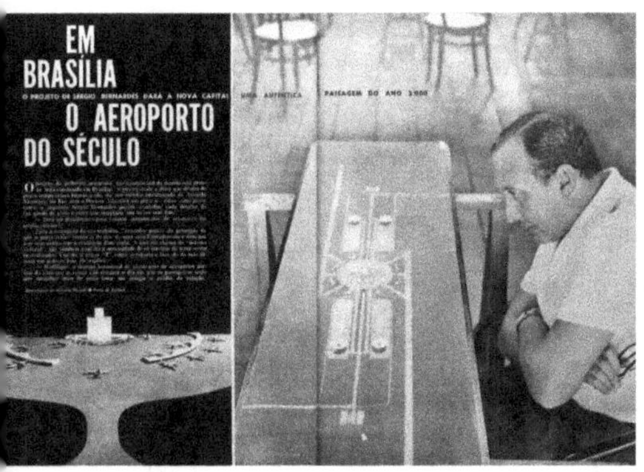

Article "In Brasília, the airport of the century," report by Ronaldo Bôscoli and photos by Jankiel. *Manchete* Magazine, no. 428, July 2, 1960, 64-65. Fausto Sombra Collection

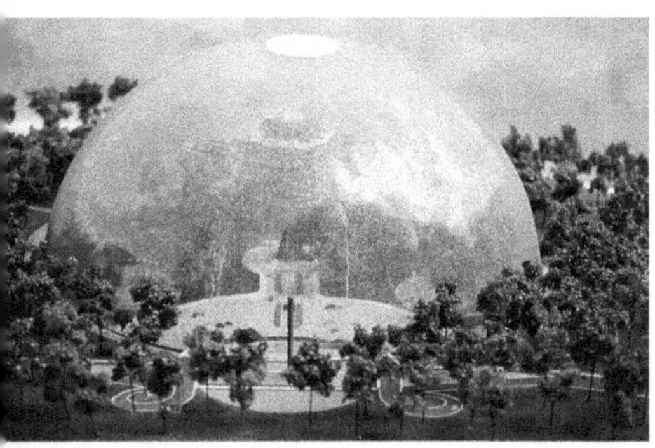

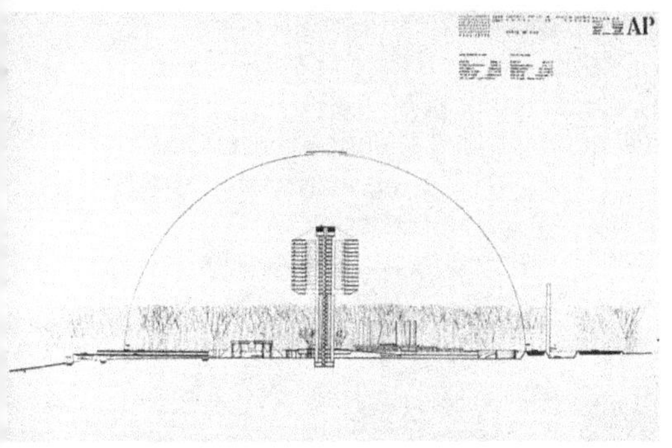

Hotel Tropical, model and section of the first version, Manaus AM, 1963. Sérgio Bernardes Collection – Memory Project / Bernardes Architecture Office

"A construction of this type could only be possible in a metallic structure. [...]

Looking at the problem, I realized that it was necessary to use a double layer reticulated structure of metallic profiles, in order to obtain sufficient rigidity.

The large dimensions of the dome and its slenderness made the action of wind expressive and imposed a tunnel aerodynamic experiment.

Technically speaking, from a structural point of view, we were in the presence of an anisotropic shell structure, with uncoupled flexural and membrane stiffness.

The surface elastic stability, that is, the possibility of its local sinking, was another important theoretical problem.

In the scientific literature of the time, and we were in the pre-computational era, there were no solutions to such problems.

It was up to me to develop the appropriate theories.

At a very young age, I was faced with an exciting challenge.

I attacked the problem with the theoretical resources of the time, and the solutions appeared.

The office of Dr. Paulo Fragoso was in charge of detailing the design. What impressed me most about everything was Sérgio Bernardes' reaction.

He had fun like a child when I explained the meaning of the theories, the results of the calculations and their relationship to the structure of the dome.

He loved scientific jargon, in which he claimed to detect a strong component of poetry.

His analytical mind grasped scientific concepts and theories with great ease, when it was possible to extract them from their mathematical formalism.

He filled me with extremely coherent questions, which I tried to answer as best I could, he called his architects to listen to the explanations around the table.

What a difference from other architects, who abhorred everything to do with theories and numbers, without which their architectural creations would never stand! [...]
The work of the Manaus dome was not accomplished, like so many other great ideas by Sérgio, because it ran into financial and technical problems.
I was a direct witness of Sérgio's suffering, in the face of not accomplishing this dream and others in the future."[74]

And he concluded, about the final version for the hotel:

"Once the impossibility of building the dome was proven, Sérgio imagined an alternative with a suspended roof, in a circular plan, from the top of the hotel tower. This solution, perhaps more beautiful than the initial one, also ended up not being accomplished. [...]
The Manaus dome marked the beginning of my long friendship and cooperation with Sérgio Bernardes."[75]

Sérgio Bernardes' avant-garde ideas for this building were such at the time that, only in 2010 – after almost four decades of the elaboration of the second version for the Manaus Tropical Hotel, in 1970 –, a building similar to that conceived by the carioca architect could be built. It is the Khan Shatyr Entertainment Center, designed by English architect Norman Foster, built in Astana, the capital of Kazakhstan, being considered the tallest tent and tensile structure in the world, with 150 meters high and an elliptical base of 200 meters.

Although many projects conceived by Sérgio Bernardes did not materialize, especially from 1960, the Tambaú Tropical Hotel is a testimony of the architect's great ability and sensitivity. Conceived in the city of João Pessoa, Paraíba, possibly between 1961 and 1971[76] – the hotel is sited on the beach of the same name, and was the result of the federal government's campaign to promote tourism "as one of the strategies of national integration in line with the modernization of the means of communication and road infrastructure."[77] "It has become a landmark of the city and an important work of Brazilian modern architecture. Not only for the preservation of urban life quality, but mainly for the relationship between technology and expression in the constructive experience."[78]

Basically composed of two concentric rings, a larger and peripheral one – structured on a breakwater that serves as a base for the suites and some social areas for rest and leisure by the sea – and a second inner ring, in which the main areas of services and support are concentrated: – similar to that proposed in the study for the Intercontinental Airport – reception, meeting rooms, administrative areas, kitchen, restaurant and others. Consisting largely of three floors, in addition to the water tank tower located in the center of the complex, and other intermediate levels intended for secondary circulations, the building is one of the most recognized postcards of the capital of Paraíba.

Strategically built at the junction of two beaches, directly on the sand, in an area protected by the Navy, its outer ring is "entirely open to the outside in its half that faces the sea and closed to the side of the city protected by a green slope, where vegetation grows."[79] It is an unusual solution that illustrates one of Sérgio's major design concerns during this period: the so-called "non-architecture", that is, the design of a building that sought to interfere visually as little as possible.

With an apparently simple solution, Tambaú Hotel is the result of controversial actions, such as its siting that happened on a public place, the beach. As it is a private undertaking, dedicated to restricted public, it presents questionable points in this regard. On the other hand, and even so, its contribution and the positive impact on its

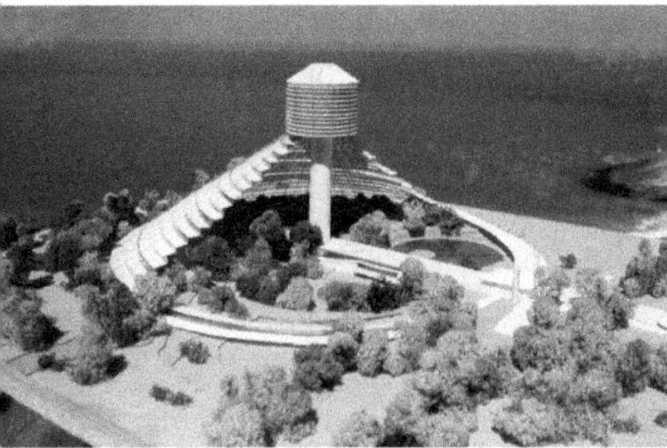

Hotel Tropical, model and section
of the second version, Manaus AM,
1970. Sérgio Bernardes Collection
– Memory Project / Bernardes
Architecture Office

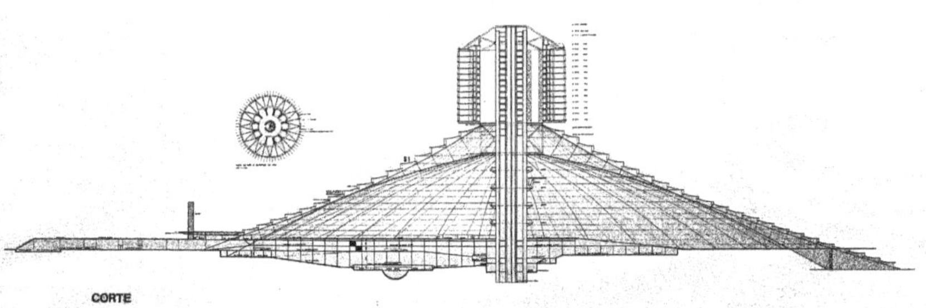

surroundings are undeniable, making it one of the most (re)
known projects within Sérgio Bernardes' work.

Currently, even with the changes of its original design
– such as the white painting on most of the walls that make
up the landscaped internal courtyards, originally designed
in exposed brick – and even though major interventions are
needed in the cluster, in order to circumvent the climatic
actions – from the wear and tear caused by the waves that
break at high tides on its basement, as well as the constant
actions of the sea air –, the aforementioned hotel could be
considered a true landmark of post-Brasilia architecture.[80]

Timidly occupying the pages of specialized books
devoted to the study of national architecture,[81] the Tambaú
Hotel was the destination for many personalities, among
them Juscelino Kubitschek. In a letter addressed to Sérgio

Bernardes, the former president congratulated the architect for his achievements in this building, claiming it to be the "most pleasant hotel not only in Brazil, but also in the world":

> "Rio de Janeiro (GB), February 22, 1972
> My dear Sérgio Bernardes,
> Among the world's architects, I consider you today one of the greatest and most ingenious.
> I have just had a proof of that, while staying a few days at the Tambaú Hotel, which, without any favors, is the most pleasant hotel not only in Brazil, but also in the world.
> I have traveled a lot, I know much about the international tourism routes, but I have never stayed in a hotel that captivated so much for the sober, elegant and friendly arrangement of all its parts.
> My congratulations are really warm, because you can be sure that, in terms of tourist hotels, no one has produced better than yours.
> Just a few months ago, I was in Torremolinos, in an excellent hotel, praised and internationally sought after. It is far from the grace of your construction lines and the pleasant atmosphere it provides.
> With my very affectionate embrace, I wish you to lavish your genius throughout this country, and produce works as interesting as the one that has marked the success of Tambaú.
> Affectionate embraces from Juscelino Kubitschek."[82]

It is understood that the honorable compliment is a consequence of the combination of the happy arrangement of materials celebrated by Brazilian modern architecture, but also the result of the atmosphere and ambience created through articulating elements, such as the galleried external walkways that give access to the suites, in addition to the

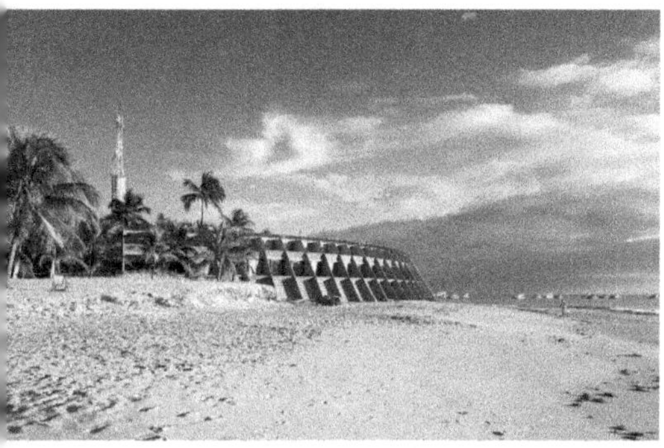

Hotel Tambaú, Southeast facade, João Pessoa PB, 1966-1971. Photo by Fausto Sombra

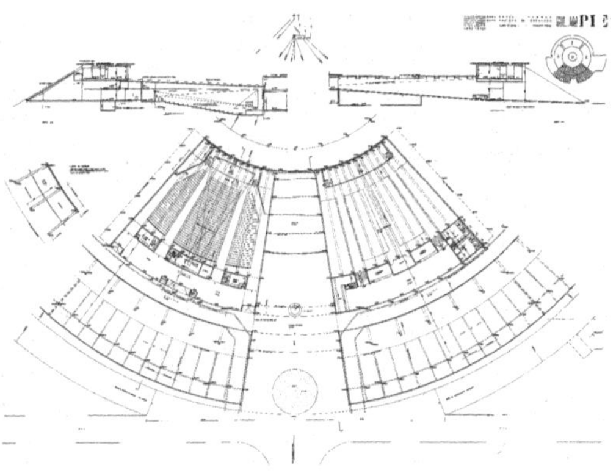

Hotel Tambaú, lower floor plan of the West section (social access), João Pessoa PB, 1967. Collection NPD FAU UFRJ / Sérgio Bernardes Fund

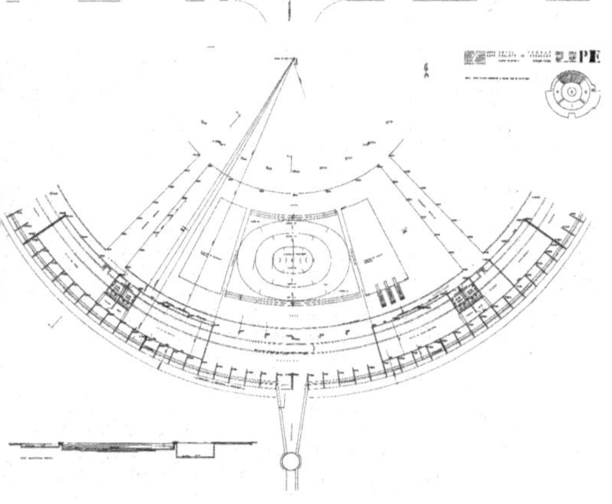

Hotel Tambaú, lower floor plan of the East section (pools), Hotel Tambaú, João Pessoa PB, 1967. Collection NPD FAU UFRJ / Sérgio Bernardes Fund

inclusion of pieces from indigenous culture, common mainly in the North and Northeast regions of the country: the hammock. This element had already been incorporated by Lúcio Costa in his sketches of unbuilt houses conceived in the early 1930s, as in the sketch of the workers' house in Vila Monlevade, in 1934, in the sketch of the House with no owner no. 1 and no. 2, in the same period, and in the Riposatevi Pavilion at the 13th Milan Triennale, in 1964.

All these factors, combined with the building's close dialogue with the site and the elements that compose it, in this case, mainly the water – through the waves that purposely touch the building at high tides, dissipating their energy on the concrete ripping that shapes the aforementioned breakwater – are characteristics and solutions that help to understand Sérgio Bernardes' way of thinking and conceiving spaces.

In addition to the many architectural designs, which his office was in charge of developing during the first half of the 1960s, Sérgio Bernardes was busy with many other crafts, such as furniture design. In an article published in *Manchete* magazine, in December 1963, it is possible to see that the architect, with other distinguished colleagues, and a decade before designing his outstanding 1975 Rampa armchair, was already dedicating part of his time to this work:

> "Lúcio Costa once said that it is easier to design a city than a chair, referring to the armchair that OCA is exhibiting alongside the new furniture models created by Sérgio Bernardes, Artur Lício Pontual and Sérgio Rodrigues."[83]

Also from the same period is the prototype car, affectionately nicknamed Bernardete, designed by Sérgio Bernardes and team. In a note published in *Manchete* magazine, in November 1964, the periodical reveals:

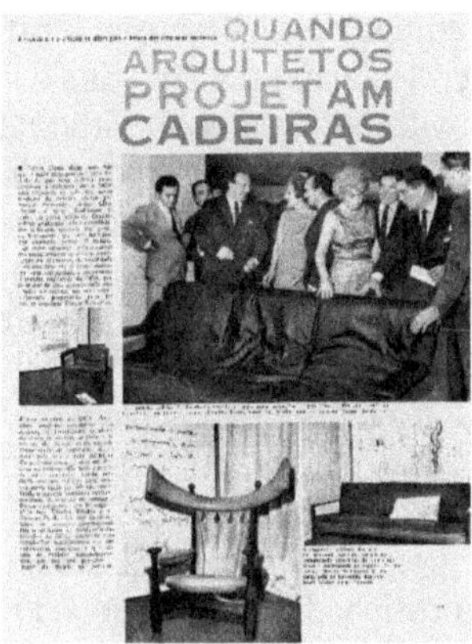

Article "When architects design chairs," published in *Manchete* magazine, no. 610, on December 28, 1963. Fausto Sombra Collection

"In the basement of his residence on Niemeyer Avenue, Rio, architect Sérgio Bernardes has researched what he calls the "pure lines of the automobile of the future". Working on a model that has been altered several times, the architect is slowly discovering the shape of a vehicle that, in addition to being comfortable and elegant, will give total security to its driver and passengers."[84]

Urban problems were already present in the work developed by the architect. In a statement published in 1966, after a storm that destroyed several houses built in risky areas in Rio, the architect already defended the necessity for cities to accept needy communities as nuclei that deserved due attention from the State. At that moment, he suggested that the squatting spaces be reorganized, allowing the adequate "installation services of water, electric light, opening of paths, canals and all public improvements. [...] The government can no longer remain silent, said Sérgio Bernardes."[85]

At least until June 1965, as shown in the excerpt below from the article "Dois famosos arquitetos residem em autênticas obras de arte", Bernardes' office still shared space with the architect's own house on Niemeyer Avenue:

"Located in an admirable, well-chosen location
– Niemeyer Avenue, facing the sea –, its construction was made with pure material, without any
coating, so that time itself can give it the final
finish. It has three floors and a swimming pool, built
above sea level and facing the ocean. It is a home
for living and for work, as his office is located in
front of it, entirely independent of the part reserved
for the home. It is a modern and bold work."[86]

However, while working in multiple lines of research,
on the most diverse programs and scales, Sérgio Bernardes
designed and built, possibly during the second half of the
1960s, the new headquarters for his office, which occupied
number 4446 Sernambetiba Avenue. Comprised of three
floors and designed in exposed concrete structure, with large
glass panels facing the sea, an entrance hall located half a
level above the street, the building stood out in the then
context of Barra da Tijuca. Engineer Jayme Mason, responsible for the project's calculations, described the conceived
space:

"Leaving the office on Niemeyer Ave, Sérgio decided to
build another one on Sernambetiba Ave, facing the sea,
on land he owned in Barra da Tijuca.
    He designed a beautiful solution in exposed rein-
forced concrete structure, with variable section beams
and large spans, covering the entire space of the architecture room. The span was surely longer than 20 m,
with the structure on display. He put me in charge of
the structural project, which I carried out with great
pleasure. [...]
    For years, he developed his projects in this office
and I was able to assist him closely, where I could be
useful.

At his total expense, he set up the LIC – "Laboratory of Conceptual Investigations" on the site, linked to his urban and geopolitical theories.

I remember having assisted, alongside our late friend Paulo Fragoso, a first session of the Laboratory, in which only Sérgio ended up speaking.

Numerous and important were the projects developed in this office, until it was handed to Banco do Brasil, to cover financing of its contracts, whose payments were not honored in time by the clients."[87]

Still about the Barra office, Sérgio Bernardes' stepson, Felipe Guanaes Rego, who from 14 to 22 years old lived with the carioca architect, then married to his mother Myriam Guanaes, recalled this generous workspace:

"Sérgio Bernardes' work room was located on a mezzanine suspended in the air, twenty meters long by five meters wide, supported by two concrete walls at the ends and with two glass sides that allowed viewing the floors below to the left, and the Atlantic Ocean to the right. A large rectangular table dominated the ambience. Sitting at the head, usually buried in drawings in front of him or in exciting presentations of new spatial concepts, was Bernardes, a strong, burly man, with an outstanding presence and fraternal eyes that drew close, inviting a good conversation."[88]

At that time, Sérgio's office in Rio had a chief coordinator, Mr. Murillo Boiabad, a professional who worked for 35 years with the carioca architect, since 1952, when the office was on the ninth floor of the Seguradoras Building, on the corner of Senador Dantas St and Evaristo da Veiga St.[89] Also around 1961, in São Paulo, and through a group of five architects organized around Ennes Silveira Mello, the office

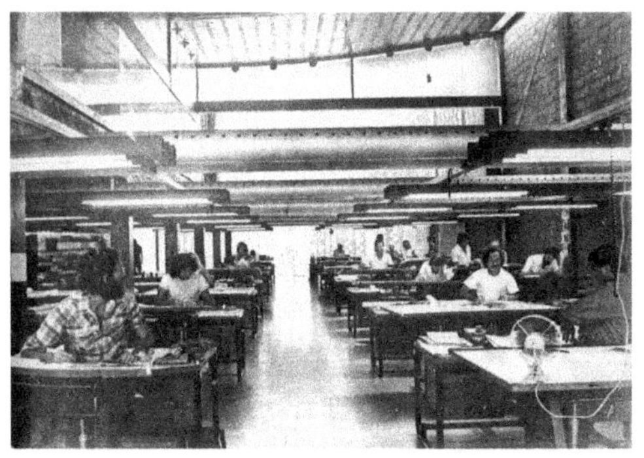

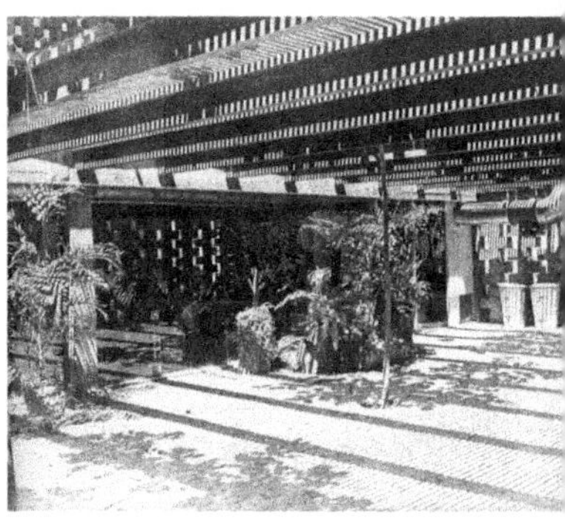

Sérgio Bernardes Associates Office / *Conceptual Investigations Laboratory (LIC)*, drawing room and backyard, Rio de Janeiro RJ, 1960s. SBA-LIC project notebooks / Sérgio Bernardes Collection – Memory Project / Bernardes Architecture Office

Sérgio Bernardes Associates Office / *Conceptual Investigations Laboratory (LIC)*, longitudinal section and plans, Rio de Janeiro RJ, 1960s. SBA-LIC project notebooks / Sérgio Bernardes Collection – Memory Project / Bernardes Architecture Office

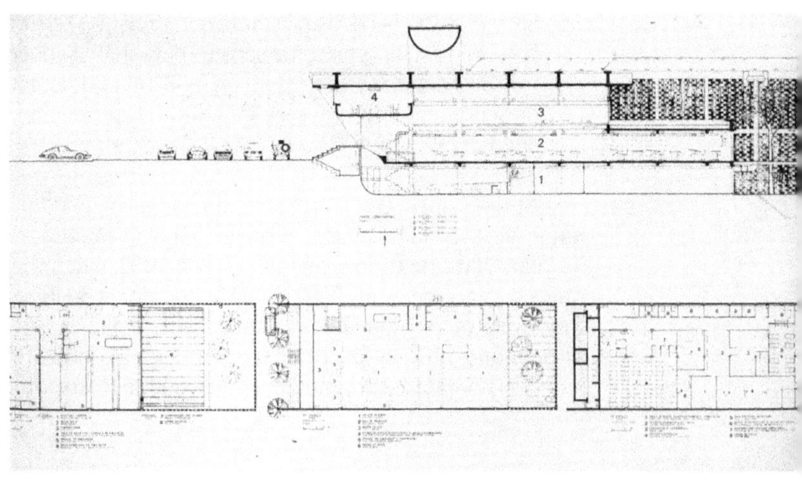

had headquarters in the capital of São Paulo,[90] thus defining
the office Sérgio Bernardes Associates – SBA.

Born in São Paulo, but graduated at the National School
of Architecture in 1963, in Rio, Silveira Mello reported
the experience of working with Sérgio after meeting him
during a series of interviews and photos he performed with
renowned architects, among them: Lúcio Costa, Niemeyer,
Reidy, Artigas, Francisco Bolonha and Oswaldo Bratke.

"All of them I had to interview, talk to them, see
what they had, what the most beautiful thing was,
photograph. I had a great deal of contact with this
whole world. And from that great contact, I naturally
fell in love with Sérgio Bernardes. A captivating guy,
a wonderful guy, an amazing guy, an intelligence,
someone amazing.
And he really was, you could say, a father to me, I
really learned a lot. In a month, I learned what I should
and should not. And I also learned about his other
side, his negative side, understand? [...] And I was his
great friend, so I could come and say things. I told him:
'Sérgio, you do not know how to stop. You have such
a strong imagination, you are designing with me, and
suddenly you change the whole concept, because you
had another idea that you want to apply' [...] For an
artist, when painting, has to know when to stop. There
is a moment when he has to stop. And Sérgio kept
continuing, understand?"[91]

Although there was no official coordinator in São Paulo,
both professionals, Murillo Boabaid and Ennes Silveira Mello,
formed a team of architects and other professionals, often
foreigners as in the case of Rio.[92] This internationalization,
inserted within the main headquarters of the office, allowed
generating different perspectives and questions to enrich
the development and result of the elaborated designs and

plans in general, and this dynamic was already present since the office on Niemeyer Avenue, as evidenced by means of an article published in 1961. In it, Sérgio's ideas for the expansion of Rio de Janeiro's capital towards Recreio was highlighted, and the introduction brought a brief overview of the carioca architect's work, and the structure of his office then, formed by several foreign scholarship holders, also his contact with renowned professionals, such as Richard Neutra.

> "Sérgio Bernardes is one of the most important Brazilian architects today. A restless but up-to-date temperament, he is always looking for new solutions in order to carry out important works, which are not simple buildings or clusters. At the same time, he is permanently concerned with the social and urbanistic side, in the highest human sense.
>
> He is internationally renowned. He gave Brazil the Grand Prize for Architecture at the Brussels Exhibition, is one of the planners of Interama, a city in Miami, designed by the greatest names in architecture in the hemisphere, and has just been invited to design the Medical School in Berlin, alongside Richard Neutra.
>
> Today, Sérgio Bernardes' office is also an international office. Japanese, Chinese, Bulgarian, Dutch, French and Brazilians work there (including scholarship holders), imbued with the concern of researching and presenting the best for architectural problems. No one is an employee there.
>
> Sérgio Bernardes and his office are increasingly embarking on the path of research, with the aim of creating a truly national architecture, taking advantage of the most relevant characteristics of our workforce, our industry, and our economic and social conjuncture."[93]

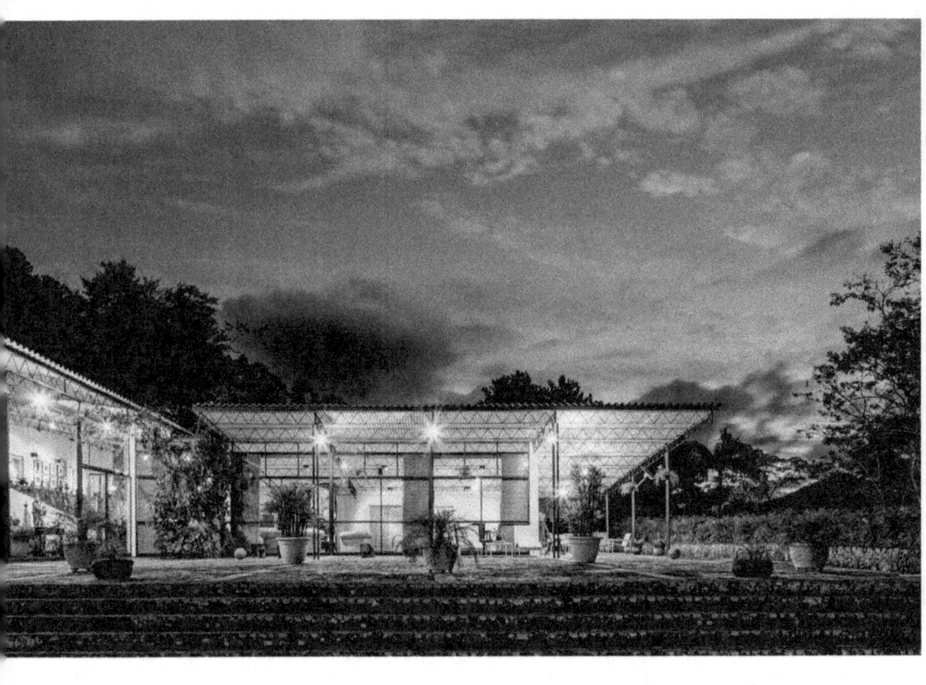

Residence Lota de Macedo Soares,
Petrópolis RJ, 1953. Photo by
Leonardo Finotti

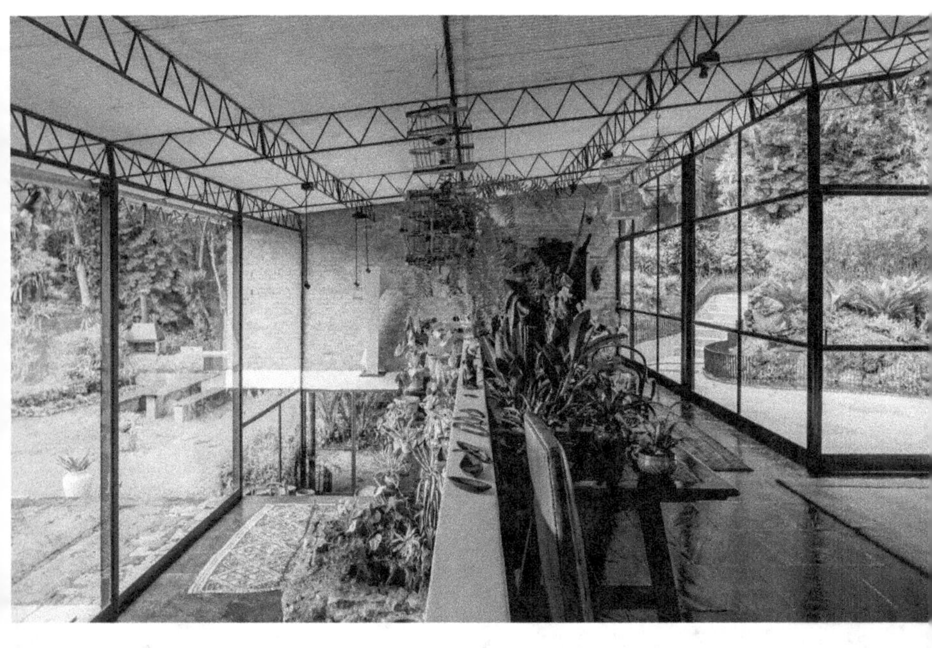

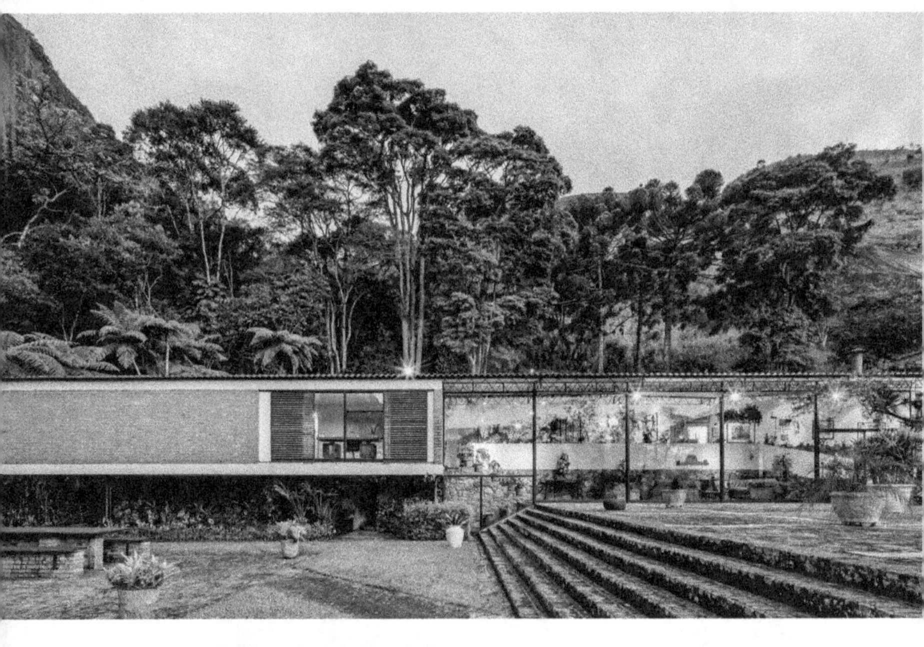

Residence Lota de Macedo Soares,
Petrópolis RJ, 1953. Photos by
Leonardo Finotti.

On the following two pages: Edifício
Barão de Gravataí, Rio de Janeiro
RJ, 1952

Edifício Justus Wallerstein, Rio de
Janeiro RJ, 1953. Photos by Leonardo
Finotti.

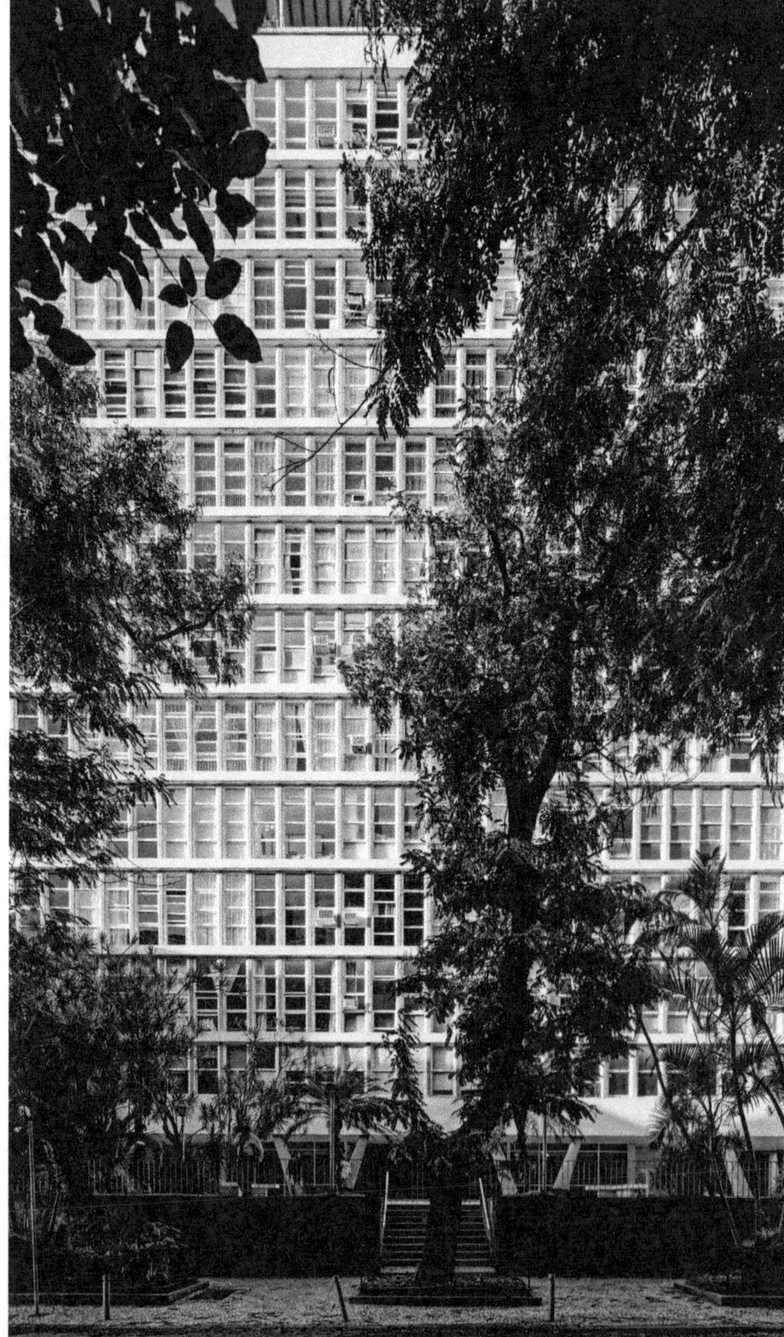

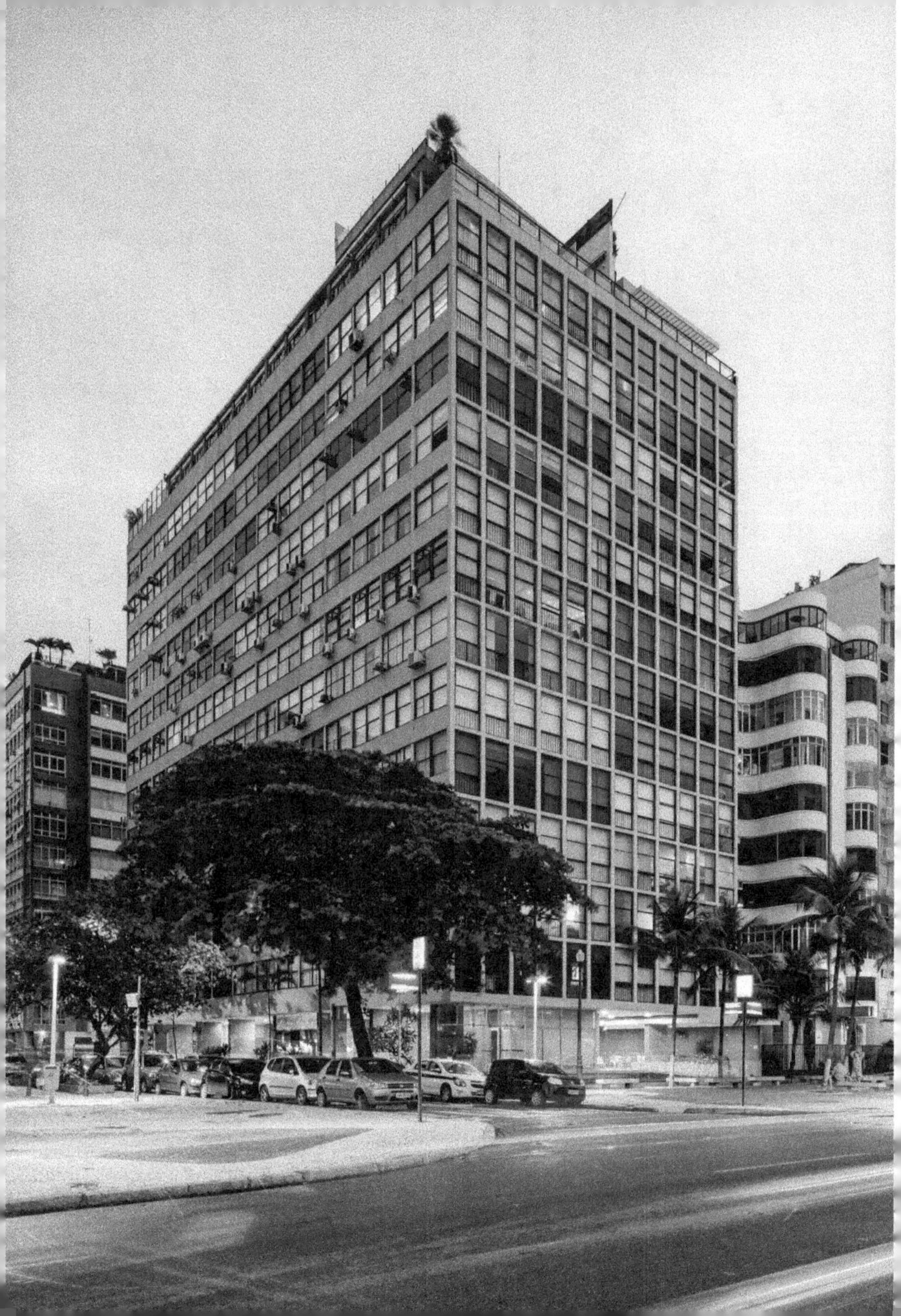

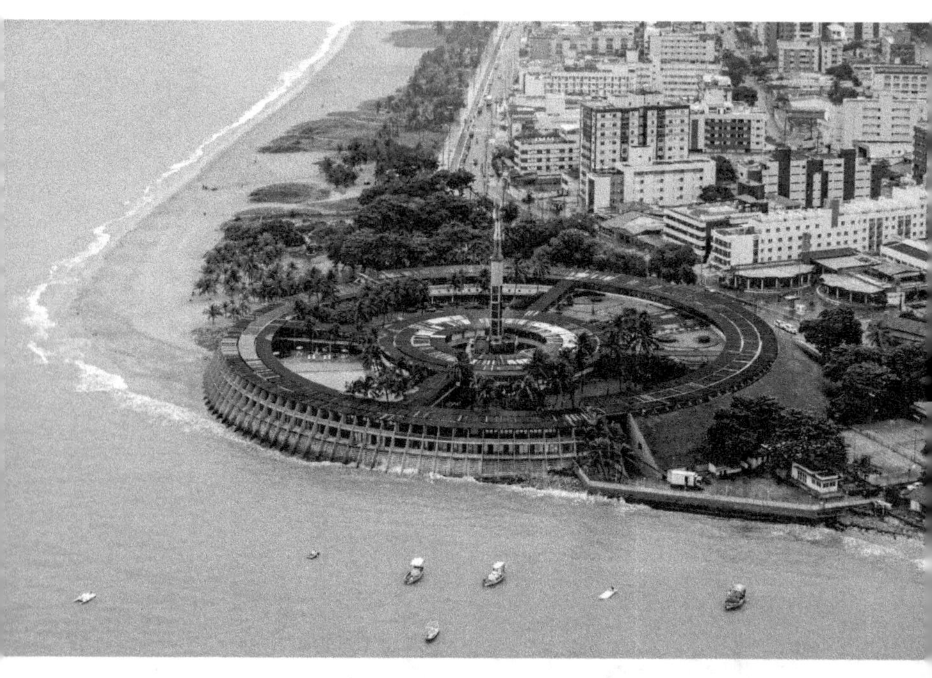

Hotel Tambaú, aerial view and rest
room, João Pessoa PB, 1966-1970.
Photos by Leonardo Finotti.

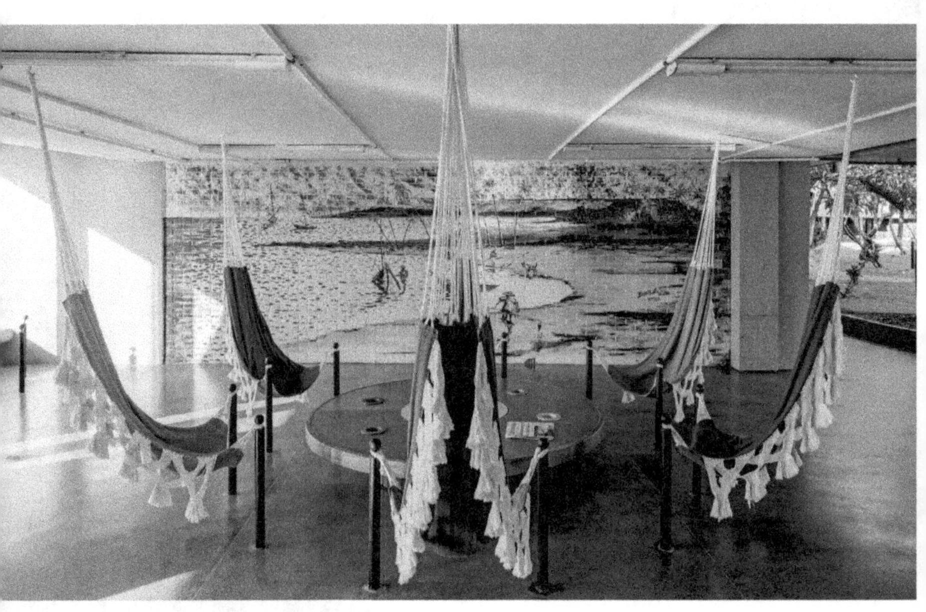

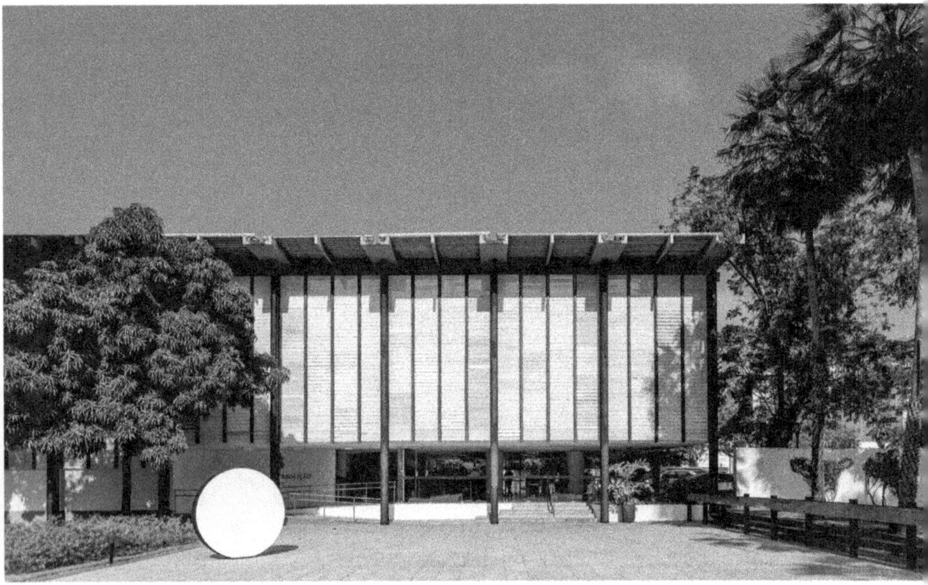

Gabinete de Despacho do Governador
(The Governor's Office), Fortaleza
CE, 1960-1970. Photo by Leonardo
Finotti.

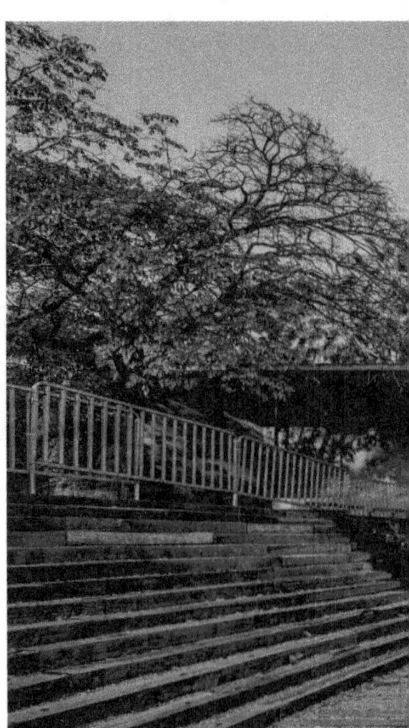

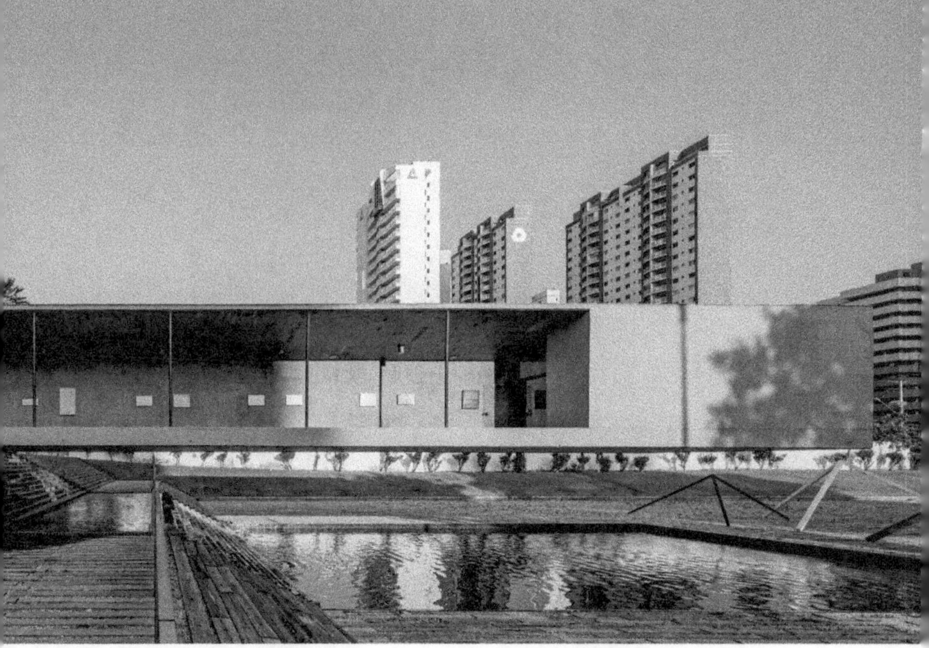

Mausoléu Castelo Branco (Castelo Branco Mausoleum), Fortaleza CE, 1972. Photo by Leonardo Finotti.

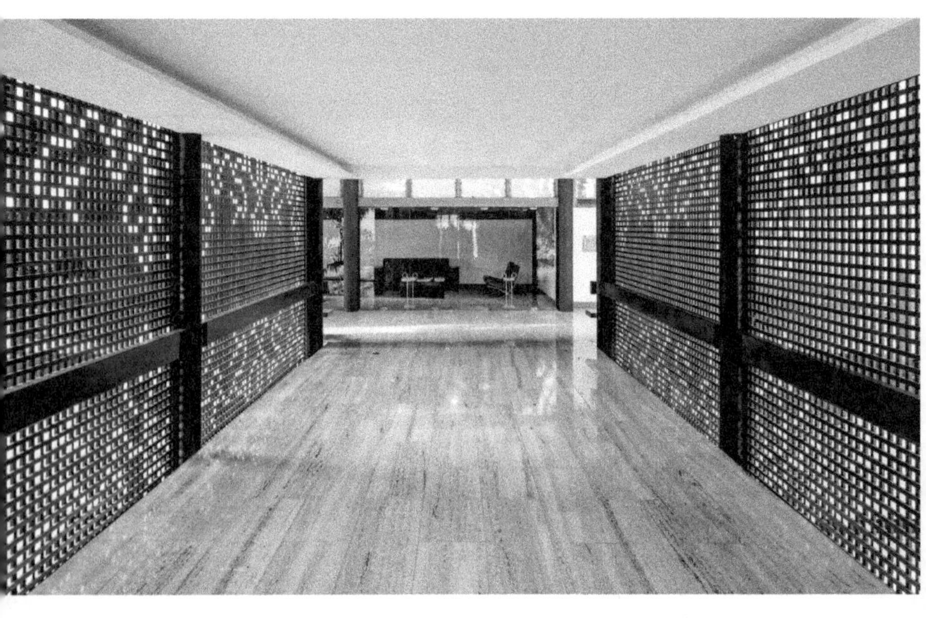

Palácio da Abolição, Fortaleza CE,
1960-1970. Photos by Leonardo
Finotti.

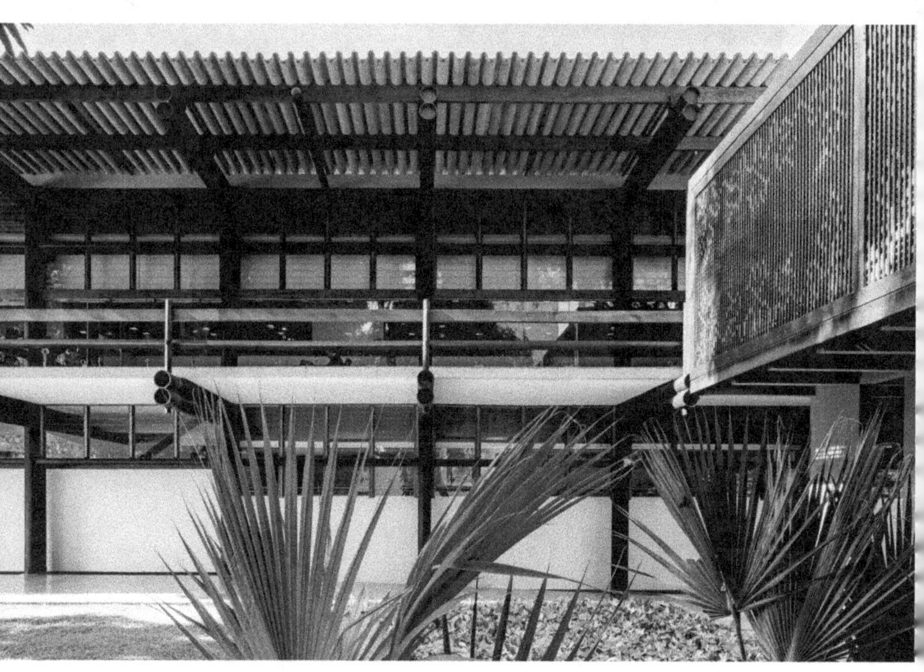

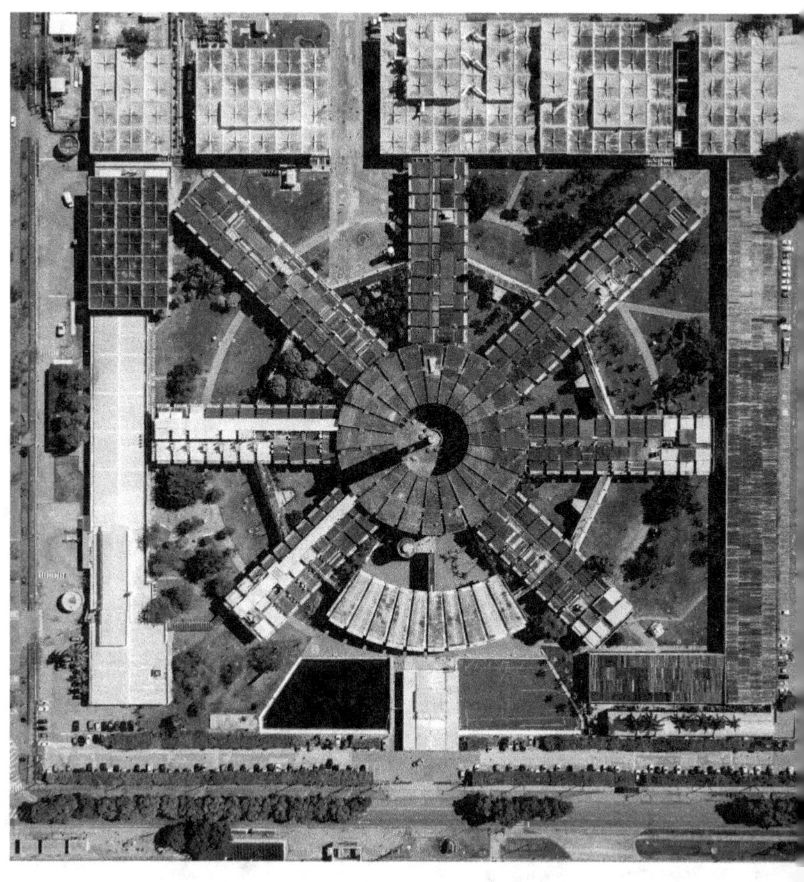

Petrobras Research Center - Cenpes,
Rio de Janeiro RJ, 1969. Photos by
Leonardo Finotti.

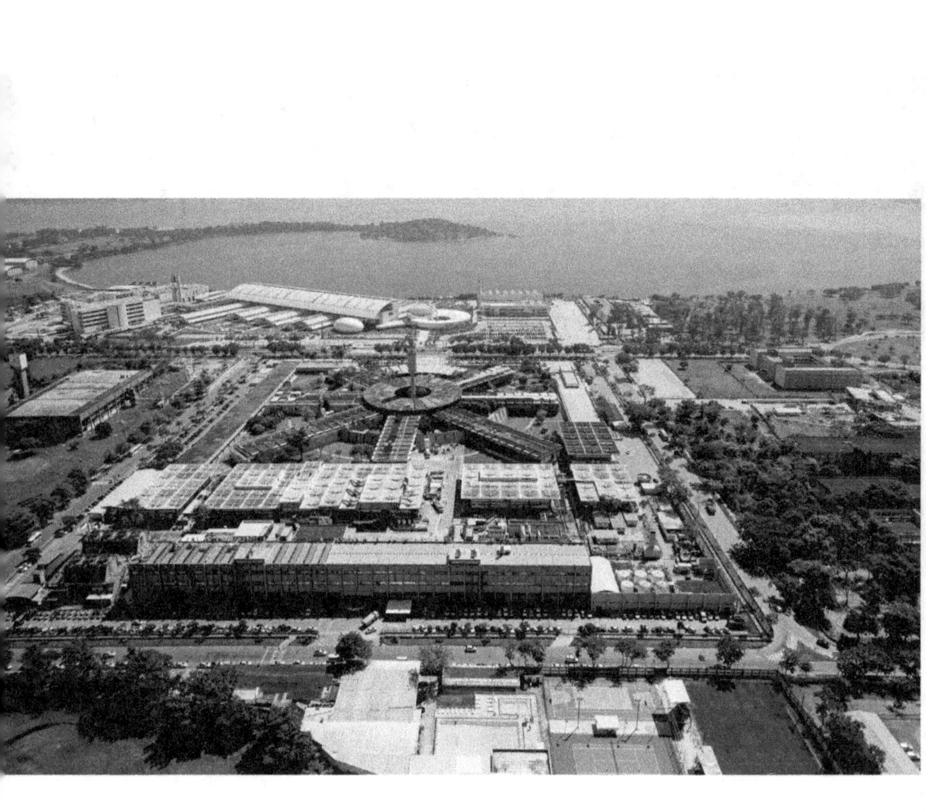

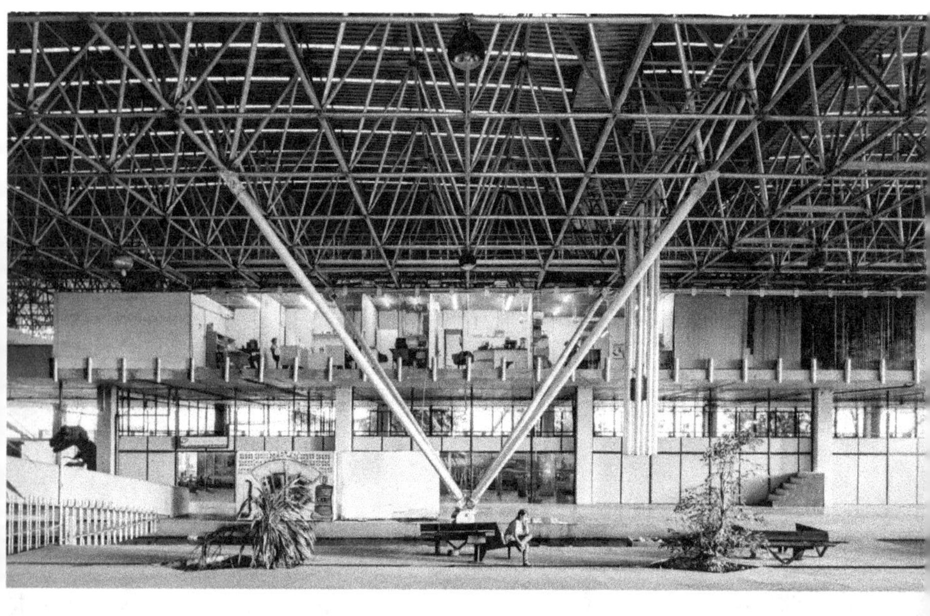

José Lins do Rego Cultural Space,
João Pessoa PB, 1980. Photos by
Leonardo Finotti.

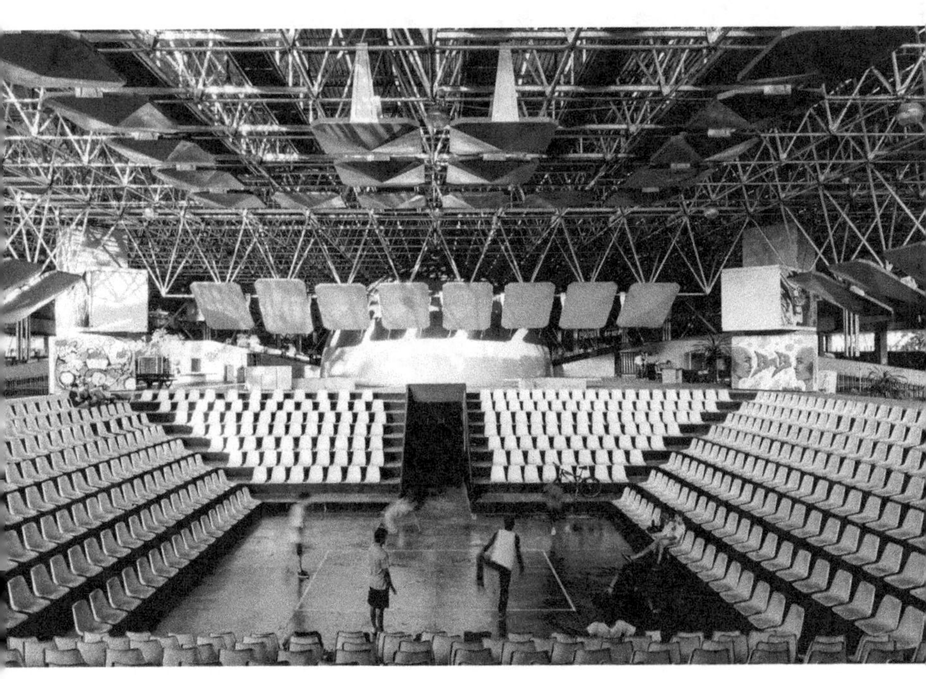

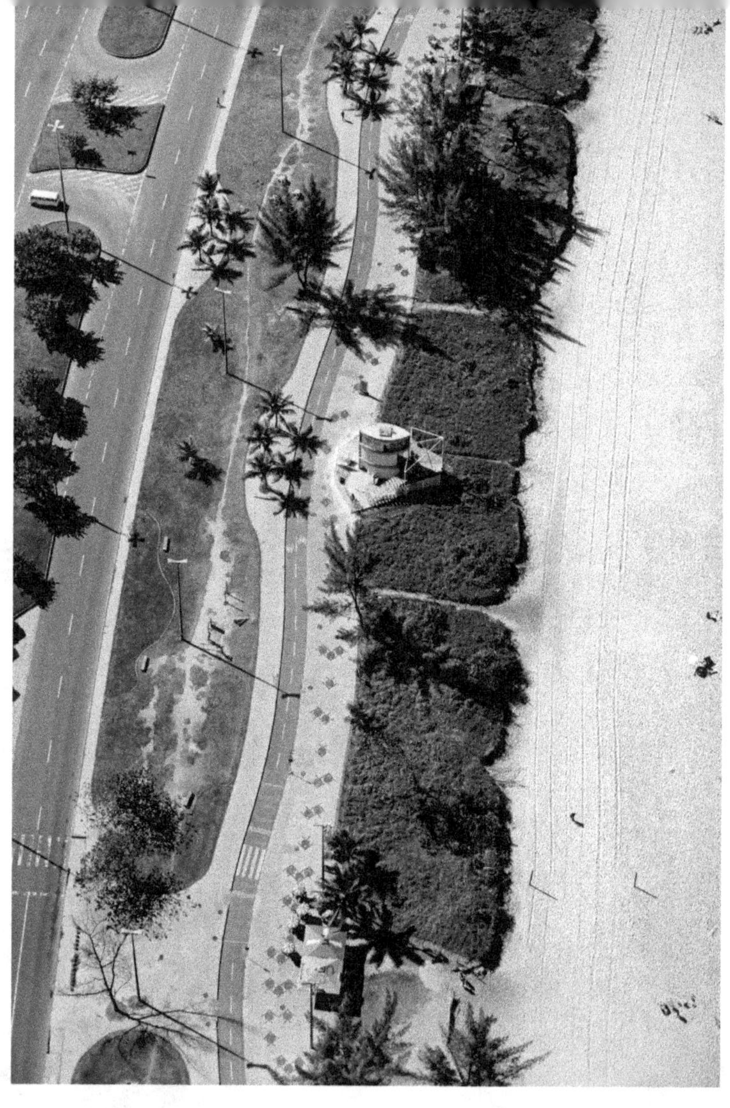

Lifeguard station, Rio de Janeiro RJ,
1976. Photo by Leonardo Finotti.

About his proximity to Richard Neutra, researcher
Fernanda Critelli has already briefly addressed this topic
in her thesis "Richard Neutra e o Brasil,"[94] also through an
undated photo when the Austrian architect and his wife,
Dione Neutra, came to the country. The image illustrates the
Austrian couple visiting Lota de Macedo Soares' house in the
company of the intellectual herself and Sérgio Bernardes.

According to correspondence authored by Dione Neutra
addressed to Sérgio Bernardes, sent from Buenos Aires on
September 29, 1959, the probable period of the aforementioned photo, there was a recent, however, apparently close
relationship established between both architects. In her

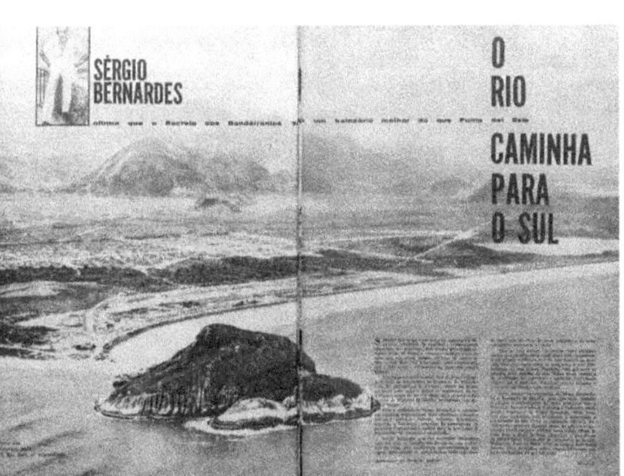

Article "Rio moves South", by
Bernardo Ludemir, published in
Manchete magazine, issue 467, on
April 1, 1961. Collection of Fausto
Sombra

letter, Dione thanked Sérgio for having confessed to Richard
Neutra how his ideas had inspired him, as well as confirmed
the date for a posterior and new visit by the couple to Rio,
on the following 2nd and 3rd.

"Buenos Aires 9.29.59
Mr. Sérgio Bernardes
Rua Tonelero, 180
apt. 104

Copacabana
Rio de janeiro, Brasil

Dear Sérgio,
I hope you allow me to be so familiar after such a short
acquaintance, but I know, you must feel the same
way as we do, how wonderful life can be that one can
recognize kindred souls immediately. I am happy for my
husband that you told him how much his thoughts on
architecture have influenced you, because he often feels
very lonely and such affirmation as yours keeps him
going and gives him new hope to continue writing and
thinking.
    It makes us both very happy to think of you and
know that you have your island to flee to and relax
there. It surely is paradise on earth and we shall always
remember with nostalgia the short time we could spend
there in company with the charming little monkeys.
    As you know by now through our telegrams, we
shall arrive Friday night 7:30 October 2 PAA flight 202.
    We should be very grateful if you could show us
some of your work next day. It is too far to drive to
Theresopolis? Our plane for Port of Spain leaves Saturday
night at 8:30 pm.
    Looking forward to be again with you
    Cordially,
    Dione [signature]."[95]

In the second half of the 1960s, Sérgio Bernardes'
office was at its highest level of activity with large-scale
works and projects in several Brazilian states. Starting with
the sketches for "Rio do futuro", published in the special
issue of *Manchete* magazine, as already briefly discussed;
the Master Plan for the Aratu Industrial Complex, in Bahia,
publicized in the same weekly magazine in November 1967,

with photos showing the evolution of the work; and the design for Corinthians Stadium in São Paulo, presented in September 1968,[96] non-built. At that point, Sérgio had resumed the topic of roofing using cables, similar to the pavilions analyzed here, however now, by means of a large longitudinal arched concrete beam, reaching 90 meters in height, and from which the steel cables would be positioned transversally with a spacing of three meters between them, elements that were launched in half a catenary until reaching the upper top of the perimeter bleachers, in a concept – keeping the due proportions, arrangement and structural solutions – similar to the one adopted in the Yoyogi National Gymnasium, in1964, by Kenzo Tange.

Other relevant projects belong to this period, among them the Recife Tropical Hotel, also in 1968, non-built, defined by a helical tower with successive setback blocks like a large staircase. The design was possibly derived from the studies carried out for the great towers of "Rio do futuro", which had recently gained supporters abroad.[97] Also the Brazilian Coffee Institute, in 1968, in Brasília, non-built; and the beautiful and technological Petrobrás Center of Investigations – CENPES, in 1969, in Rio.

Moving into the 1970s, the aforementioned projects National Pavilion Monument, in Brasília; and the Castelo Branco Mausoleum, in Fortaleza, both inaugurated in 1972. The same year dated the original design for the Cultural Center of Brasília, an interesting exemplar of the list constructed by Sérgio Bernardes, and which – with the adoption of steel cables – maintained certain formal and sometimes technical similarities with the pavilions studied here. However, after undergoing major interventions and expansion of its facilities in the early 1990s, the design authored by the office Mayerhofer & Toledo Architecture, ended up suffering a great loss of characterization and became the Ulysses Guimarães Convention Center.

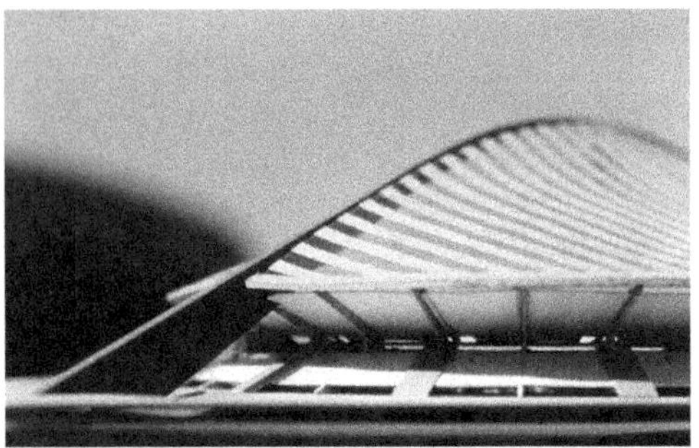

Corinthians Stadium, model of the unbuilt project, São Paulo SP, 1968. Collection of Sérgio Bernardes - Memory Project / Bernardes Architecture Office.

The manipulated sheets referring to the executive drawings for this project, prepared by Sérgio's team and filed at the NPD, indicated on the stamp the date of October 2, 1977, that is, suggesting that its inauguration had taken place later on.[98] This long process established between the beginning of its original conception and its development, for at least five years, was partially revealed through the article published in the newspaper *O Estado de S. Paulo*, on November 16, 1972. With the title "Cultura é esquecida, mas tem novo projeto",[99] questions were raised concerning the then military government's neglect of culture in Brasilia, the development of the study by Sérgio Bernardes, and why it was not granted to colleague Oscar Niemeyer, who, according to the text, had already designed "a conference room and an exhibition hall"[100] to compose the then "Cultural Sector" of the city.

Throughout the 1970s, Sérgio Bernardes still designed several other buildings, many of them non-built, such as the War School in Brasília, in 1972, having only its foundations built; Paquetá Hotel, in 1974, non-built; the headquarters for the computer company IBM in Rio, also in 1974 and non-built; in addition to the lifeguard stations on the beachfront in Rio, in 1976, with an elegant oblong shape, designed to clear the view from the interior towards the beach as little as possible.[101] The Sports Headquarters for the Aeronautics

Club, the Zoo and Hotel, both in Rio, from 1978, also ended
up not materializing.

In 1974, on the other hand, Sérgio conceived the industrial complex for Schering pharmaceutical company, in
Jacarepaguá, Rio de Janeiro. With a simple design defined by
a large roof composed of spatial trusses, totalling "almost 47
thousand square meters,"[102] the building had a large quadran-
gular opening measuring 50m x 50m in its central portion,
under which there was a large water mirror. Its spatial roof
preceded by some years the Cultural Space José Lins do Rêgo,
from 1980, as well as the Castro Pinto Airport, from 1981 –
which is currently quite uncharacterized –, both authored by
Sérgio Bernardes and located in the capital of Paraíba.

Although conceived more than a decade after Anhembi
Convention Center, in São Paulo, designed by Jorge Wilheim
and Miguel Juliano in 1968, the Cultural Space José Lins
do Rêgo, as well as the Schering complex, are examples
of concerns with spatial ambience and humanization that
Bernardes sought to imprint on the buildings and places he
designed. If in these two exemplars, the carioca architect
adopted the spatial roof as a structuring element of the

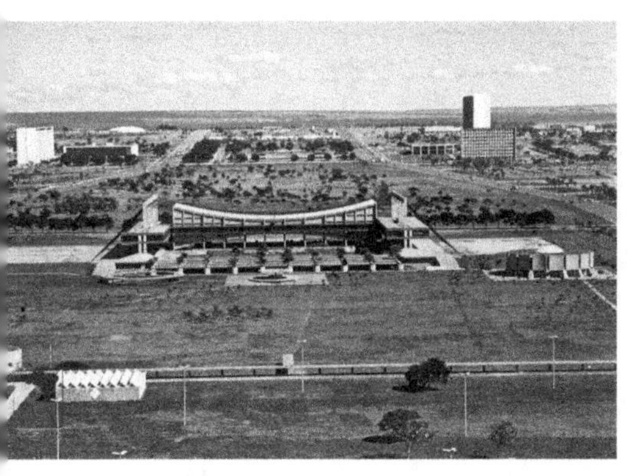

Brasília Convention Center, postcard
from Edicard Editora Cultural Ltda,
Cultural Diffusion Sector, undated.
Collection of Fausto Sombra

building, the role given to water – through the presence of water mirrors and the explanation and treatment of the leading and falling pipes over them –, has conceptually revealed equal relevance. Allied to these characteristics, the idea of flexibilizing the use of spaces through the adoption of "prismatic volumes that do not denounce their function,"[103] and the use of light structural materials are characteristics that, adapted to the climate and technical-financial conditions, approach the high-tech logic mainly pursued from the late 1970s, with the Pompidou Center in Paris. Such intentions, albeit incipient, could be found in the Volta Redonda Pavilion, as is attested by the description of this movement:

> "The use of metal and glass is a key feature of high-tech architecture, which proposes a kind of inverted approach, in which honesty of expression is desirable even when it comes to revealing the building's internal structure – the bones. Such a conception embodies ideas about industrial mass production, according to which building elements can be standardized in a factory, before being assembled at the construction site. One of the priorities of high-tech architecture is flexibility of use. This means that the emphasis is on space functionality rather than social or artistic advantages, as exemplified at the Pompidou Center in Paris by Richard Rogers and Renzo Piano. High-tech buildings, therefore, have designs that are more focused on efficiency and constructive functionality than serving a specific purpose. If Le Corbusier described the house as 'a machine for living', but he struggled to achieve it, high-tech exemplifies the potential of this maxim: the machine is a metaphor that presents applied technology and serves as a source of inspiration and imagination. Aesthetics do not reflect what happens inside these buildings, having little to do with their surroundings and context."[104]

During this period, in 1979, the Laboratory of Conceptual Investigations – LIC, a non-profit entity, was officially created, settling with the office Sérgio Bernardes Associates – SBA. At that moment, the carioca architect and his team of interdisciplinary professionals began to focus even more on the development of studies and urban,

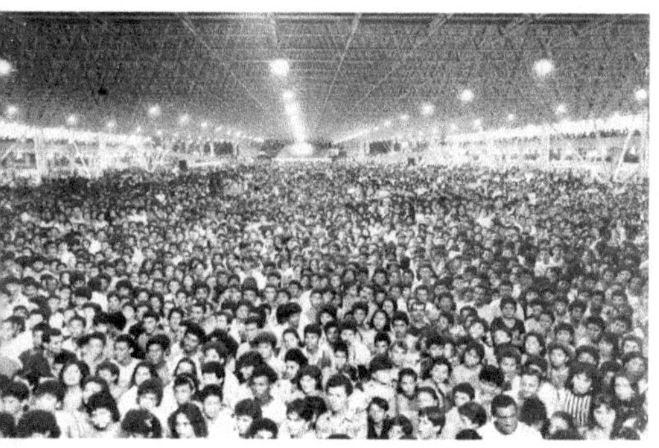

José Lins do Rego Cultural Space, Jorge Altinho concert at the closing of the Paraiban Craft Fair, João Pessoa PB, 1980. Collection of Sérgio Bernardes – Memory Project / Bernardes Architecture Office

José Lins do Rego Cultural Space, installation and detail of the spatial structure, João Pessoa PB, 1980. Collection of Sérgio Bernardes – Memory Project / Bernardes Architecture Office

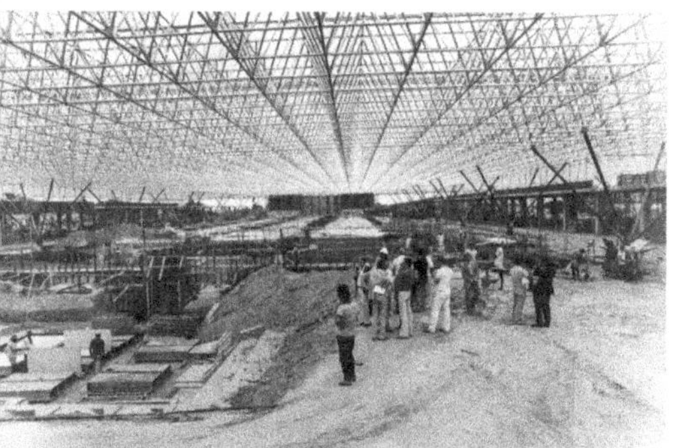

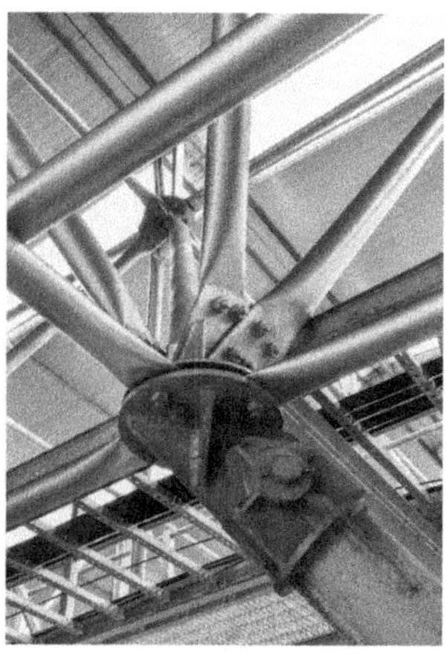

regional and national plans, underwater capsules, cities in the Arctic, and other projects of great complexity, a unique and little seen organization in the Brazilian or even international architectural universe. This work structure could be compared, at that time, to that suggested by the Office of Metropolitan Architecture – OMA, founded by Rem Koolhaas in 1975, after associating with his colleagues Elia and Zoe Zenghelis and Madelon Vriesendorp.[105]

Briefly explaining the actions by LIC, below is an excerpt of the text published in the special edition of *Módulo* magazine, dedicated to Sérgio Bernardes in 1983, defining the creation of this entity, whose content denoted Sérgio's distress with the paths of his profession, thus proposing the application of research as a means of developing plans more suited to the needs and realities of the urban environment.

Laboratory of Conceptual Investigations – LIC

"Architecture and urbanism today have nothing to do with cities – but 80 percent of the Earth's population is heading towards the cities. While urbanism only creates viaducts and neuroses, trying to order chaos, architecture cannot be healthy. Architecture and urbanism, therefore, are today the final art of great inertia – the speed of scientific and technological advances is crushed by the slow evolution of concepts for the organization of urban life and society in its political, economic, social and cultural plurality.

It was from this observation and from the need to intervene in the natural tendency of every Government to generate guidelines only after events or happenings – as the solution of the viaducts symbolically illustrates – that the LIC – Laboratory of Conceptual Investigations was born in 1979, a non-profit entity whose only capital is an idea – the idea of being a nucleus of thought to intervene in the current reality, and suggest how Man can better organize in space, by harmonizing work, circulation, housing and leisure, elementary conditions of his well-being.

LIC is fed by mistakes to design changes. But changes that are based on Man's naturalness, which is evolution, and not revolution, which is the lack of naturalness to admit that same evolution. Inspired by experiences accumulated by Humanity, but also by the perception that we live in a moment when only chaos is planned, the LIC does not prescribe palliative or analgesic prescriptions, nor does it indicate remedies only for the sick parts of the social and urban tissues. Rather, we imagine that cities, for instance, are like Man, an organism that must be studied and medicated as a whole, in a systemic way.

The LIC has an even broader vision. We think that Man is an extension of the Universe, and consider the Earth his capital asset. Therefore, we understand that Man has the right to receive all the fruits of the Earth's transformation, until the natural fusion between the two systems – Man and Earth, is consummated.

Based on a permanent investigation of concepts – because concepts expire at a surprising speed – the LIC develops projects that offer new horizons to the potentialities that the Earth and each country in particular offer. These are proposals that ignore momentary economic crises, because they are indications of definitive solutions that generate employment, provide social well-being and make cities viable."[106]

From the point of view of the present study, it is not necessary to extend the narrative regarding the relevant role of the LIC and other themes that Sérgio Bernardes would still undertake at the end of his long professional career – such as the plan entitled Rings of balance, from 1979 , for Rio;[107] the competition for Parc de la Villette, 1982, in Paris;[108] the

studies for "A city on the train line" and Lagocean, both from
1983, in Rio; in addition to his candidacy for mayor of the
state capital, in 1985, by the National Mobilization Party.

Finally, it is noteworthy that one of the last works Sérgio
Bernardes developed, already at the turn of the century, that
is, close to his passing, was the reconstruction design for
Volta Redonda Pavilion, an emblematic building, as well as
its peers from the second half of the 1950s, which will be
revisited in the three subsequent chapters that compose and
properly define the theme of analysis in the present research,
a relevant moment of inflection in the vast work by this
professional.

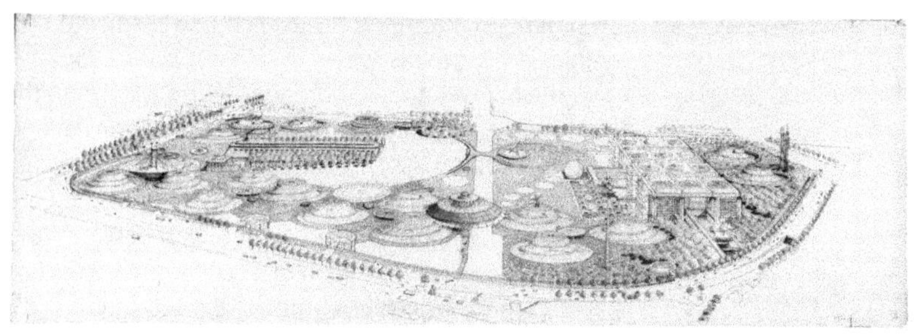

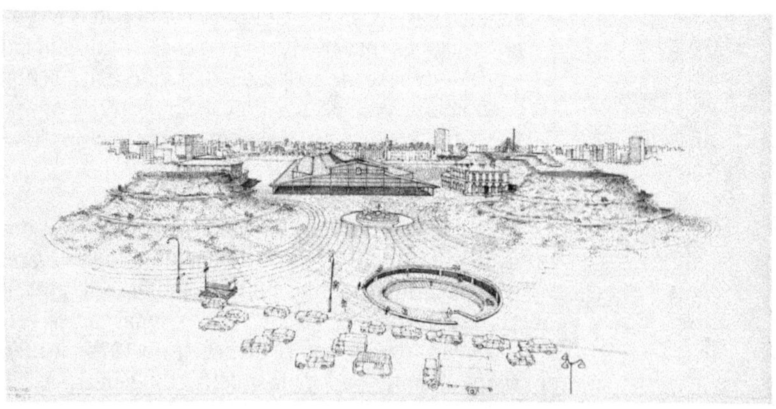

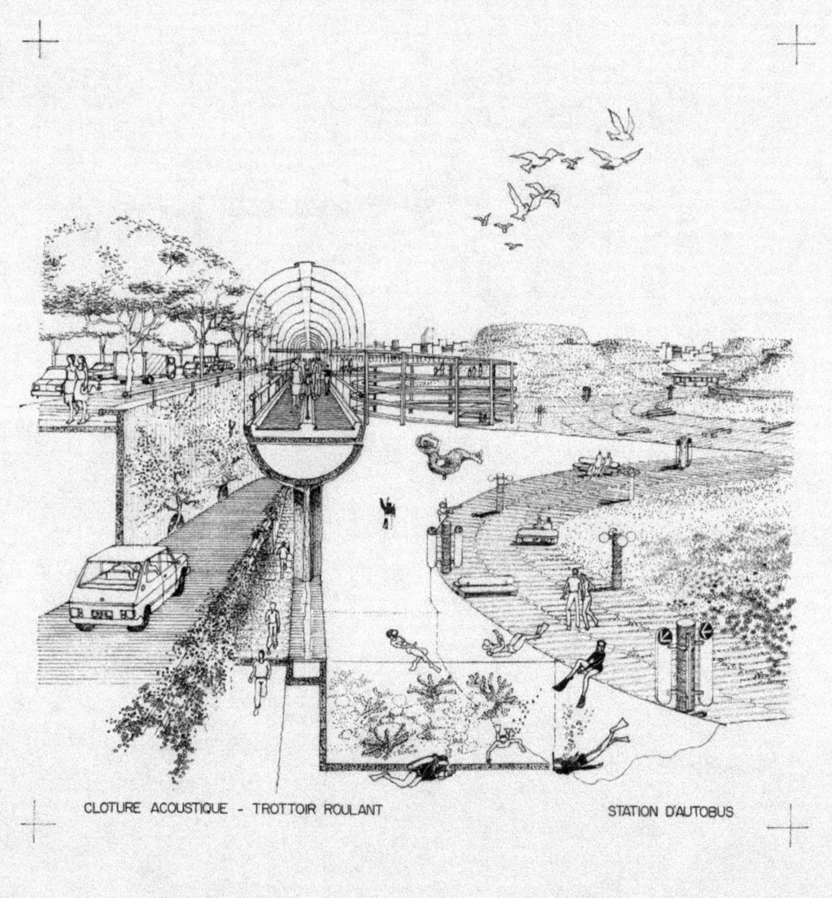

Parc De La Villette, competition drawings, unbuilt project, Paris, France,
1982. Collection of NPD FAU UFRJ /
Sérgio Bernardes Fund

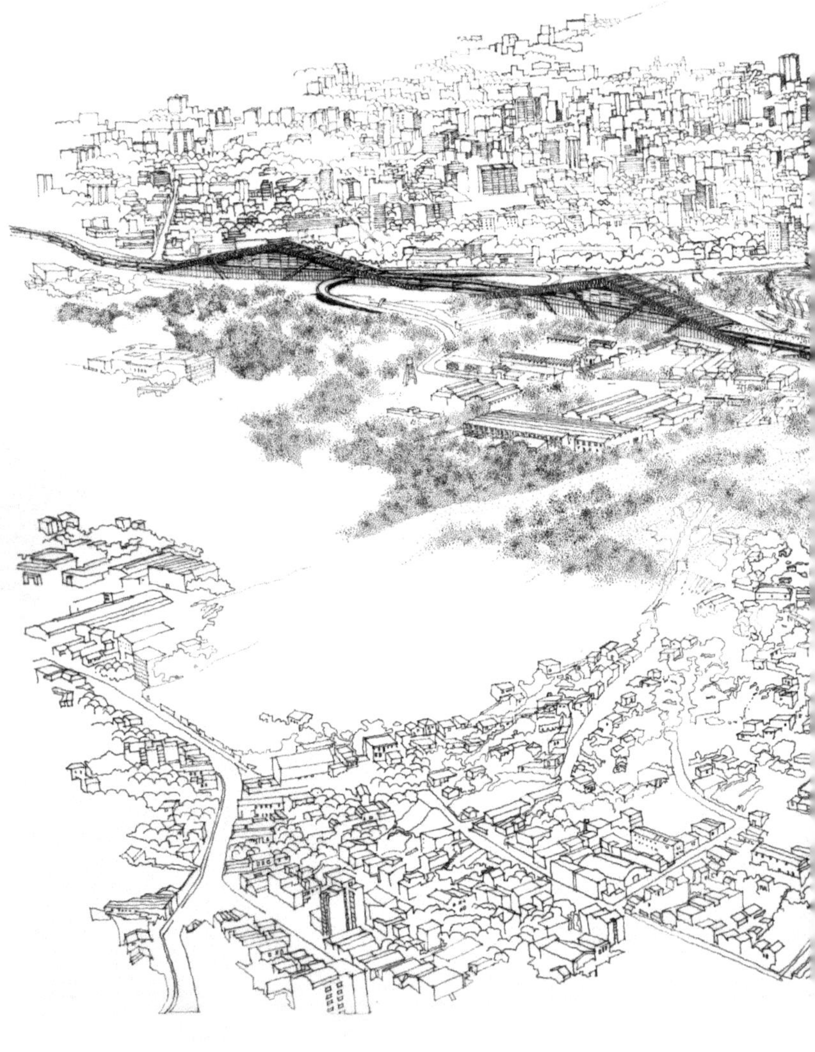

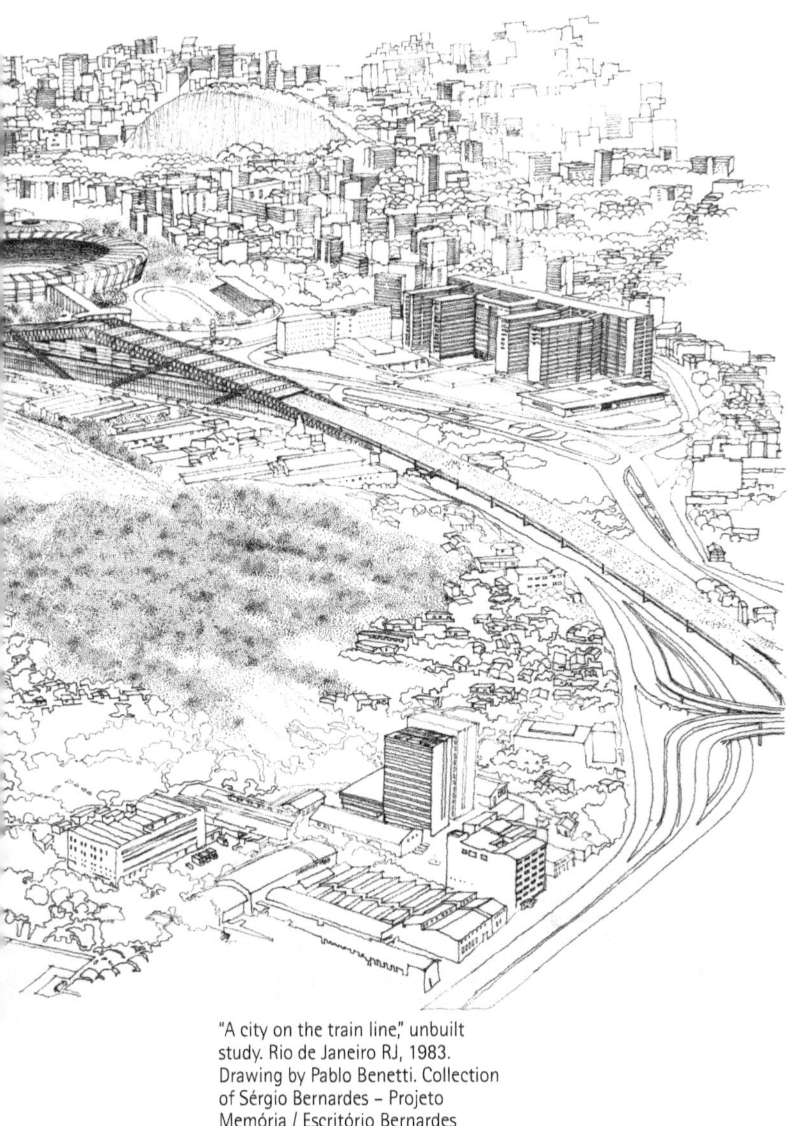

"A city on the train line," unbuilt
study. Rio de Janeiro RJ, 1983.
Drawing by Pablo Benetti. Collection
of Sérgio Bernardes – Projeto
Memória / Escritório Bernardes
Arquitetura

Notes

1. José Lira, in his book about Gregori Warchavchik, recalled the history that involved the construction of the House on Santa Cruz St: "It is worth remembering the epic of the event [...]. To obtain the building permit from the facade censors, the architect had simulated a conventional compositional solution, claiming at the end of the work the lack of resources to carry out the planned ornamentation". José Lira, *Warchavchik: fraturas da vanguarda*, 151.

2. Abilio Guerra, "Lúcio Costa, Gregori Warchavchik e Roberto Burle Marx: síntese entre arquitetura e natureza tropical", 315.

3. Ibid., 313.

4. Ibid., 313.

5. Ibid., 313.

6. Aracy Amaral, *Artes Plásticas na Semana de 1922*, 151.

7. According to testimony by Luis Saia to Aracy Amaral, quoted in Amaral, *Artes Plásticas na Semana de 1922*, 151.

8. Silvio Colin, "A arquitetura na Semana de Arte Moderna de 1922".

9. Amaral, *Artes Plásticas na Semana de 1922*, 157.

10. Ibid.,157.

11. Guilherme Malfatti, quoted in Amaral, *Artes Plásticas na Semana de 1922*,151.

12. About the neocolonial style, see Maria Lucia Bressan Pinheiro, *Neocolonial, modernismo e preservação do patrimônio: debate cultural dos anos 1920 no Brasil*.

13. About the constitution of the MES building, see Roberto Segre, *Ministério da Educação e Saúde: ícone urbano da modernidade brasileira (1935-1945)*.

14. Henry-Russell Hitchcock. *Latin American architecture since 1945*, 31.

15. Redação, "Brésil".

16. TN: *Tupiniquins* are an indigenous people of Brazil.

17. Mário de Andrade, "Brazil Builds".

18. Rino Levi, "A arquitetura e a estética das cidades: uma carta de um estudante brasileiro em Roma".

19. This fact demonstrates the precariousness of the Brazilian technical development at the time in the face of the rationalist style disseminated by avant-garde schools in Europe, such as the Bauhaus, extinguished early in 1933 by the Nazis.

20. Originally published respectively in *Revista da Diretoria de Engenharia da PDF* and in the opening issue of *Revista do Serviço do Patrimônio e Histórico e Artístico Nacional*.

21. Lauro Cavalcanti, *Quando o Brasil era moderno: guia da arquitetura 1928-1960*, 12-14.

22. Segre, "Sérgio Bernardes (1919-2002)".

23. Lydio de Souza, "Brasil potência arquitetônica", 22.

24. Alexandre Bahia has presented in his research a list of designs by Sérgio Bernardes organized in a chronological and typological way, a significant contribution in the intention of reorganizing the vast projectual production by Bernardes. Vanderlei, "Sérgio Bernardes".

25. Bernardes and Cavalcanti, eds., *Sérgio Bernardes.*

26. Murillo Boabaid, "Pavilhões", 54-63.

27. Bruand, *Arquitetura contemporânea no Brasil*, 259-261.

28. Ibid., 260.

29. Ibid., 260-261.

30. Ibid., 261.

31. Cavalcanti, *Sérgio Bernardes*, 38.

32. Edward Denison, ed., *30-Second Architecture: 50 estilos fundamentais explicados de forma clara e rápida*, 106.

33. About high-tech architecture, see Colin Davies, *A New History of Modern Architecture*, 344-361.

34. Vicente Mas et al., "Conversación con Paulo Mendes da Rocha", 115.

35. Carlos Guilherme Mota and Adriana Lopez. *História do Brasil: uma interpretação*, 610.

36. On Brazil's involvement in Second World War, especially on the naval conflict between Brazil and Germany in that period, when Hitler stated that "in Brazil, all the conditions for a revolution that would allow to transform the State governed and inhabited by mestizos into a Germanic possession". Roberto Sander, *O Brasil na mira de Hitler: a história do afundamento de navios brasileiros pelos nazistas*, 15.

37. Claiton Márcio da Silva, "Nelson Rockefeller e a atuação da American International Association for Economic and Social Development: debates sobre missão e imperialismo no Brasil", 1697.

38. See Lina Rodrigues de Faria, "Os primeiros anos da reforma sanitária no Brasil e a atuação da Fundação Rockefeller (1915-1920)".

39. "One of the reasons why Roosevelt hired Nelson, in August 1940, to work in his government as coordinator of the Office of the Coordinator of Inter-American Affairs" had nothing to do "with the fact that he was the heir to one of the greatest fortunes in the world, but because of the good traffic he maintained with the Latin American elite". Tota, *O amigo americano*, 17.

40. See Silva, "Nelson Rockefeller e a atuação da American International Association for Economic and Social Development".

41. The Venice Triennale is an apparently mistaken term used by Sérgio Bernardes as the name for another event, not identified by the research, in which he won the architecture prize for the Hélio Cabal residence in Rio.

42. Redação, "A expansão de São Paulo se fez explosivamente".

43. A document present in the architect's collection – a letter dated Jul. 3, 1956, sent by Companhia Imobiliária Kosmos, addressed to Sérgio Bernardes, "to the care of Comissão Executiva da Exposição Internacional de Indústria e Comércio" – mentions the "study of tablets (sic) that will be fixed on the work in question", which confirms that at that time Bernardes is already in charge of the Pavilion design. Companhia Imobiliária Kosmos, correspondence to Sérgio Bernardes, Rio de Janeiro, 3 Jul. 1956, Sérgio Bernardes collection.

44. Between 1956 and 1958, the Brazilian GDP increased from 2.9% to 10.8%. See Redação, "Brasília 50 anos".

45. Pedro Bloch, "A humanização da arquitetura", 101.

46. The newspaper *Gazeta de Notícias,* a periodical with wide circulation at the time, was smeared in 1931 during the provisional government of Getúlio Vargas, for taking a direct stand against the actions of the intervener. For a brief history of the newspaper, see Carlos Eduardo Leal, Gazeta de Notícias (entry).

47. Regina Bittencourt was born on May 9, 1922.

48. Backhauser, "A obra de Sérgio Bernardes".

49. About Sérgio Bernardes' father, see Redação, "Um dicionário hilariante", 76-77.

50. TN: Currency of the period.

51. Marly Berg, Lúcia Vasconcelos, and Celso Arnaldo Araújo, "O que eles sonharam para os filhos. Para a escolha de uma profissão, a influência dos pais pode não ser um fator positivo", 52.

52. Bloch, "A humanização da arquitetura," 98.

53. Ibid., 98.

54. Ibid., 98.

55. See Ana Lúcia Cerávalo, "Paulo de Camargo e Almeida: arquitetura total na trajetória de um arquiteto brasileiro".

56. Bloch, "A humanização da arquitetura," 98.

57. Ibid., 98.

58. Sérgio Bernardes still had a fourth child out of wedlock, a girl named Bernarda Van Allen Guaraná Bernardes, born in 1975. The architect dedicated his book *Cidade: a sobrevivência do poder* to his four children.

59. Bloch, "A humanização da arquitetura," 98.

60. Jayme Mason, *Humanismo, ciência, engenharia: perspectivas, depoimentos, testemunhos,* 225-226.

61. Redação. "Sérgio Bernardes: Country Club e Petrópolis".

62. Costa et al., "O sanatório de Curicica".

63. Ibid. Also see Malaquias, "Sérgio Bernardes e o Sanatório de Curicica".

64. The house was renovated and adapted by architect Guilherme Lemke Motta for the current resident, artist Jacqueline Aronis, who gave testimony for this research. Jacqueline Aronis, testimony to Fausto Sombra at the artist's atelier-residence, São Paulo, 21 Sep. 2019.

65. Bloch, "A humanização da arquitetura," 98.

66. Mason, *Humanismo , ciência, engenharia*, 226

67. Redação, "Aeroporto Intercontinental América do Sul-Brasília".

68. Ibid., 12.

69. Ronaldo Bóscolo, "Em Brasília, o aeroporto do século," 64.

70. Ana Luiza Nobre, "Malhas, redes, cabos e triângulos," 37.

71. Researcher Marcelo Jabor proved that Sérgio Bernardes happened to propose at least three solutions for the Manaus Tropical Hotel. Marcelo Jabor de Oliveira Almeida, "Vestígios de um futuro (ou o Hotel Tropical de Manaus de Sérgio Bernardes sob a óptica do redesenho)".

72. In Brazil, in the dome of Conjunto Nacional, a 1955 design by David Libeskind and Austrian engineer Hans Eger, the pioneering use of these innovative roofing systems could already be observed.

73. Nobre, "Sérgio Bernardes," 40.

74. Mason, *Humanismo, ciência, engenharia*, 223-224.

75. Ibid., 224.

76. At the main entrance to the hotel, a sign posted on the wall near the reception clarifies: "Tambaú Hotel João Pessoa, built in the government of João Agripino, 6 Mar. 1971, and inaugurated in the government of Ernani Sátyro, 11 Sep. 1971, Secretariat of Transport, Communications and Works, SUPLAN". Suplan, Placa de inauguração do Tambaú Hotel, João Pessoa, Governo Estadual da Paraíba, 11 Sept. 1971.

77. Rocha, Tinem, and Cotrim, "Hotel Tambaú, de Sérgio Bernardes".

78. Ibid.

79. Ibid.

80. The hotel's fate is still indefinite. Recently, after the property was auctioned, the City Hall of João Pessoa expressed its intention to expropriate, list, restore and preserve the building. G1-PB, "Prefeitura de João Pessoa transforma Hotel Tambaú em bem de utilidade pública: em meio a disputas judiciais, Prefeitura quer manter a preservação do local. Próximo passo é tentar desapropriar o prédio".

81. Maria Alice Junqueira Bastos and Ruth Verde Zein, *Brasil: arquiteturas após 1950*, 147.

82. Juscelino Kubitschek, "Carta a Sérgio Bernardes", Rio de Janeiro, Feb. 22, 1972, Sérgio Bernardes Collection.

83. Redação, "Quando os arquitetos projetam cadeiras", 101.
84. Redação, "Posto de escuta", 102.
85. Juracy Costa, Muniz Sodré, "Favela cinco vezes inferno", 30.
86. Redação, "Dois famosos arquitetos residem em autênticas obras de arte", 58.
87. Mason, *Humanismo, ciência, engenharia*, 227.
88. Guanaes, *Sérgio Bernardes*, op. cit., 12.
89. Murillo Boabaid, Testimony to Fausto Sombra through electronic message, Rio de Janeiro, Nov. 22, 2019.
90. According to Ennes Silveira de Mello, the office in São Paulo was organized as follows: "I organized the office, who coordinated the work was Edla Van Steen, my wife, Modesto Carvalhosa lawyer, my uncle Antônio accountant. Lew Parrella photographer, Luís Baravelli perspectives, Zoltan Snowsky detailing. Architects: Henrique Pait, Arthur Fajardo, Dácio Ottoni, Eduardo Almeida, Ennes Silveira Mello. My idea was to create an architecture studio and not an architecture office. We were all partners, there were no employees. It worked for seven years". Ennes Silveira de Mello, Testimony to Fausto Sombra through electronic message, São Paulo, Nov. 22, 2019.
91. Cf., Ennes Silveira de Mello, Testimony to Fausto Sombra at the architect's residence, São Paulo, Feb. 6, 2018.
92. Information confirmed by architect Antônio Claudio Pinto da Fonseca, former collaborator of Sérgio Bernardes in Rio de Janeiro, and Joan Villà, architect and former collaborator of Sérgio Bernardes in São Paulo, in testimonies given on the same day to a small audience in the lobby of the School of Architecture and Urbanism at Mackenzie Presbyterian University. Cf. Antônio Claudio Pinto da Fonseca, Depoimento em palestra, São Paulo, FAU Mackenzie, Oct. 9, 2018; Joan Villa, Depoimento em palestra, Sao Paulo, FAU Mackenzie, Oct. 9, 2018.
93. Bernardo Ludemir, "O Rio caminha para o Sul", 64.
94. Fernanda Critelli, "Richard Neutra e o Brasil", 167.
95. English original, Sérgio Bernardes collection (in possession of Kykah Bernardes at the time of the research).
96. João Pedro Backheuser, "Estruturas que se lançam no espaço", 66.

97. See Redação, "Un nuevo edificio
conformará el paisaje de Puebla,
México: Torre Helea".

98. The original design was from
1972-1973, after several
program and area adjustments,
it was inaugurated in 1979.
Redação, "Centro de Convenções
Ulysses Guimarães: neste
icônico projeto, Sérgio Bernardes
contemplou a vista de Brasília
com uma grande construção
horizontal".

99. Redação, "Cultura é esquecida,
mas tem novo projeto".

100. Redação, "Cultura", 18.

101. The stations can still be found,
with greater or lesser mischar-
acterization, on the beaches
of Copacabana, Ipanema and
Leblon.

102. Nobre, "Sérgio Bernardes," 43.

103. Ibid., 43.

104. Denison, ed., *30-Second
Architecture*, 116.

105. See Redação, Rem Koolhaas
(entry).

106. Redação, "LIC – Laboratório
de Investigações Conceituais",
15-16.

107. Alfredo Britto, "Sérgio Bernardes
e o Rio", 132.

108. See Vieira, "O Parc La Villette na
concepção de Sérgio Bernardes".

Chapter 2
Volta Redonda Pavilion
1954–1955

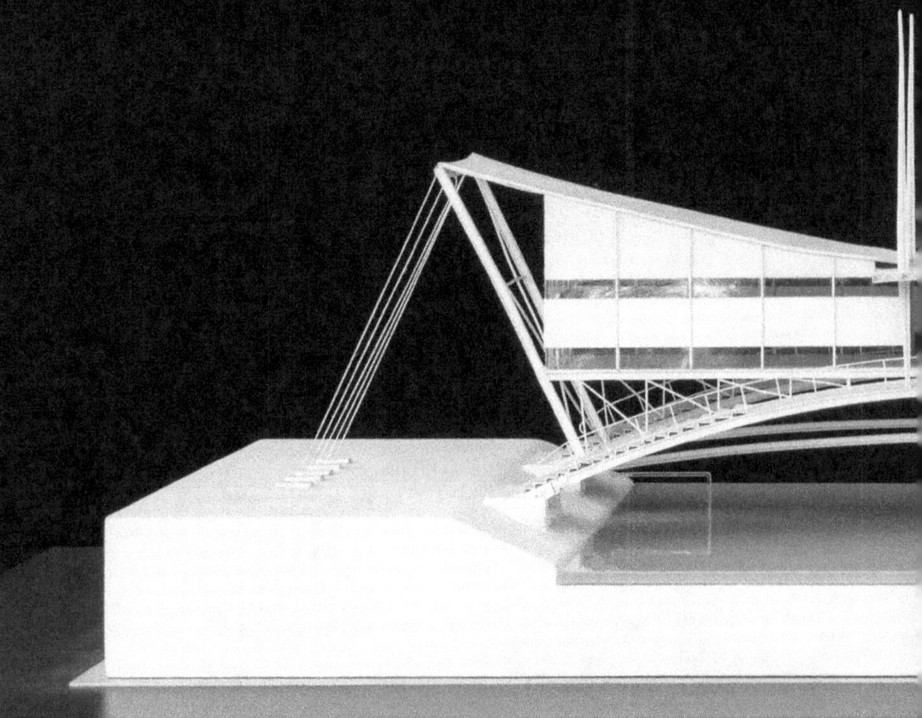

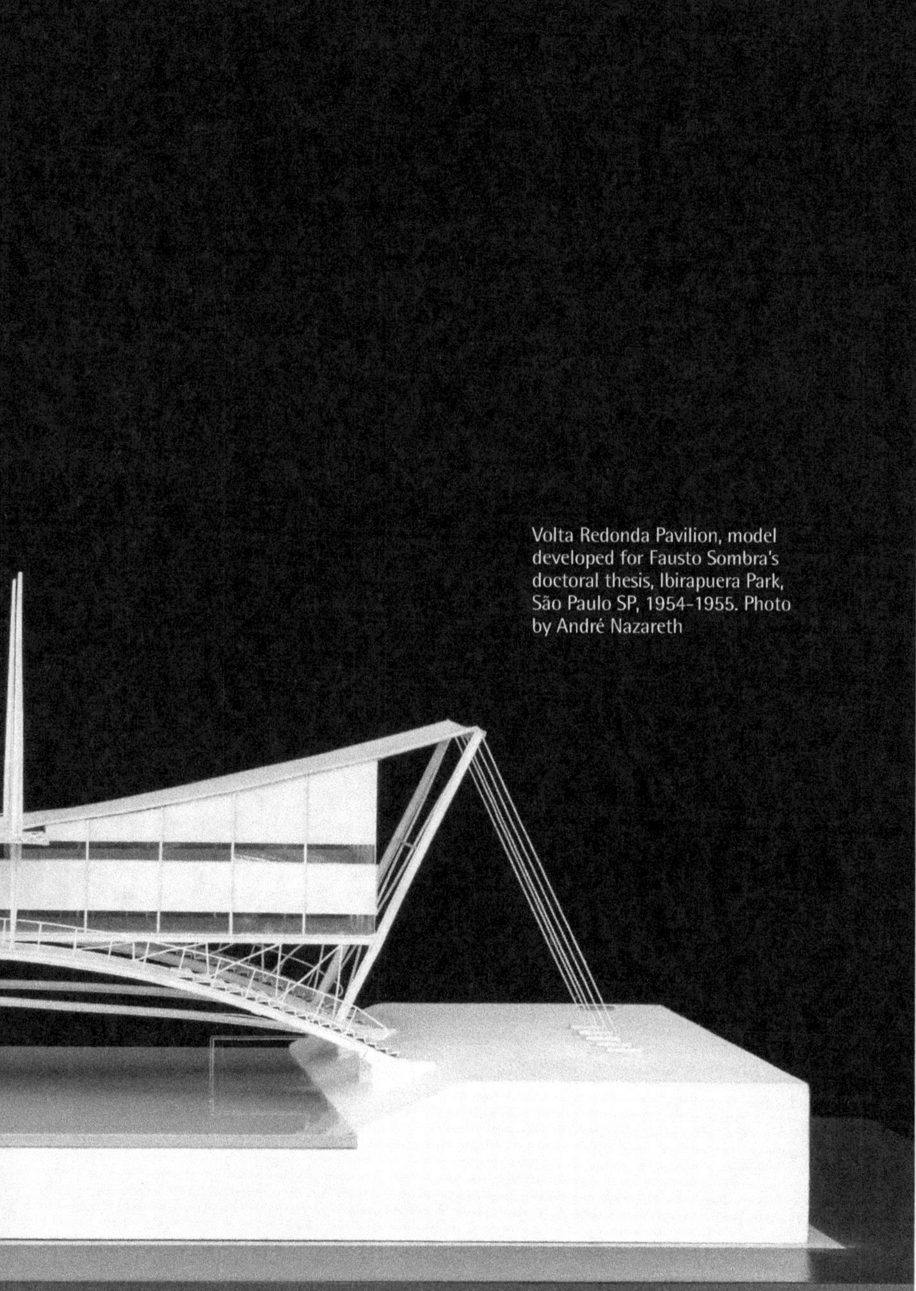

Volta Redonda Pavilion, model
developed for Fausto Sombra's
doctoral thesis, Ibirapuera Park,
São Paulo SP, 1954–1955. Photo
by André Nazareth

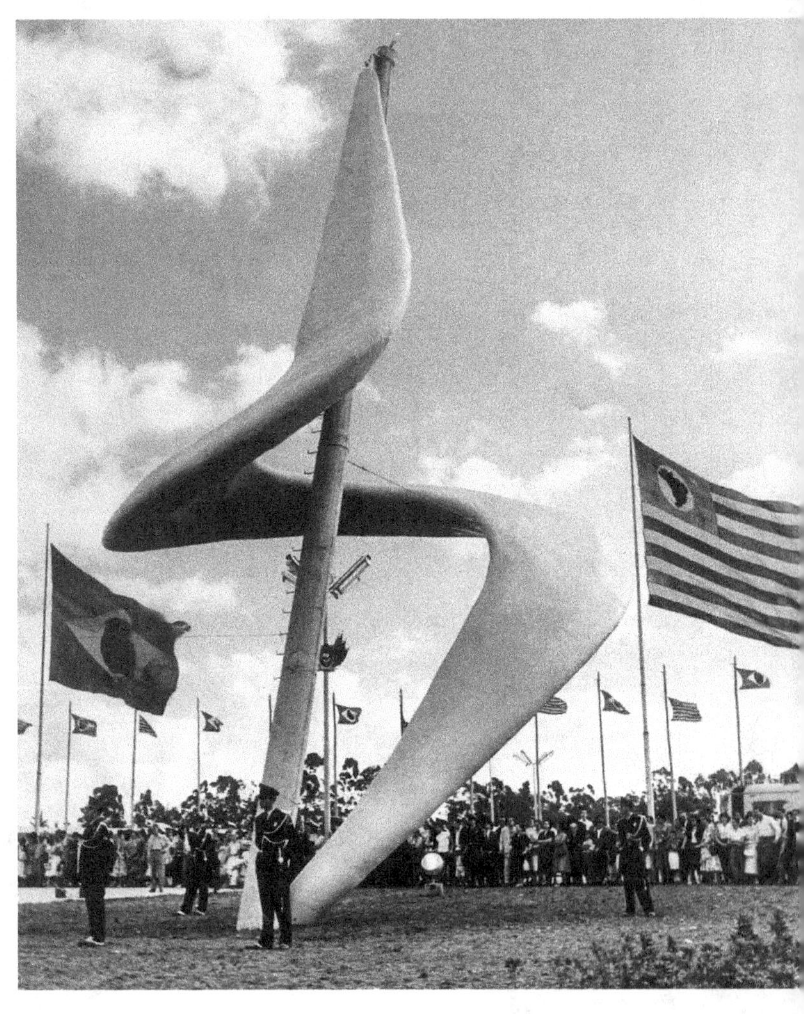

Ibirapuera Park, sculpture symbolizing
the 400th Anniversary of São Paulo,
São Paulo SP. Oscar Niemeyer, 1954.
Wanda Svevo Historical Archive / São
Paulo Biennial Foundation

Relevance of Volta Redonda Pavilion

It is not uncommon to identify contributions from the so-called carioca school in the consolidation of modern paulista architecture during the mid-20th century, including the important works attributed to Oscar Niemeyer, such as Copan,[1] 1951-1966, and the Ibirapuera Park complex,[2] 1951-1953, both designs are directly linked to the commemorative festivities of the 4th Centenary of São Paulo City.[3] Sérgio Bernardes – creator of his own language, understood, according to Lauro Cavalcanti, as "concurrently organic and rational,"[4] referring to the work of Mies van der Rohe and Frank Lloyd Wright – was part of this exquisite group of professionals who, like other talented architects from Brazil and abroad, left major works on the Piratininga plateau.[5] In this context, the present publication aims not only to recover and emphasize the relevance of Sérgio Bernardes' work in its general scope, but also to value the architect's contribution to the modern architectural avant-garde of São Paulo.

To this end, the still little (re)known Volta Redonda Pavilion has become our object of study. This ephemeral exemplar was idealized and built fundamentally with metallic profiles and elements at the invitation of the National Steelworks Company – CSN, being inaugurated on February 15, 1955 and serving as a promotional stand for the state-owned company at the 1st São Paulo International Fair. An outstanding event, the fair was installed in Ibirapuera Park and officially opened to the public on August 21, 1954.[6] In addition to bringing together museums, bars, restaurants, circus, rodeo area, amusement park and other diverse attractions, there were also pavilions that hosted and represented 28 nations – some were individual, such as the Uruguay and Japan Pavilions –, and other outstanding pavilions representing eleven states of the federation,[7] such as Minas Gerais Pavilion and Rio Grande do Sul Pavilion.

Other smaller buildings, linked to sponsoring companies, such as Ford, Philips, Coca-Cola, Shell, General Electric, Companhia Antarctica Paulista, Mercedes-Benz, Nestlé and Eternit, were built in the park, and it seems that the vast majority was dismantled at the end of the event. Exception only to the Japan Pavilion, Rio Grande do Sul Pavilion, and Volta Redonda Pavilion. The latter, for being intelligently positioned on the narrowing of Sapateiro stream, before opening up to the large lake of the park, was also used as a crossing for users in a central and strategic point of this urban facility, considered at that time, by many critics, as one of the best architectural complexes in Pauliceia.[8]

The scenario that made possible the constitution of this great show, and consequently the construction of the

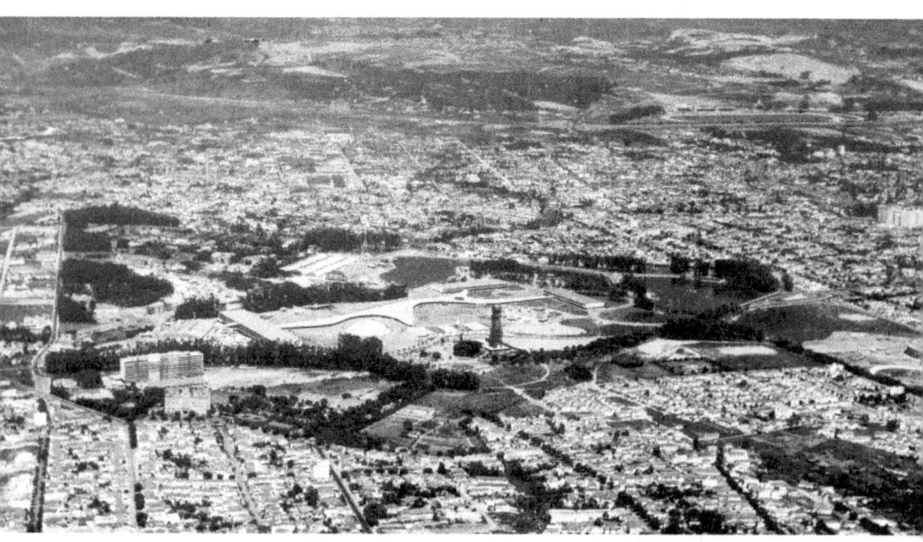

Ibirapuera Park at the time of its inauguration, São Paulo SP, 1950s. Photo by Vasclo Photographic Agency. Wanda Svevo Historical Archive / São Paulo Biennial Foundation

CSN Pavilion, had a complex network of actions promoted by influential patrons and intellectuals, cultivated under a favorable environment for the development of the city of São Paulo, seeking, since the 1922 Modern Art Week,[9] to place itself economically and culturally ahead of its direct competitor, the then Federal capital, Rio de Janeiro.

Immersed in an intense process of immigration[10] since the late 19th century, mainly with a large number of jobs arising from the cultivation of coffee and other crops in the paulista countryside – a fact that allowed, years later, the accumulation of capital necessary to accelerate the process of development of its industrial park, and the process of metropolization, forged, among other factors, by the break and resignification of values and social organization commonly found in more traditional cities –, "São Paulo no meio do século 20 (São Paulo in the Mid-20th Century)"[11] was undergoing a bustling cultural development as result of the most diverse manifestations. Among them, the creation of the outstanding museums: MASP (1947) and MAM-SP (1948), and the accomplishment of the Art and Architecture Biennials from 1951 onwards. This process, carried out along the lines of the Venice Biennale and which took place first in the renovation and expansion[12] of the old eclectic building by architect Ramos de Azevedo, the Belvedere Trianon, from 1916, on Paulista Avenue; whereas from the late 1953,[13] in its second edition, it started to be held in the recently inaugurated Palace of Nations and Palace of States, both in Ibirapuera Park.[14]

Characterized among several other factors by the constitution of these renowned museums, materialized by the idealization of the journalist from Paraíba, Assis Chateaubriand, and by his competitor, the São Paulo businessman Francisco Matarazzo Sobrinho,[15] in this period of the early 1950s, in which the "eyes of the world" turned to São Paulo, the state capital had a population of approximately 2.2 million inhabitants,[16] reaching 2.5 million in 1954.

At that time, it also had 40% of the workers in Brazilian industry, and its production corresponded to 54% of the total manufacturing production in the country.[17] Industry in the state of São Paulo was a source of pride, and its capital constantly sought to express the progress of its economy's numbers:

"São Paulo is the capital of the state of the same name, whose territory covers only 3% of the area of Brazil. It is the 2nd city in the country, 3rs in South America and 14th in the world in terms of population (2,500 inhabitants – 1,000 inhabitants per km^2). The municipal revenue forecast for 1954 is two billion three hundred million cruzeiros,[18] 17,415 industries, 173,000 motor vehicles. São Paulo is the fastest growing city in the world!"[19]

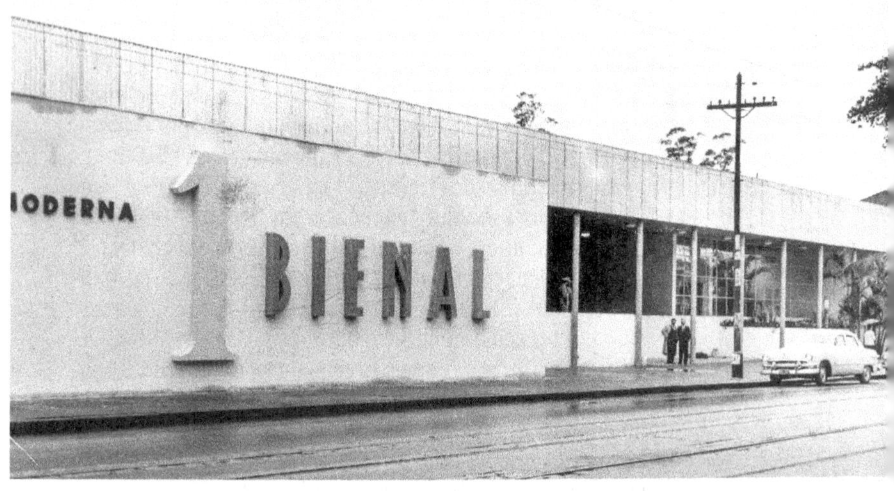

Pavilion of the 1st Biennial of the Museum of Modern Art, São Paulo SP. Luís Saia and Eduardo Kneese de Mello, 1951. Wanda Svevo Historical Archive / São Paulo Biennial Foundation

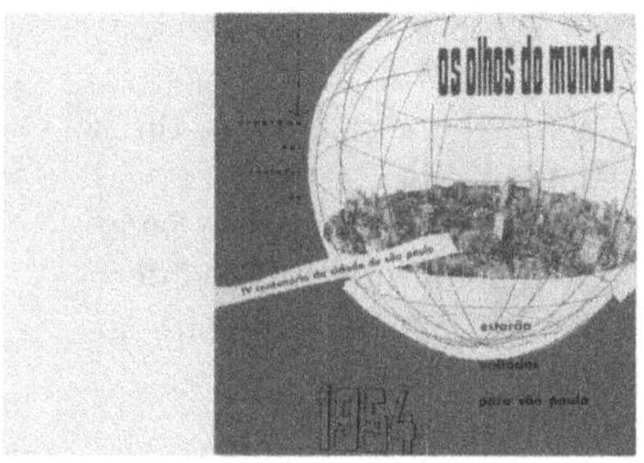

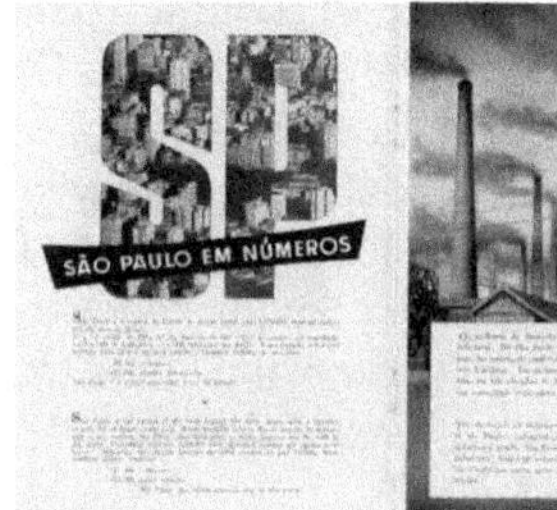

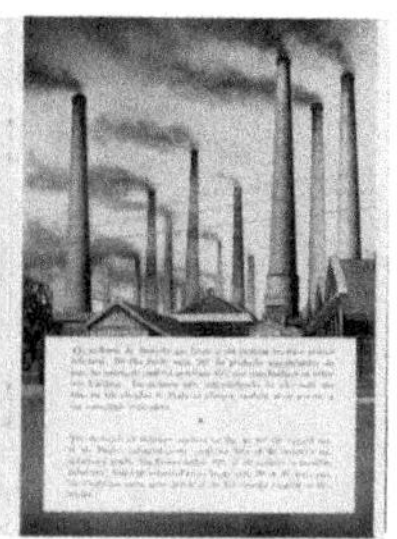

Folders "The Eyes of the World" and "São Paulo in Numbers". 4th Centenary Commission of the City of São Paulo, 1950s. Wanda Svevo Historical Archive / São Paulo Biennial Foundation

A theme already addressed by researcher Alexandre Bahia in his article "Pavilhão da CSN 1954: recorrência técnica e manifesto da modernidade,"[20] the study could be considered one of the few that seek to understand in depth the phenomena related to the constitution of that pavilion. In his text, there is a brief excerpt extracted from the book *Brasil: arquiteturas após 1950*, in which researcher Ruth Verde Zein summarizes part of the issues explained above:

"Despite its exponential demographic and economic growth throughout the 20th century, the metropolis of São Paulo, currently one of the five largest urban agglomerations in the world, played a secondary role in the Brazilian cultural scene until the 1940s. With the progressive concentration of wealth resulting from the rise of its rural and later industrial bourgeoisie, and the formation of an extensive proletariat comprising migrants and immigrants, São Paulo had consolidated, throughout the first half of that century, a growing importance in the definition of the country's economic directions, with increasingly relevant repercussions on cultural issues.

[...] But it would only be in the late 1940s, with the creation, by Assis Chateaubriand, of MASP (São Paulo Museum of Art), in 1947, and with the creation by the Matarazzo family in 1948, of MAM-SP (Museum of Modern Art of São Paulo), and in 1951, of the São Paulo Art Biennial – institutions that quickly reached an international name – that São Paulo began to have a strong presence in the international art circuit."[21]

The researcher also complemented her reasoning by highlighting the great intellectual and ideological clash undertaken in the first Biennials, part of it linked to the very artistic movements that the city hosted, "the concrete artist and his controversial manifestos, and then the clashes between concrete and neo-concrete ones, when the direction is reversed, with cariocas contesting the predominance of paulistas."[22] This conflict of ideas had had its origin with the theme of adoption of abstract art[23] in the 1st Biennial and its relationship with North American imperialism, a process previously highlighted by researcher Leonor Amarante in her book *As Bienais de São Paulo: 1951-1987*, from 1989.

At the beginning of her text, Amarante addresses the clash between the critic from Pernambuco Mário Pedrosa and architect João Vilanova Artigas, who at that time was part of the editorial committee of the *Fundamentos* magazine.[24] A vehicle linked to the Brazilian Communist Party – PCB, it was responsible for disseminating and defending the precepts defined by the so-called August Manifesto.[25]

"Brazil was experiencing yet another of its socio-political-economic turmoil, and the Biennial, in a way, served as a pretext for some intellectuals to demonstrate against certain attitudes of the government, especially those that restricted freedom. On the one hand, the carioca critic Mário Pedrosa – a friend of Trotsky's and one of the main promoters of his ideas in Brazil –, with a more international vision of art, defended the Biennial and the abstractionist movement that dominated the first edition. On the other hand, the radical architect J. B. Vilanova Artigas considered the Biennial the "expression of bourgeois decadence". [...]

At that time, the book *O mundo da paz*, by Jorge Amado, was released, and soon seized, and architect Oscar Niemeyer could not get a professorship in Brazilian universities. Newsstands were raided by the police in search of *Fundamentos* magazine, to which Artigas was a contributor. 'Alongside these measures, the program of a variant sounds like a seamaid tale. It is in this misleading line of argument that the São Paulo Biennial is placed, a great exhibition of abstract art in Brazil, with the massive attendance of heroes of the decadent art of the bourgeoisie, which transforms our country into the headquarters of cosmopolitism,' he [Vilanova Artigas] wrote outraged."[26]

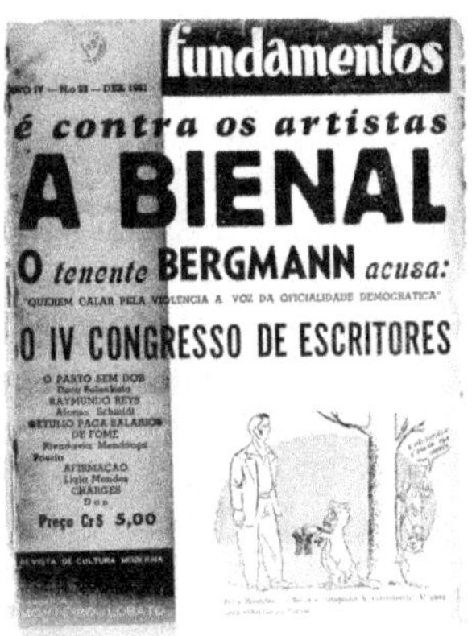

Cover and article "The Biennial is Against Brazilian Artists", published in the magazine *Fundamentos*, no. 23, December 1951. Hemeroteca Digital Brasileira / Fundação Biblioteca Nacional

Leonor Amarante has also complemented on João Vilanova Artigas' speech:

"American imperialism, which traces the police measures of Getúlio Vargas' government, which demands our young people for war, which sucks our economic resources and reduces our people to the blackest misery, is behind all these maneuvers, applauding the provincial sagacity of their representatives in our homeland."[27]

Under such ideological divergences, based on the canons of the arts in their most diverse manifestations, and partly constituted and articulated by the presence of external figures and forces – such as the aforementioned presence of magnate Nelson Rockefeller –, the processes of metropolization and industrialization in São Paulo and in a few states of the Union would be strengthened. This phenomenon was initially observed in the constitution of the National Steelworks Company,[28] during the Estado Novo regime, in the government of Getúlio Vargas,[29] since part of the capital that allowed the installation of the largest steelworks in Latin America,[30] throughout the 1940s, in the municipality of Volta Round, would come from "US credits, granted by the Export-Import Bank".

"The implementation of the Volta Redonda Plant and the form of its constitution were defined in July 1940. It was financed by American credits, granted by the Export-Import Bank, and by resources from the Brazilian government. Its control was in the hands of a mixed-capital company, the National Steelworks Company, organized in January 1941. This solution did not result from a clear definition by the government since the beginning of Estado Novo, nor was there a uniform thought in the governmental machine about

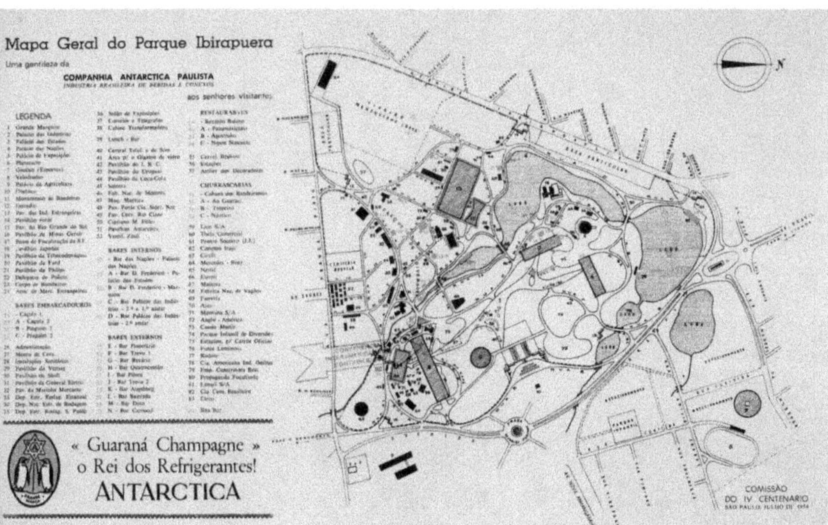

General Map of Ibirapuera Park, São
Paulo SP. 4th Centenary Commission
of the City of São Paulo, July 1954.
Wanda Svevo Historical Archive / São
Paulo Biennial Foundation

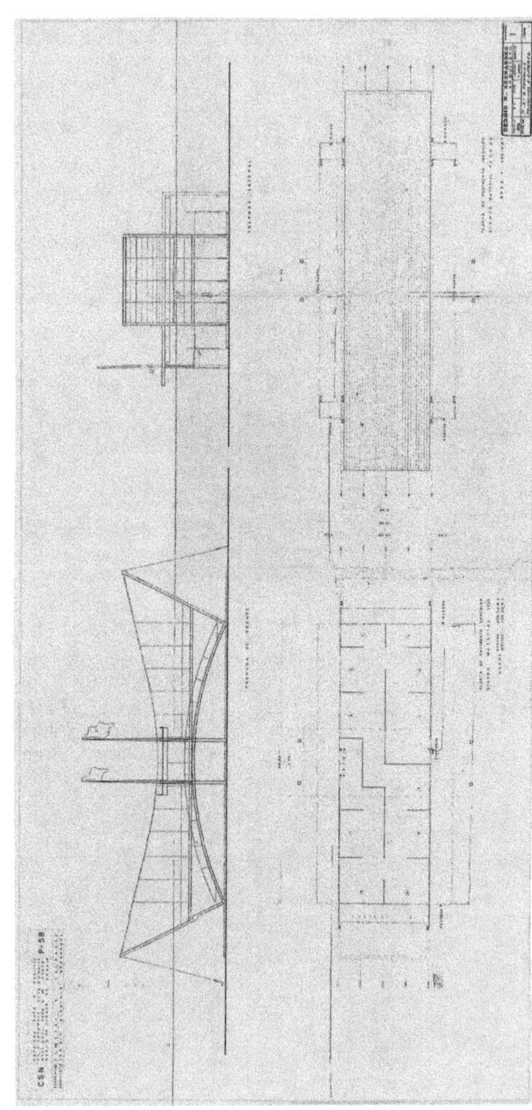

Volta Redonda Pavilion, *Drawing 1*, initial study at 1:100 scale, Ibirapuera Park, São Paulo SP, 1950s. Collection NPD FAU UFRJ / Sérgio Bernardes Collection

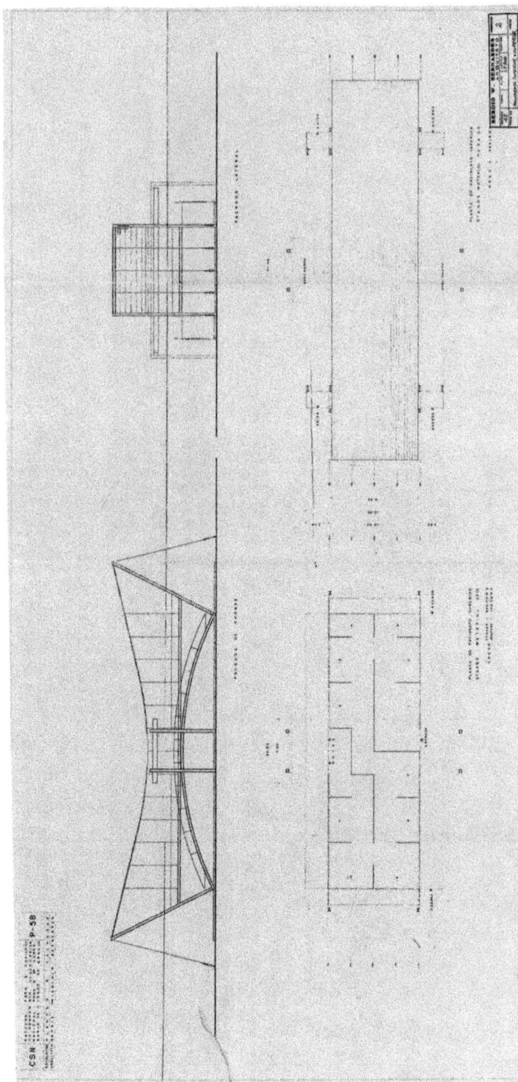

Volta Redonda Pavilion, *Drawing 2*, initial study at 1:100 scale, Ibirapuera Park, São Paulo SP, 1950s. Collection NPD FAU UFRJ / Sérgio Bernardes Collection

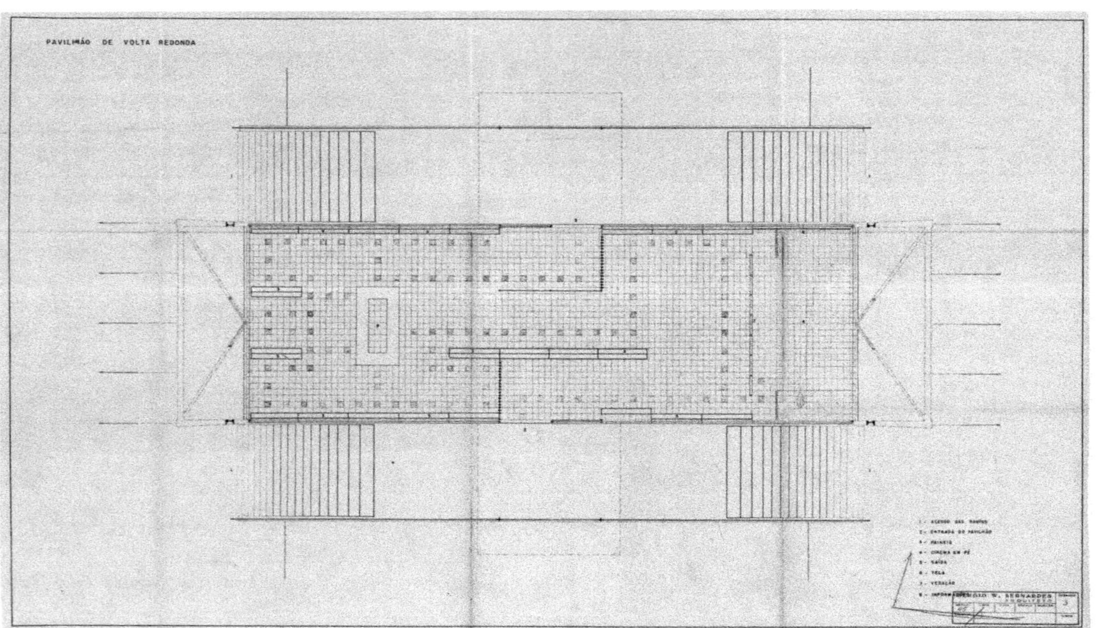

Volta Redonda Pavilion, *Drawing 3*, final upper level plan at 1:50 scale, Ibirapuera Park, São Paulo SP, 1950s. Collection NPD FAU UFRJ / Sérgio Bernardes Collection

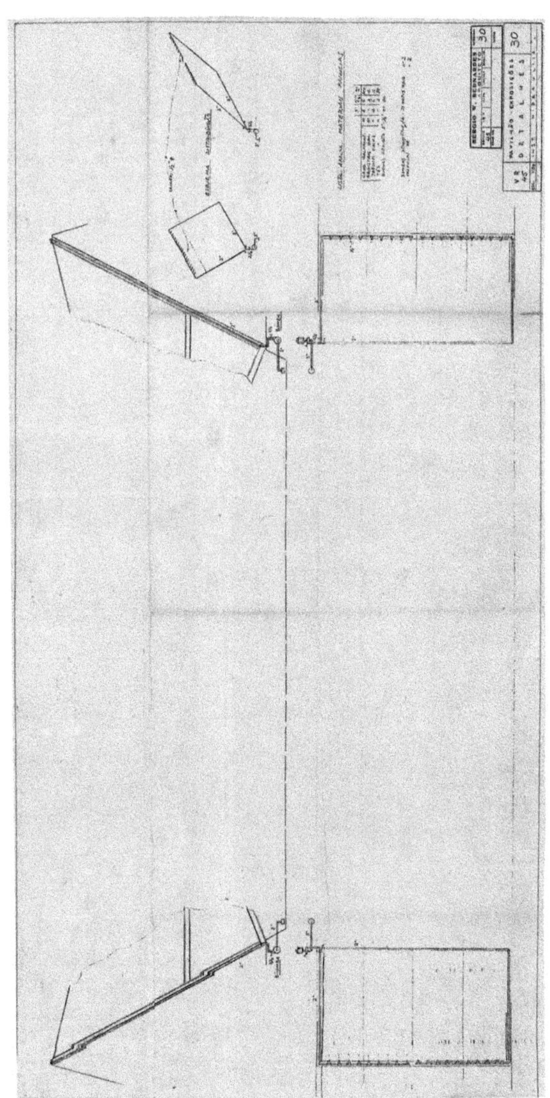

Volta Redonda Pavilion, *Drawing 30*, hydraulic installations at 1:50 scale, Ibirapuera Park, São Paulo SP, 1950s. Collection NPD FAU UFRJ / Sérgio Bernardes Collection

147

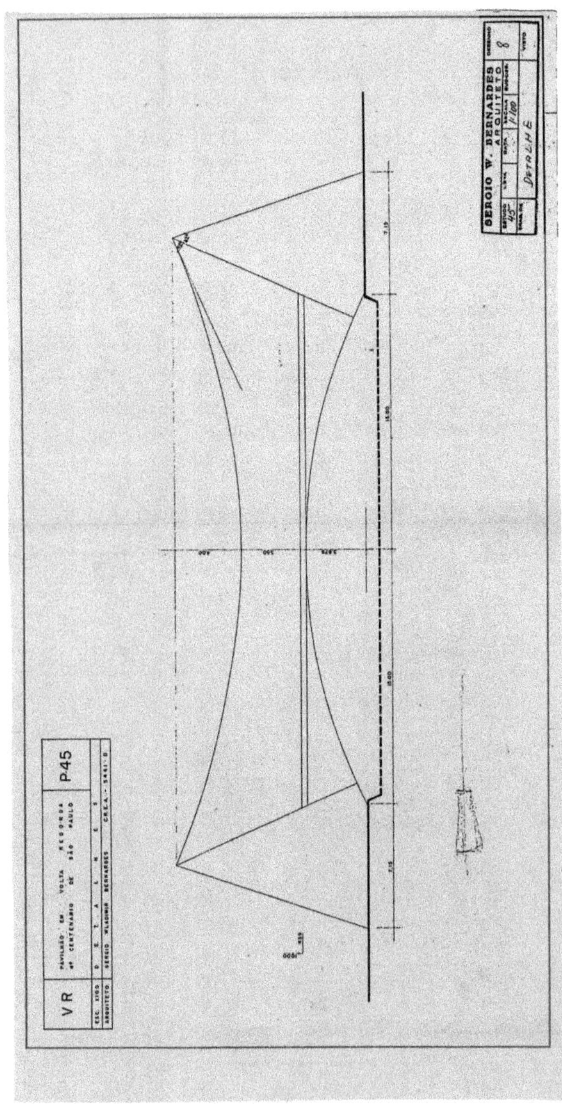

Volta Redonda Pavilion, *Drawing 8*, side elevation at scale 1:100, Ibirapuera Park, São Paulo SP, 1950s. Collection NPD FAU UFRJ / Sérgio Bernardes Fund

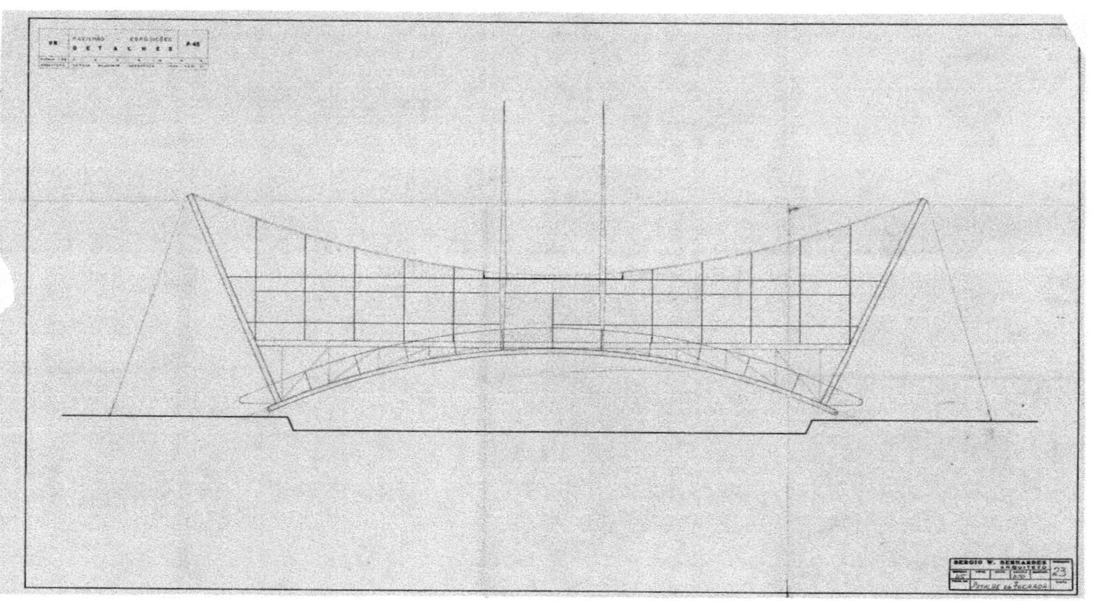

Volta Redonda Pavilion, *Drawing 23*, elevation at scale 1:50, Ibirapuera Park, São Paulo SP, 1950s. Collection NPD FAU UFRJ / Sérgio Bernardes Fund

Volta Redonda Pavilion, *Drawing 34*, detail of the tying of the submerged internal footings at scale 1:100, Ibirapuera Park, São Paulo SP, 1950s. Collection NPD FAU UFRJ / Sérgio Bernardes Fund

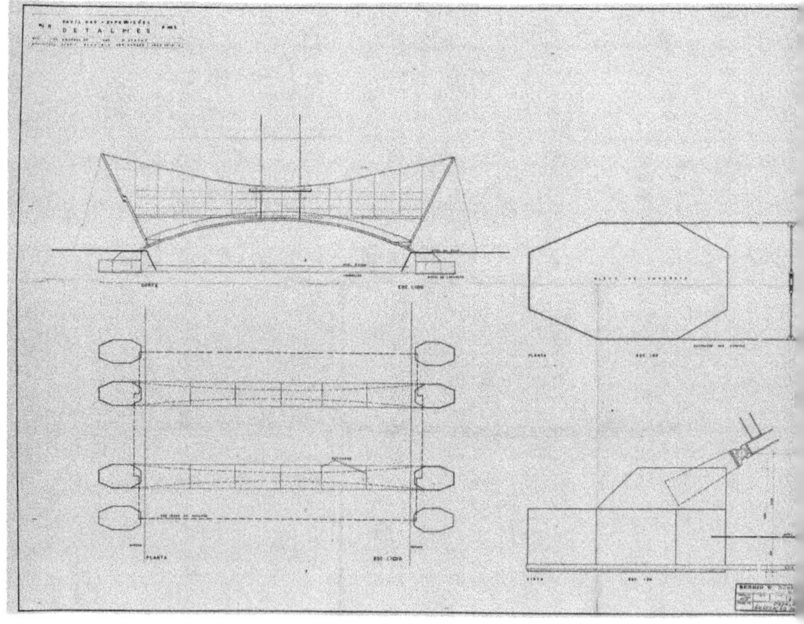

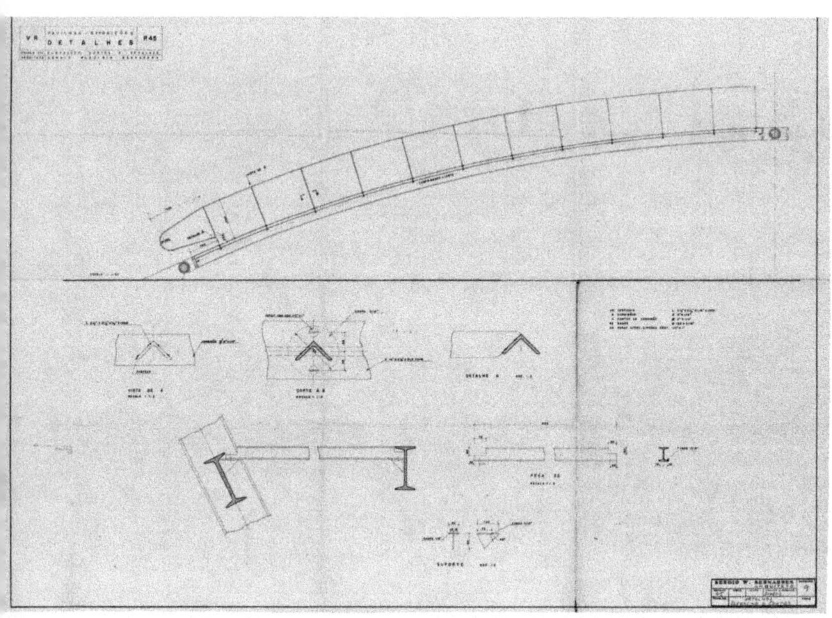

Volta Redonda Pavilion, *Drawing 9*, details of the balustrades at scales 1:2, 1:5, and 1:20, Ibirapuera Park, São Paulo SP, 1950s. Collection NPD FAU UFRJ / Sérgio Bernardes Fund

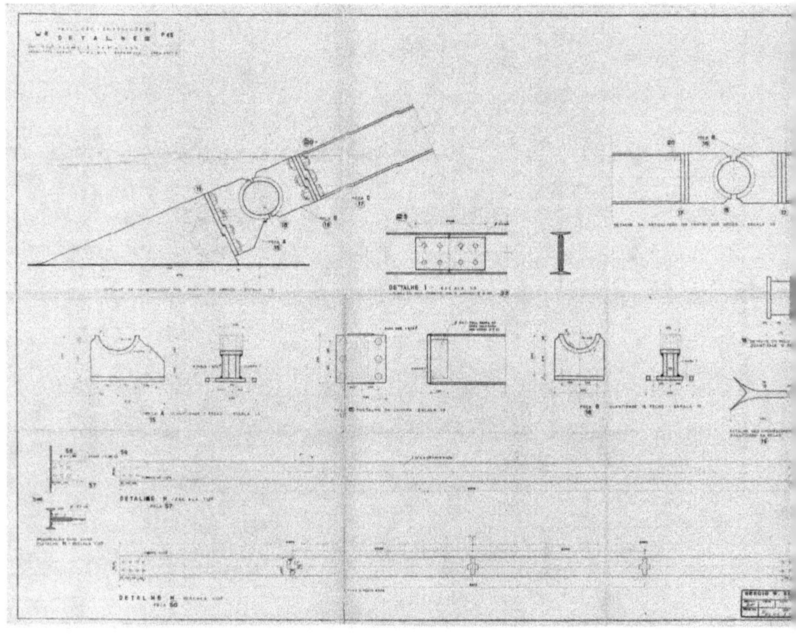

Volta Redonda Pavilion, *Drawing 13*, details of the arch joints of the bridges at scales 1:5 and 1:12.5, Ibirapuera Park, São Paulo SP, 1950s. Collection NPD FAU UFRJ / Sérgio Bernardes Fund

Volta Redonda Pavilion, *Drawing 25*, plan and detail of the roof bracing at scales 1:2 and 1:50, Ibirapuera Park, São Paulo SP, 1950s. Collection NPD FAU UFRJ / Sérgio Bernardes Fund

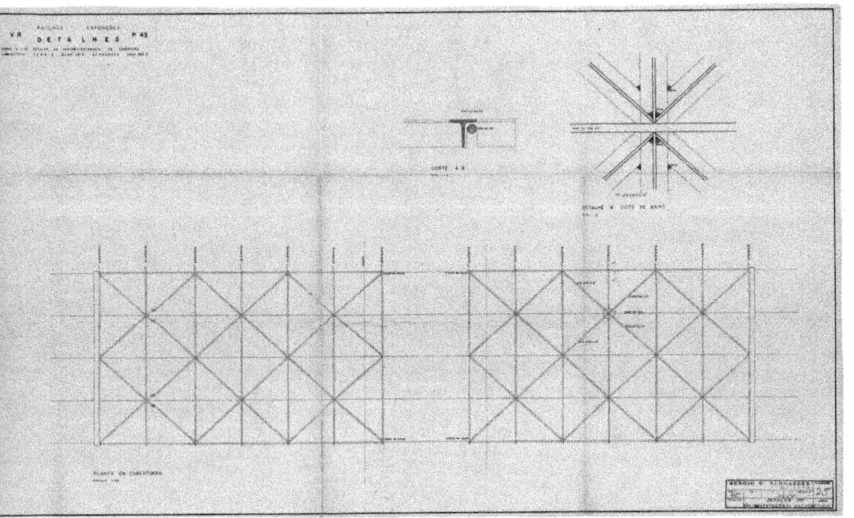

Volta Redonda Pavilion, *Drawing 14*, plan and facades showing the position of metal elements at scale 1:100, Ibirapuera Park, São Paulo SP, 1950s. Collection NPD FAU UFRJ / Sérgio Bernardes Fund

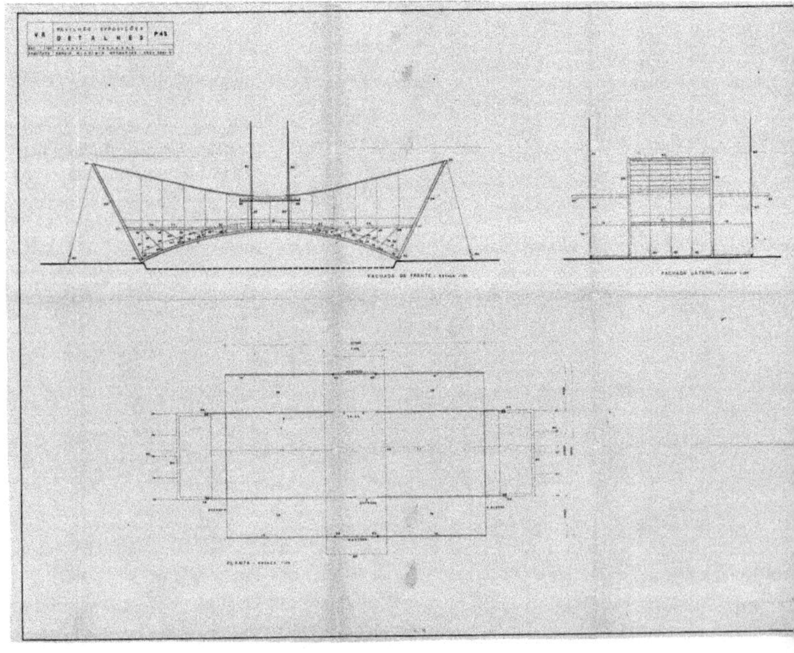

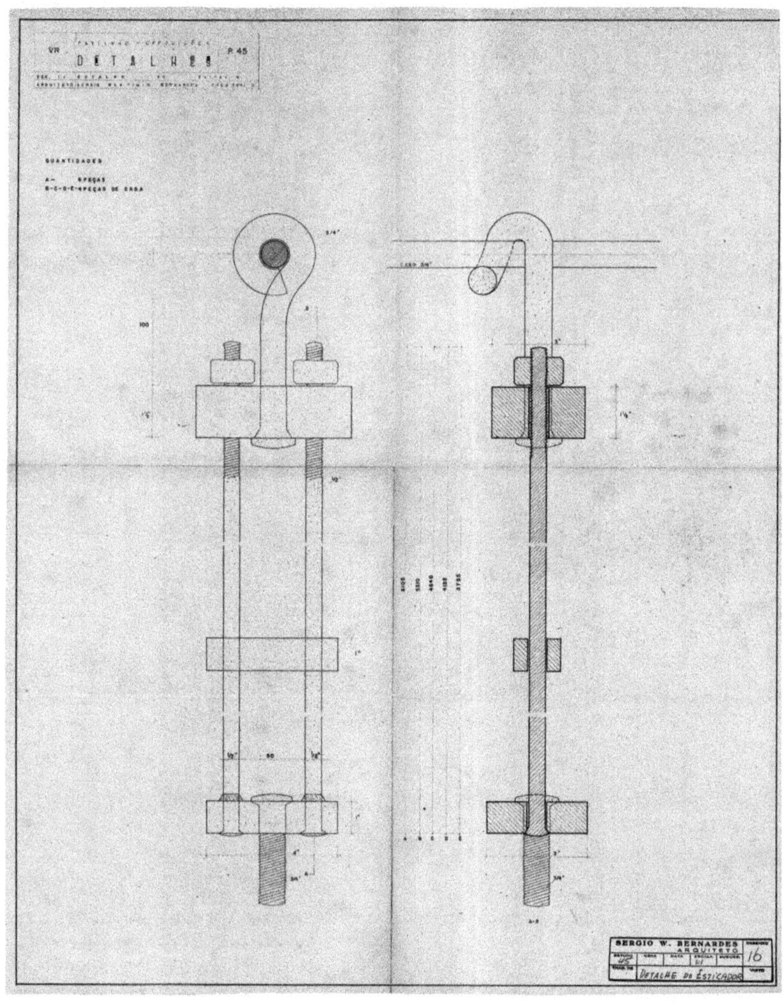

Volta Redonda Pavilion, *Drawing 16*,
turnbuckles types A, B, C, and D at
scale 1:1, Ibirapuera Park, São Paulo
SP, 1950s. Collection NPD FAU UFRJ /
Sérgio Bernardes Fund

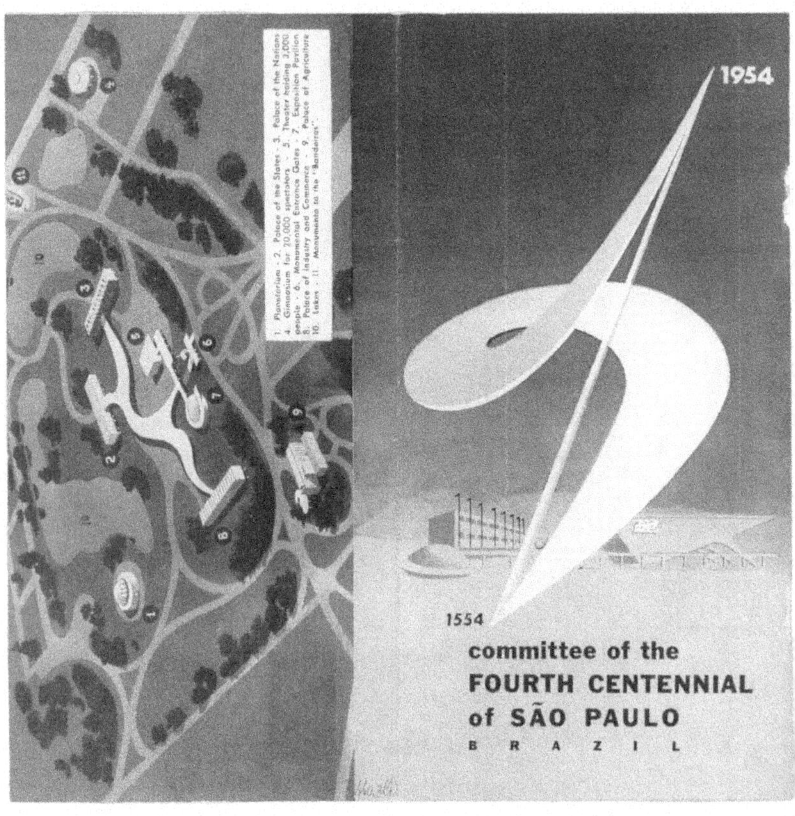

Folder of the Celebrations of the 4th Centenary of the City of São Paulo. Committee of the Fourth Centennial of São Paulo, Brazil. Wanda Svevo Historical Archive / São Paulo Biennial Foundation

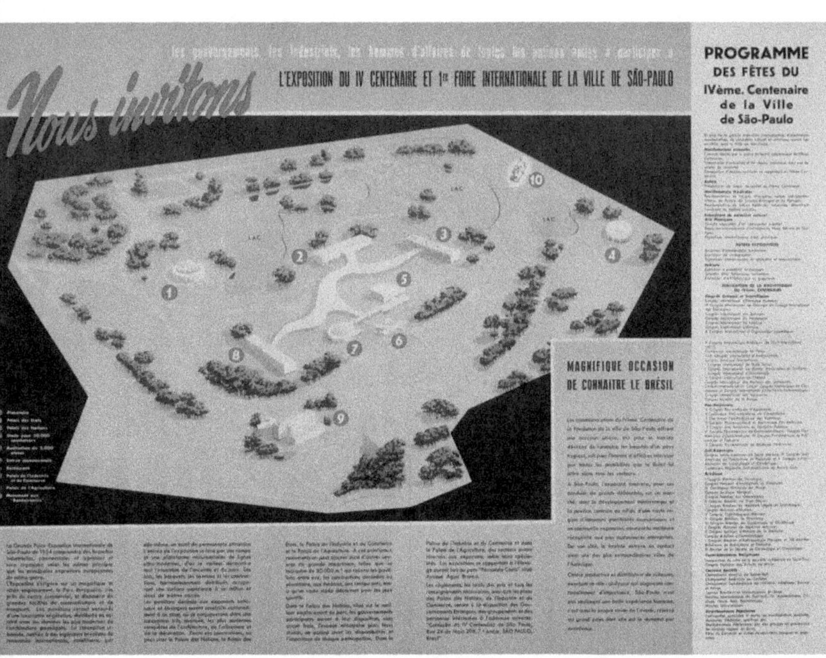

Brochure of the celebrations of the 4th Centenary of the City of São Paulo. Programme des fêtes du IVème. Centenaire de la ville de São Paulo. Wanda Svevo Historical Archive / São Paulo Biennial Foundation

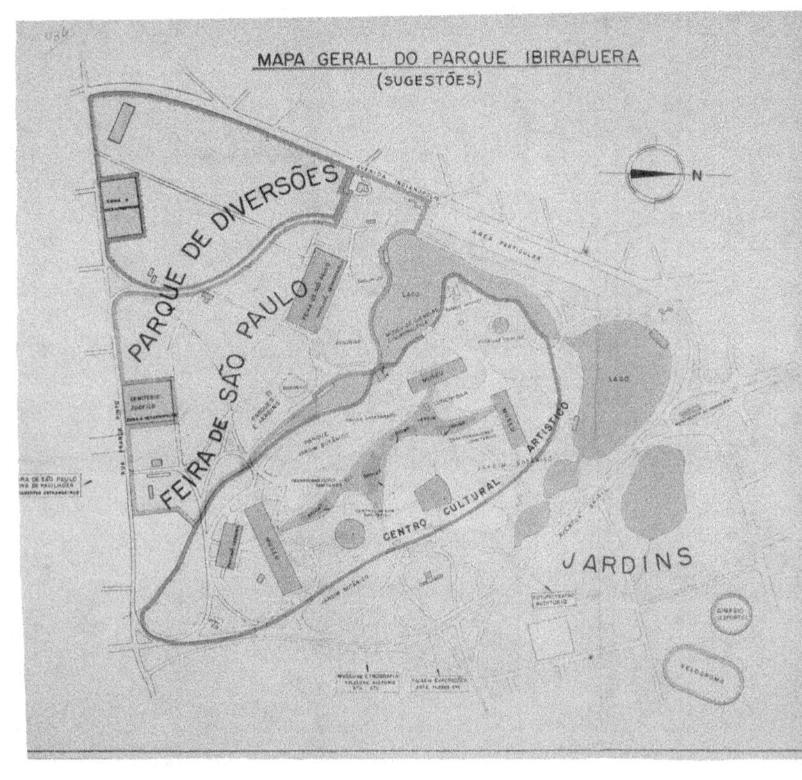

General Map of Ibirapuera Park –
suggestions, 1950s. Wanda Svevo
Historical Archive / São Paulo Biennial
Foundation

the subject. The different groups only agreed to recognize the need to expand and diversify the steel production. The expansion of transport services and installation of heavy industry depended on solving the problem; in addition, steel imports represented an increasing burden on the continually unfavorable balance of payments."[31]

It was in such scenario that the first Art and Architecture Biennials flourished, and on which researcher Helio Herbst discussed throughout his dissertation, *Pelos salões das bienais, a arquitetura ausente dos manuais: expressões da arquitetura moderna brasileira expostas nas bienais paulistanas (1951-1959)*, from 2007, published as a book in 2011.[32] The same theme was briefly addressed by researcher Ruth Verde Zein, when the author emphasized the importance of the first five editions of the Biennial during the period that awarded outstanding architects, such as the Franco-Swiss Le Corbusier; the Germans Mies van der Rohe and Walter Gropius; the Italian Bruno Zevi; the Swiss Max Bill; and Americans Philip Johnson, Craig Elwood and Paul Rudolph.[33]

Recalling that Rudolph was awarded at the 2nd Biennial, in 1954, with the Young Foreign Architect award, granted for the design of the Walker Guest House, in Senibal Island, Florida,[34] while Sérgio Bernardes took the Young Brazilian Architect award for the design of Lota de Macedo Soares' house.

It was also in this universe, sometimes troubled by ideas contrary to those developed in the general context of the first Art and Architecture Biennials, initially with a strong link to the dogmas developed in the editions of the International Congresses of Modern Architecture – Ciam – recalling the fierce criticisms made by Max Bill on his visit to Brazil in June 1953, when he "caused controversy by denouncing the socially uncompromising tone of much of Brazilian architecture", of "whimsical and gratuitous curves", referring to

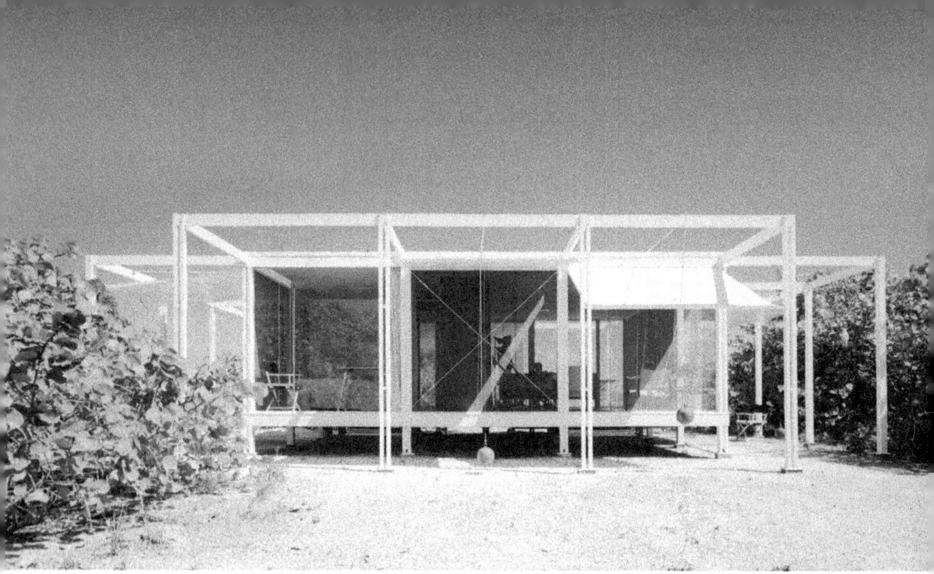

Walker Guest House, Sanibel Island, Florida, 1952-1953. Paul Marvin Rudolph. Wanda Svevo Historical Archive / São Paulo Biennial

Foundation Lota de Macedo Soares Residence, Petrópolis RJ, 1953. Photo by Leonardo Finotti

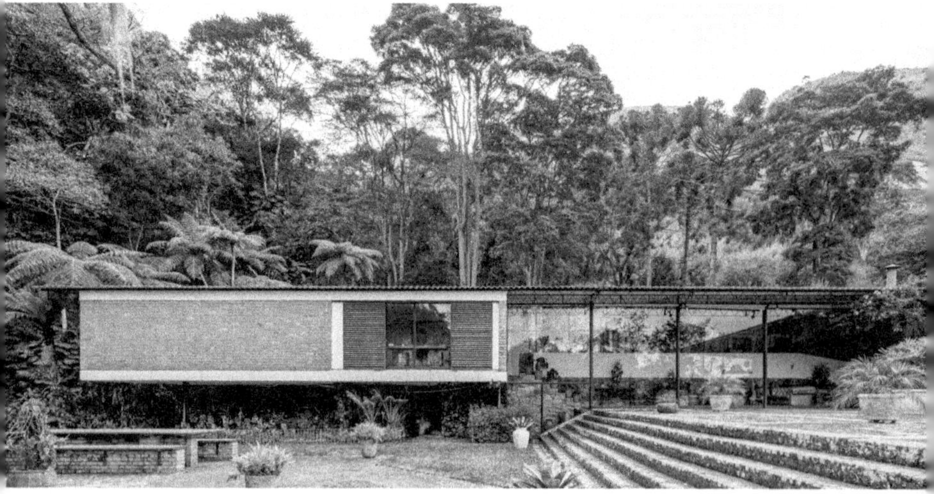

Pampulha[35] –, that the Volta Redonda Pavilion was constituted. In other words, Sérgio Bernardes enjoyed the positive
repercussions achieved by the Lota Macedo Soares house
project – with some proto-industrial key elements,[36] so to
speak, – to design a pavilion conceived under a program and
ideal of extreme industrialization, in a discourse closer, but
not exclusive, to that proposed by the architects representing
the Bauhausian school, such as that of its founder Walter
Gropius.

In this way, and celebrating the festivities of the four
hundredth anniversary of the capital of São Paulo, the Volta
Redonda Pavilion, a unique bridge-building in the list of
Brazilian modern buildings, was conceived. Composed of
two parallel bridges 5 meters wide and 10 meters apart,
each one composed by a pair of arched and tri-articulated
"I" profiles,[37] approximately 30 centimeters high – a system
that made it possible to increase the span a hundred times
longer, of generous 30 meters –, the building had at the
ends of its two internal arches the support points for the
two main transversal inclined porticos that structurally
connected both bridges. These elements were responsible
for determining the perimeter of the floor deck – defining a
surface of 30m x 10m – as well as the catenary roof of the
exhibition area. This, in turn, was formed by five steel cables
that were anchored on each side of the stream, extending
parallel to each other and longitudinally over the pavilion.
To provide stability, the cables were locked by a system of
thin "T" profiles that formed a rigid triangular mesh, and
on which the corrugated metal plates rested, thus config-
uring the roof. The aforementioned plates were arranged
longitudinally in the building, with their grooves facing the
transverse marquee positioned in the center of the building –
marking the accesses to the stand –, to which the water was
conducted on rainy days and/or after being pumped from
the stream below, allowing, in addition to the improvement

in thermal performance due to the cooling of the roof, the
phenomenological effect of the waterfall returning to the
Sapateiro stream, located just below.[38]

Although slightly similar to existing structures, such as
La casa sobre el arroyo[39] by the distinguished Argentinian
architect Amancio Williams, built in reinforced concrete in
the form of an arched bridge over the La Chacras water-
course in the city of Mar del Plata in 1946, for his father
pianist Alberto Williams; or also the Coocon House[40] by Paul
Rudolph, built in the State of Florida in 1950, with a catenary
roof, also with the use of cables, similar to the Volta Redonda
Pavilion – but a rather smaller scale –, Sérgio Bernardes'
conception and power of synthesis in this building, in terms
of form, technique, materiality and program, surprised
the most rigorous scholars and critics, factors that led the
project to be published by the specialized media of the time,
as in the magazine *Arquitetura e Engenharia* no. 36, July/
August 1955; *Módulo* magazine no. 2, August 1955;[41] as well
as being mentioned in Henrique E. Mindlin's popular book
Modern Architecture in Brazil, 1956.[42]

Such qualities, as well as the strategic siting of the
building over the stream in the central region of Ibirapuera
Park, most likely contributed for one of the bridges to survive
the dismantling of the rest of the pavilion at a moment
that has not yet been properly explained.[43] In addition, and
as already mentioned, the conditions that involved the
constitution of the Volta Redonda Pavilion, and the events
that followed allow it to be equated with the context of
the construction and dismantling of the German Pavilion in
the city of Barcelona in 1929, as well as its reconstruction
in 1986, as part of the centenary celebrations of its creator
Mies van der Rohe, because similarly to what happened with
the famous European architect, Sérgio Bernardes was invited
by the National Steelworks Company, probably in 1999, for
the reconstruction project of the Volta Redonda Pavilion
in its original location. However, and unlike the German

architect, Bernardes suggested radical adjustments to the 1954 project, opting, in his own words, for a "conceptual revision compatible with current technological advances."[44] This new proposal – which was accessed through contact with Kykah Bernardes and researcher Monica Paciello Vieira, an intern at Sérgio's office during the years 1998 and 1999[45] – despite the support of recognized professionals, as discussed later on, it eventually did not get off the ground.[46]

Announced with enthusiasm by the journals of the period, regardless of the outcome of the episode, the existing bridge on the North side, still today a catalyst for a large audience on weekends and holidays, was, in the early 21st century, again the target of its creator Sérgio Bernardes, at the age of 80. He spent time and effort in the fight for its reconstruction, reinforcing and emphasizing the relevance of the work as a vanguard exemplar of modern architecture in São Paulo and Brazil.

Initial Sketch and Conjectures on Site Choice

The 38 sheets corresponding to the executive project of the Volta Redonda Pavilion, according to material preserved in the Sérgio Bernardes Collection, at the NPD UFRJ, have suggested that at least two different studies were developed for the conformation of the pavilion.

The first study has two floors, the first at ground level and the second elevated to approximately four meters high. As this initial study has indicated – with similar geometry and spatiality to the built project –, at first, the architect did not think of siting it over the Córrego do Sapateiro stream, as a bridge, but directly on dry land.

Structured by a set of four concurrent arches and two porticos with their upper beams inclined towards the outside of the building, in addition to the catenary-shaped roof with its five longitudinally arranged steel cables – similar to the arrangement observed in the built project –, this arrangement allowed more than doubling the total measurement of the exhibition area to be explored by the National Steelworks Company, from 300 to approximately 690 square meters.

The sheet that illustrates this option, entitled *Drawing 2*, undated and in 1:100 scale, has two elevations: front and side, in addition to the plans of the two floors. The sheet also highlights the ground level serving as a "heavy material stand", and its upper level for a "light material stand", a logical distribution due to the lower overload foreseen for the upper floor deck, and in this sense, the possibility of using slimmer profiles with less visual expression in the main body of the building.

Unlike the conceived final project, this study presents four extra central supports that start from the ground in the form of two parallel porticos, rising a little above the central marquee, structuring it as a pair of inverted beams – a solution which, despite being plastically expressive, provided less lightness to the set when compared to the built project.

In addition, the aforementioned study, which has two parallel ramps for access to the upper floor, 2.5 meters wide and in the form of an arch, that is, with half the width of the stairs later adopted in the built project, in a way, has contradicted – as researcher Alexandre Bahia Vanderlei had already proposed in his article on the subject[47] – the idea that the project was conceived, from the beginning, on the park's stream. In this sense, it seems plausible to suggest that this study, although undated, as well as the vast majority of the other sheets for this project, points to a natural evolution condition of the architectural project, that is, of its development throughout the process, with the improvement of technique, composition, rearrangement of the main elements that compose the final object, and even, in this case, the definitive site of its construction.

Still on this initial version, but now defined on a new sheet entitled *Drawing 1*, we can see, through the intervention of a hand sketch, the suggestion that two of the four central supports should be raised as masts. This condition, in addition to breaking the predominance of the building's horizontal lines, favors the creation of visual elements that expand the pavilion's exposure to visitors and users. Two other hand-drawn interventions on the same study, already suggest increasing the width of the ramps and transforming the transverse marquee into a gutter, an element that later started to function as a means of capturing and conducting rainwater.

Even without specifying the elaboration dates of the drawings illustrated above, it is possible to establish, still with a certain margin of imprecision, that the initial study was prepared around January or February 1954, since the contract for the elaboration project of the Volta Redonda Pavilion – established between Sérgio Bernardes and the National Steelworks Company, consisting of two pages and dated April 28, 1954 – has confirmed that a good part of the specifications would have already been forwarded with the "preliminary study by the architect, in a letter addressed to the Company, dated March 5, 1954,"[48] that is, almost two months before the date indicated in the aforementioned document.

Initially defined as "construction of a CSN pavilion, for the Exhibition of the 4th Centenary of São Paulo City," right afterwards, the contract established precisely the work to be developed and delivered by the architect:

"Architect Sérgio Wladimir Bernardes.
74 Senador Dantas Street, – 11th floor.
Rio de Janeiro – DF.

By the present VR-SE, the National Steelworks Company, hereinafter referred to as COMPANY, has commissioned Architect Sérgio Wladimir Bernardes, hereinafter referred to as ARCHITECT:

Item 1: Elaboration of complete design and supervision of construction for a Pavilion to represent the Company in the 4th Centenary of São Paulo City.

Item 2: Supply and placement of decoration material, including flooring and lighting, in the Pavilion mentioned in Item 1 above.

I:
The complete Pavilion Design includes:
a-) Preliminary Study.
b-) Preliminary Project.
c-) Project.
d-) General Details.
e-) Structural Projects.
f-) Facilities Design.
g-) Specifications and budgets.

II:
The architect will provide the Company with the originals and a copy of each original of all drawings referring to the project.

III:
The decoration services mentioned in item 2 will consist of the supply and placement of panels and other decorative elements, including photo-montages, graphs, captions, counters for distributing prospectuses, support for the presentation of showcases, composition of rails, flooring, lighting fixtures, all in accordance with the specifications presented with the preliminary study by the Architect, in a letter addressed to the COMPANY, dated March 5, 1954 and which will remain an integral part of this VR-SE."[49]

Another relevant detail about this exemplar – and unlike the documents handled for the Brazil Pavilion in Brussels, which will be discussed later on – is that on the sheets of the Volta Redonda Pavilion project there are no indications of the North orientation, nor are there any illustrations of siting in the surroundings that point to a precise place for the construction of the building. In this case, and based on the information present in the contract between the parties, it seems plausible to suggest that architect Sérgio Bernardes had been initially invited to develop a simple study for the pavilion, still without a specific site, based on a possible program of preliminary needs forwarded by CSN. Following this reasoning, and with the positive feedback given by the company through the aforementioned document, Sérgio Bernardes would have had more time to properly evolve the pavilion's design and even define, possibly with the event's organizers, and the park's own team of architects, the most suitable and convenient position for the building.

At this point, it is necessary to recall that the original design for Ibirapuera Park, conceived by Oscar Niemeyer and his team of paulista architects, would undergo considerable adjustments, including the cancellation of the landscape study by Roberto Burle Marx, dated 1953, replaced in that same year by the design of the paulista agronomist Otávio Augusto Teixeira Mendes.[50] Among other relevant works, he authored the gardens in the residence of Maria Luisa and Oscar Americano, in a generous lot located in the neighborhood of Morumbi, in addition to being, at that time, the Head of the State Forest Service.

As a reflection of these and other inconveniences, shortly afterwards, the first issue of *Módulo* magazine, in March 1955, published the article "Mutilado o conjunto do Parque Ibirapuera (The Ibirapuera Park Complex Was Mutilated)." Accompanying its critical text, there are photos of the models for the preliminary project and the approved project of the park. Differences between both proposals are noticeable, because, while the one in the preliminary project illustrates the large marquee with five ends, and

the restaurant occupying the same lakeshore as the other
outstanding buildings in the park – then called Palaces –,
the one in the approved project illustrates the marquee
composed of only four ends and the restaurant moved to the
opposite shore. Common points are also identified between
both sketches, such as the presence of the auditorium –
which would only be built half a century later –, in addition
to considerable adjustments in the geometry of the lakes in
comparison to the final executed project.

Moreover, on the aforementioned sketches, no crossing
was proposed close to the location of the future siting of the
Volta Redonda Pavilion, only two more peripheral crossings,
one of them always close to the restaurant, a building that,
in the end, was never made possible.

In other words, buildings considered relevant in the
architectural concept of the park, such as the restaurant
and the aforementioned two thousand-seat auditorium –
which would even have a tapestry specially designed by Le
Corbusier for its interior, and would be built at the entrance
of the park, opposed to Oca – ended up being definitively
canceled at the time. Even the bridge planned to be built
next to the non-built restaurant, ended up not getting off
the ground. Thus, the idea that, with the scarcity of funds
and the political-ideological disputes between Christiano
Stockler das Neves, who even drafted a proposal for the park
in 1951,[51] and Francisco Matarazzo Sobrinho – who ended up
leaving the presidency of the 4th Centenary Commission,[52]
being replaced by writer Guilherme de Almeida, who "could
remedy very little"[53] – this condition, unfavorable at first, in
the final result seemed to have contributed positively to the
success of the Volta Redonda Pavilion.

Although needing more supporting facts, evidence has
suggested that Sérgio Bernardes and his collaborators hit
two targets with one shot. In other words, by deciding to site
the pavilion in a central point of the park, over the Sapateiro
stream, which shapes and feeds the lakes, and considering

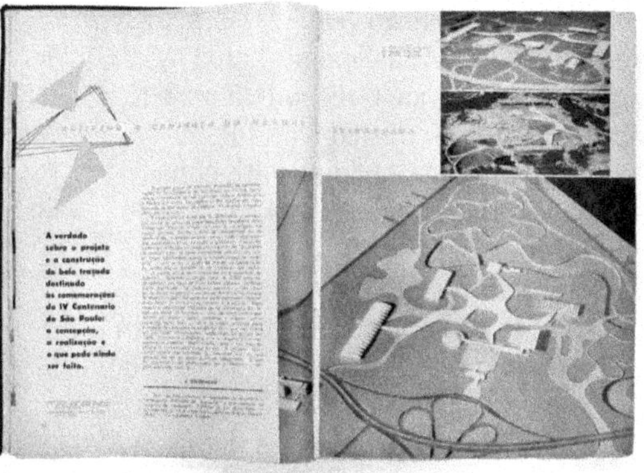

Ibirapuera Park, models of the preliminary design and the approved
project, São Paulo SP, designed by
Oscar Niemeyer and team, published
in *Módulo* magazine, no. 1, in March
1955. Collection of the FAU USP
Library

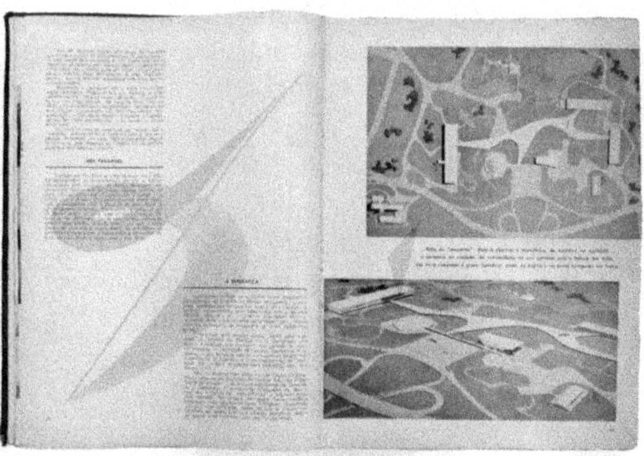

that, at that point, no element of transposition of the water-
course had been foreseen, the project started to reach a
strategic solution, of high aesthetic degree and interest.

Thus, combined with the different buildings that defined
the main character of the park: the Palaces of Industries,
Nations, States, Agriculture, etc., the cluster would be joined,
in addition to the CSN Pavilion, by other pavilions provision-
ally built for the 1st International Fair of São Paulo. Two were
outstanding, the Pavilion of Foreign Industries – more for

its dimensions, since its compositional aspect was extremely simple – and the Rio Grande do Sul Pavilion authored by architect Jayme Luna dos Santos,[54] idealized with a mixed system of cables and steel profiles, covered with tiles, resulting in an interesting penthouse building with curvilinear features, "resembling a riding saddle" and technically defined as a "revolution hyperboloid."[55]

Within this context and through a more mature and definitive design concept, Sérgio Bernardes developed, with the support of the Technical Engineering Office Adolfo A. de Aguiar – responsible for the calculations of the Lota house[56] – and his consultants at the National Steelworks Company, the technical-structural solutions for the Volta Redonda Pavilion. Now, no longer an exemplar sited on dry land, but as a bridge-building in which water would become, like steel, an element of great technical and formal expression.

The Definitive Project

After the elaboration moment of the initial study for the Volta Redonda Pavilion that was certainly prepared before April 28, 1954, originally proposed to be built on dry land with two levels, and in parallel with the definition of the site, the other 36 sheets of drawings referred to what would be the definitive project of the pavilion.

Starting with the sheet named *Drawing 3*, illustrated at 1:50 scale, and referring to the floor plan of the building's upper level. It shows the internal distribution of the floor, and according to the few available internal and external images, it largely matches the design of the Volta Redonda Pavilion. In addition to incorporating the hand-sketched ideas in *Drawing 1*, previously presented – that is, the increase in the width of the access ramps from 2.5 meters to five meters, in which the incorporation of seventeen steps in their initial sections can also be observed –, the plan also defines the access and exit doors of the building, both under

two dashed areas that illustrate the transverse marquee posted on the axis of the set, an element that is defined as *gutter*. In the referred plan, the internal checkered floor in two colors could be observed as responsible for defining the visitors' path, and a caption in the lower right corner simply describing the accesses and the elements represented inside, as follows: 1) access to ramps; 2) entrance to Pavilion; 3) panels; 4) standing cinema; 5) exit; 6) screen; 7) sealing; 8) information.

Also undated, this drawing, on the other hand, presents two parallel vertical lines that are interrupted by four access stairs to the building, elements that represent and define, albeit symbolically, the existence of the stream below. And even if a situation or guidance plan is not illustrated, the brief caption, which defines the entrance to the pavilion as the door in the lower part of the drawing, and the exit of the pavilion as the door in the upper part of the drawing, such information allows concluding – through the position of the cinema projection area – the correct orientation of how the project was sited in the park. To be more precise, when analyzing the photographic records of the pavilion's exterior, one can observe that the light – which should flow through the crystal glass panels that formed part of the building's facade – clearly does not have the same intensity on both sides.

This fact is due to the internal seal that was applied to the glasses of this portion of the building – in this case, the right side of the floor plan in *Drawing 3* –, making it possible to create an internal environment with little light, necessary for visitors to be able to properly watch projections of films inside the pavilion. The two photos illustrated here, depicting the two main facades of the building (North and South), allow us to observe properly one of the darker sides, which is certainly the side of the projection area.

By analyzing the geometry of the lakes and the buildings that appear at the background in the photos, and crossing them with the elements and information extracted from the aerial photos of Ibirapuera Park at the time of the 4th Centenary, one can determine precisely that the area destined for the projections inside the Volta Redonda Pavilion was close to the shore on which the Rio Grande do Sul Pavilion was located, thus determining that the access to its interior was through the North bridge, overlooking the Japanese Pavilion, and the exit from the Pavilion through the South bridge, overlooking the Palace of Industries, currently known as the Biennial building. This analysis becomes more consistent when one observes the two photos of the pavilion's interior published in *Arquitetura e Engenharia* magazine no. 36, July/August 1955.

Before moving on to other drawings, and the conception of the pavilion itself, other details can be observed on the upper-level plan, such as the bracings placed diagonally and inside the two inclined porticos that, in turn, create the inflection points of the five roof cables and, consequently, shape the geometry of the catenary, as will be seen below.

Also, through the plan, it is possible to identify a pattern of twelve modules, measuring 2.5 meters, distributed in the longitudinal direction of the building, totaling 30 meters in length, and eight modules, distributed in the transversal of the building, with four modules destined for the floor of the exhibition area, and four modules that define the space for the two access ramps, totaling twenty meters wide.

This metric, visible in the pair of rebars that structure the corrugated steel sheet panels that shape and define the facades, as well as the crystal glass panels – arranged in two horizontal lines, positioned at the base of the floor, and at its highest portion next to the lower face of the marquee/gutter, each 90 and 70 centimeters high, respectively – created a blind strip at half height, 1.6 meters high, surrounding the entire perimeter of the building, allowing the placement of a large part of the Pavilion's expography. This, to a large extent, would be formed by suspended panels made of thin metallic

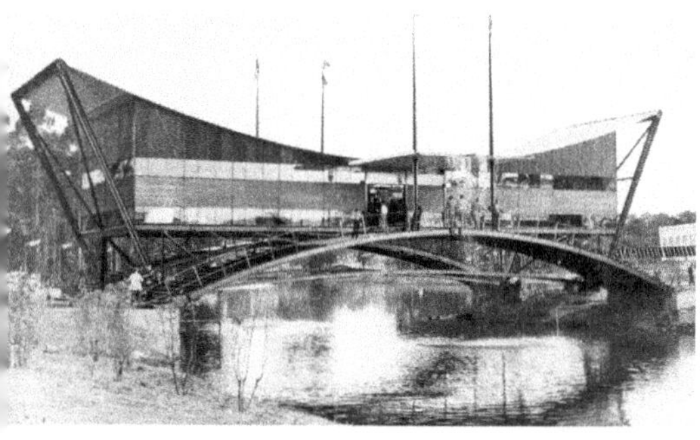

Volta Redonda Pavilion, North and
South facades, interior with exhi-
bition design, Ibirapuera Park, São
Paulo SP, 1954-1955. Collection
Sérgio Bernardes – Memory Project /
Bernardes Architecture Office

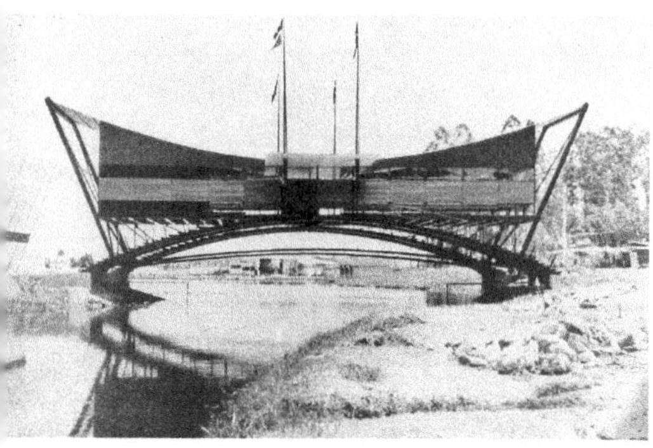

Volta Redonda Pavilion, Ibirapuera
Park, São Paulo, 1954-1955, published in the magazine *Arquitetura e
Engenharia*, no. 36, July and August
1955. Collection FAU USP Library

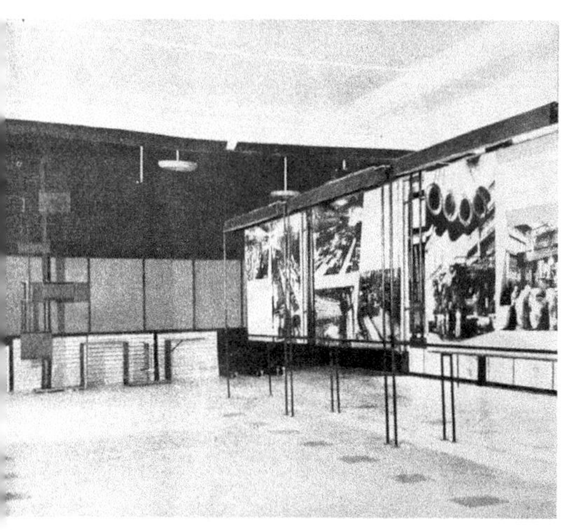

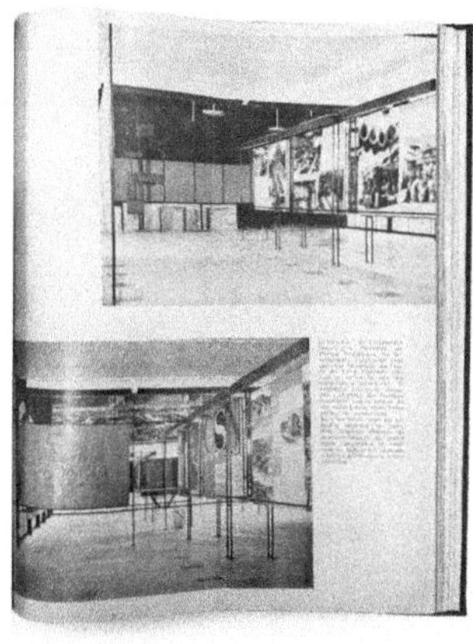

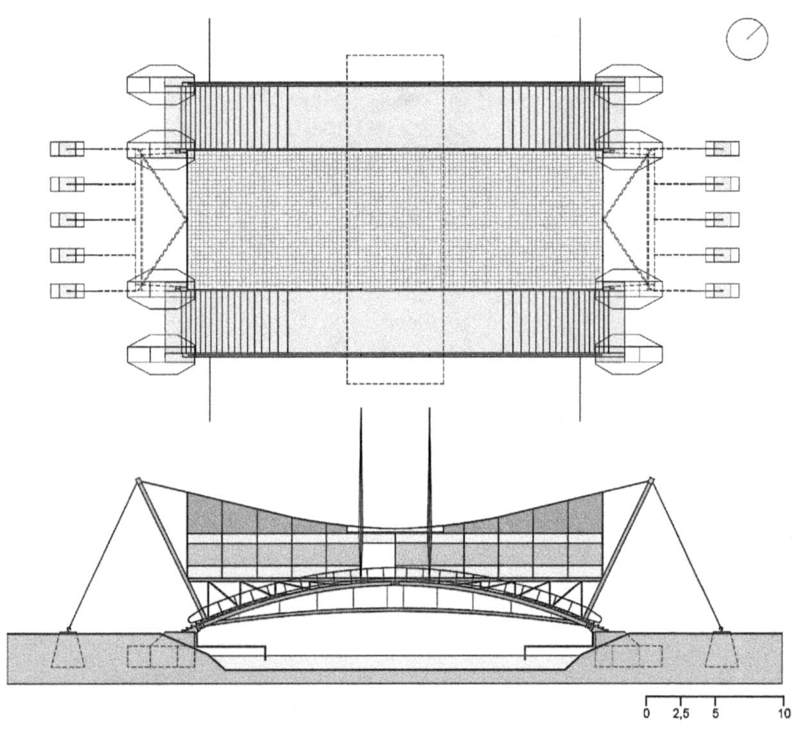

Volta Redonda Pavilion, plan and
elevation, Ibirapuera Park, São Paulo
SP, 1954-1955. Redrawn by Fausto
Sombra

tubes that rose from the floor, structuring photos and information about the then growing production of metallic elements and profiles produced by the National Steelworks Company.

Many of these panels also had, in their highest portion, and as can be seen in the photos of the Pavilion's interior, delicate metal rails apparently intended to accommodate lamps for direct lighting of these elements, a solution idealized by the Portuguese architect and artist, born in Lisbon, Eduardo Anahory, as revealed in the article published in the newspaper *O Estado de S. Paulo* the day after the building was inaugurated, transcribed in full below:

"The Pavilion of the National Steelworks Company was inaugurated yesterday afternoon in Ibirapuera. Designed by architect Sérgio Bernardes, the 'Steelworks' Stand' consists of a daring metallic structure that connects the two shores of the large lake, functioning as a bridge of ultramodern lines, giving an appearance of extreme lightness and elegance. The interior decoration comprises 27 panels, executed by painter Anahory. The act was attended by numerous personalities from the civil and military world, and the inauguration was carried out by the vice president of CSN, Mr. Ismael Coelho de Souza, substituting the president, General Macedo Soares, who is in Europe. Declaring the pavilion inaugurated, the Company's vice-president gave a brief speech describing the company's evolution and extolling the progress of São Paulo."[57]

The mention of the military, including the presence of CSN's vice president, has confirmed the strategic, economic and military importance of the country's company since the Estado Novo regime, a topic that would be addressed by historian Boris Fausto in his book *História do Brasil*:

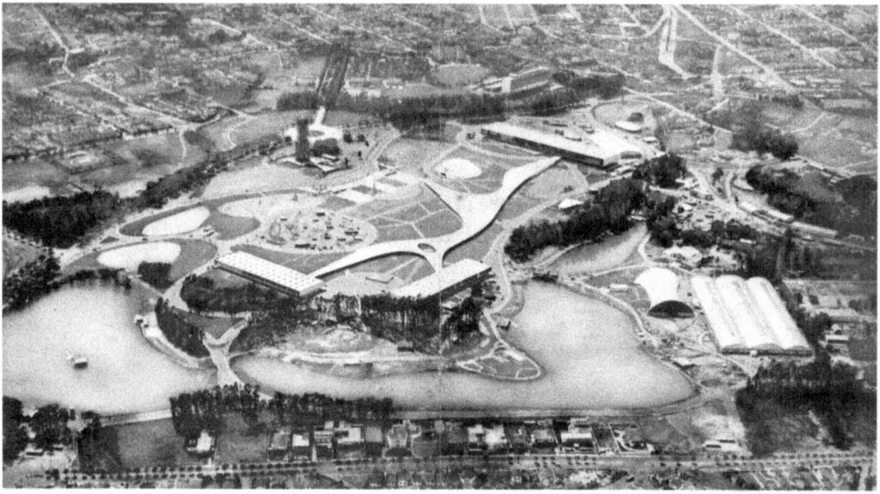

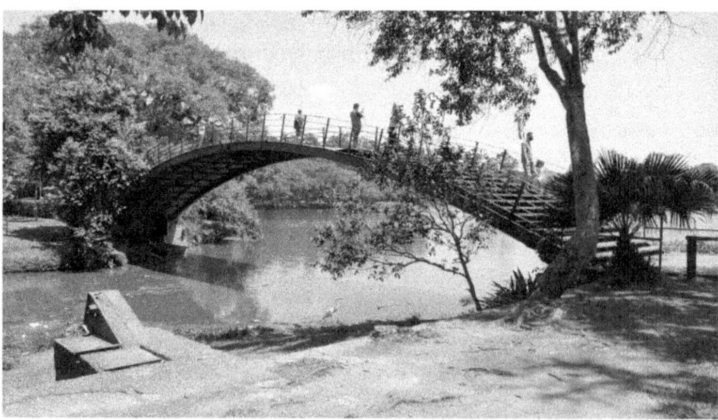

Ibirapuera Park, aerial view, São Paulo SP. Special issue "IV Centenary of São Paulo" of *Manchete* magazine, 1954. Wanda Svevo Historical Archive / São Paulo Biennial Foundation

Volta Redonda Pavilion, remaining North bridge, São Paulo SP, 1954–1955. Photo by Fausto Sombra

"We can synthesize the Estado Novo under the socio-economic aspect, saying that it represented an alliance of the civil and military bureaucracy with the industrial bourgeoisie, whose immediate common objective was to promote the industrialization of the country without major social upheavals. The civil bureaucracy defended the industrialization program for considering that it was the path to the country's true independence; the military because they believed that the installation of a base industry would strengthen the economy – an important component of national security, the industrialists because they ended up convinced that the incentive to industrialization depended on an active intervention by the State."[58]

Other newspapers circulating at the time have also highlighted the inauguration of the Volta Redonda Pavilion, and these texts are important sources of records and information about the project and about socioeconomic issues that permeated its constitution. It is the case of *O Lingote* newspaper, no. 48, dated March 10, 1955[59] – a vehicle produced by CSN itself – and the extensive article published in *Folha da Manhã* newspaper, on February 17, 1955,[60] two days after its inauguration. The latter, in addition to praising the elegant design by Sérgio Bernardes and including the transcript of the speech by vice president Ismael Coelho, quoted in the previous article, also mentioned a detail that is clearly visible in some of the photos of the building, including the one that the article shows – but which, until now, has gone unnoticed by the researchers. It is about the water pumping from the Córrego do Sapateiro stream to its roof.

Divided into five parts, due to the relevance and richness in the description of the details present in that article, although with some ineligibility in some excerpts, we chose to transcribe its two initial excerpts:

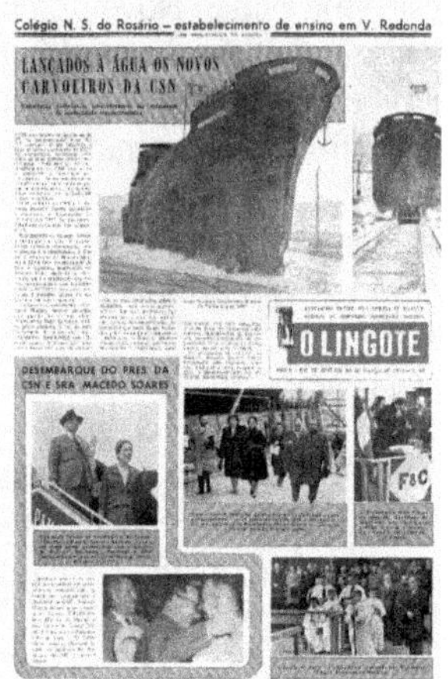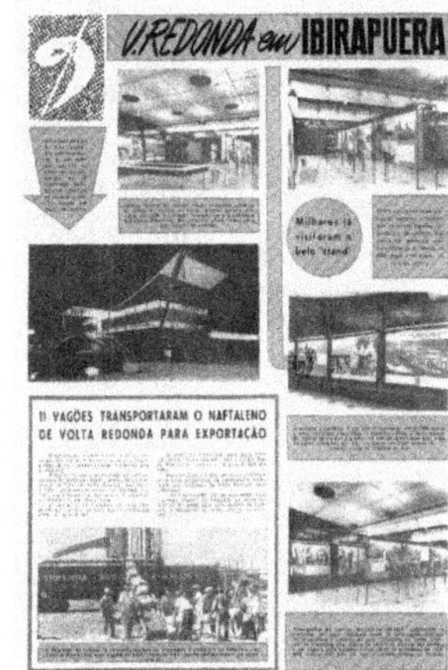

Cover and promotional article of the Volta Redonda Pavilion in the newspaper *O Lingote*, March 10, 1955.

Corporate Documentation Center – CEDOC / Companhia Siderúrgica Nacional – CSN

"The ceremony on the day before yesterday was attended by the acting president of CSN – an all-steel structure of Volta Redonda.

In a ceremony held in the afternoon of the day before yesterday [15/02/1955], the pavilion built by the National Steelworks Company was inaugurated in Ibirapuera. The act was attended by the company's acting president, Mr. Ismael Coelho de Souza. In addition to high civil and military personalities and representatives of governmental entities and the producing classes.

The pavilion was assembled on one of the lakes, flanked by two bridges, in a location that constitutes a natural passage for visitors to the exhibition. Its structure is all-metal and its visible coating is made of steel plates, all material from the blast furnaces of Volta Redonda. The support arches have movable joints at the center and at the bases, in order to compensate for expansion and contraction caused by temperature variation. With the aim of cooling the structure, but resulting in an appreciable aesthetic effect, jets of water constantly slide over the covering plates, running entirely into two waterfalls.

Inside the pavilion, there is a [series of large expographies and shelf pictures] assembled, also products manufactured by the CSN are exhibited. The exhibition highlights the magnitude of the work carried out in Volta Redonda – 'which is heading towards the production of one million tons per year' – the effort made to reach this result, the quality of the products manufactured there, the importance they have for national industry, in particular, for the railways and the construction industry, and the economic relations of the plant with the industrial park of São Paulo, its biggest consumer. Employer relations in force in the company and the social health assistance provided to employees are also illustrated."[61]

Being clearly proven by the water jet present in the photos, the water pumping also becomes visible by the presence of the pair of pipes positioned under the North bridge, both also visible in photos of the period. In addition, the project's sheet of hydraulic installations, defined as *Drawing 30*, on a 1:50 scale, illustrates perfectly how this system was idealized, with two pumps next to the foundation of the external arch of the North bridge, of 35 thousand liters/hour, one on each bank of the stream.

This ingenious solution, in which water is an integral part of the project, follows closely the rest of the bold architectural and structural design conceived for the Volta Redonda Pavilion, which is synthetically illustrated by lines and their main measures in *Drawing 8*, represented on a 1:100 scale. In it, for the first time, it is possible to observe the representation of the stream below the pavilion, with a width of 30 meters, and the angles of 42 degrees that make up the catenary.

The aforementioned drawing and the plan of the upper level, presented at the beginning of this chapter, are now complemented with the elevation of the building through *Drawing 23*, represented at 1:50 scale. In it, it is possible to observe what the constructed building would be like, but with some lacking elements that would be incorporated later during its execution, and not illustrated in any of the manipulated sheets. Firstly, it is the two arched profiles located under the internal arches that received the two inclined porticos forming the roof, and which would have the function of bracing the building, preventing the stress of the main loads of the pavilion, which were transferred to the four reinforced concrete footings on the ground, from moving horizontally and gradually in the opposite direction, with the eventual consequence of the pavilion's structural collapse.

These bracings are clearly visible in all the photos of the building's exterior, but they are no longer present on the remaining North bridge in Ibirapuera Park. However, with simple prospecting through site visits, the marks left by the removal of one of the bracings on the internal arch beam that formed the North bridge could be identified, proving the position and precise junction of these elements in the architectural cluster.

Also through the photos of both facades of the pavilion, we can see the presence of very slender vertical elements distributed with orderly spacing, perhaps at each module of 2.5 meters, and positioned, it seems, always in pairs between the arched beams and referred bracings. This detail has already been observed in the final part of the subchapter "Methodological issues" of the Introduction to this text, when the need for such elements was defended in the questioning of attentive researcher Alexandre Bahia Vanderlei.

Still referring to the theme of foundations, a new sheet defined as *Drawing 34* illustrates a second form of bracing proposed for the four internal footings of the building. In the title of the drawing, indicated as "Detailed bracing of the footings", four elements could be observed, similar to a type of strap, perhaps made of steel, which would be braced in two pairs among the four internal footings of the building.

Unlike the bracing under the internal arches, however, these would be located below the water level of the stream, and each pair would be connected by five turnbuckles in the transverse direction, evenly distributed along the length of the bracing straps. Regarding this system, it is possible to assume that, because it is located under the water and is consequently more complex to execute, it has been replaced by the exposed bracing system directly above the water.

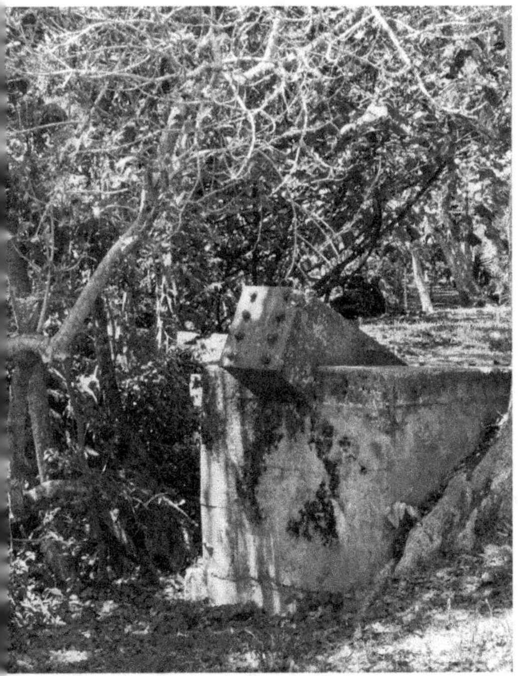

Volta Redonda Pavilion, base of the removed South bridge, São Paulo SP, 1954-1955. Photo by Fausto Sombra

However, only more detailed surveys to be carried out in the stream could definitively respond to this question.

Another element that is not present in the handled sheets referring to the project, but visible in the remaining North bridge, are the beam wagons executed under the steps and the arched floor at the top of the bridge. These elegant and delicate structural elements, with six "X" bracings along the entire length of the bridge, are not illustrated in *Drawing 9*, in which are presented only the profiles that make up the guardrails and the "I" joists that structure the bridge's floor steel plates. These joists, at least on paper, follow a precise alignment with the vertical uprights of the guardrails, occurring approximately every 1.2 meters, but with a visible approximation of the vertical uprights close to the transverse axis of the bridges.

Many other sheets that illustrate the project and its elements are relevant, and worth mentioning here. First, the truss beams that were positioned under the "I" beam that formed the lateral bases of the exhibition floorboard on the upper level, *Drawing 20*. The sheet that illustrates the three joints that were positioned on the axis and on both bases of the four "I" profile arches that formed both bridges, *Drawing 13*, these elements are still present in the remaining bridge. Also noteworthy are the sheets referring to the details and location of the footings, *Drawings 31* and *32*, being the only sheets that are dated, May 30, 1954 and May 10, 1954, respectively, both stamped by engineer Adolfo A. de Aguiar – the only one who is actually mentioned in the handled documents.

In addition to these, two more sheets are worth mentioning. The first, *Drawing 25*, referring to the pavilion's roof, illustrates an ingenious system of "T" profiles arranged diagonally and transversally to the building, all structured by five steel cables that make up the catenary roof. This design allowed the system to gain rigidity, while creating the necessary support points for fixing the corrugated steel sheets that made up the roof. The second sheet, defined as *Drawing 14*, is not necessarily a project, but rather a guide illustrating the side and front facades, and a schematic plan, all full of numbers. Each number corresponds to a metallic element that makes up the building, functioning, in this sense, as a guide to the location of the parts, a simple but intelligent solution, which perfectly organizes the assembly system, of industrial nature, proposed for this exemplar.

All 38 sheets of the project, kept in the architect's collection, many of them related to details of the elements that make up the building, represented in scales ranging from 1:1 to 1:20, ratify the concern of Sérgio Bernardes and his team for the development of unique and personalized details in his buildings. This is the case, for example, of the detail corresponding to turnbuckles, *Drawing 16*, conceived to join

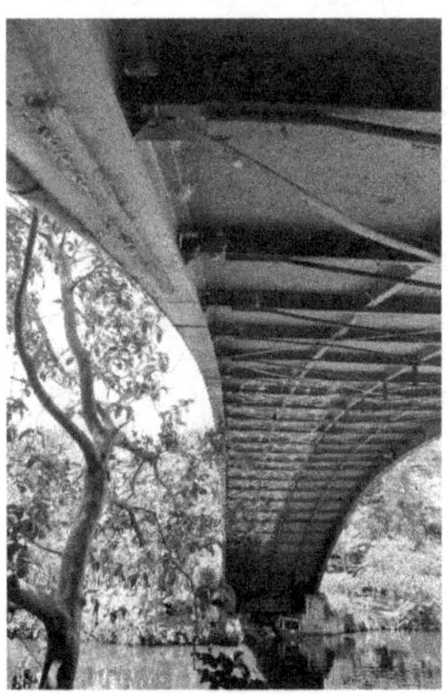
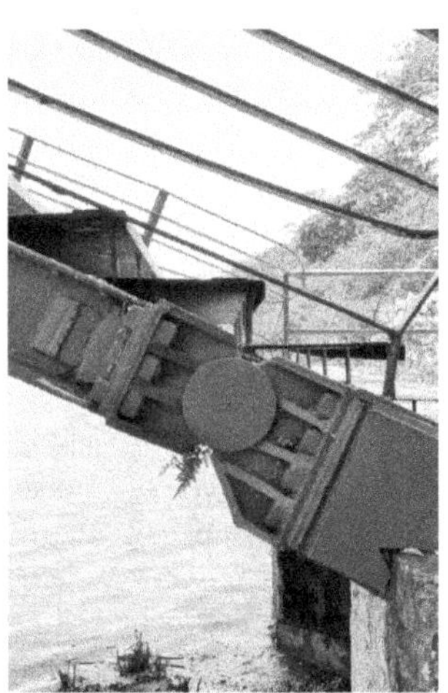

Volta Redonda Pavilion, underside and base joint of the re-emerging North bridge, Ibirapuera Park, São Paulo SP, 1954-1955. Photos by Fausto Sombra

the five cables – which made up the catenary cover – to the ground. These elements were anchored on both banks, in ten large blocks of reinforced concrete foundations with a trapezoidal drawing, a geometry specially designed to receive the tension stress coming from the cables.

Being representative elements of the project, as a complementary exercise, following the procedures carried out with physical models – the models of the buildings in 1:100 scale –, the machining of one of the turnbuckles in 1:1 scale was requested so that it could symbolically materialize the pavilion made of steel, an elaborated work by FEG Brasil Company. The result, after the turnbuckle was redesigned in its different views, is a piece of approximately six kilos and 50 centimeters long, a measure that can present some variation depending on the pair of threaded rods needed to precisely and individually tension each of the five cables.

According to preliminary simulations based on single-line three-dimensional models – an exercise developed by Márcio Sartorelli, an architect-engineer student at the Polytechnic School at the University of São Paulo,[62] and with the advice of engineer Yopanan – each of the three different cable positions – external cables, intermediate cables and central cable – was subject to a different magnitude of stress. This finding may be the way to understand why the turnbuckle board pointed out the need to produce a total of 22 turnbuckles, six of which are the same as the largest size (type A), and sixteen more turnbuckles with four different types of lengths (types B, C, D and E).

A simple hypothesis for this issue would be if the calculators had simply requested different turnbuckles and in greater quantity – originally there would have been only ten turnbuckles – so that tests could be carried out during the assembly of the building. In this way, any corrections – more complex to calculate at the time, such as, for example, the action of the winds – could simply be corrected by replacing one or more turnbuckles.

However, this is a topic that requires new and broader analyses, and it is not up to the present study, both in terms of deadline and values involved, to carry it out. On the other hand, the question that arises seems relevant for a deeper understanding of this intriguing exemplar, which, after its construction and dismantling, would once again gain attention from the National Steelworks Company and its idealizer in the late 1990s.

Dismantling and the Idea of Reconstruction

The Volta Redonda Pavilion, as seen, opened its doors to the public on February 15, 1955 in a ceremony attended by distinguished guests, and approximately eleven months after the date defined in the contract signed between the National Steelworks Company and Sérgio Bernardes. This process took place during an interval when other relevant participating pavilions opened their spaces, such as the already mentioned Rio Grande do Sul Pavilion, officially opened months earlier, on September 20, 1954,[63] and the Uruguay Pavilion, opened almost three months later, on December 11, 1954.[64]

These and other ephemeral exemplars were conceived to remain built during the first São Paulo International Fair, an event that was officially opened on August 21, 1954,[65] after many setbacks, budget cuts, adaptations, and even after cancelling the construction of relevant buildings idealized in the original conception of the project, such as the afore-mentioned Auditorium, and the restaurant at the end of the lake, cuts that irritated Oscar Niemeyer and his team of collaborators.

Even under such circumstances, the adjustments carried out ensured the maintenance of most of the events and congresses scheduled for 1954, like the 2nd Biennial, from December 13, 1953 to February 26, 1954, with Ibirapuera Park still under construction, and an extensive program of activities that would be regularly and systematically disseminated by the 4th Centenary Commission, through posters, pamphlets, periodicals, etc., also in French and English, as well as documentation preserved in the Wanda Svevo Historical Collection in the Biennial Foundation of São Paulo.

Other documentary sources allow us to understand that not only the public buildings suffered from a lack of funds and cuts, but also the Volta Redonda Pavilion went through

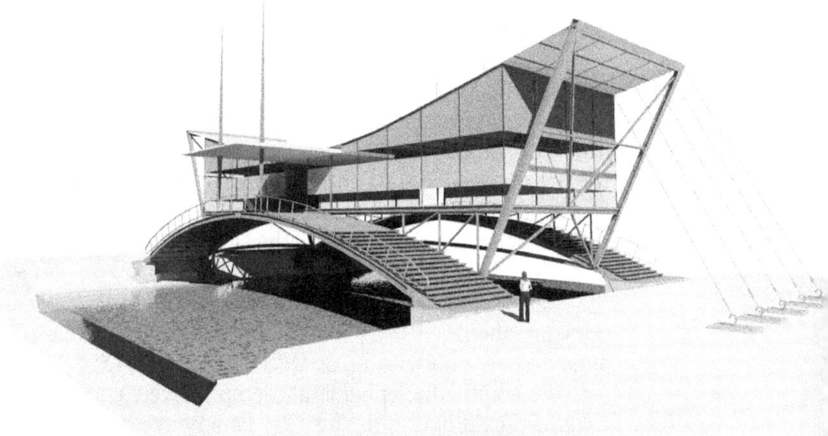

Volta Redonda Pavilion, perspective, elevation, and foundation in 3D model, São Paulo SP, 1954-1955. Drawings by Fausto Sombra

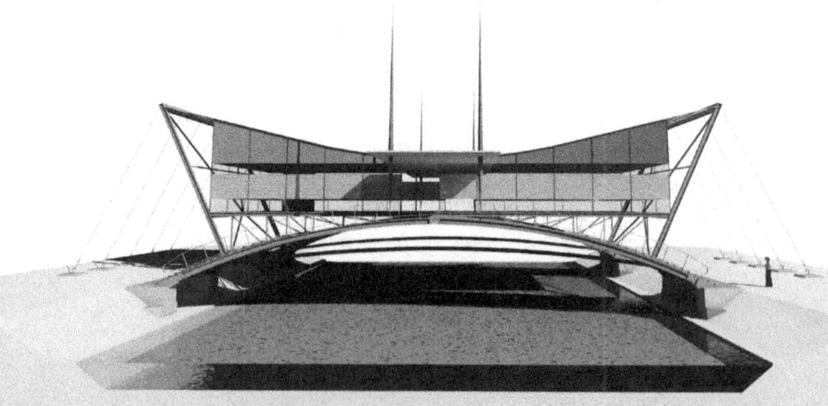

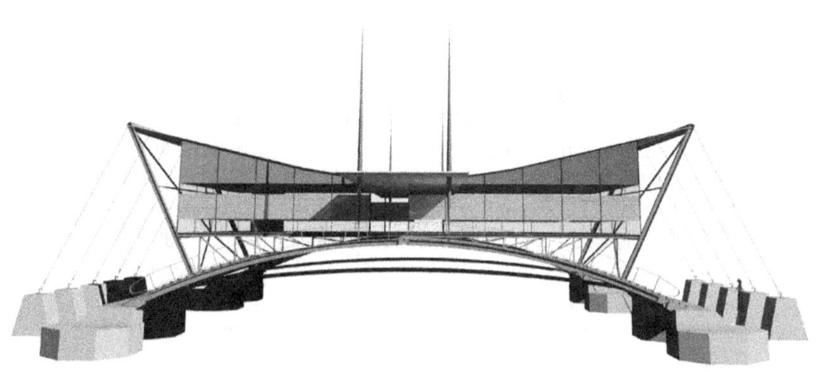

considerable delay in the estimates initially defined for its inauguration. Through the *Folha da Manhã* newspaper, dated August 4, 1954, already close to the official opening of Ibirapuera Park, the periodical praised the construction of the Bernardes' pavilion through a brief description that confirms the information presented so far, complementing and defining, however, that the Pavilion would be inaugurated on the September 7, Brazil's Independence Day.

"Designed by architect Sérgio Bernardes, the C.S.N. stand is being built with exposed metallic structure, covered with sheets from Volta Redonda, and will connect the two shores of the great lake of Ibirapuera at the point where they are closest to each other. Its structure weighs 93 tons and is being prepared at the Volta Redonda Metallic Structure Plant, while foundation piles are being driven in place. The nature of the terrain required special measures to guarantee the stability of the stand in view of its depressed arch, in its original form. The opening of the pavilion is scheduled for the September 7. At one end of the stand, there will be a balcony for showing films about the activities of the National Steelworks Company."[66]

Based on this article, it appears that the considerable gap that occurred in relation to the initially planned date for its opening until its official completion, in February 1955, is a topic that requires attention, as it is a difference of more than five months, a delay that led the aforementioned building to be – observing the dates of the Rio Grande do Sul and Uruguay Pavilions – one of the last pavilions to have its doors open, when more than a year had passed since the official opening celebration of the 4th Centenary of São Paulo City on January 23, 1954.[67] Even so, with the great success of its forms, and being very useful as crossing for

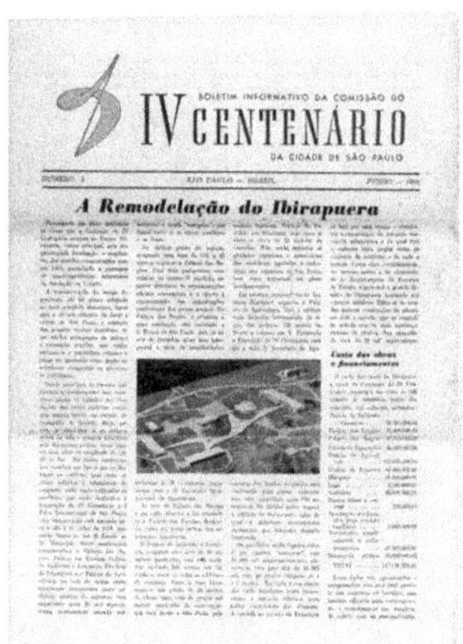

Brochure of the Celebrations of the 4th Centenary of the City of São Paulo. *Committee of the Fourth Centennial of São Paulo*, Brazil. Wanda Svevo Historical Archive / São Paulo Biennial Foundation

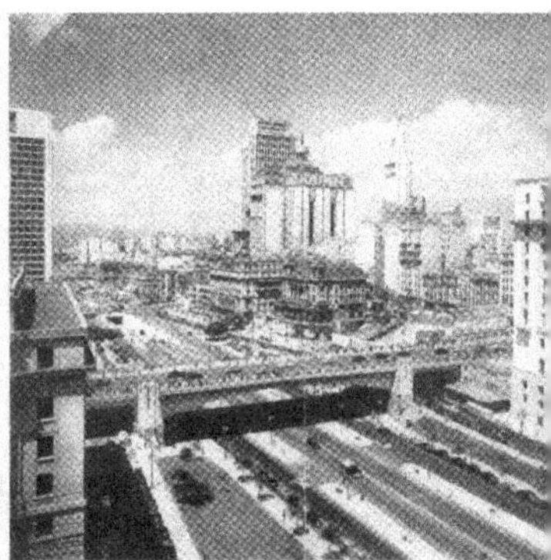

Brochure of the Celebrations of the 4th Centenary of the City of São Paulo. *São Paulo, the world's fastest growing city*. Wanda Svevo Historical Archive / São Paulo Biennial Foundation

users in the heart of the park, and unlike most of the other pavilions,[68] the Volta Redonda Pavilion could be listed as a permanent building for the Ibirapuera Park.

Among the documents handled in the Wanda Svevo Collection, of which there are practically no records about the Volta Redonda Pavilion, a small map stands out. With the title "General Map of Ibirapuera Park – suggestions", undated, the drawing illustrates the park divided into three large groups: Artistic Cultural Center; São Paulo Fair; and Amusement Park. It points out and summarizes the possible destinations for the most relevant constructed buildings, most of which were planned to be transformed – more generally – into museums. Two other buildings, such as the Rio Grande do Sul Pavilion, are designated as "dismountable pavilion". Whereas the Volta Redonda Pavilion is one of the few buildings to receive a more precise destination: the Science and Aeronautics Museum.

In the end, nevertheless, as can be seen today, only the Palaces and the Japanese Pavilion were preserved, and most of the other buildings were dismantled or partially dismantled, including the Volta Redonda Pavilion, of which only the North bridge survived. However, the moment when this dismantling process would have actually occurred is still, according to the present research, an issue that has not been properly addressed.

At least three facts seem to call into question the commonly found assertion that Sérgio Bernardes' building was dismantled shortly after the 1st International Fair. The first is the map described above, in which the intention to preserve it is noted. The second fact is an article published in the newspaper *O Estado de S. Paulo*, in September 1955, with the title "Coisas da cidade – O destino do Ibirapuera", authored by Luís Martins, in which the writer describes the possibilities on the future of the park, while considering the high value spent on the construction of this great facility, and the need observed in so many parts of the growing metropolis. Still in the text, the author emphasizes that, since the "architectural complex of great beauty" had been built, ideally, it should be transformed into a definitive center of culture and leisure, giving examples similar to those found in the city of Paris. However, Luís Martins warned readers, stressing that:

> "Low-key politicians, lead-foot administrators are already seriously considering installing public offices in Ibirapuera, putting in accounting machines where Picasso's paintings once shone, typewriters where there were sculptures by Laurens, and possibly Public Cleaning donkeys where the venerable documents of the Historical Exhibition were shown..."[69]

Luís Martins' reflections would become reality, as seen in a new article published three years later – the third fact just mentioned –, more precisely on September 28, 1958, when the precariousness of Ibirapuera Park was described. This situation would have started after Adhemar de Barros was elected mayor of the capital, when he transferred a good number of public offices to Ibirapuera, in a process of abandonment and contempt for what was once one of the greatest prides of São Paulo residents.

From this long article, two low-quality photos and their explanatory texts draw attention. The first photo, with piles of rubble in the foreground, is accompanied by the following description: "The immense dunghill that now covers the areas close to the majestic Rio Grande do Sul Pavilion". And the second photo, illustrating a section of one of the bridges of the Volta Redonda Pavilion, including the presence of the arched bracing profile under it, is followed by the title: "A saddening view of the lake that passes under the pavilion built by the Volta Redonda Plant".

Both photos and their respective texts suggest that the aforementioned pavilions would still be present at that moment, a proposition that gains strength with the testimony of Sérgio Bernardes' former partner in São Paulo, Ennes Silveira de Mello, in an interview with the author. Mello stated that, during the assembly of the special room dedicated to the work of Sérgio Bernardes, at the 7th Biennial – held at Parque Ibirapuera, in 1963[70] –, the Volta Redonda Pavilion was still fully standing, and this was topic of conversation between both professionals on that occasion:

> "It was at that time that I, strolling with him, strolling around Ibirapuera, at the stage of the exhibition that I was doing for him – because he used to travel – I was doing the exhibition here for him, that is, setting up the exhibition. On a tour that we were taking, we passed by that pavilion and he [Sérgio] said: 'wow, how beautiful this pavilion is.' I said: 'beautiful, beautiful Sérgio.' He said: 'wow, what if we could do it.' I was looking for a house to do a project. To do it. We did it, right? Sérgio and me. I made an office here with him, and I was looking for a house – and he said: 'wow, I'll try to talk to the guy from Volta Redonda, from the Steelworks – I have a friend there – and I'll see if I can make an office here.'"[71]

Since it was a simple dialogue and without great pretensions, logically Sérgio Bernardes did not manage to set up his São Paulo headquarters in this public place, and as Ennes Silveira de Mello reported, it occupied a townhouse in the Jardins neighborhood.

The facts presented above, in addition to an old video recently rescued by researcher Abilio Guerra – more precisely, episode 34 of the TV series *O Vigilante Rodoviário*, a program produced and presented between 1961 and 1962, in which the Volta Redonda Pavilion is the setting for one the recorded sequences,[72] – confirm that, possibly, until at least

1963 – year of the 7th Biennial – the Bernardes' Pavilion was fully standing in Ibirapuera Park.

Even so, without new clues that allow specifying the moment when this exemplar suffered its almost total dismantling, the referred Pavilion started to live only in the memory of those who had the opportunity to visit it, being its remaining North bridge the testimony of the capacity and efforts by its idealizer and team.

More than four decades after its inauguration, at the end of the 1990s, Sérgio Bernardes once again focused on the plans and projects developed for this originally ephemeral pavilion. At a certain age, close to his eighties, but full of energy and very willing to work, Sérgio was invited by the already privatized National Steelworks Company, through its then president, Maria Silvia Bastos Marques, to draw up plans for the reconstruction of the small exemplar over the Sapateiro stream.

This fact belatedly recovered a common theme in significant works of the modern movement around the world, especially regarding the group of buildings of the pavilion typology. Referring here, for example, to the L'Esprit Noveau Pavilion by Le Corbusier, built at the International Exhibition in Paris in 1925, and rebuilt in the Constitution Square at the Bologna Fair in Italy between 1975 and 1977, with the "consent of Le Corbusier Foundation."[73] As well as the German Pavilion, by architect Mies Van der Rohe, a building constructed in Montjuïc Park during the Barcelona International Exhibition in 1929, and rebuilt on the same site between 1981 and 1986 by the team of architects Ignasi de Solà Morales, Cristian Cirici and Fernando Ramos, as already discussed. Among other well-known examples, there was also the Pavilion of the Spanish Republic, a building designed by architects José Lluís Sert and Luis Lacasae, built for the Universal Exhibition in Paris in 1937, during the Spanish Civil War – which received the Guernica painting by Pablo Picasso – and was rebuilt for the 1992 Olympic Games in the

Vall d'Hebron Park, in Barcelona, through the team formed by architects Miquel Espinet, Antoni Ubach and Juan Miguel Hernandez de Leon.[74]

In the popular book by architect Moisés Puente, entitled *Pabellones de Exposición: 100 años*, published in 2000, fifty recognized projects of pavilions originally built between the years 1900 and 2000 are gathered. Unfortunately, none of the three pavilions designed by Sérgio Bernardes, pictured here, was included in this select list. However, in the text that opens the book authored by Catalan architect and curator Carles Muro, there is a rich synthesis of the ephemeral role of the pavilions and the fairs for which they were designed, in addition to the relevance of the photographic record of these exemplars in face of the possibility of rebuilding them. Muro, in his final paragraph, questions exactly the theme of reconstruction of these exemplars, a phenomenon that, according to the author, began "to appear a few years ago in southern Europe":

> "In this sense, as if there were an inversion of the concept of exhibition time, the pavilions remained exposed long enough to be captured in series, often reduced, of photographs. This book gathers exactly those photographs. Through them, a new exhibition is proposed where one can find, in their natural habitat – the printed-paper –, the pavilions seen at different times and places.
>
> Perhaps this book favors these pavilions more than their reconstructions, which, like a curious collection of butterflies held forever by the entomologist's long pin, began to appear a few years ago in southern Europe."[75]

With a similar thought to the one presented by Professor Carles Muro and unlike many architects, such as Mies van Der Rohe, who accepted, in 1959, the invitation to rebuild the Barcelona Pavilion following what would be the "original plans" – work which ended up not materializing[76] –, Sérgio Bernardes accepted the task of rebuilding the pavilion in Ibirapuera, and proposed technical adaptations compatible with the new available technologies, generating a conceptually similar building, but considerably different when compared to the original.

In an undated document entitled *Descriptive Memorial*, Sérgio revealed his intentions about the new challenge:

> "When I received the invitation from CSN to redesign the Pavilion, built in Ibirapuera Park in 1954, on the commemorations of the 4th Centenary of São Paulo City, I realized that I could carry out a conceptual revision compatible with the current technological advances.
>
> The pavilion, which I now propose, is composed of two arched bridges that span the length over the park's river, and structure a flat surface protected by frames and glass. The mixed roof (steel and concrete) is supported by lattice beams and metal pillars.
>
> Access to the exhibition area is through staircases, located on the arched bridges that lead to the pavilion entrances. Attached to the stairs, protected by the large catenary cover, we have motorized platforms for the disabled.
>
> At the ends of the supporting arches and perpendicular to them, four steel pillars form an inclination of 65 degrees with the floor. These pillars meet the two connecting upper trusses that span the smaller length of the pavilion, also serving as support for the 36 tie rods anchored to the floor.
>
> The roof, in turn, is composed of 36 steel cables forming the catenary and connected by "T" profiles, which support the precast concrete plates ($80 \ kg/m^2$), which will receive the waterproofing. This catenary

forms a large gutter to receive rainwater, which is poured into the river through its central ends.

In the center of each of the access curves (bridges), two masts mark the center of the circumference forming the roof catenary.

The implementation of this pavilion will mark the technological advances available at the moment, opening space for advanced technology for the population.

Sérgio Bernardes."[77]

Complementing this description, a second letter on CSN letterhead, also undated, but probably from the year 2000, summarizes the Steelworks' desire to rebuild the aforementioned building, naming people such as the then president of the Company, Maria Silvia Bastos Marques; Ricardo Ohtake, then municipal secretary of green and environment; and Oscar Niemeyer, who would have been consulted and given his approval for intervention in the park, then already listed by the state protection agency Condephaat, and the municipal agency Conpresp.[78]

Both documents help to clarify the idea of reconstruction of this representative exemplar, and allow us to understand the forms resulting from the operations, and the new rearrangement of the pieces proposed by the already octogenarian carioca architect, being one of his last studies carried out before his passing on June 15, 2002, aged 83.

Less elegant than its original design, in part resulting from the increase in the suggested new scale, and logically no longer representing the golden moment of its avant-garde design – in which not only the Volta Redonda Pavilion was conceived, but also its later counterparts – , the new proposal for the pavilion in Ibirapuera emphasized, however, a striking feature in Sérgio Bernardes' posture: that the architect rarely seemed to look at his work with a nostalgic feeling, which would prevent him from moving forward and suggesting adaptations and transformations. This, perhaps, is one of the qualities that best defines the carioca architect, that is, being a professional with convictions always focused on the future, towards new challenges and solutions, in line with the rapid changes of the contemporary world.

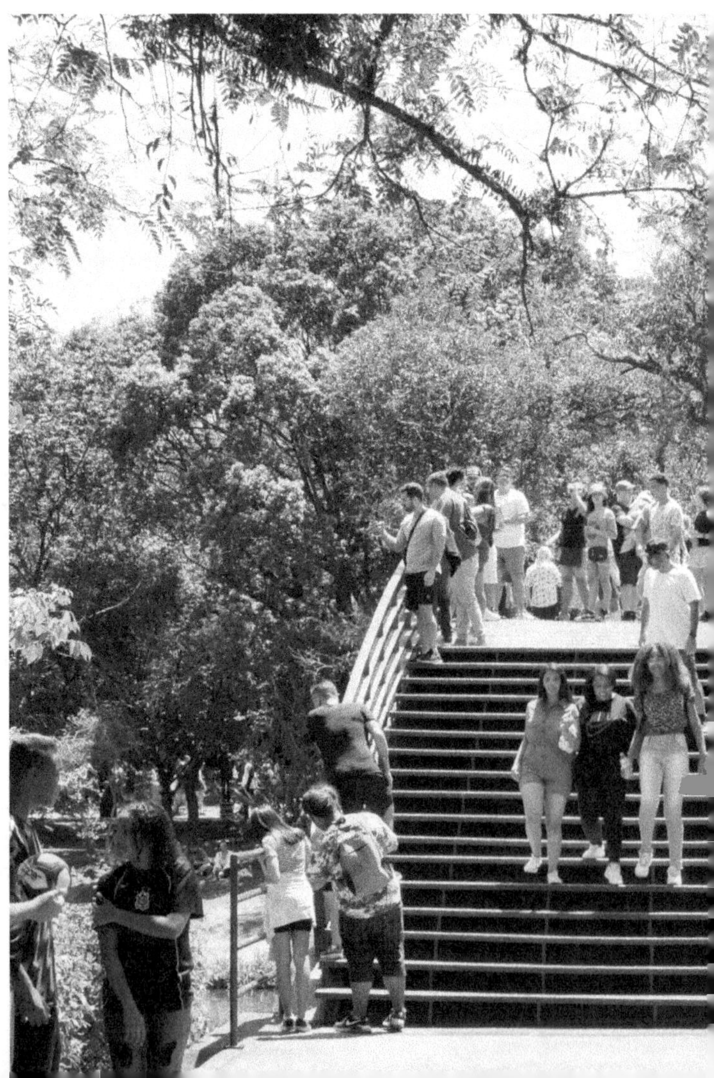

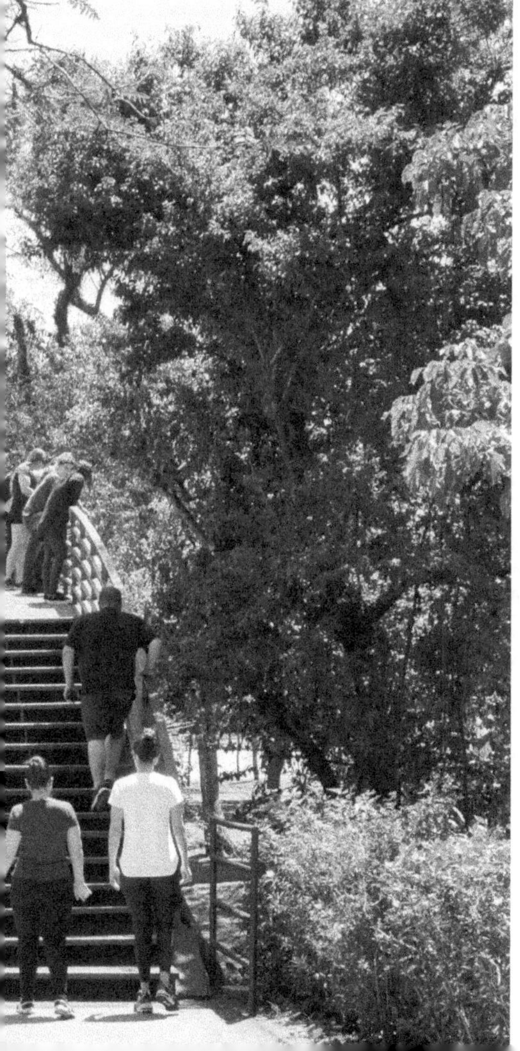

Volta Redonda Pavilion, remaining North bridge, São Paulo SP, 1954-1955. Photo by Fausto Sombra

Notes

1. About the history of Copan, see Carlos Alberto Cerqueira Lemos, *Trilogia do Copan: a história do edifício Copan.*
2. About the constitution process of Ibirapuera Park, see Regina Meyer, "Metrópole e Urbanismo: São Paulo anos 50"; Arruda, *Metrópole e cultura* (full professorship dissertation and book); Fabiano Lemes de Oliveira, "Os projetos para o Parque Ibirapuera: de Manequinho Lopes a Niemeyer (1926-1954)"; Fabiano Lemes de Oliveira, "O Parque do Ibirapuera: projetos, modernidade e modernismo"; Cecília Rodrigues dos Santos, "Teatro do Parque Ibirapuera: em nome de quem?"; Ana Cláudia Castilho Barone, *Ibirapuera: parque metropolitano (1926-1954)* (dissertation and book).
3. See *Manchete* magazine (edição especial 4º Centenário), Rio de Janeiro, 1954 <https://bit.ly/36IOVHs>.
4. Cavalcanti, *Sérgio Bernardes*, 13.
5. About the contribution of renowned foreign architects, mainly during the 1930s and 1960s in São Paulo, see Raul Juste Lores, *São Paulo nas alturas*; Moracy Amaral e Almeida, "Pilon, Heep, Korngold e Palanti: edifício de escritórios (1930-1960)"; Marcelo Consiglio Barbosa, "Adolph Franz Heep: um arquiteto moderno" (dissertation and book).
6. See Redação, "Inaugura-se hoje, em São Paulo, a exposição do IV Centenário", 9. Interestingly, Belgium – the country where the Brazil pavilion designed by Sérgio Bernardes would have great prominence in 1958 – had a prominent participation in the 1954 exhibition at Parque do Ibirapuera. Redação, "Pavilhão da Bélgica no Ibirapuera"; Redação, "Homenagem da Bélgica à cidade de S. Paulo no seu IV Centenário".
7. See Fernanda Curi, "60 anos do Parque Ibirapuera".
8. Although the construction of Ibirapuera Park resulted in great frustration for Oscar Niemeyer in the face of "the builders' greed and the idiocy of the centenary commission", which combined to lose half of the beauty of the originally idealized project, even so, the critic and sociologist Darcy Ribeiro argued that this architectural complex was considered the "best in Paulicéia". Darcy Ribeiro, *Aos trancos e barrancos: como o Brasil deu no que deu,* (entry) 1374. See also Redação, "Conjunto do Ibirapuera: clamorosamente mutilado o projeto inicial do grupo arquitetônico comemorativo do 4° Centenário de São Paulo", 18.

9.	Historians Carlos Guilherme
Mota and Adriana Lopez recalled
a series of facts – beyond the
Modern Art Week – that point
to the political dissatisfaction in
the state of São Paulo between
the late 1910s and the end
of the 1930s: "The extensive
workers' strike of 1917, in the
State of São Paulo, had opened
a new period in the history of
Brazil. Subsequently, the foundation of the Brazilian Communist
Party, the Modern Art Week in
1922, the Tenentista movements
of 1922, 1924 and 1926, the
Revolution of 1930, and the
Constitutionalist Revolution of
1932, the communist uprising
of 1935, the integralist revolt of
1937, and the implementation
of Estado Novo (1937-1945)
signal a long, intense and
contradictory process of tran-
sition from an oligarchic-rural
order to a society marked by
urban-industrial forces. Or from
a society of estates and castes
to a society of classes. São Paulo
was the main center of these
renovation attempts. In fact,
in this period, there was an
attempt to build a new identity
and a new historical-social and
political memory. A new, mark-
edly urban and cosmopolitan
mentality was defined; in the
words of Richard Morse, there
was the establishment of a
'temperament of the metropolis',
title of a chapter in his classic
work, *Formação histórica de São
Paulo*. Mota and Lopez, *História
do Brasil*, 676.

10.	Pedro Cunha, a figure who
supported the organization
of actions promoted by the
4th Centenary Commission,
summarized the importance
of immigrant participation in
shaping the capital of São Paulo:
"Brazil owes a lot to foreigners
who from various parts of the
world came to complete the
work begun by the Portuguese
at the time of its discovery.
Especially in the state of São
Paulo, which has the densest
population of 'aliens', this debt
is recognized and taken into
account. It is precisely here that
one could best appreciate the
value of the cooperation of
foreign children, whose intelligence and hard work strive in
the multiple aspects of life in
the place, both in terms of the
culture of the spirit and of the
activities of industry, commerce
and agriculture. With regard to
the Japanese, from the passage
of the fourth centenary of the
foundation of the city of São
Paulo, another recognition is
imposed: that of gratitude on
the part of the natives of the
State. The important historical
event brought all the foreign
colonies a good opportunity to
express their feelings towards
the people who received them
and welcomed them to their
bosom. Not a few colonies, on
that occasion, took advantage
of the opportunity for these
manifestations, in various ways
sharing the joys of the people.
There was one, however, that
surpassed all the others in this
kindness. It was the Japanese

colony, precisely the one that was most recently formed. It exceeded everything; in the sum of financial resources spent, in the construction, and donation to the Municipality, of one of the most beautiful and expressive palaces that the city has today, and in the brilliance represented in all cultural manifestations by great men of thought and notable figures of their artistic medium". Pedro Cunha, "A colônia que melhor contribuiu para as festas do IV Centenário".

11. Such as the subtitle borrowed from the professor's dissertation and book by sociologist Maria Arminda do Nascimento Arruda, *Metrópole e cultura: São Paulo no meio século XX.*

12. The expansion and renovation project for Belvedere Trianon was in charge of architects Luís Saia and Eduardo Kneese de Mello. See Sombra, "O pavilhão da I Bienal do MAM SP"; Sombra, "Luís Saia e o restauro do Sítio Santo Antônio"; Abilio Guerra and Fausto Sombra, "Avenida Paulista, 1951: cenário da 1ª Bienal de São Paulo".

13. The 2nd Biennial was opened to the public on December 12, 1953, with the official opening of Ibirapuera Park on August 21, 1954. Curi, "60 anos do Parque Ibirapuera".

14. The 2nd Biennial had 24,000 m² of exhibition area and support, encompassing the Palace of Nations and the Palace of States. Helio Herbst, *Pelos salões das bienais, a arquitetura ausente dos manuais: contribuições para a historiografia brasileira (1951-1959),*185.

15. See Sombra, "O pavilhão da I Bienal do MAM SP"; Daniele Pisani, *O Trianon do MAM ao Masp: arquitetura e política em São Paulo (1946-1968).*

16. In 1910, São Paulo had 314 thousand inhabitants, and in 1920, 550 thousand. Data from the American Chamber of Commerce for Brazil published in *Acrópole* magazine, no. 157, May 1951. Redação, "A cidade que mais cresce no mundo", s/p.

17. COMISSÃO DO 4º CENTENÁRIO DA CIDADE DE SÃO PAULO. São Paulo em números. Wanda Svevo Archive, São Paulo Biennial, Fundo FMS_0441-06.

18. TN: currency of the period.

19. COMISSÃO, São Paulo em números.

20. Vanderlei, "Pavilhão da CSN 1954".

21. Bastos and Zein, *Brasil,* 36-37.

22. Bastos and Zein, *Brasil,* 37.

23. "In visual arts, concretism appeared as an evolution of abstractionism and not as an opposition to the movement. It must be understood as part of the modern abstractionist movement, with roots in experiences such as that of the De Stijl group, created in 1917 in Holland by Piet Mondrian, Theo van Doesburg, among others". Redação, "Movimento Concretista nas artes plásticas".

24. In his article in *Fundamentos* no. 23, Vilanova Artigas criticized harshly the 1st Biennial. See João Batista Vilanova Artigas, "A Bienal é contra os artistas brasileiros", 10.

25. The August Manifesto was signed by leader Luiz Carlos Prestes, on August 1, 1950, on behalf of the National Committee of the Communist Party of Brazil. Publication, Luiz Carlos Prestes, "Prestes dirige-se ao povo brasileiro".

26. Leonor Amarante, *As Bienais de São Paulo: 1951-1987*, 16.

27. Amarante, *As Bienais de São Paulo*, 17.

28. For a synthesis of the conformation of the National Steelworks Company – CSN, see Regina da Luz Moreira and Maurette Brandt, *CSN: um sonho feito de aço e ousadia.*

29. About Getúlio Vargas, see the trilogy: Lira Neto. *Getúlio 1882-1930: dos anos de formação à conquista do poder;* Lira Neto, *Getúlio 1930-1945: do governo provisório à ditadura do Estado Novo*; Lira Neto, *Getúlio 1945-1954: de volta pela consagração popular ao suicídio.*

30. The growth of the activity carried out by the National Steelworks Company, from 1953 onwards, was published by the newspaper *O Lingote*. See Fábio Salgado Araújo, "A Companhia Siderúrgica Nacional e as políticas sociais de lazer para os trabalhadores: os clubes sociorrecreativos".

31. Boris Fausto, *História do Brasil*, 371.

32. Herbst, *Pelos salões das bienais, a arquitetura ausente dos manuais: contribuições para a historiografia brasileira (1951-1959).*

33. Bastos and Zein, *Brasil*, 37.

34. According to the November 1953 issue of *Acrópole* magazine, Paul Rudolph was awarded at the 2nd Biennial in 1954 with the Young Foreign Architect Award for the design of the Walker Guest House in Senibal Island, Florida, while Sérgio Bernardes received the Young Brazilian Architect Award for the design of Lota de Macedo Soares' house. The inconsistency in the dates—the November 1953 magazine announcing winners declared in January 1954—is likely due to the delayed publication of the issue. See: Redação. Awards from the 2nd International Exhibition of Architecture of the 2nd Biennial of the São Paulo Museum of Modern Art, p. 328. Thanks to the collaboration of researcher Helio Herbst, the Jury Minutes (doc.: 01-00723) were located at the Bienal Foundation, dated January 4, 5, 6, and 7, 1954, and signed by the jurors Walter Gropius, Josep Lluís Sert, Alvar Aalto, Ernest N. Rogers, Affonso Eduardo Reidy, and Oswald Arthur Bratke (president), where it is clear that Rudolph was awarded for the three projects presented: Guest House, 1953; Winter House, 1951; Club Cabin, 1953. Interestingly, the announcement of the winners by *Acrópole* magazine occurred more than a month before the date on the Minutes, which opens up two possibilities for the event: the delayed

publication of the magazine issue or the analysis of the projects done by correspondence among the jurors, who only arrived in São Paulo in January 1954. Regarding the brief stay of Gropius in Brazil, see: Rodrigo Marcondes Rocha. *Walter Gropius in Brazil: Revisiting Critiques.*

35. Herbst, *Pelos salões das bienais, a arquitetura ausente dos manuais: contribuições para a historiografia brasileira (1951-1959)*, 197.

36. Here referring to the pavilion system of metallic trusses and pillars used by Sérgio Bernardes.

37. Engineer Yopanan Conrado Pereira Rebello presented a synthesis of the characteristics and behavior of the tri-articulated arch: "The tri- articulated arches can adapt well to changes in shape, better absorbing the stress variation. They are arches that, because they can be assembled in parts, allow a simpler execution. On the other hand, these arches are more sensitive to buckling, requiring greater care in their stabilization". Yopanan Conrado Pereira Rebello, *A concepção estrutural e a arquitetura*, 94-95.

38. In an article reporting the inauguration of the pavilion, there is a brief quote about the water pumping system from the stream towards its roof. Redação, "Inaugurado na exposição do Ibirapuera o Pavilhão da Cia. Siderúrgica Nacional", 10.

39. About Casa sobre el Arroyo, see Daniel Merro Johnston, *La casa sobre el arroyo: Amancio Williams en Argentina.*

40. About Cocoon House, see Christopher Domin and Joseph King, *Paul Rudolph: the Florida Houses*, 96-100.

41. At the time, the board of directors and technical advice in the magazine *Arquitetura e Engenharia* included names such as Sylvio de Vasconcelos, Afonso Eduardo Reidy, Álvaro Vital Brasil, Eduardo Kneese de Mello and Rino Levi. Whereas *Módulo* magazine had names like Joaquim Cardoso, Oscar Niemeyer, Rodrigo Mello Franco de Andrade and Zenon Lotufo.

42. Other later publications high-lighted the construction of the Volta Redonda Pavilion; Bruand, *Arquitetura contemporânea no Brasil*, 261; Adrian Forty, *Brazil's Modern Architecture*, 89; Luís Andrade de Mattos Dias, *Edificações de aço no Brasil*, 200.

43. According to an article published in the newspaper *O Estado de S. Paulo*, on April 19, 2000, the Volta Redonda Pavilion remained assembled in the park for two years. Marisa Folgato, "SP ganha no aniversário presente que havia sumido", 26. This state-ment is going to be refuted later, in the chapter that closes the analysis of the referred exemplar.

44. Excerpt from the Descriptive Memorial for the new version of the CSN Pavilion project. Source: Sérgio Bernardes Collection.

45. A few years later, researcher Mônica Paciello presented in her thesis on the work of Sérgio Bernardes, plans and elevations of the new study for the CSN Pavilion. See Vieira, "Sérgio Bernardes," 145.

46. Architect Monica Paciello, a former intern at Sérgio Bernardes', told the author about the reconstruction of the pavilion: "I do not recall how the negotiations between CSN and the São Paulo City Hall took place, nor why the project was not carried out. But I am sure they did not expect a new project. They wanted to 'only' rebuild the 1954 pavilion. Perhaps this fact contributed for the project not to advance". Monica Paciello Vieira, Testimony to Fausto Sombra, electronic message, Porto, May 2, 2018

47. Vanderlei, "Pavilhão da CSN 1954".

48. Excerpt from the final paragraph of the contract established between CSN and Sérgio Bernardes, Apr. 28, 1954. Quoted in Vanderlei, "Sérgio Bernardes", 280.

49. Full contract established between CSN and Sérgio Bernardes, Apr. 28, 1954. Quoted in Vanderlei, "Sérgio Bernardes", 279-280.

50. See Cássia Mariano, *Preservação e paisagismo em São Paulo: Otávio Augusto Teixeira Mendes*.

51. Oliveira, "O Parque do Ibirapuera".

52. After the then mayor Armando de Arruda Pereira left office on Apr. 7, 1953.

53. Oscar Niemeyer, "Mutilado o conjunto do Parque Ibirapuera", 20.

54. Luna dos Santos used a mixed roofing system with cables and steel profiles, covered with corrugated tiles, however, in this case, to build a more generously sized ground floor pavilion, measuring 5,000 square meters, being 120 meters long by 60 meters wide at both ends. Its two main facades rose up to twenty meters high, with its lowest central point at ten meters. See Redação, "Será oficialmente instalada amanhã a grande exposição do IV Centenário", 13.

55. Dias, *Edificações de aço no Brasil*, 200.

56. Engineer Adolfo A. Aguiar was also responsible for calculating the structure of the Lota de Macedo Soares residence. See NPD UFRJ, SB-004, Caixa-002.

57. Redação, "Inaugurado ontem no Ibirapuera o Pavilhão da Companhia Siderúrgica", 12.

58. Fausto, *História do Brasil*, 367.

59. Redação, "V. Redonda em Ibirapuera".

60. Redação, "Inaugurado na exposição do Ibirapuera o Pavilhão da Cia. Siderúrgica Nacional".

61. Ibid., 10.

62. Calculation memorial Ibirapuera Exhibition Pavilion – Analysis performed: In order to carry out the structural analysis of the pavilion, it was necessary to consider the geometric nonlinearities of elements without bending stiffness under large displacements, such as the cables. Such consideration is essential to evaluate the efficiency of the tensioned structure, where a linear structural analysis can indicate very imprecise values. Conventional linear analyzes use the assumption that the deformed configuration of a structure is small enough to approximate the deformations in linear relationships, which is valid for most structures, but not for cables and membranes, whose structural performance depends exclusively on their shape, while presenting much more pronounced displacements than rigid elements. With the help of the finite element program ANSYS, it is possible to simulate these effects with the help of non-linear structural solution tools. For the calculation, properties of conventional structural steel were considered.

63. About the inauguration of Rio Grande do Sul Pavilion, see Redação, "Os festejos populares marcados para hoje e amanhã no Ibirapuera".

64. Redação, "Aberto o Pavilhão do Uruguai na 1ª Feira Internacional de São Paulo".

65. See Redação, "Será oficialmente instalada amanhã a grande exposição do IV Centenário".

66. Redação, "Pavilhão da Companhia Siderúrgica Nacional", 4.

67. Redação, "Abertura dos festejos do IV Centenário: flutuarão sobre o Anhangabaú na manhã de hoje quatro grandes bandeiras nacionais".

68. In an article published in the newspaper *O Estado de S. Paulo* on June 15, 1957, the text raises doubts about whether the Rio Grande do Sul Pavilion would remain built in Ibirapuera Park until that moment, as it was designed to be dismantled after the event and reassembled in the state of Rio Grande do Sul, the cost of transporting the parts and elements that made up the building, according to the article, would be more expensive than the cost of the pavilion itself. See Redação, "Pavilhão do R. Grande do Sul no Ibirapuera".

69. Luis Martins, "Coisas da cidade: o destino do Ibirapuera".

70. The 7th Biennial was held from Sep. 28 to Dec. 22, 1963. See BIENAL DE SÃO PAULO, "7ª Bienal de São Paulo".

71. Cf. Ennes Silveira de Mello, Testimony to Fausto Sombra at the architect's residence, São Paulo, Feb. 6, 2018.

72. The series, originally shown on TV Tupi, was produced by Indústria Brasileira de Filmes – IBF and directed by Ary Fernandes. Thirty-eight episodes were filmed between 1961 and 1962. In the episode "A repórter", partly recorded in Ibirapuera Park, the Volta Redonda Pavilion appears intact in three sequences in the range from 17'36" to 18'26". See *O vigilante rodoviário*, Ep. 34, "A repórter".

73. Ana Carolina Santos Pellegrini, "Bolonha, Barcelona, Firminy: quando o projeto é patrimônio", 205.

74. Ibid., 208.

75. Carles Muro, Presentación. About the theme related to the reconstruction of important pavilions, see also Ascensión Hernández Martínez, *La clonación arquitectónica*.

76. According to the records of Ignasi de Solà-Morales and team, in 1959, Grup R, through its secretary Oriol Bohigas, approached architect Mies van der Rohe, proposing the reconstruction of the German Pavilion. Its idealizer immediately accepted it without charging fees, even suggesting that the coordination of the work was his responsibility. However, due to lack of support from the institutions involved, the work ended up being suspended. Solà-Morales, Cirici, and Ramos, *Mies van der Rohe*, 26.

77. Sérgio Bernardes, "Pavilhão da Companhia Siderúrgica Nacional no Parque Ibirapuera – SP", Rio de Janeiro, s.d. Acervo Sérgio Bernardes.

78. Companhia Siderúrgica Nacional, "CSN assina convênio para reconstruir um espaço cultural no Parque Ibirapuera", Volta Redonda, c.2000, Acervo Sérgio Bernardes.

Chapter 3
Brazil Pavilion in Brussels 1957–1958

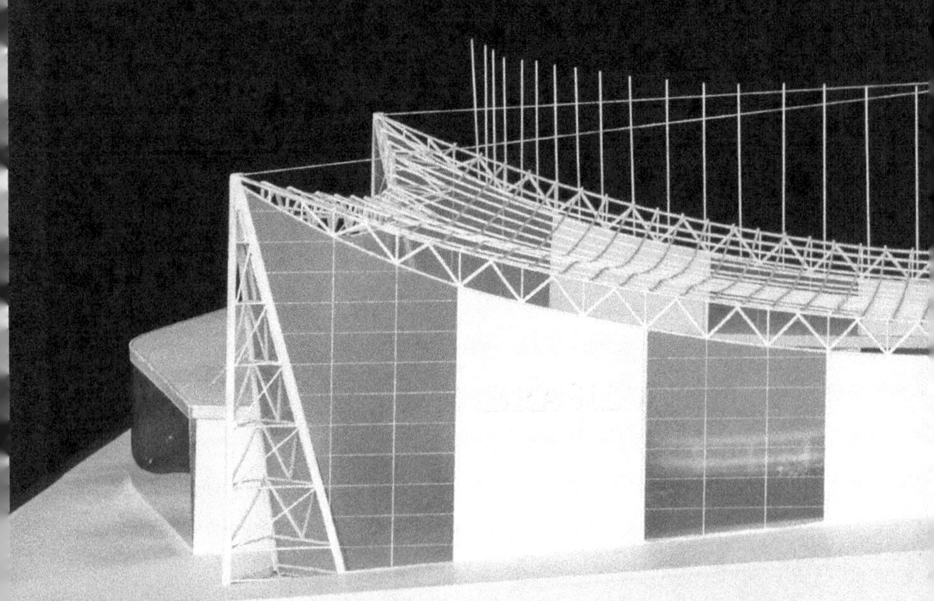

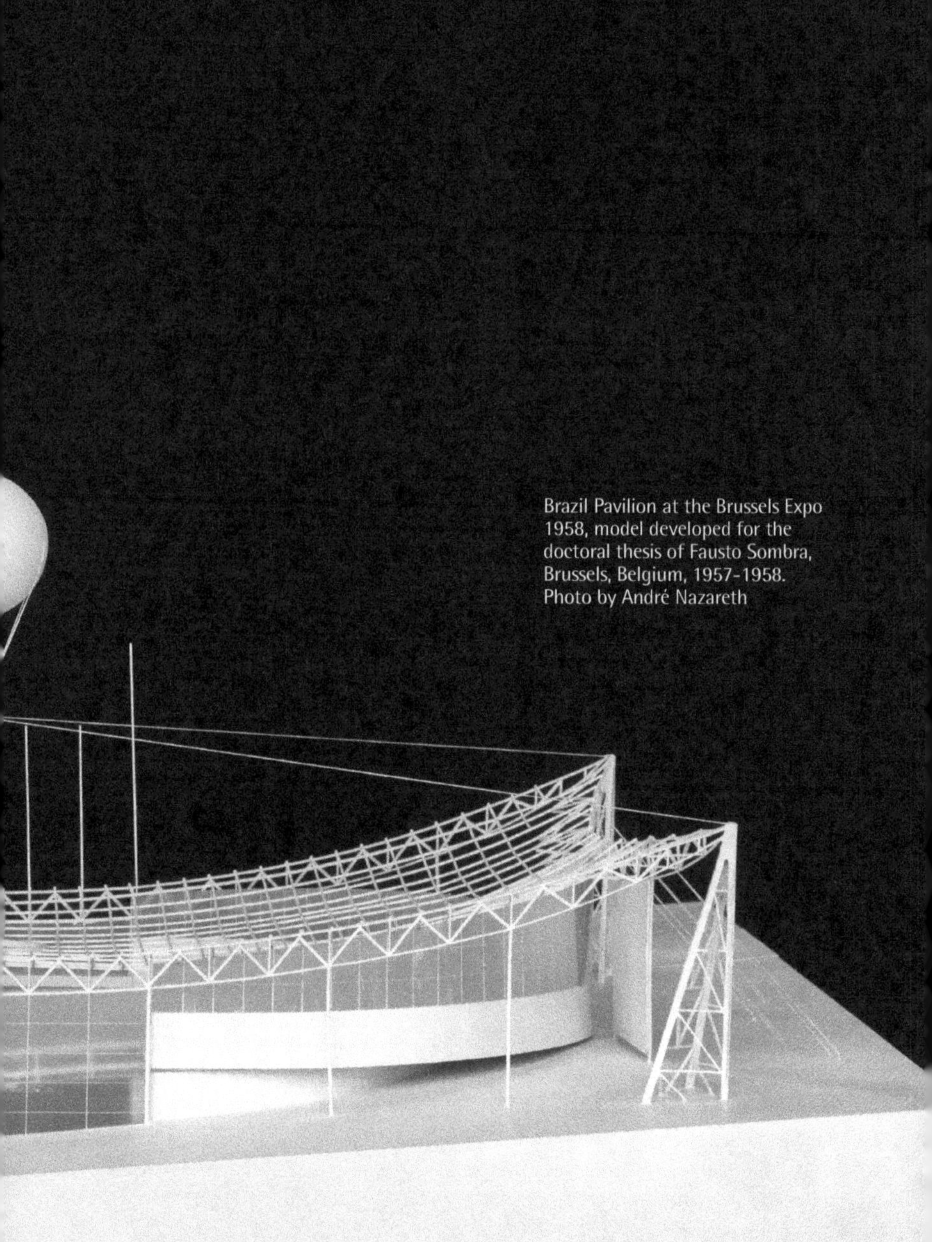

Brazil Pavilion at the Brussels Expo
1958, model developed for the
doctoral thesis of Fausto Sombra,
Brussels, Belgium, 1957–1958.
Photo by André Nazareth

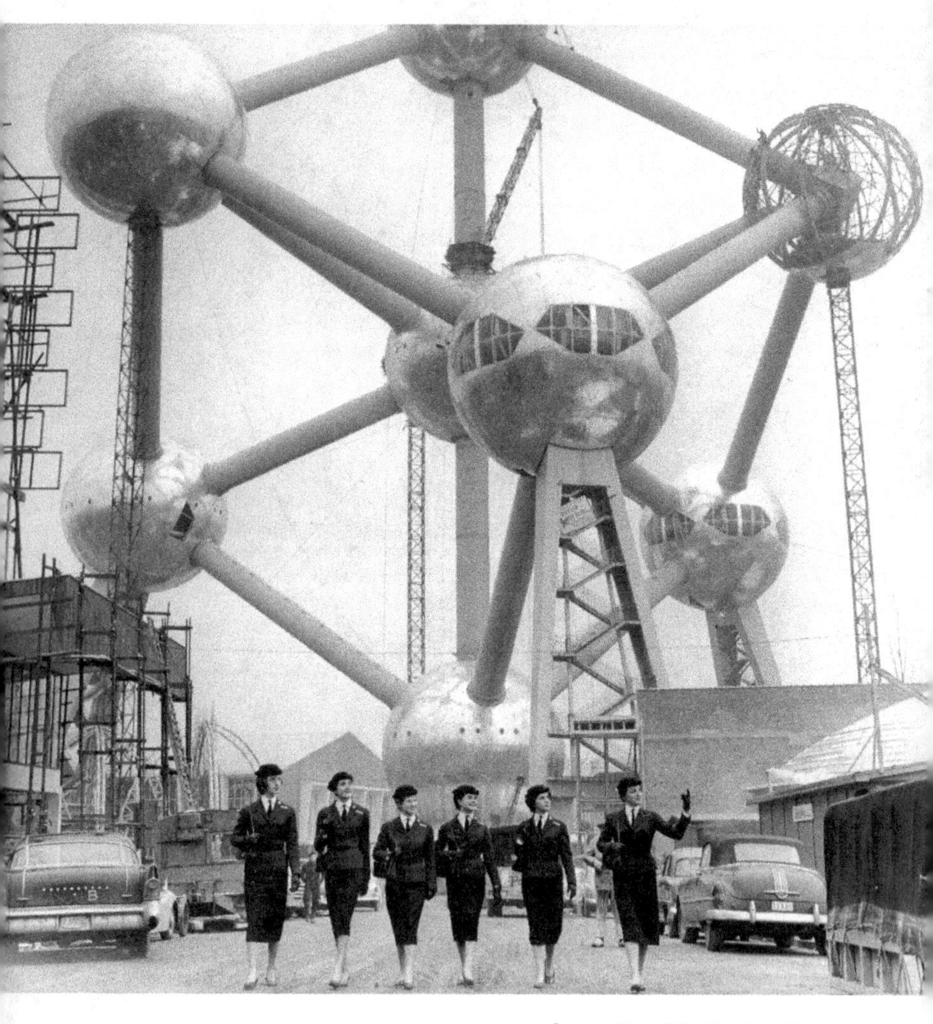

Construction of the Atomium, Parc de Laeken, Brussels Expo 1958. Photo by Pieter Vandeweyer. Wikimedia Commons license CC-BY-SA-4.0 https://bit.ly/3TegbZn

Brazil Pavilion at the Brussels Universal and International Exhibition

Located in Heysel, in the northern region of the Belgian capital, a little more than six decades ago, at the Brussels Universal and International Exhibition – the first major exhibition held after the Second World War and amid the Cold War – one of the most surprising projects was built in concrete and steel as part of the extensive list of works by architect Sérgio Bernardes. It is the award-winning Brazil Pavilion, a building located on irregular terrain with a steep slope in the southern portion of Parc de Laeken, on a currently grassy lot between the Avenue des Seringas and Trembles Abele, next to the small chapel of Sainte-Anne and its fountain.

As with the Volta Redonda Pavilion, the amount of information and details about the actions that involved the elaboration of this project are considerably scarce compared to the relevance of this exemplar in the Brazilian and

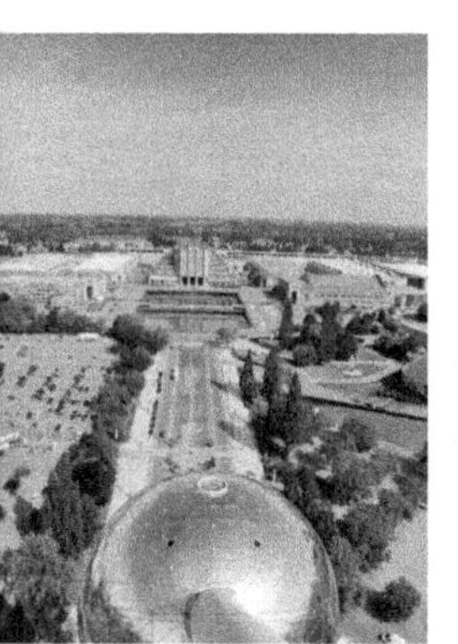
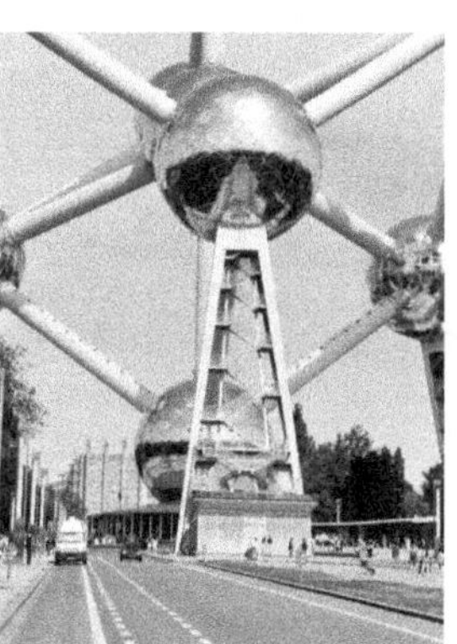
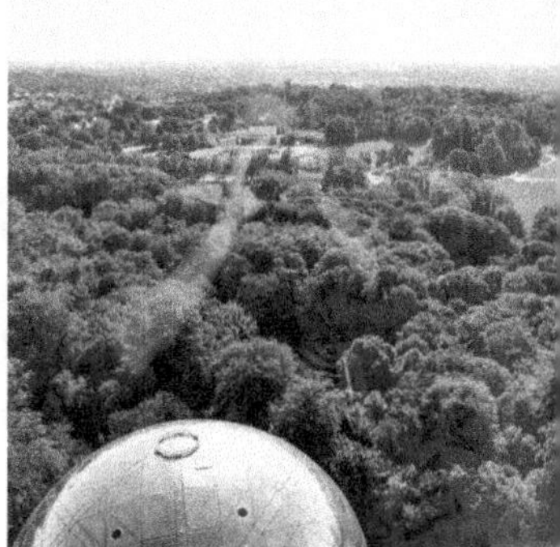

Brussels Expo 1958, Atomium and views of the exhibition grounds, Parc de Laeken, Brussels, 1958. Photos by Fausto Sombra

international architectural milieu. Subject of a single light publication dedicated exclusively to the building, "Expo 58: the Brasil Pavilion of Sérgio Bernardes," in addition to other aforementioned scarce studies carried out through postgraduate courses, we seek to deepen and contribute with new analyzes and interpretations on this still incipient critical panorama,[1] dedicated to the iconic building by the architect and his collaborators. In fact, the aim is to correlate his design actions with those of its peers: Volta Redonda Pavilion and São Cristóvão Pavilion.

It is appropriate to emphasize that the lines that follow, to a large extent, were taken from our article "Sérgio Bernardes e o pavilhão brasileiro na Exposição Universal e Internacional de Bruxelas, 1958: industrialização,

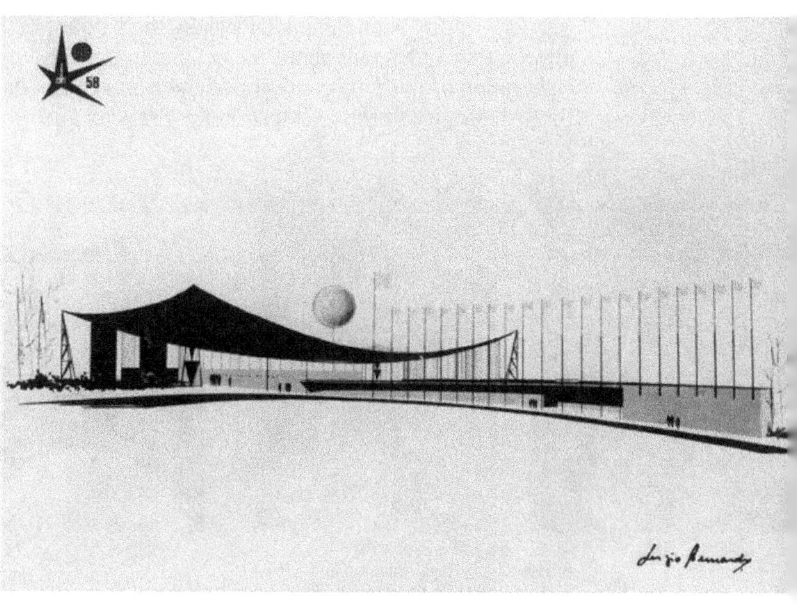

Brussels Pavilion, undated perspective signed by Sérgio Bernardes. Collection of *Correio da Manhã* / Arquivo Nacional

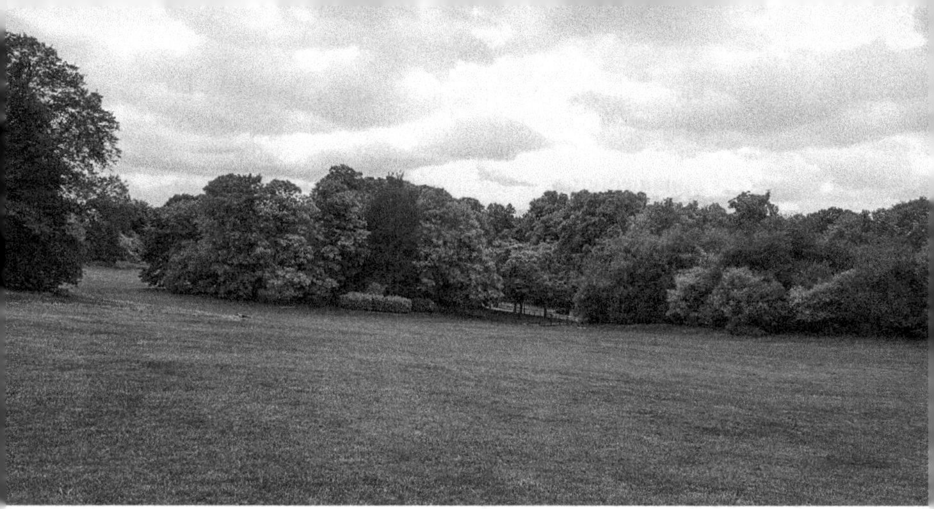

Expo Brussels 1958, construction site
of the Brazil Pavilion, Parc de Laeken,
Brussels. Photo by Fausto Sombra

Brazil Pavilion, sketch, Parc de Laeken,
Expo Brussels 1958. Collection
Sérgio Bernardes – Memory Project /
Bernardes Architecture Office

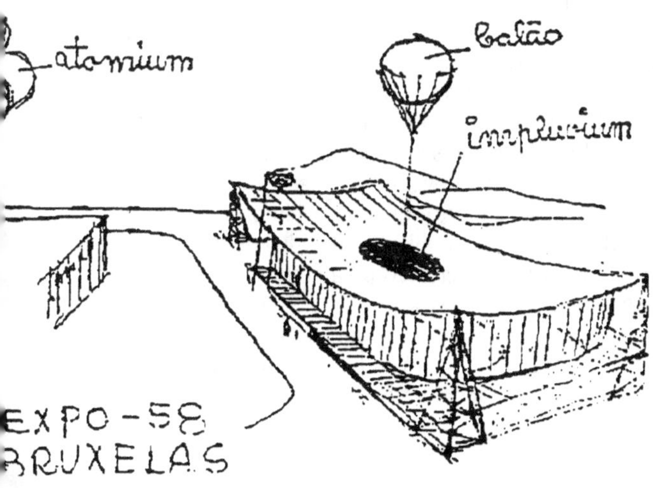

211

inventividade e experimentação", presented at the 5th
Enaparq, in October 2018, and republished in *Arquitextos*
magazine.[2] In addition to the ideas expressed in the
aforementioned article, research on this exemplar have
progressed punctually in some themes, such as Sérgio's idea
of conceiving the ramp that occupied the center of the
building in wood structured on scaffolding, allowing the
rapid assembly, disassembly and reuse of much of the material used; or as the visit made to the site where the Pavilion
was built in August 2019. This last fact has made it possible
to broaden the understanding of the Brazilian Pavilion and
its dialogue with the surroundings, including the Atomium as
a symbolic monument of the aforementioned event, which
was illustrated by Sérgio Bernardes in a sketch with the Brazil
Pavilion.

Following the same techniques used in the approxi-
mations and analyzes carried out on the pavilion built in
Ibirapuera Park, that is, through extensive documental analysis of the original files related to the project; in addition
to publications – such as the book *L'Architecture Moderne
à l'Expo 58: pour un monde plus humain*, in 2006, by Rika
Devos and Mil de Kooning –; newspapers and journals of the
period; elaboration of digital models and physical model of
the building; machining of a representative section of the
building on a 1:1 scale; and analysis of the available iconog-
raphy – some of them unpublished, we intend to emphasize,
at the end of this chapter, among other points, that certain
elements of relevance present in this ephemeral exemplar,
such as the red balloon hovering over its light roof – a
creative, low-cost artifice of great visual impact, a resource
that is often not properly linked to the idea of architectural
design –, would have been incorporated during or even close
to the completion of the work.

This hypothesis seems to demonstrate and reinforce, in
the present understanding, in addition to inventiveness, a
certain degree of detachment on the part of the architect.

For, even though Sérgio Bernardes proposed to develop a solution architecture with a certain degree of industrialization for the then Brazilian reality – in many cases, with budgetary concerns –, he has also mixed, not infrequently and in many cases with happy results, purely experimental elements and solutions. In this sense, Bernardes approached the artisanal and unique labor that has characterized, on a large scale, his vast and varied architectural and intellectual production.

The Exhibition, Foreign Nations and Brazil

With an expressive audience of approximately 41 million visitors over the six months of the event,[3] since the opening of its "monumental gates" on April 17, 1958 – in a ceremony by the then King of Belgium, His Majesty Baudouin[4] –, until October 19, of that same year, the Brussels Universal and International Exhibition took place through a long process – which began a decade earlier, more precisely on May 7, 1948 –, when, through the proposal of the Burgo-Master of the city of Brussels, the Belgian capital was designated as the headquarters of the next Universal Exhibition. After more than four years and already after the appointment of the Commissioner General of the Government,[5] on "November 20, 1952", the year of the great event was determined: 1958, a symbolic date that would mark the "fiftieth anniversary of the re-annexation of Congo to Belgium."[6] After the creation of the "Exhibition Society" on March 4, 1954, presided by Baron Van de Menlebrock, with the definition of the various committees that would be responsible for organizing topics such as accommodation, transport, media, tourism, etc.,[7] the foundations were laid for the realization – four years later – of the largest of the Universal Exhibitions held so far.[8]

The vast siting area was 175 hectares, defined near and around the Heysel palaces, a place 7 kilometers away from the city center of Brussels, "magnificently wooded", comprising – in addition to the Plateau du Heysel and the buildings that were already there – the Forest Park, the Laeken Public Garden and the Belvédere Domain. Its organizers adopted as the official theme and motto of the exhibition "to encourage men of any country, race or religion, to which they belong, in relation to certain humanist demands more imperative than ever".[9] This concern with the well-being of others, among other factors, result of the recurring wars that had taken place in the previous five decades – since the First World War, a conflict that involved for the first time a significant number of nations with a great impact on the geopolitical distribution of important regions in the planet – sought to bring peoples closer to the desire for peace and solidarity, through a change in scale and visions, supported by the progress of science and techniques applied to the service of mankind:

> "The alteration of technical progress drives the world irresistibly towards its unity. It is necessary, from now on, to adopt a global perspective for all problems. It is under this sign of the future that the 1958 Exhibition takes its position from the start.
>
> The march towards world unity obviously calls for a more authentic and universal humanism, which initially implies maximum contact and understanding between individuals and peoples. From now on, individuals and peoples should be empowered with the solidarity of their destiny. Worldwide collaboration becomes an obligation. It is no longer possible to think about the future on a local and national scale. Reciprocal understanding and tolerance among all peoples are indispensable to peace.
>
> We must confront the achievements of recent decades, the most characteristic projects of time, with the need for a profound return to man, through culture and the promotion of specifically human values. The

Brussels Exhibition of 1958 must therefore emphasize the need for an exhaustive human activity, in terms of mutual understanding, the development of social sense and authentic personality. If this target is reached, the Exhibition shall be a landmark in history. It shall have contributed to creating a chain of faith in man's destiny, a climate of friendship between individuals and peoples.

Perhaps it could also encourage the beginning of a new stage in which the progress of science and technology is resolutely placed at the service of man in the most complete and noble conception of the term."[10]

Within this generous perspective in favor of the celebration of diversity and respecting "scrupulously" the existing tree masses, an extensive program of attractions and buildings was developed to be implemented in the main accesses and roads of the exhibition, among them, the Palace of International Cooperation, the Palace of Science, The Palace of Arts – designed to reinforce the plurality of nations, peoples and cultures – as well as the buildings corresponding to the Belgian section, including Congo and Luanda-Urandi, both colonies of the event's host until then.

As the main area of its exhibitions and shows, Belgium settled in the great palaces of Heysel. Whereas the Congolese section – to which the exhibition gave great prominence for dissemination of the pioneering Belgian effort carried out in central Africa, in the "course of industrial equipment of a vast territory," in the "sense of constant improvement of living conditions of indigenous populations, their education and social and cultural development"[11] – would be located in a generous area in the western region of the exhibition, concentrated close to Porte Mondiale and next to the Atomium, which was positioned in the central portion of the event, as illustrated in the general plans.

In addition to these structural buildings, a parking area for thirty thousand vehicles[12] and many other attractions, such as the beautiful gardens and an amusement park, approximately 200 thousand square meters of the exhibition's territory were dedicated to foreign countries.[13] Positioned from the Monumental Road, passing between the Forest Park and the Laeken Garden, ending at the limits of the Chausére de Meyesse, in order, at least in speech, according to the geographical distribution, it is visible in the General Plan of the Exhibition, large areas granted to countries such as the Netherlands, Great Britain, Italy, France, and mainly the United States and the extinct Soviet Union. The two nations – immersed in their ideological, military, economic disputes, as well as inserted in the aerospace race that characterized part of the protracted conflict between the two countries – were placed side by side at the Brussels Exhibition "in a live community."[14]

This distribution, that is, the general terms that defined the siting areas for foreign nations, would be defined according to a report signed by the Belgian Moens de Fernig, Commissioner General of the Belgian government. The document, translated by Luiz Galvão do Valle, clarifies:

> "During the month of May 1954, invitations were sent through diplomatic channels to all the countries with which Belgium maintains diplomatic relations.
>
> Each participating country will have to, in its presentation, obey the theme of the Exhibition, showing everything that its activity entails that is truly human in the economic, social, cultural and spiritual order. [...]
>
> The particular character of the Exhibition implies a series of contacts prior to the collaboration of the foreign sections in its site. Therefore, it is certainly recommended that each country should examine, as soon as possible, the principle of its participation and designate the Commissioner General in charge of representing it before the Commissioner General of the Belgian Government.

The choice of locations reserved for foreign countries shall be based on the acceptances received by the Commissioner General.

Since a number of important participations have been acquired, it is in the best interest of each interested country to take its position without delay."[15]

Also contributing to this understanding, Francine Latteur, in a translated copy of her article published in the Belgian magazine *Presence* in 1958, stated about the then distribution of nations in the event, explaining the distant position of the countries – Venezuela, Colombia, Uruguay and Peru – who then represented Latin America:

"Visitors will recognize the Netherlands, near its harbor and dykes, Austria for its bridge-shaped pavilion, France for the elegance of its futuristic architecture, Canada for the transparency of its palaces, Russia and the countries of Central Europe for their maples and tundra, the United States for its monumental eloquence.

From a distance, the Holy See will look like a fortified city, with its bell-shaped walls. Switzerland will hide its chalets in the green, sheltered by huge granite blocks, on the edge of a small lake. Spain, Portugal, Monaco, Italy, Greece, Yugoslavia will have a Mediterranean sweetness; colonnades, hanging gardens, marble, mosaics will give the cradle of European Civilization its powerful seduction. Great Britain, thanks to its huge glass roof, will reflect the smallest ray of sunlight. As far as the eye can reach, the visitor will perceive a corner of the world; at the far end, Latin America, the Middle East and the countries of the Levant."[16]

Without specifically mentioning any member country in Latin America, Latteur's text only sheds light on the secondary participation of this group in the aforementioned

exhibition. However, the marking in pen with the name of
Brazil on the lots initially destined for Uruguay and Peru, as
seen in the lower right section of the General Plan of the
Exhibition, as well as the plan confirming the final geometry of the Brazilian lot, according to its planialtimetric
survey, allow an approximation – albeit without explaining
the withdrawal of the Uruguayan and Peruvian participation with their pavilions – to the reason why the Brazilian
pavilion would be defined as the furthest away of all in the
exhibition.

As it was also possible to verify through the reading of
other documents and official letters preserved in the NPD
collection, the effective confirmation of the Brazilian participation in the General Commission of the Exhibition, as well
as the studies of the pavilion, would take a long time to start.
The correspondence exchanged between the then Brazilian
ambassador to Belgium, Hugo Gouthier de Oliveira Gondim,
and Olavo Falcão, then director of the National Department
of Trade and Industry of the Ministry of Labour, dated
January 31, 1957, expressed the ambassador's concerns
about the delay of the Brazilian delegation compared to
other countries:

> "Dear friend Dr. Olavo,
> [...]
> As you may have seen from the other information I sent,
> almost all countries already have their designs ready
> and some have already started construction. I wish
> to disclaim my responsibility for any delay to prevent
> Brazil's efficient and timely participation. The architec-
> tural part and any delay in your arrival and that of the
> architect could result in incalculable losses for Brazil.
> Sincerely."[17]

Whereas in correspondence sent a week later, on
February 7, 1957 and addressed to the Secretariat of State

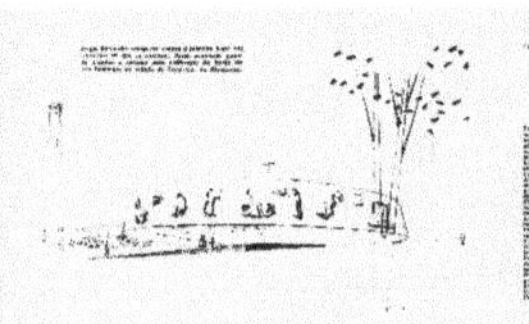
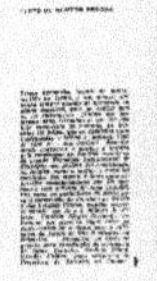
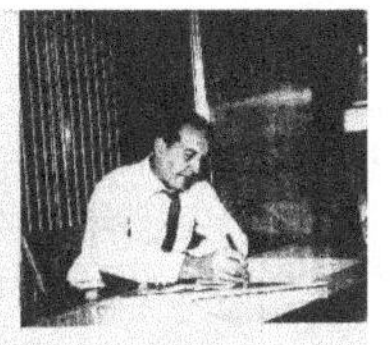
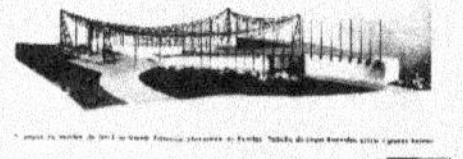
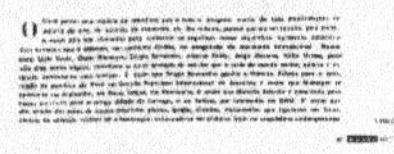

Article "Brazilian Architecture, an Export Product," report by Newton Freitas, published in the Rio de Janeiro magazine *O Mundo Ilustrado*, no. 16, on April 16, 1958. Hemeroteca Digital Brasileira / Fundação Biblioteca Nacional

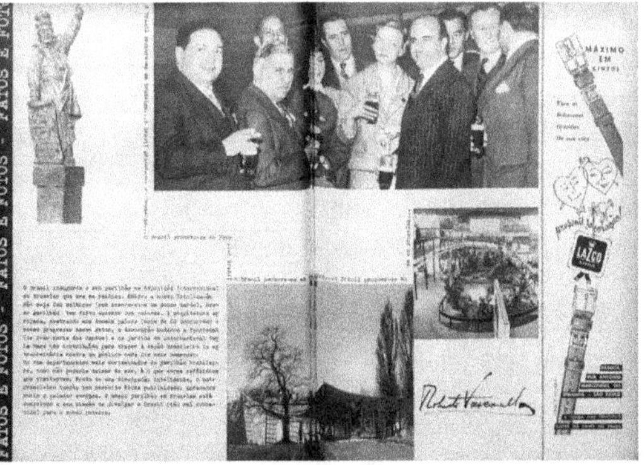
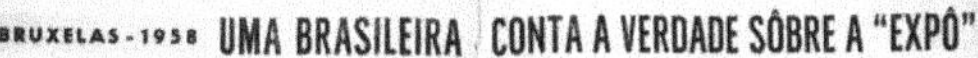

Article "Facts and Photos," report by Roberto Vasconcellos, published in the Rio de Janeiro magazine *Jóia*, no. 14, on June 14, 1958. Hemeroteca Digital Brasileira / Fundação Biblioteca Nacional

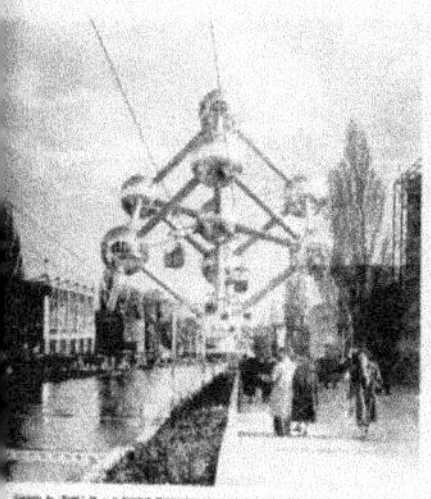
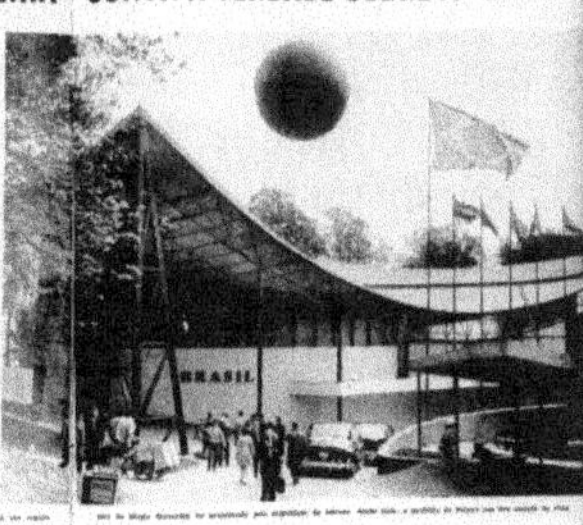

Article "A Brazilian Tells the Truth about the Expo," report by Leila Marise, published in the Rio de Janeiro magazine *Revista da Semana*, no. 29, on July 19, 1958. Hemeroteca Digital Brasileira / Fundação Biblioteca Nacional

for Foreign Affairs, once again Gouthier expressed the importance of Brazil's participation in the aforementioned exhibition, alerting that the then neighbor Mexico had already started the construction of its pavilion and that their architect was already in Brussels. In that three-page letter, Gouthier, among other points, also ratified that the Soviet Union would spend a total of fifty million dollars on its participation, and that the United States would spend five million dollars just on the construction of its pavilion.[18]

Expressive numbers for the time, and in the opposite direction to most of the powerful nations, the Brazil Pavilion, due to problems of funding availability – recollecting that the works of Brasília had already started[19] – would adopt as precept a much more economic project, brilliantly designed by Sérgio Bernardes and his collaborators,[20] a fact that would lead the Brazilian building to win "all twelve awards offered, including aesthetics, functionality, materials used and better environmental conditions".[21] This performance was summarized in the article "Brazil Pavilion at the Brussels International Fair", published in the Minas Gerais magazine *Arquitetura e Engenharia* no. 48, January/February 1958, which also emphasized the financial difficulties:

> "Architect Sérgio Bernardes was chosen to execute the project, but as soon as it started to be created, the usual difficulties appeared.
>
> A first obstacle was soon overcome due to Sérgio Bernardes' pertinacity and courage: when special-ists were working on the construction calculations, the Ministry of Labor announced that there were no funds. Sérgio assumed responsibility for the calculation expenses, while the Brazilian ambassador to Belgium, Hugo Gouthier; the secretary, Vladimir Murtinho, from the Cultural Division of Itamarati; Alonso Brandão, from the Ministry of Labor; and Francisco Figueira Melo, from the Federation of Industries; did everything they could

to remedy this difficulty as soon as possible, and to prevent the appearance of new obstacles. Soon after, however, with no way of finding new funds, and while approaching the deadline for the start of construction in Brussels (Brazil would look very bad in the eyes of the world if it gave this public demonstration of bankruptcy: abandoning the exhibition for lack of money to build the pavilion), it was necessary for Sérgio to leave for Brussels, where he spent a month and a half doing everything to get the construction started right away. This is what happened: arrangements, compromises, and a Belgian firm working hard to build the pavilion in one hundred pre-established working days. Individual enthusiasm prevailed in Brussels over government sluggishness and indifference. Ambassador Hugo Gouthier; the resident commissioner-general, minister of economic affairs Caio Lima Cavalcanti; the head of the commercial office in Beneluz, Jorge Carvalho de Brito; Michael Joseph Corbert as a representative of Itamarati; and Otto Lara Rezende, have all joined this team with Sérgio Bernardes. And the pavilion is being built and will be ready on the required date."[22]

The figure of the Brazilian ambassador to Belgium proved to be relevant in the process of implementing the construction of the Brazil Pavilion. In his book *Presença*, the diplomat described his experience and memories during the process of conceiving and inaugurating the pavilion alongside Sérgio Bernardes, when he confirmed the financial difficulty reported in the previous article:

"My first move was to invite Sérgio Bernardes to design the Brazil pavilion. This man I have always admired, who has left the mark of his genius spread throughout the world in memorable works of architecture, has created bonds of definitive friendship with me. For we are

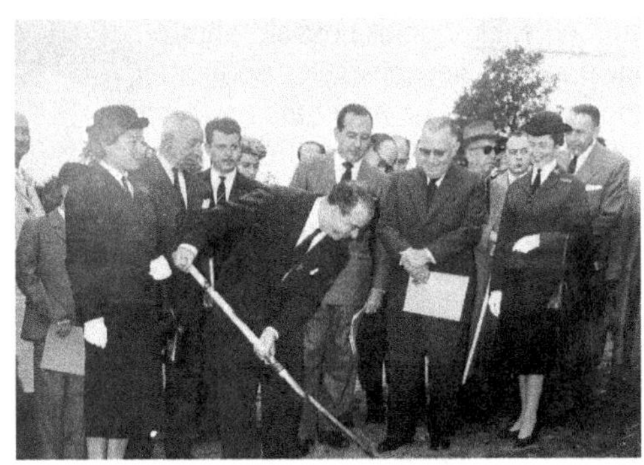

Brazil Pavilion, groundbreaking ceremony with Brazilian ambassador Hugo Gouthier, shovel in hand, and Sérgio Bernardes, at the center, Expo Brussels 1958. Gouthier Family Archive

Next page: Brazil Pavilion, main access and balloon floating over the roof, Expo Brussels 1958. Photo by Julien Willems. Mil De Kooning Collection

alike in many ways, including feverish enthusiasm and rhythmic, meticulous work. Neither he nor I are afraid of problems if we decide to tackle them one by one, as they arise.

Sérgio immediately accepted my invitation by going to Brussels, where he stayed with us to outline the initial plans. [...]

We ended up setting up at the Embassy a real office at the service of the Brazil pavilion. Sérgio entrusted the structural part to Paulo Fragoso and Eduardo de Barros.

And I was there, making an effort for my country to play a beautiful role in that show. Distressed because the money had not arrived from Brazil, I signed a promissory note endorsed by Sérgio, and we raised the money for the initial expenses in a bank. We looked like a bunch of fanatics out to save the world, working night and day. And we managed to achieve everything, thanks not only to my commitment, but above all, to Sérgio's tireless oceanic ability."[23]

Complementing his account, Gouthier also gave a detailed description of others involved in the project, both political figures and part of the technical staff responsible for the pavilion project:

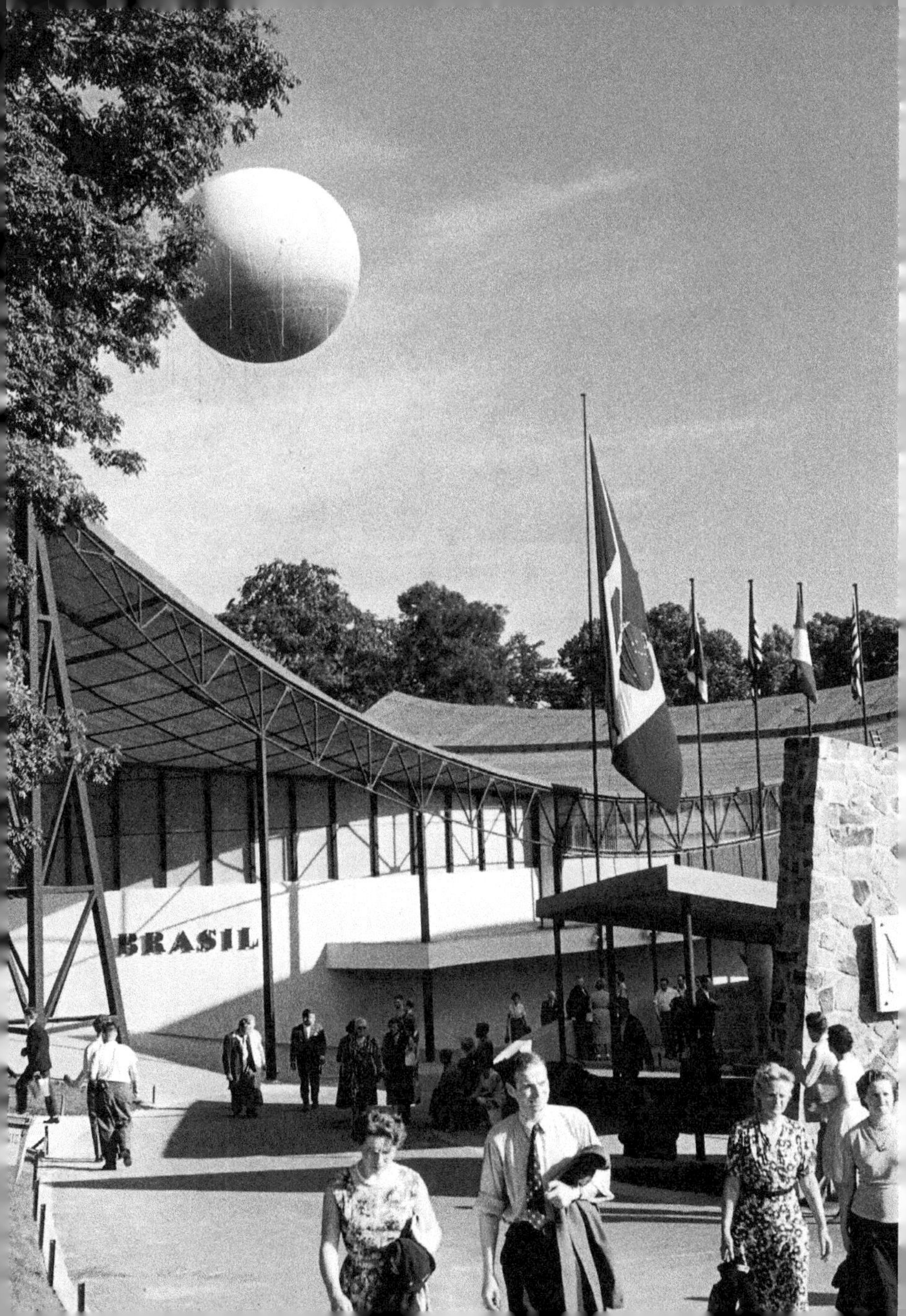
BRASIL

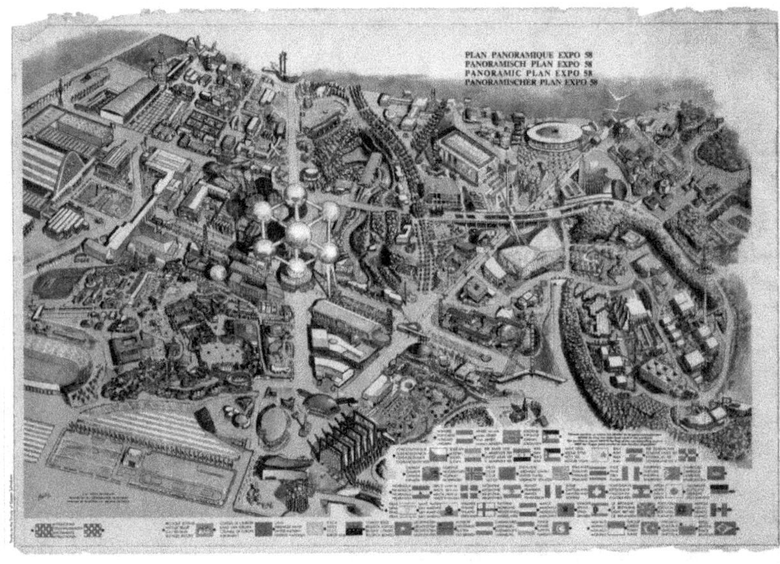

Expo Brussels 1958, panoramic
plan of the exhibition grounds, Parc
de Laeken, Brussels, 1958. Gaston
Schoukens Family Archive / Atomium
Museum

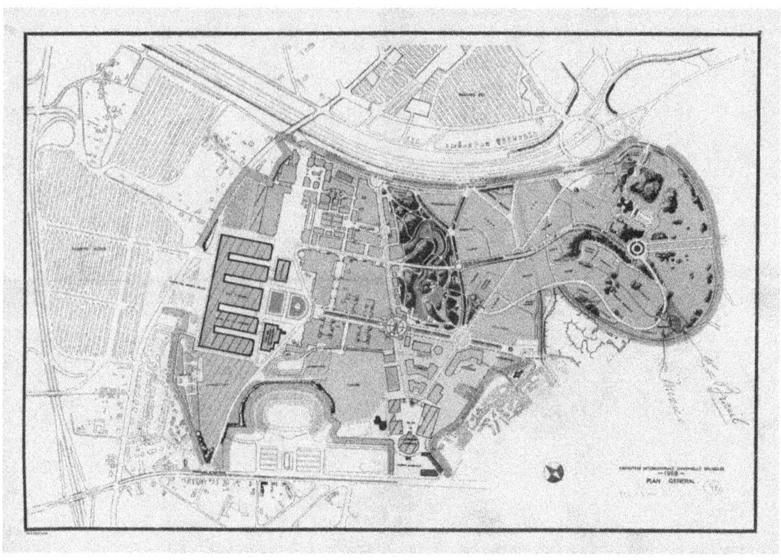

Expo Brussels 1958, general plan
of the exhibition at a 1:5000 scale.
NPD FAU UFRJ Collection / Sérgio
Bernardes Fund

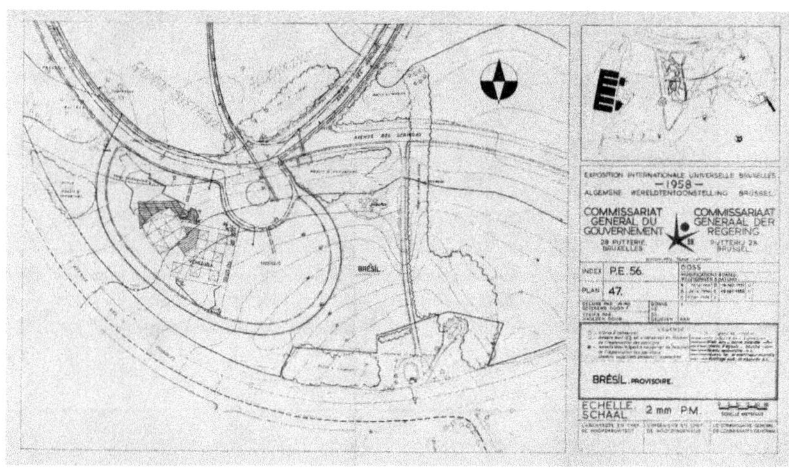

Brazil Pavilion, one of the five revisions of the planialtimetry of the Brazilian pavilion lot dated between April 10 and December 19, 1956, Expo Brussels 1958. NPD FAU UFRJ Collection / Sérgio Bernardes Fund

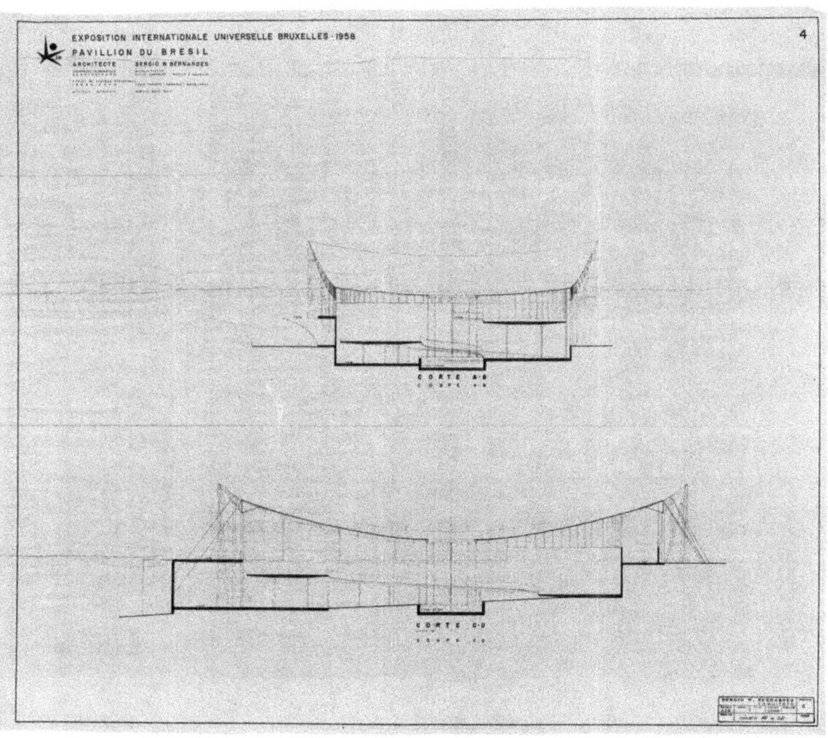

Brazil Pavilion, *Drawing* 4 with cross and longitudinal sections at a scale of 1:100, undated board, Expo Brussels 1958. NPD FAU UFRJ Collection / Sérgio Bernardes Fund

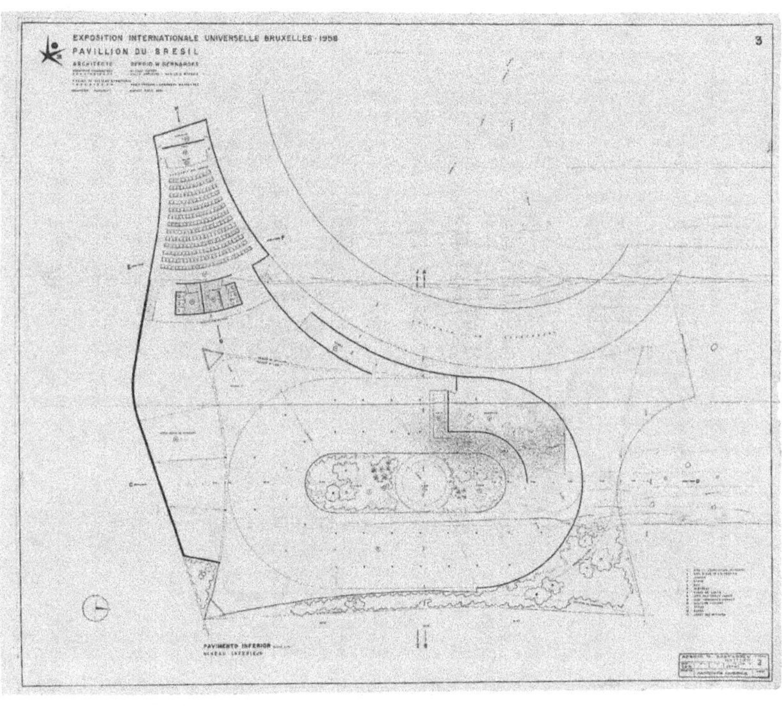

Brazil Pavilion, *Drawing 2* with lower floor plan at a scale of 1:100, undated board, Expo Brussels 1958. NPD FAU UFRJ Collection / Sérgio Bernardes Fund

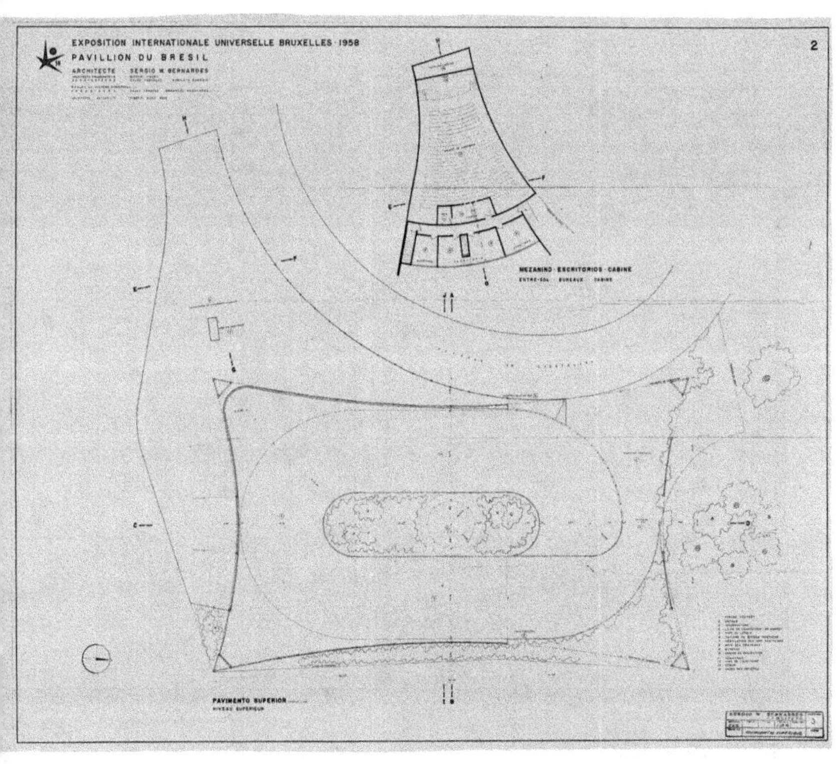

Brazil Pavilion, *Drawing 3* with plans for the access floor and mezzanine at a scale of 1:100, undated board, Expo Brussels 1958. NPD FAU UFRJ Collection / Sérgio Bernardes Fund

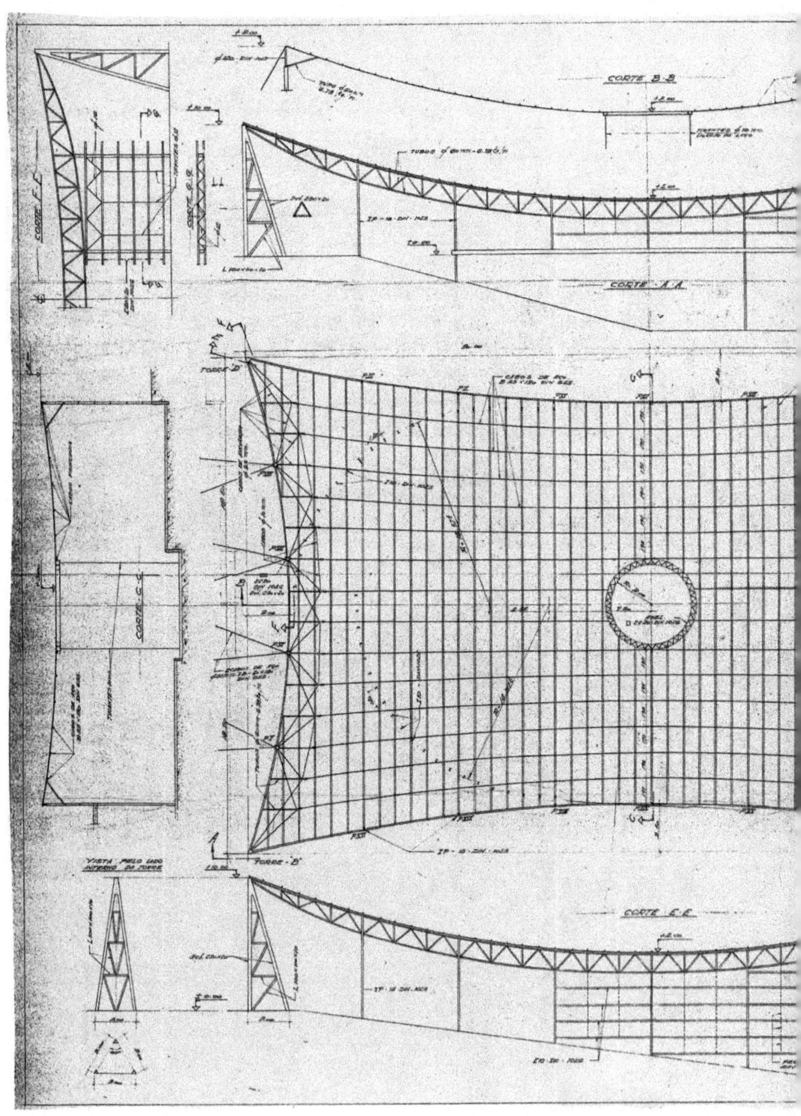

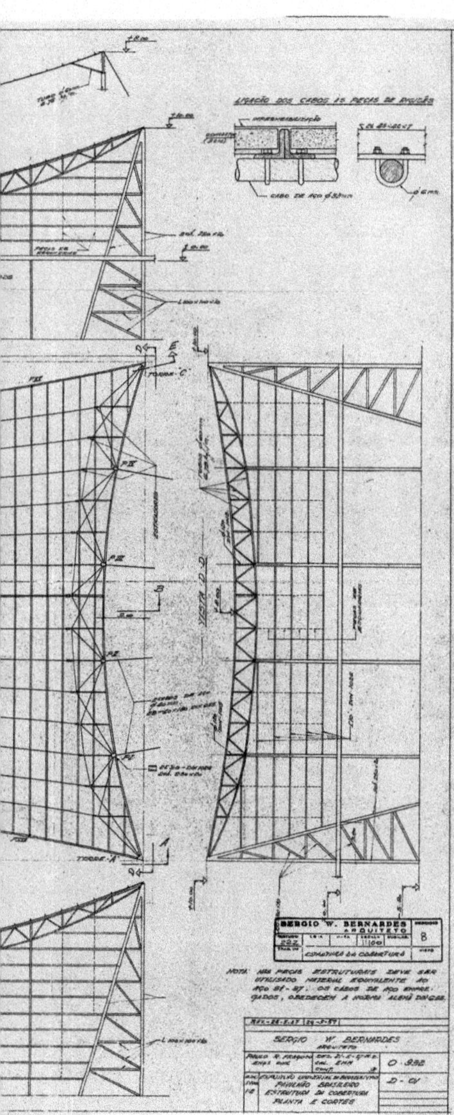

Brazil Pavilion, *Drawing 8* with structure at a scale of 1:100, engineer Paulo Fragoso, May 29, 1957, Expo Brussels 1958. NPD FAU UFRJ Collection / Sérgio Bernardes Fund

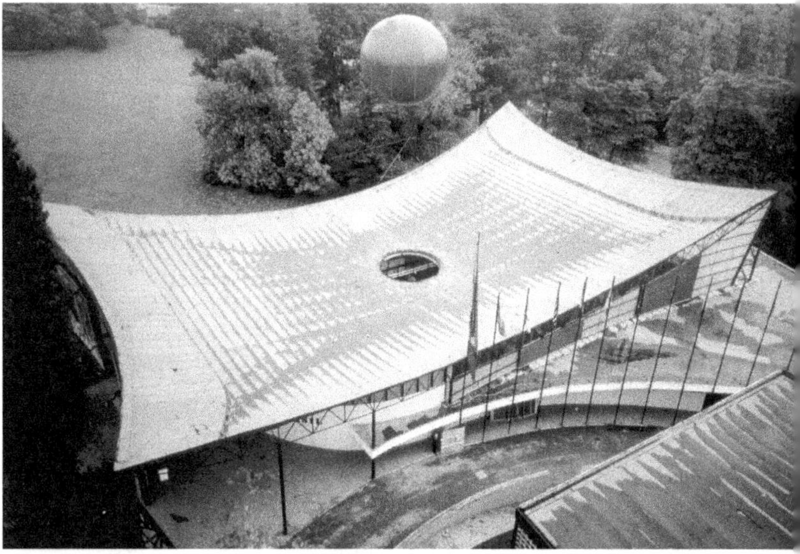

Brazil Pavilion, floating balloon and roof with impluvium, Expo Brussels 1958. Sérgio Bernardes Collection – Memory Project / Bernardes Architecture Office

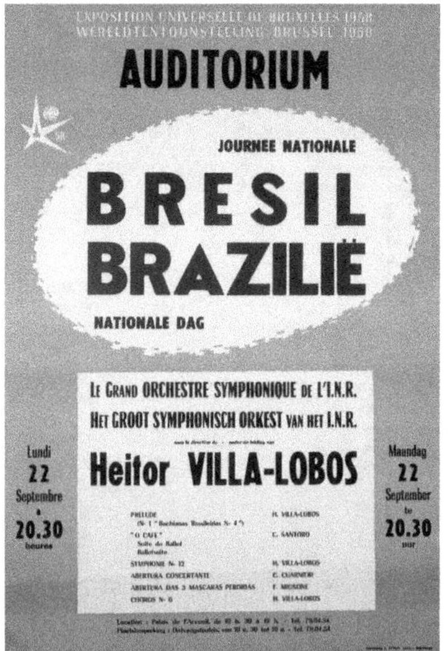

Expo Brussels 1958, promotional poster for the Brazilian pavilion's cultural program. Mil De Kooning Collection

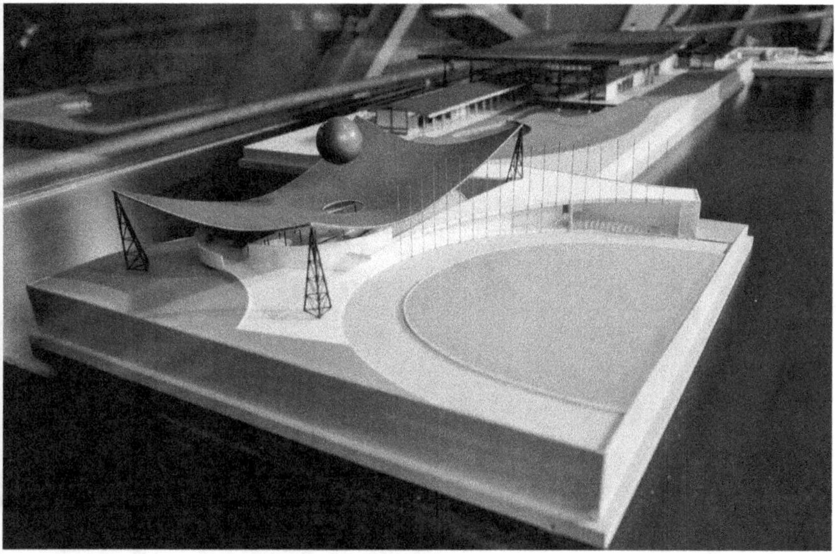

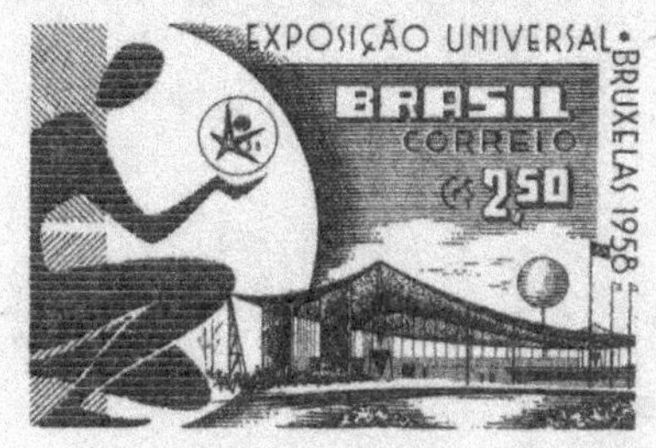

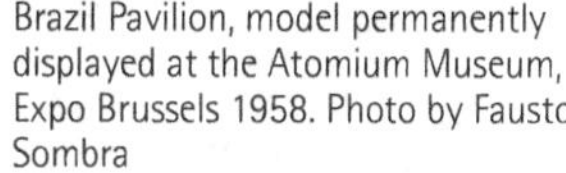

Brazil Pavilion, model permanently displayed at the Atomium Museum, Expo Brussels 1958. Photo by Fausto Sombra

Commemorative stamps from Panama and Brazil illustrated with designs of the Brazilian pavilion, Expo Brussels 1958. Mil De Kooning Collection

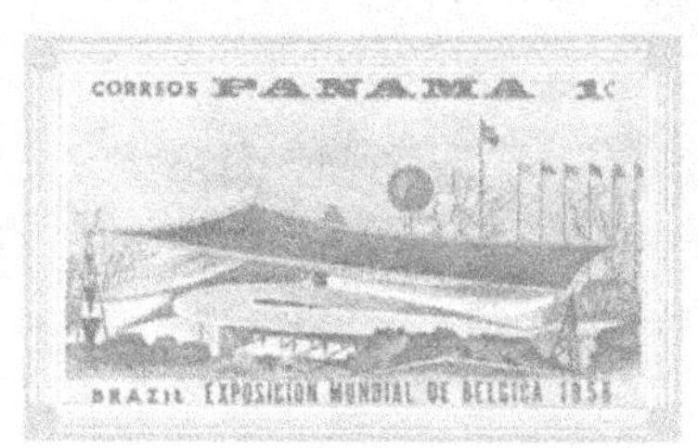

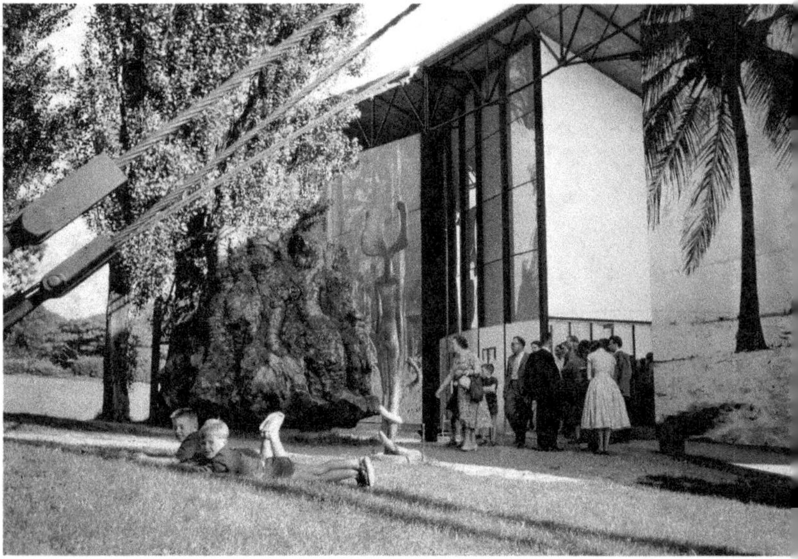

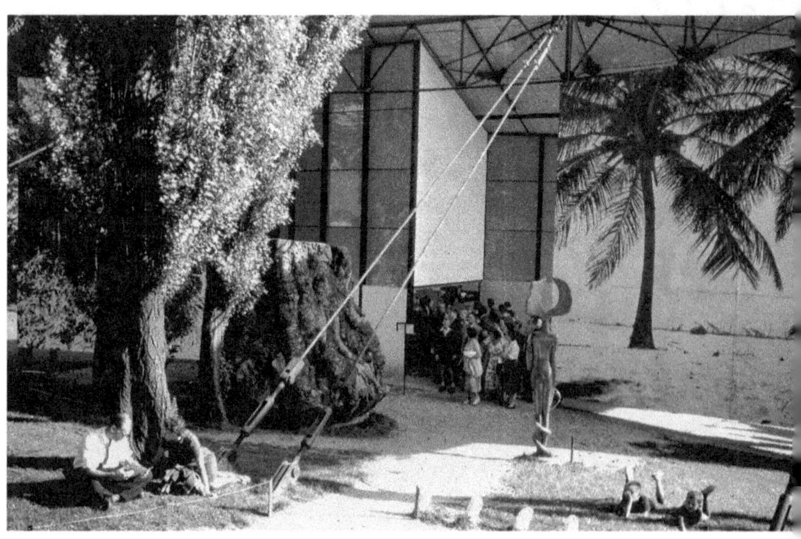

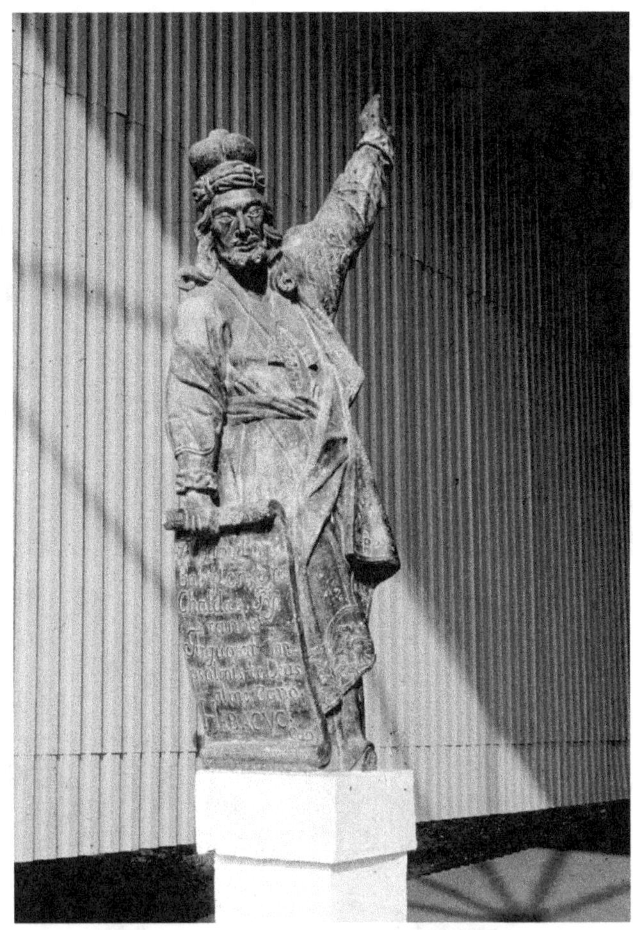

On the left, Brazil Pavilion, sculpture by Maria Martins and the large base of the cumaru trunk displayed at the North entrance, Expo Brussels 1958. Sérgio Bernardes Fund - Project Memory / Bernardes Architecture Office

Above, Brazil Pavilion, replica of Aleijadinho's sculpture in one of the entrances, Expo Brussels 1958. Photo by Julien Willems. Mil De Kooning Collection

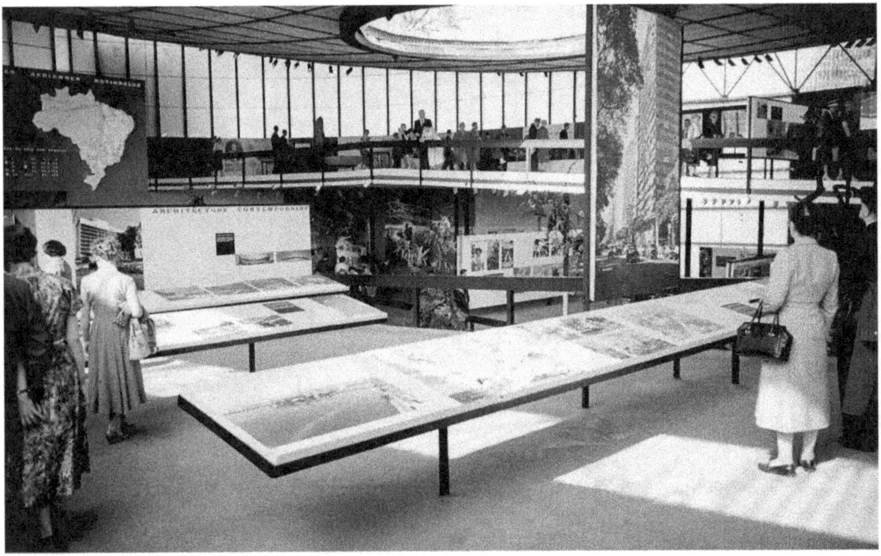

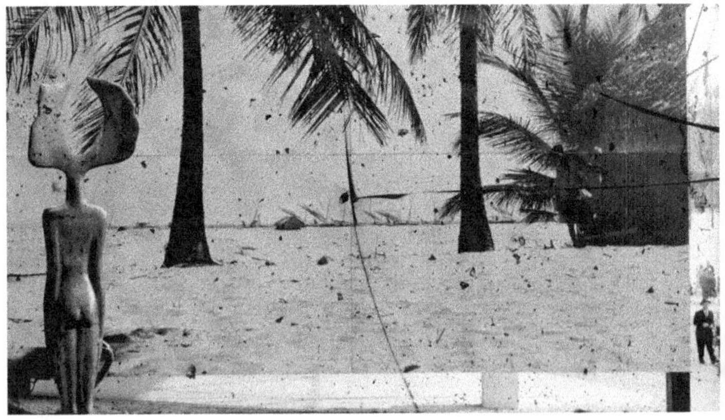

Brazil Pavilion, interior with exhibition and tropical garden by Roberto Burle Marx, Expo Brussels 1958. Photo by Julien Willems. Mil De Kooning Collection

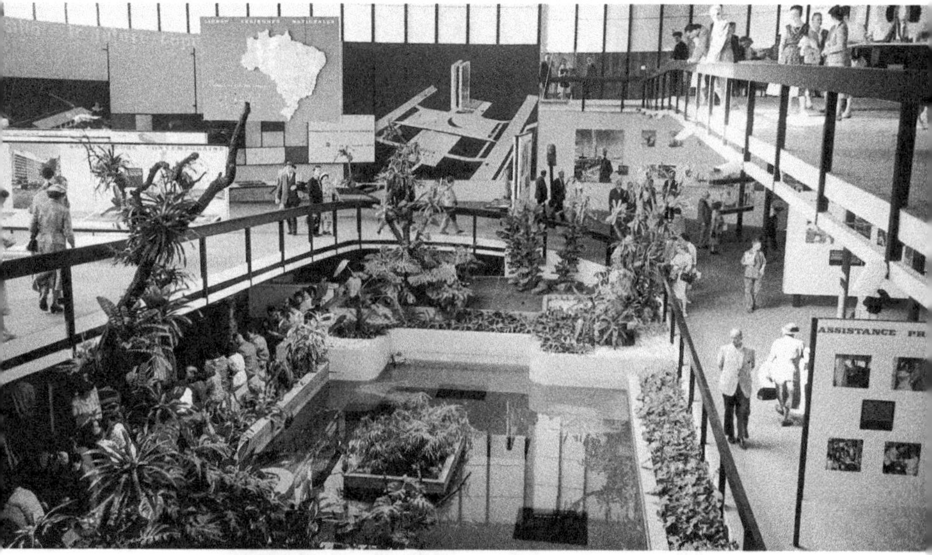

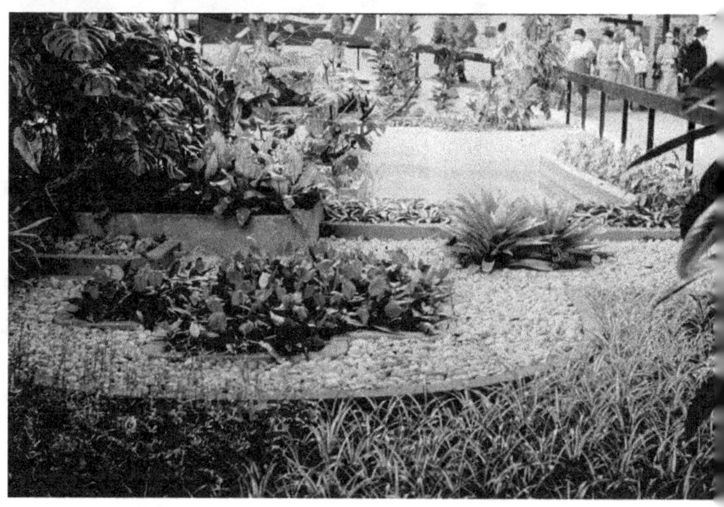

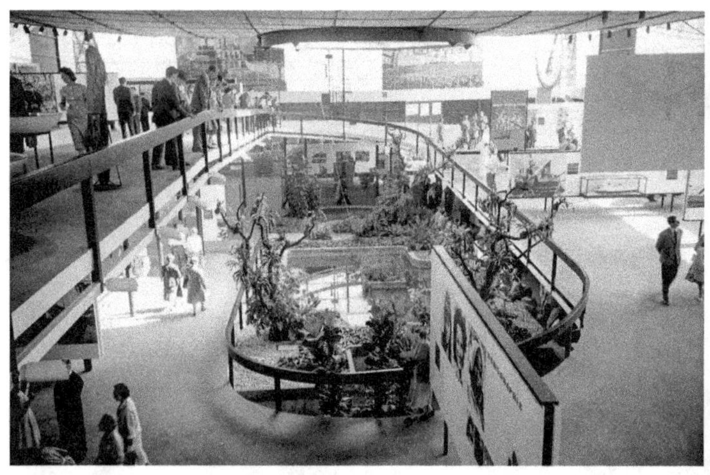

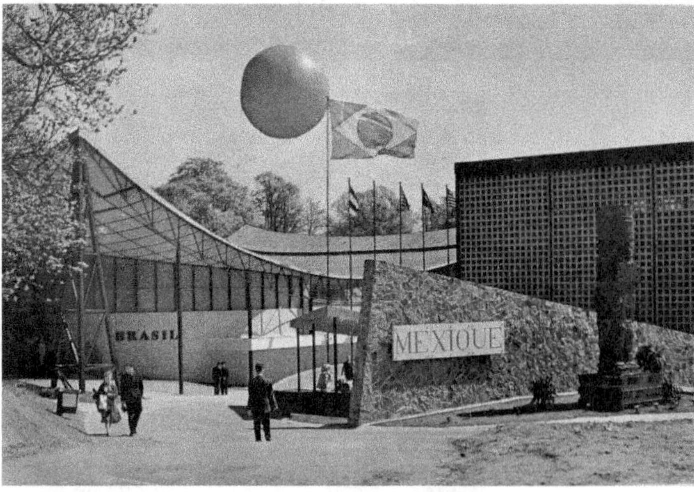

Brazil Pavilion, tropical garden by Roberto Burle Marx, Expo Brussels 1958. Photo by Julien Willems. Mil De Kooning Collection

Brazil Pavilion next to the Mexican Pavilion, Expo Brussels 1958. Collection NPD FAU UFRJ / Sérgio Bernardes Fund

"We did not only believe in Brazil, but we also believed in ourselves and in the vibrancy of our companionship, where I highlight the cooperation of Caio de Lima Cavalcanti, Minister of Economic Affairs, the most scrupulous and demanding person I appointed to watch over the application of resources – that ended up arriving from Brazil – destined for the construction of the pavilion.

Wladimir Murtinho, now Ambassador, was in charge of the decoration phase. And the gardens were the responsibility of the genius Roberto Burle Marx, whose talent was able to trace them wonderfully within the same line of creativity that had presided the bold design of architecture.

For Commissioner-General, Dr. Edgar Batista Pereira was chosen, a dynamic and correct man, who proved to be unsurpassable in the fulfillment of his duties. [...]

The other members of the Commission were the following: Technical Committee – Wladimir Murtinho, President; Sérgio Wladimir Bernardes, Chief Architect; Nicolai Fikoff, Assistant Architect; Max Winders, Consulting Architect; João Maria dos Santos, Chief Decorator; Eduardo Anahory, Assistant Decorator; Jack van de Beuque, Assistant Decorator; Artur Lício Pontual, Assistant Decorator; Libble Smit, in charge of lighting; Mario Dias Costa, in charge of Publications Service; Special Services – Herculano Borges da Fonseca, from Banco do Brasil; Octavio Cintra Leite, from Instituto do Café; Fernando Balaguer, from Instituto do Mate; Orlando Gomes Calaza, from the Ministry of Education; Jorge de Carvalho Britto Davis, Commercial Information; Secretariat – Stella Baptista Pereira, Renée Prueffer, Maria José Nonnenberg and Lucy Teixeira."[24]

Still in the report, the Brazilian ambassador to Belgium concluded with a synthesis of the concept for the pavilion idealized by Sérgio Bernardes:

"It is not surprising that the Brazil pavilion – which reproduced the economic cycles of our history – has won the grand prize at the Brussels Universal Exhibition 1958. It should be noted that the Brazil Pavilion cost around USD $200,000, while pavilions like the United States and Russia cost around USD $5 million."[25]

It should be noted that the name of Sérgio Bernardes officially appears for the first time as the pavilion's architect only in the correspondence dated February 17, 1957, in which Mr. Van Achte and Mr. Vende Walle forwarded information about the future pavilion. The document, as well as the publication of the newspaper *O Estado de S. Paulo*, on March 7, 1957, with the article "Brazil will participate in the Brussels Fair," allow us to affirm that Sérgio Bernardes, unlike most other architects and delegations of the event, had a considerably reduced time interval for the elaboration of the study, approval and development of the projects:

"Brazil will participate in the Brussels International Exhibition with its own pavilion, which will represent the various sectors of the national activity in the last twenty years. The Brazilian Embassy in the Belgian capital informed the General Commission for Exhibitions and Fairs that our country already has a place to build its pavilion, reserved by the organizers of the international event.

At the Department of Trade and Industry, the General Commissioner for Exhibitions and Fairs convened the Planning Commission, who will begin work on the organization of displays, graphics, etc., for public bodies or private entities. The design of the Brazilian pavilion will be presented briefly by architect

Sérgio Bernardes, author of the national project for Trade and Industry to be carried out during this year."[26]

Belonging to a rich and extensive context only briefly revisited here, the constitution of the Brazilian pavilion by Sérgio Bernardes, and the recognition granted to him by the various prizes awarded by the organizers of the Brussels Exhibition, would lead his majesty, King Baudouin, on September 22, 1958, to grant the carioca architect the title of *Chevalier de la Couronne Belge*.

Among so many bold pavilions built at the Brussels Universal and International Exhibition, at high costs and often with complex structural solutions[27] – such as the pavilion of Philips company, designed by Le Corbusier –, the Brazilian pavilion "stands out for being perfectly suited to the concept of the exhibition and the space in which it was sited."[28] Sérgio Bernardes' sensibility, despite the adverse working conditions, has been translated into the solutions and arrangement of the architectural program adopted in the Brazilian pavilion, as synthesized below.

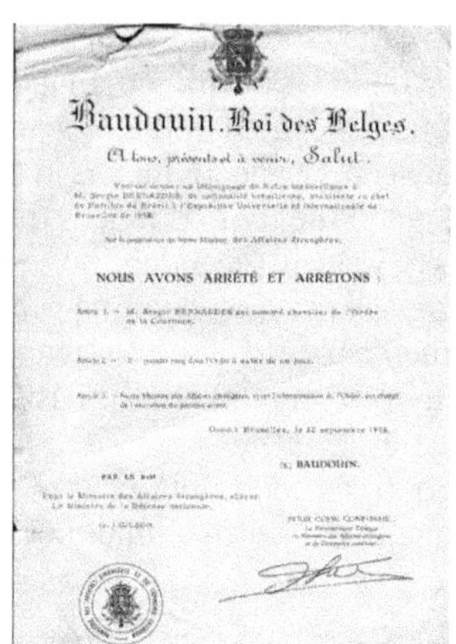

Chevalier de la Couronne Belge, decoration by King Baudouin to Sérgio Bernardes for achievements in the design of the Brazil Pavilion at the Universal and International Exhibition in Brussels, September 22, 1958. Collection Sérgio Bernardes – Project Memory / Bernardes Architecture Office

The Brazil Pavilion: a Brief Synthesis

Idealized to host exhibition areas, a coexisting space with café, restrooms, an administrative area and an auditorium for projections, totaling an implementation area of approximately 2,645 square meters, the pavilion was composed of a large basement with irregular elevation. With six meters in its highest portion, the Brazil Pavilion was made of concrete and masonry, being partially embedded in the ground in an "L" shape following the geometry of the lot. Its sweetened and curvilinear perimeter was reflected in the main roof, with a delicate rectangular and independent drawing, parked just above, structurally free from the translucent perimeter closures that partially composed the facades. Also free of internal supports, the roof was composed of four concave faces and its ends were tensioned and raised in relation to the central portion, like a sheet of generous dimensions of 60m x 37m. This element, with an accurate technical solution, constituted by a thin layer of concrete, was structured by a set of 43 pairs of small "L" profiles arranged transversely and superimposed on fourteen steel cables arranged in the longitudinal direction, both transmitting their stress to four large trussed beams of variable sections and curved inward direction, reaching a height of 1.5 meters in its longest stretch. These, in turn, were interconnected and structured around the four lattice towers – with a triangular base and pyramidal elevation – located at the four vertices of the roof. Varying between 12 and 16 meters in height,[29] these supports structured the roof, as well as the other 22 intermediate supports, visually secondary, but essential for structuring the cluster, all positioned on the periphery of this large roof and symmetrically distributed in two lines of seven and four pillars each, corresponding to the East/West and North/South laterals, respectively.

On the North/South facades, eight pairs of steel cables were extended on one side – North – until they met the

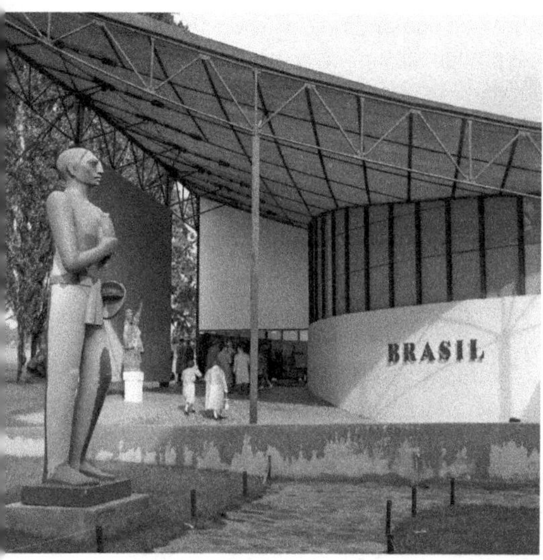

Brazil Pavilion, sculpture of the Mexican pavilion in front of the Brazilian pavilion, Expo Brussels 1958. Photo by Wouter Hagens. Wikimedia Commons license CC BY-SA 3

ground and on the other – South – until they crossed the top of the concrete slab that formed the auditorium's roof, element that extended along the south and west laterals of the building. At this point, the aforementioned slab met the narrow circular-shaped external street – which gave access to the building – and the 21 flagpoles with the flags representing the States that made up the Federation at the time,[30] as well as the Brazilian flag. It would be hoisted on a higher mast, fluttering next to the building and marking the entrance to the pavilion with the name "Brasil", written in Portuguese and delicately fixed to the facade below.

Occupying the central region, still on the main roof, there was a large metal ring measuring 6 meters in diameter, which, without cables, profiles and the thin layer of concrete that formed the main roof, efficiently allowed the entry of light and the renewal of air inside the building, in addition to capturing and conducting rainwater in the form of a water-fall, the so-called *impluvium*.

Below it, inside the building and on the lower floor, there
was an exotic tropical garden, designed by artist and landscaper Roberto Burle Marx, structured in a 27m x 8m linear
bed, formed by its central water mirror and small setback
plateaus, defined by thin walls of delicate geometric composition, idealized to accommodate regional plant species and
some adapted – such as papyrus, water lilies, ficus religiosa,
bromeliads, dracaena fragrans, mosteras deliciosas, asplenium
nidus, platycerium bifurcatum, agave, native anthuriums,
cryptanthus, among others,[31] a cluster that – in addition to a
generous ramp in reinforced concrete, which was developed
for a turn and a half around it and in the form of a semi-
spiral –, formed the structuring elements of the project.

Structured by 31 pillars and protected by guardrails
of an elementary and intelligent drawing, devoid of any
adornments, this ramp, with a gentle slope and starting
meters after the line with three doors that gave access to
the building, in the North portion, still outside, positioned
right after a replica of the statue of Prophet Habakkuk – by
sculptor Aleijadinho from Minas Gerais –, allowed visitors
to enjoy a favorable point of contemplation of the interior
of the building, also marking the beginning of the walk
towards the lower floor and the exhibition itself, in a course
of approximately 115 meters in length. At the garden level,
a location that also had an exhibition area, there were the
popular coffee and mate counters – both positioned under
a lower stretch of the ramp –, the restrooms, the administrative area – intelligently positioned on the mezzanine
with access through two linear stairs –, the auditorium for
229 seats, storage areas, and even the exit of the building, a
narrow corridor of 2.5 meters in width contained between
two parallel and competing windowless walls, in a small path
with a gentle curved slope towards the outside, leading to
a shaded recess on the main façade. This program and its
triangular distribution provided space for the concentration
of visitors, in an analogy to the casual bars and cafes of

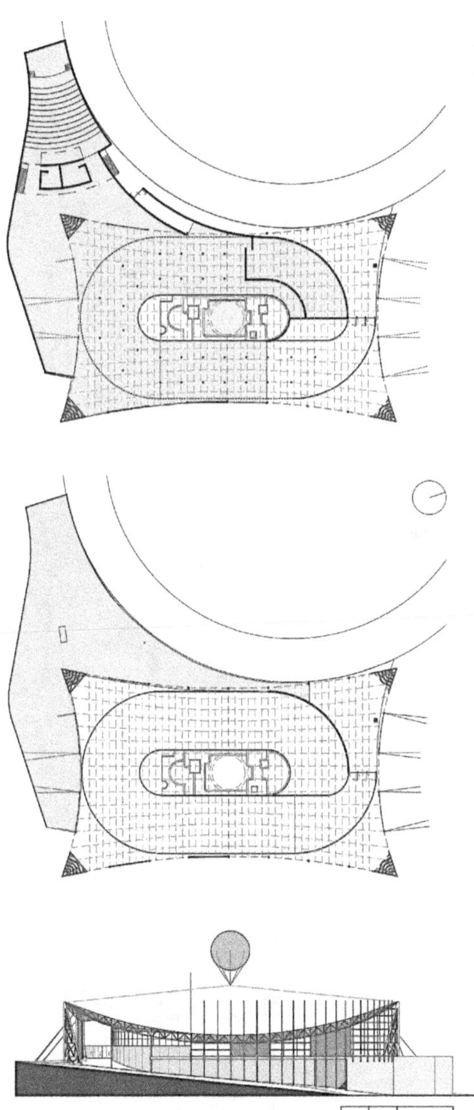

Brazil Pavilion, plans and West
facade, Expo Brussels 1958. Redrawn
by Fausto Sombra

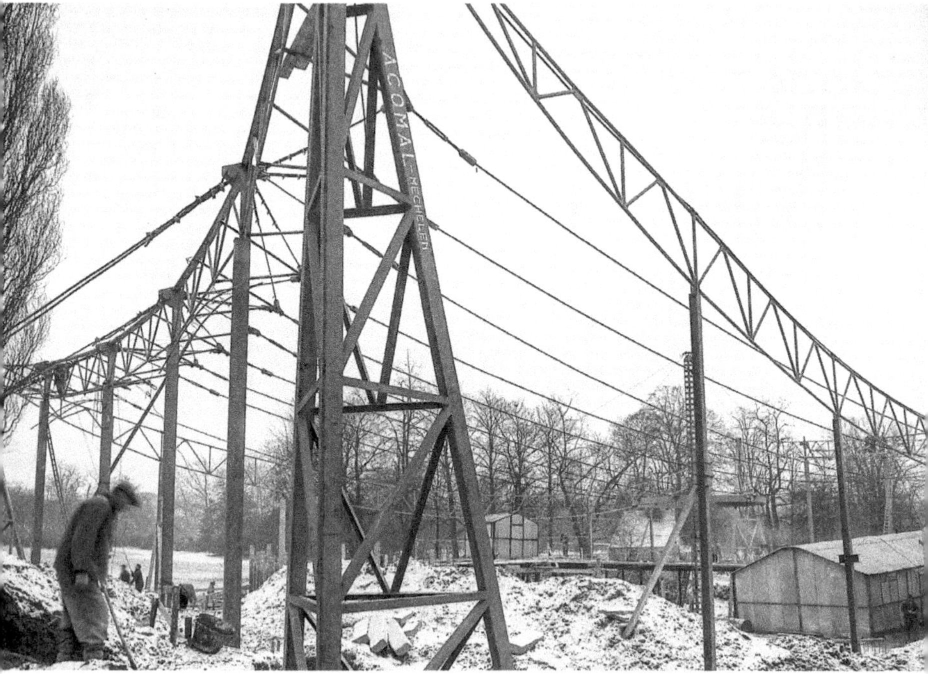

Brazil Pavilion, construction, Expo
Brussels Brussels 1958. Collection
Dept. A&S, Faculty of Engineering and
Architecture, Ghent University

Brazil Pavilion, construction, Expo
Brussels Brussels 1958. Photographer
unknown. Mil De Kooning Collection

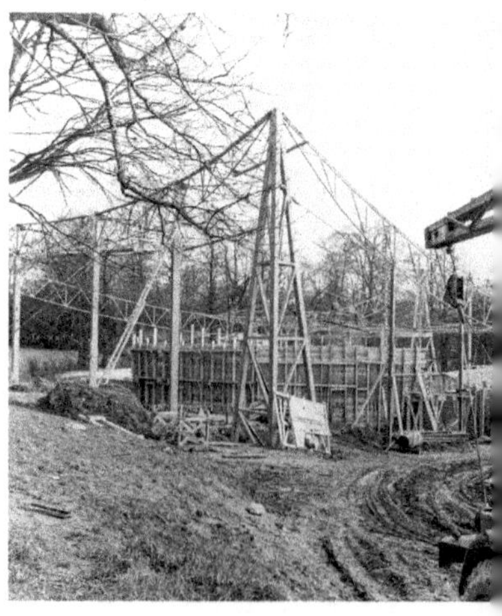

the time, reinforcing the receptivity and friendly Brazilian character, in "its cordial naturalness."[32] During much of this journey, even outside the building – through two large photos of natural landscapes fixed between the four pillars of the North façade – visitors had access to the pavilion's expography, which was composed of various advertising panels and elements on display about Brazilian biodiversity, its people, culture and folklore, education, economy, agriculture, industry, steelworks, transport, technological advances, in addition to the emphasis given to the vertiginous growth of its cities, a theme illustrated by photos of modern Brazilian buildings and mainly through the model of the future federal capital under construction, Brasília. It was the exhibition entitled "Brazil builds a western civilization in the tropics".[33]

Whereas outside the building, positioned above the metallic ring and rising more than 25 meters above the ground, connected to the pavilion through a set of four main radial cables, a large red balloon, 7 meters in diameter and filled with helium gas, sought to wave from afar to the great visiting public, in an effort to create a formal and ludic dialogue with the main symbol of the exhibition, the Atomium.

As material testimony of the exhibition held there, representative of the positivist and scientific spirit that characterized this great event, this monument, located approximately 900 meters away from the Brazilian pavilion and conceived by Belgian engineer André Waterkeyn, was built close to the two main entrances of the fair, at the convergence of its two main avenues.

Soaring to 102 meters in height with its nine aluminum spheres of eighteen meters in diameter each – simulating an iron crystal cell magnified 165 million times, with an infinity of luminous points revolving around it at night, just like the movement of electrons around the nucleus of the atom – this grandiose monument expressed the "prodigious force of atomic energy", understood as the "latest conquest of man over matter".[34]

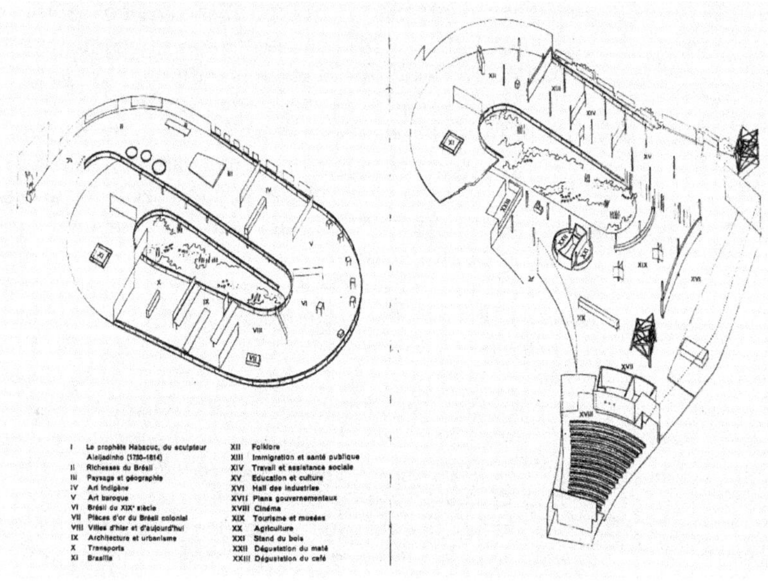

Brazil Pavilion, exhibition design
project, Expo Brussels. Brussels 1958.

Collection NPD FAU UFRJ / Sérgio
Bernardes Fund

Industrialization, Inventiveness and Experimentation

Officially opened to the public on a Saturday, May 3, 1958, at 11 am,[35] the architecture that characterized this ephemeral building would be recognized worldwide for the simplicity and efficiency with which it was accommodated in a distant lot, with a great slope, with an irregular perimeter and through a lean budget.[36] Surprisingly, as he had already achieved in previous designs, Sérgio Bernardes sought to combine his keen creativity with certain architectural industrialization solutions, followed by sensory and visual experimentation, making the Brazil Pavilion at the Brussels Exhibition 1958 one of the most recognized and visited spaces of the great event.

Sérgio Bernardes, in an article published in *Cultura* magazine no.1 in 1970, synthesized his design by stating:

"The Brazil Pavilion at Expo-58 in Brussels had its idea from the analytical and logical side. In an exhibition of enormous distances, man is totally despised in his ability and limitations to walk, and when arriving at the Brazilian Pavilion, he would be very tired. Nothing could be more natural than making him enter the high point of arrival and leave through the low point, which is why there was a ramp whose elliptical shape had symbolic connotations with the economic and cultural cycles

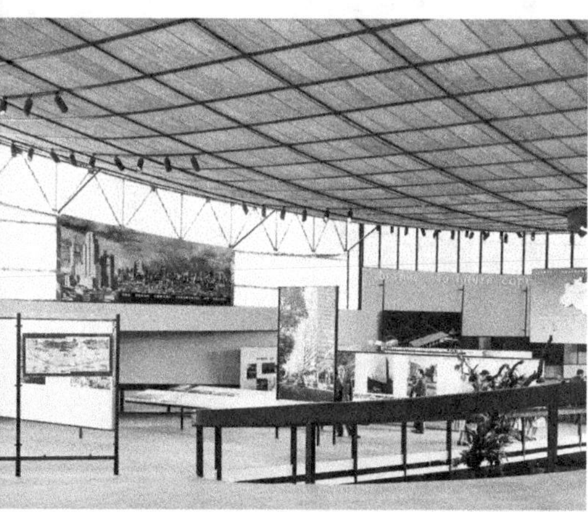

Brazil Pavilion, interior with exhibition, Expo Brussels 1958. Collection Dept. A&S, Faculty of Engineering and Architecture, Ghent University

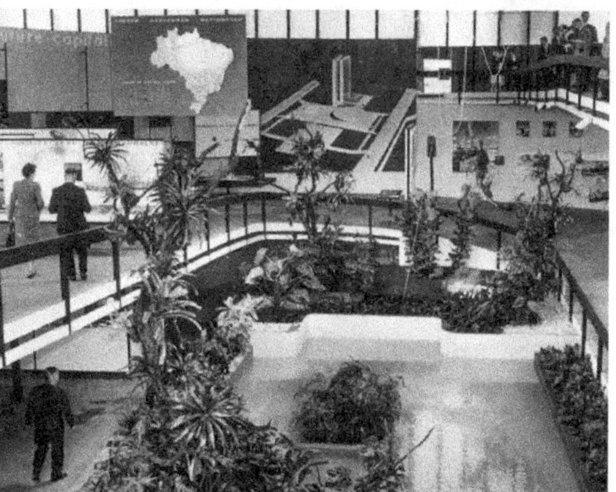

Brussels Pavilion, photo published in the Rio de Janeiro newspaper *Correio da Manhã*, on August 6, 1958. The caption highlights the "new, vigorous, inventive" architecture by Sérgio Bernardes and the "excellent central garden by Roberto Burle Marx". Collection Correio da Manhã / Arquivo Nacional

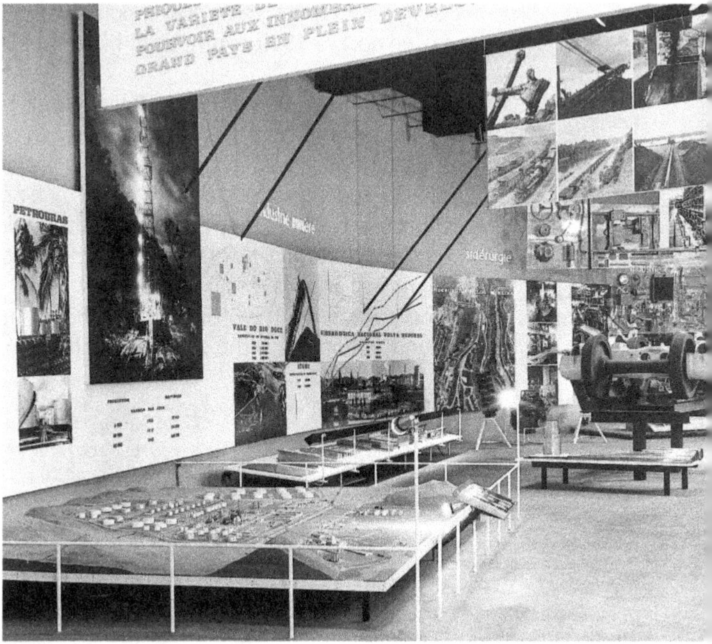

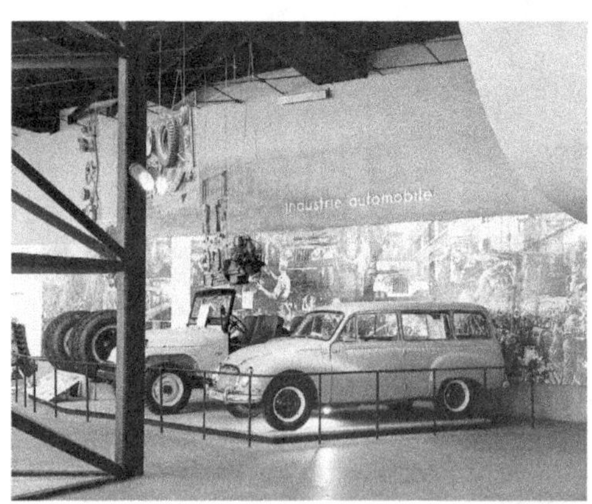

Brazil Pavilion, interior with exhibitions of the commodities and automotive industries, Expo Brussels 1958. Collection Dept. A&S, Faculty of Engineering and Architecture, Ghent University

of Brazil. As he walked this ramp, he hit the ground again, practically dragging his foot, guided by the law of gravity without making the slightest effort, at the same time he descended around the tropics, which were the gardens."[37]

As essential clarification for understanding the concept adopted in the Brazilian pavilion, this brief synthesis ends up not mentioning three elements of relevance for the

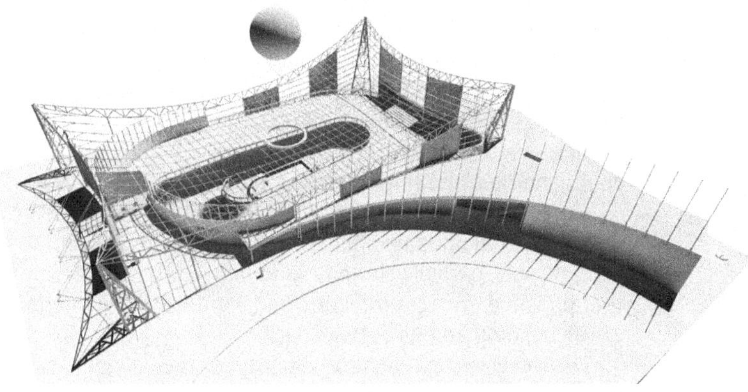

Brazil Pavilion, West and East facades
in 3D model, Expo Brussels 1958.
Drawing by Fausto Sombra

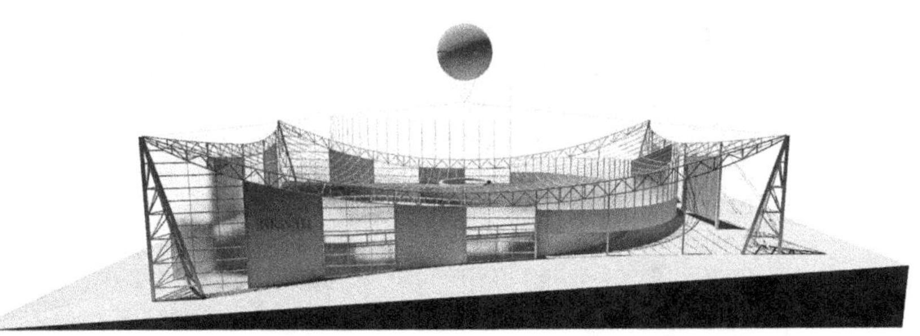

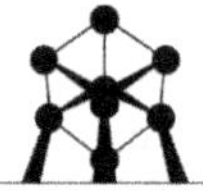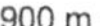

Distance and scale comparison between the Atomium and the Brazil Pavilion, Expo Brussels 1958. Drawing by Fausto Sombra

project. Firstly, its ingenious roof, similar to that used in the Volta Redonda Pavilion, with the use of steel cables in the form of a catenary, produced externally and assembled on site, an element that practically gave the pavilion its image. Secondly, the assimilation of water as a central design element, present both in the water mirror of Burle Marx's central garden, and through the *impluvium* on rainy days. And thirdly, the large balloon, which hovering over the delicate roof, even on rainy or cold days, was lowered using a central cable, partially closing the *impluvium*, a mechanism that provided greater protection and comfort to the interior of the building and its users.

However, the moment of adoption of the balloon, an element so opportunely incorporated into the building, is worthy of a brief reflection. As proposed by Alexandre Bahia Vanderlei in his article about the Volta Redonda Pavilion, "Pavilhão da CSN 1954: recorrência técnica e manifesto da modernidade"[38] – an analysis in accordance with the present understanding and as already discussed in chapter 2 –, this building might have been initially designed to be built on solid ground and not on the Sapateiro stream. Recollecting, this questioning was duly posed after the analysis of the initial studies of the aforementioned pavilion built in Ibirapuera, because though the sketches did not illustrate the stream under the two bridges, they did illustrate the four masts – which structured the two central transverse marquises – starting from the ground, that is, assisting in the structuring of the whole cluster, in a structural concept different from the final developed project, and from the built building.

In due proportions, when relating this event to the building here in vogue, after analyzing a considerable range of drawings and documents on the Brazilian pavilion in Brussels, no one found – except the undated illustrated sketch of the Brazil Pavilion by Sérgio Bernardes, next to the Atomium – another drawing or text mentioning the balloon in the project. Even the executive drawings and models, illustrated in the various publications at the time of the building's construction, do not suggest this relevant element. Only with the publication of the article "Pavilhão do Brasil na Exposição Internacional de Bruxelas", in the *Módulo* magazine no. 9, February 1958,[39] with just two months to go before the opening of the pavilion, the balloon was briefly mentioned, even so, in text accompanied by drawings without the balloon. In fact, the longitudinal section that accompanies the referred mention suggests that the circular ring that defined the *impluvium* had a set of eight tubes or chains distributed in a radial way, responsible, in a first and slight analysis, for properly conducting the rainwater coming from the roof to the water mirror below; a solution similar to that adopted by Sérgio Bernardes, years later, in the rainwater descents present at the José Lins do Rêgo Cultural Space, in João Pessoa, Paraíba in 1980.

However, a closer look at the sheet referring to the detailing of the roof, a drawing signed by engineer Paulo Fragoso, confirms that the illustrated lines were steel rods with a diameter of 10 millimeters, and although not incorporated into the built project, such as attested by the photos from inside the building, these elements probably had the original function of stabilizing the roof, for on days of intense wind, it could suffer from upward vertical stress, common in architectural elements with such characteristics.[40]

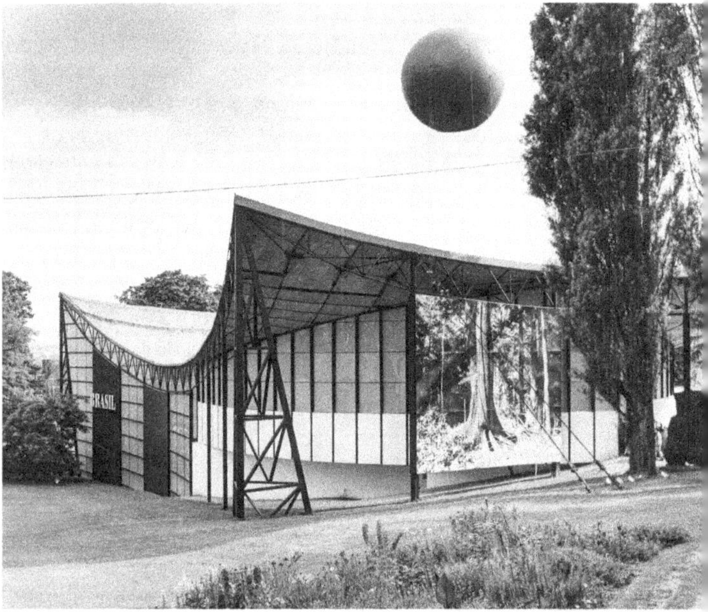

Brazil Pavilion, balloon floating above
the roof, Expo Brussels 1958. Photo
by SADO. Rigolle Collection

Brazil Pavilion, Roberto Burle Marx
garden and balloon closing the
impluvium of the roof, Expo Brussels
1958. Photo by Reginald Hugo de
Burgh Galwey. Collection of the
British Architectural Library / Royal
Institute of British Architects

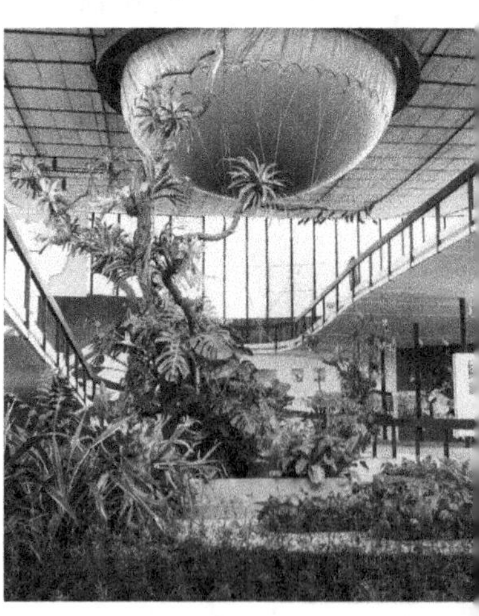

This information should include the testimony of former partner, Murillo Boabaid[41] – a team member responsible for the drawings of the Brazilian pavilion in 1958 – stating that the idea of this ephemeral and playful element was inspired by the film *Le Balon Rouge* from 1956, also highlighting, without mentioning dates, that it was the suggestion to incorporate it into the project.[42]

Even without specifying the moment at which Sérgio Bernardes and his team would definitely adopt the balloon as an integral part of the architecture of the Brazilian pavilion, the result is a building of exceptional design and character, of elementary importance for International and Brazilian architectural historiography, standing out in a wide range of vehicle network at the time, and thus praised by the weekly *Manchete*, in October 1958, close to the end of the great show:

"Our Country was the last to decide on its participation in the great international exhibition in Brussels. When our technicians arrived there, the best areas of what would become Latin America Avenue were already occupied. We were left with a green basin, almost outside the limits of the Park, between two small cypress groves. A wall of the Mexico Pavilion covered our façade like a kind of Andes Mountain Range. But the Brazilian architects, led by Sérgio Bernardes, did not lose inspiration and, with ingenuity and art, managed to build a modern, original, daring pavilion, in terms of lines and design, which would surprisingly become one of the main aesthetic attractions of the Expo-58.

Another serious difficulty: lack of money. Our government had voted an insignificant amount for the Pavilion. The credits, as always happens, arrived in installments and the work was in a hurry. Few Brazilian private industries and organizations have taken a concrete interest in the subject. The material that we were supposed to exhibit proved to be extremely limited from the beginning, almost inexpressive in relation to the importance of the event. But the organizers of our representation arranged the elements at their disposal, improvised here and there, and ended up composing a cluster worthy of being visited by European crowds, and of saving Brazil's prestige. Today, on the eve of the Exhibition's closing, we can claim victory: the International Committee that is judging the 102 Brussels Pavilions has reserved to ours, several prizes, including the Grand Prize of Architecture. In the overall points count, Brazil is in ninth place, which is a real success. Above all, if we consider that we are placed immediately after France, whose pavilion was one of the most expensive built in the park. First place went not to the Russian and American Molochs, of gigantic dimensions, but to small Czechoslovakia, whose Pavilion was a marvel of good taste and beautiful organization, in the spirit of Expo-58: 'showing the world what each country has done for the betterment of life and human well-being.'

In the Brazilian Pavilion, Europeans admired the impressive functional design of the internal ramp, which, descending from the upper floor, allows a view of all the stands without causing any fatigue. So much so, that in a short time, our pavilion gained a reputation for being a peaceful and restful place within the immense Exhibition. Absolute success in order: the Brazilian coffee (20,000 cups a day), the iced mate (unknown in Europe until then), and the exhibition of precious and semi-precious stones, which could be purchased by the public."[43]

Concluding the arguments and themes about the Brazil Pavilion in Brussels and before moving on to the considerations on the São Cristóvão Pavilion, we highlight that, as previously mentioned, originally Sérgio had idealized the ramp, which skirted the central garden of the Pavilion, in

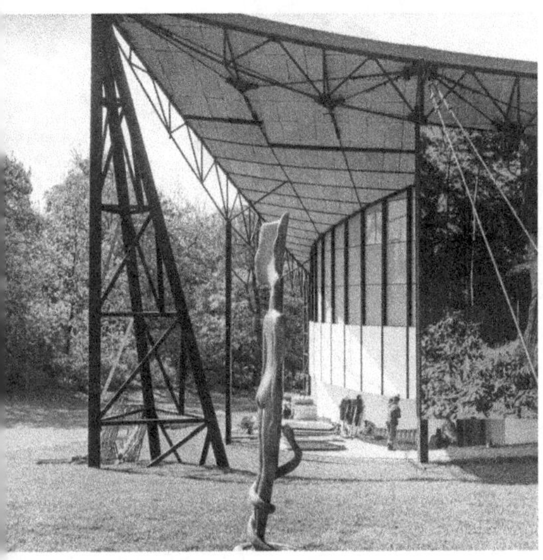

Brazil Pavilion, sculpture by Maria Martins at one of the entrances, Expo Brussels 1958. Photo by Reginald Hugo de Burgh Galwey. Collection of the British Architectural Library / Royal Institute of British Architects

wood and structured on Mills scaffolding. This decision and design information is relevant, emphasizing the degree of experimentation by the carioca architect, also clarifying why there is diverse material on this construction system in the folders of that project preserved in the architect's collection at the NPD.[44] This finding is based on a document provided by Kykah Bernardes, more precisely on the undated curatorial text by Marco Gallery, on an exhibition by Sérgio Bernardes of the building constructed in Brussels. The brief text accurately describes the design of the project and the materials used in it:

"The solution adopted by Sérgio Bernardes, which became victorious, was one of the most remarkable, since all the problems (plastic, economic, topographic, execution time, period of use, etc.) were brilliantly solved by the structural solution and the use of materials. Starting from the slope of the terrain, the architect

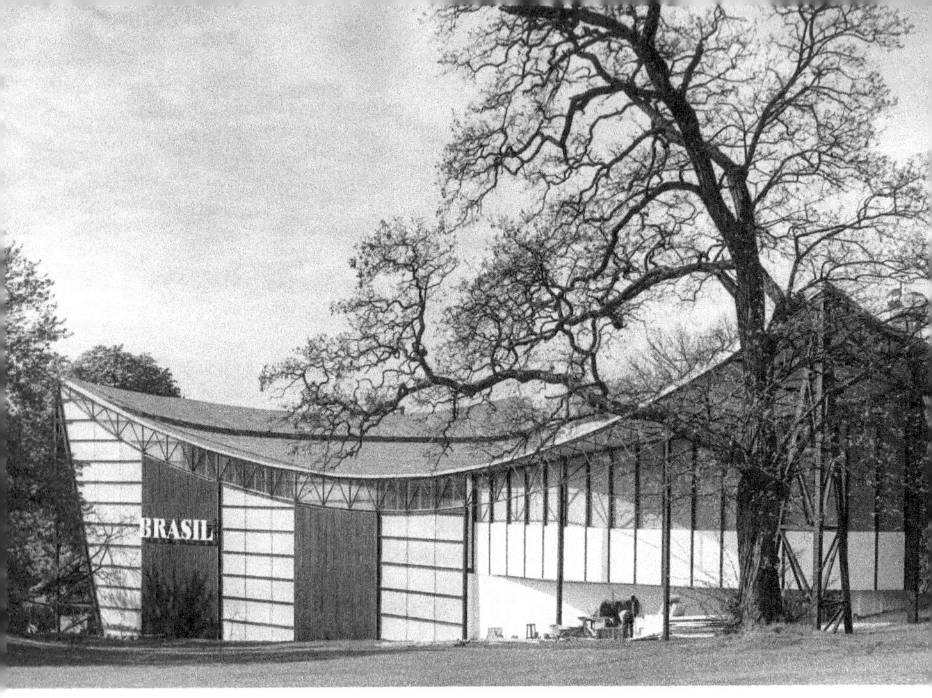

Brazil Pavilion, view of the lawns on the east side with a balloon floating above the roof, Expo Brussels 1958. Photo by Reginald Hugo de Burgh Galwey. Collection of the British Architectural Library / Royal Institute of British Architects

launched a descending ramp (4%) around a tropical garden and surrounded by panels displaying the development of our civilization. This arrangement also offered the public, whose access was at the highest part, a total and constant view of the interior, with a feeling of space and freedom. This ramp, initially designed in wood supported by Mills scaffolding aimed not only at economic and time reduction, but also at the posterior use of the material; but local legislation did not allow it, as it was a combustible material, so reinforced concrete was adopted. Having solved the problems of the internal

environment and circulation, the architect conceived
the structure and roof, which, according to him, was
similar in content to a circus, as it was only a 6-month
show, to be demolished afterwards. Based on this idea,
he thought of a rectangular tarp supported on 4 corners,
with a circular opening over the garden. Engineer
Paulo Fragoso, his direct collaborator, found the solution in a metallic structure composed of 4 supports
at the extreme points and a metal lattice cover filled
with concrete plates, sealed together with neoprene,
and waterproofed with epoxhypalon plastic paint. The
pavilion's cladding would be with 'Cocoon' (plastic paint
on reinforced screen), but due to certain technical difficulties plexiglass plates were used. Above the circular
opening in the roof, the pavilion had a captive balloon,
with vertical movement, with a larger diameter (7 m).
This balloon, which was made of red nylon, stood out in
the gray sky of Brussels, attracting the visitor from the
entrance of the park, situated at a higher level than the
Brazilian pavilion."[45]

The thought-provoking possibility of adopting scaffolding in the pavilion, even without drawings that materialize this decision, refers to the idea of the ramps of the
ephemeral building designed by Carla Juaçaba and Bia Lessa
for the Humanidade Pavilion, built in Rio de Janeiro in 2012.
This design vanguard is ultimately ratified by the statement below by architect Paulo Mendes da Rocha. Published
in the Spanish magazine *En Blanco* and pointing out the
inspirations of the Brazilian pavilion in the design of the
Atlético Paulistano Club Gymnasium, the thought seems to
reinforce the words uttered by Roberto Segre – presented
in the Introduction – about Sérgio's strong influence "on
architecture students in search for alternative paths to the
sterile formalism of our time." Mendes da Rocha's speech is
as follows:

"The first question: the size of the space to play and how
to cover a large void in a non-heavy way. At that time,
tensioned structures were fashionable and I thought
about them simply because there was a lot of talk about
this type of structure. I did some experiments, and
there was even a very interesting pavilion already built
by Sérgio Bernardes for the International Exhibition
in Brussels. Bernardes made a concave pavilion, with
tensioned cables in the form of a 'tent', with a circular
impluvium in the center. It was very interesting from
the point of view of tensions, because that steel circle
in the center was subjected to homogeneous tensions
throughout, that is, it enjoyed the indeformability of the
circular shape. By compression or by tension, the circle
is indeformable. I thought I could do it that way too,
light, and I created a structure to house a square, which
I imagined excavated, to make the building lower, where
the steps went down and the roof was suspended above.

In Bernardes' building, interestingly, the roof was
eventually closed by a helium balloon with a diameter
a little larger than the *impluvium*. The balloon was
attached to a cable that left the center of this large
space and floated announcing the pavilion. If it rained,
they collected the cable and the balloon closed the
space.

At the São Paulo gymnasium, I tried to, at least, use
the ingenuity of that project."[46]

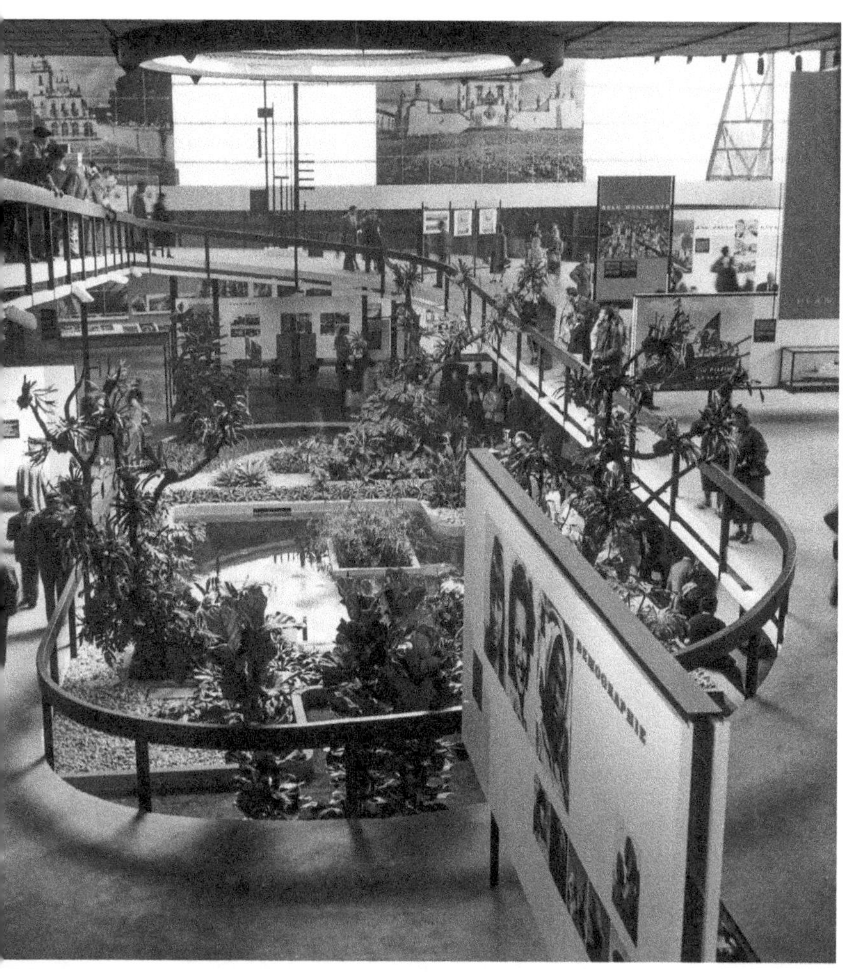

Brazil Pavilion, tropical garden by
Roberto Burle Marx, Expo Brussels
1958. Photo by Reginald Hugo de
Burgh Galwey. Collection of the
British Architectural Library / Royal
Institute of British Architects

Notes

1. There are only two books published exclusively about the work of Sérgio Bernardes that briefly highlight the Brazil Pavilion in Brussels: Cavalcanti, *Sérgio Bernardes*; Bernardes and Cavalcanti, eds., *Sérgio Bernardes*. The magazines *Módulo, Habitat* and *Arquitetura e Engenharia* also published articles on the pavilion at the time: Redação, "Pavilhão do Brasil na Exposição Internacional de Bruxelas"; Redação, "O pavilhão da engenharia civil em Bruxelas"; Redação, "Pavilhão do Brasil na Feira internacional de Bruxelas". And the pavilion had the merit of an exhibition in 2012 at the Atomium Museum in Brussels, in the 1958 exhibition circuit. Europalia Brasil, Cur., *Sérgio Bernardes. Expo'58 – Brazil Pavilion*, International Arts Festival, Belgium, Atomium Museum, Oct. 2011/Jan. 2012

2. Sombra, "Sérgio Bernardes e o pavilhão brasileiro na Exposição Universal e Internacional de Bruxelas, 1958" (annals and magazine).

3. The Shanghai Exhibition, held between May and Oct. 2010 in China, had 73 million visitors. Cf. Redação, "Expo Xangai 2010 termina como a mais visitada da história".

4. Pierre Lambert, "Bruxelas: capital do mundo por seis meses".

5. The Commissioner General of the Government, Baron de Moens de Fernig, would be "responsible for ensuring, in the name and under the authority of the Minister of Economic Affairs, the conception, realization, organization and administration of the Exhibition". Georges Moens de Fernig, "Brussels Universal and International Exhibition". Translated by Luiz Galvão Valle, Brussels, Kingdom of Belgium, Permanent Commission for Exhibitions and Fairs Abroad, Apr. 24, 1957, 5.

6. Ibid., 4.

7. The following Special Committees were created: Advertising and Publicity; Circulation of Roads and Ways and Parking lots; and Superior of Tourism. The latter was subdivided into the Accommodation Committee; Transport Committee; and Reception and Documentation Committee. Ibid., 6-7.

8. Ibid., 5-8.

9. Ibid., 8.

10. Ibid., 8-9.

11. Ibid., 11.

12. Ibid., 6.

13. Ibid., 8.

14. Francine Latteur, "Comissariado Permanente de Exposições e Feiras no Exterior: Exposição Universal e Internacional de Bruxelas". Also see Redação, "Exposição de Bruxelas – 1958".

15. Moens de Fernig, "Brussels Universal and International Exhibition", 12-13.

16. Latteur, "Comissariado Permanente de Exposições e Feiras no Exterior", 3.

17. Hugo Gouthier, Correspondence to Olavo Falcão, Brussels, Jan. 31, 1957. NPD FAU UFRJ Collection.

18. Hugo Gouthier, Correspondence to Secretariat of State for Foreign Affairs, Brussels, Feb. 7, 1957. NPD FAU UFRJ Collection.

19. The text corresponding to the researches of Paul Meurs, Mil de Kooning, Ronny de Meyer, summarize the moment of construction of the Brazilian Pavilion, mentioning the accelerated rhythm of the JK era, the establishment of the automobile industry, Cinema Novo, Bossa Nova, the Brazilian team with its first world title and Brasília becoming reality through the sketches of Lúcio Costa and Niemeyer. Meurs, Kooning, and Meyer, "Expo 58"; "Esse Brasil grande e ambicioso se apresentou em Bruxelas num pavilhão de aço e concreto, projetado por Sérgio Bernardes". Meurs, "O pavilhão brasileiro na Expo de Bruxelas, 1958".

20. The sheets of the executive project for the Brazilian pavilion appoint the following professionals as responsible: Sérgio Bernardes as architect; Nicolaï Fikoff as collaborating architect; Kylzo Carvalho and Murillo C. Boabaid as draftsmen; Paulo Fragoso and Emmanoel Magalhães as structural design engineers; and Roberto Burle Marx as landscape architect.Paul Meurs lists the following additional team members: Max Winders, consultant; João Maria dos Santos, interior design; Eduardo Anahory, Jack van de Beuque, and Artur Lício Pontual, assistants; Libbe Smit, lighting. Paul Meurs. *The Brazilian Pavilion at the Brussels Expo, 1958: Architect Sérgio Bernardes* (op. cit.).

21. Geraldo Casé, "Sérgio Bernardes", 127.

22. Redação, "Pavilhão do Brasil na Feira internacional de Bruxelas", 22.

23. Gouthier, *Presença*, 153-154.

24. Ibid., 154-155.

25. Ibid., 155.

26. Redação, "Participará o Brasil na Feira internacional de Bruxelas", 26.

27. The French magazine *L'Architecture d'Aujourd'hui*, no. 78, of June 1958, presents a synthesis of the outstanding pavilions in the exhibition. Redação, "Bruxelles 58". See also Rika Devos and Mil de Kooning, *L'Architecture Moderne à L'Expo 58: pour un monde plus humain*.

28. Backhauser, "A obra de Sérgio Bernardes".

29. Only the two towers on the south facade were 15.8 m. The two lattice towers on the north facade, due to the elevation of the land, measured approximately 10.80 and 11.80 m.

30. In 1958 there were 21 Brazilian states, being: Alagoas, Amazonas, Bahia, Ceará, Espírito Santo, Goiás, Guanabara (extinct in 1975), Maranhão, Mato Grosso, Minas Gerais, Pará, Paraíba, Pernambuco, Piauí, Rio de Janeiro, Rio Grande do Norte, Santa Catarina, São Paulo and Sergipe. Redação, "Eleições gerais no Brasil em 1958" (entry).

31. As identified with the help of architect and landscaper Karla Lopez, the mentioned species correspond respectively to Nymphaea ssp, Asplenniun nidus, Ciperus papirus, Bromeliaceae ssp, Dracaena marginata, Monstera deliciosa, Platyce- rium bifurcatum, Agave attenuata, Anthuriun ssp, Cryptanthus ssp. Karla Lopez Álvarez, testimony to Fausto Sombra, Bernardes Architecture office, São Paulo, Jun 7 2018.

32. Novais Teixeira, "O Pavilhão do Brasil", 7.

33. Meurs, Kooning, and Meyer, "Expo 58".

34. Latteur, "Comissariado Permanente de Exposições e Feiras no Exterior", 2.

35. Gilles Lapouge, "Inaugurado o pavilhão do Brasil em Bruxelas".

36. The budget difference of the Brazilian pavilion compared to the other pavilions of the event is considerable. While the average pavilion was built for 10,000 francs/m^2, the pavilion conceived by Bernardes was budgeted at 2,900 francs/m^2. The difference in the amount of steel would be a preponderant point in this equation, because, while the pavilions used around 200 kg/m^2 of steel in their roofs, the Brazilian pavilion consumed only 25 kg/m^2. Redação, "Pavilhão do Brasil na Feira internacional de Bruxelas", 22-23.

37. Sérgio Bernardes, "Vanguarda: perspectiva e busca," quoted in Backhauser "A obra de Sérgio Bernardes".

38. Vanderlei, "Pavilhão da CSN 1954".

39. Redação, "Pavilhão do Brasil na Exposição Internacional de Bruxelas".

40. It is possible to suggest that the non-adoption of the tie rods is related to the presence of the impluvium, which by allowing the air passage in the central region of the roof, combined with the ballast coming from the thin layer of concrete that formed it, and the weight of the structuring profiles – totaling 85 tons – would allow a decrease in wind pressure and consolidation of the cluster. The elimination of these rods would also make it possible to change the geometry of the central water mirror, constantly illustrated as a circular drawing in the different plans of the project – following the circular and radial distribution of the rods –, finally being erected with more orthogonal lines.

41. Murillo Boabaid, testimony to Fausto Sombra at Bernardes Architecture Office, Rio de Janeiro, Apr. 19, 2017.

42. Murillo Boabaid, "Pavilhões", 60.

43. Martins Justino, "Talento, armado: Brasil em Bruxelas".

44. See SB 140, Pavilhão Brasileiro da Exposição Universal de Bruxelas, CX 30, Revistas e Apostilas, Acervo Sérgio Bernardes, NPD.

45. Galeria Marco. Marco Gallery opening its permanent exhibition of architecture, engineering, urbanism and decoration, sponsors the exhibition of the Brazilian Pavilion at the 1958 Brussels International Exhibition by architect Sérgio W. Bernardes. Rio de Janeiro, n.d. Sérgio Bernardes Collection.

46. Mas et al., "Conversación con Paulo Mendes da Rocha," 115.

Chapter 4
São Cristóvão Pavilion
1957–1960

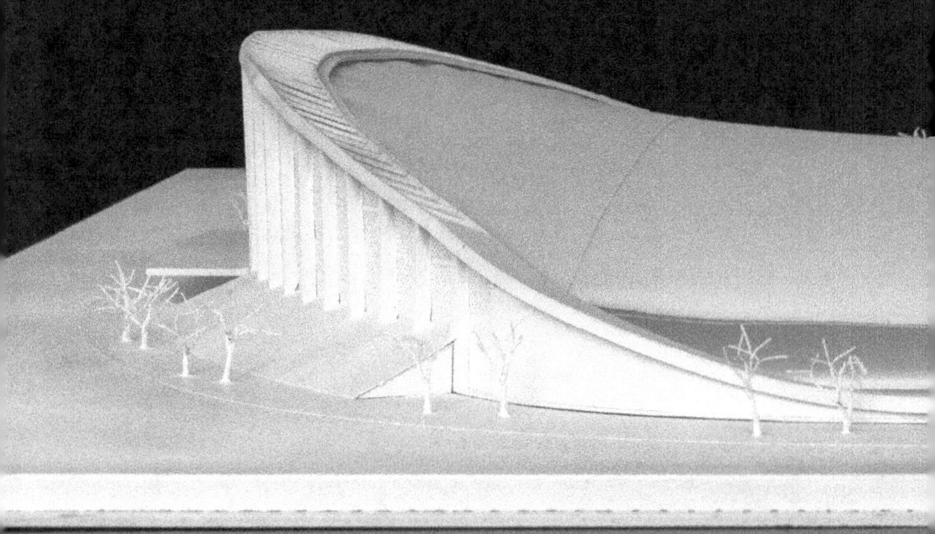

São Cristóvão Pavilion, model developed for Fausto Sombra's doctoral thesis, Rio de Janeiro RJ, 1957-1960. Photo by André Nazareth

Assembling a Puzzle

With the positive results obtained by the pavilion design for the National Steelworks Company in Ibirapuera Park, and only two years after the opening, in 1957 and under the government of Juscelino Kubitschek, Sérgio Bernardes received two commissions of supreme relevance, the just revisited Brazil Pavilion in Brussels – opened in May 1958 – and the Pavilion for the International Trade and Industry Fair, opened to the public in December 1960 in Rio, also known as São Cristóvão Pavilion.[1]

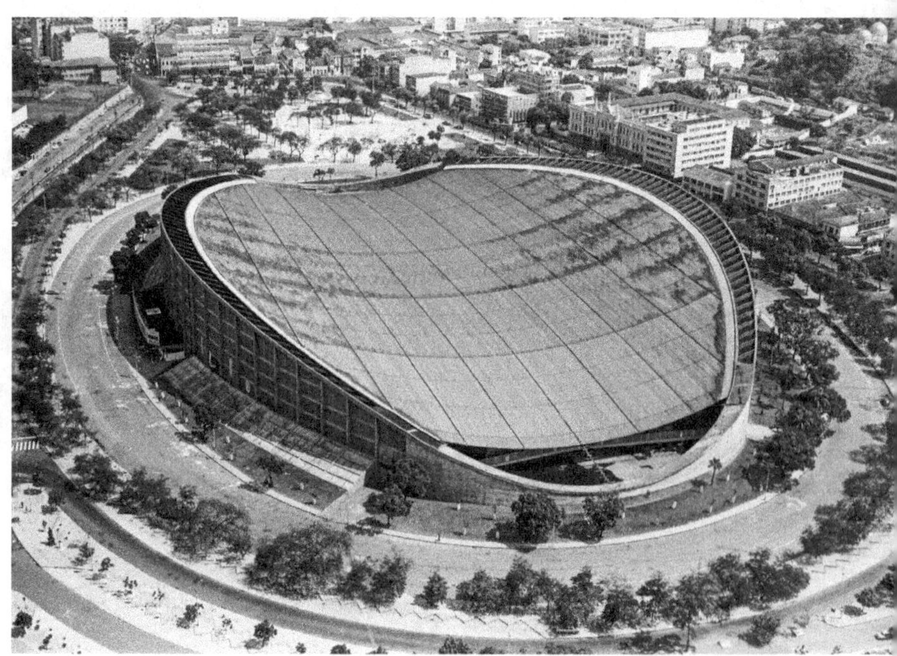

São Cristóvão Pavilion, aerial view of the building with the roof, Rio de Janeiro RJ, 1957-1960. Photo by Celso Omena Brando

The two last exemplars were contemporary in terms of
conception, however they were concluded at different times,
this temporal difference could be justified by three important
reasons: the first is the fact that the Brazil Pavilion in
Brussels was an ephemeral building, scheduled to be opened
and dismantled – even if its inauguration did not match the
official opening of the event –; the second, the fact that
the Brazil Pavilion in Brussels had a considerably smaller
measurement than the São Cristóvão Pavilion, and therefore
involving technical issues of considerably lower magnitude; and the third, probably due to the labor used in the
construction of the Pavilion in Brussels, for a significant part
of the companies involved in the construction and manufacture of its metallic components belonged to the host country
– Belgium – at that time already considered an expert in the
manufacture and application of steel, as confirmed by the
construction of the Atomium.

Thus, unlike the exemplar in Brussels, the construction
process of the São Cristóvão Pavilion was presented in a
much more complex way and full of mishaps, remaining
to this date a rare topic studied and deeply analyzed by
researchers and critics. Its relevant contribution to Brazilian
modern architecture has only recently been of interest for
specialized media, as seen in the book published abroad
by Brazilian researcher Renato Anelli entitled *Architettura
contemporanea: Brasile* in 2008;[2] in *Monolito* magazine no.
31, compiled by editor Fernando Serapião, entitled *Escola
carioca: arquitetura moderna no Rio de Janeiro* in 2016;[3]
and through the book-catalog of the exhibition *Infinito vão:
90 anos de arquitetura brasileira*, 2019, also by Fernando
Serapião in partnership with critic Guilherme Wisnik,[4] all
already mentioned in a footnote in the book's introduction.
In general, however, these publications, as well as a few
others, end up dealing with the aforementioned exemplar in
a superficial way, focusing on a limited number of images[5]
known to the researchers, and dedicating little or not even

any keen contextualization of the work to the period of its conception.

With this critical scarcity about the São Cristóvão Pavilion, as already initially mentioned, however, the work developed by researcher Ana Luiza Nobre has stood out through her PhD dissertation "Fios cortantes: projeto e produto, arquitetura e design no Rio de Janeiro (1950-70)" from 2008, more precisely in the subchapters "Malhas, redes, cabos e triângulos."[6] In it, the author approaches the carioca pavilion, describing in a pioneering[7] and practically exclusive way – except for the biographical book authored by researcher João Perdigão[8] and Euler Corradi, as shall be addressed later – the process that involved the conception of the two distinct roofs designed for this outstanding building in the capital of Rio de Janeiro, including access to plans prepared by engineer Paulo Fragoso responsible for the building's general structural calculation. Unfortunately, the present research was not able to access these original materials. This fact occurred even after contact with researcher Ana Luiza Nobre, and some unsuccessful attempts with the collections linked to the Laboratory of Structures at the School of Engineering of São Carlos, LE EESC USP, institution cited in the dissertation of the referred researcher as responsible for carrying out "six measurements of the tension in the cables"[9] of the São Cristóvão Pavilion during the period between 1960 and 1981,[10] work conducted by engineer Dante Martinelli.

Part of this report, dated July 1974 and signed by engineer Dante Martinelli on its final page, coincidentally, has reached the present research through architect Thiago Bernardes, Sérgio's grandson. Due to its relevance in relation to the care required by the roof of this building, the conclusions described in its final pages were extracted, and made clear the need to carry out, at that moment, little more than thirteen years after the inauguration of the building, maintenance actions on the pavilion's roof, as well as monitoring

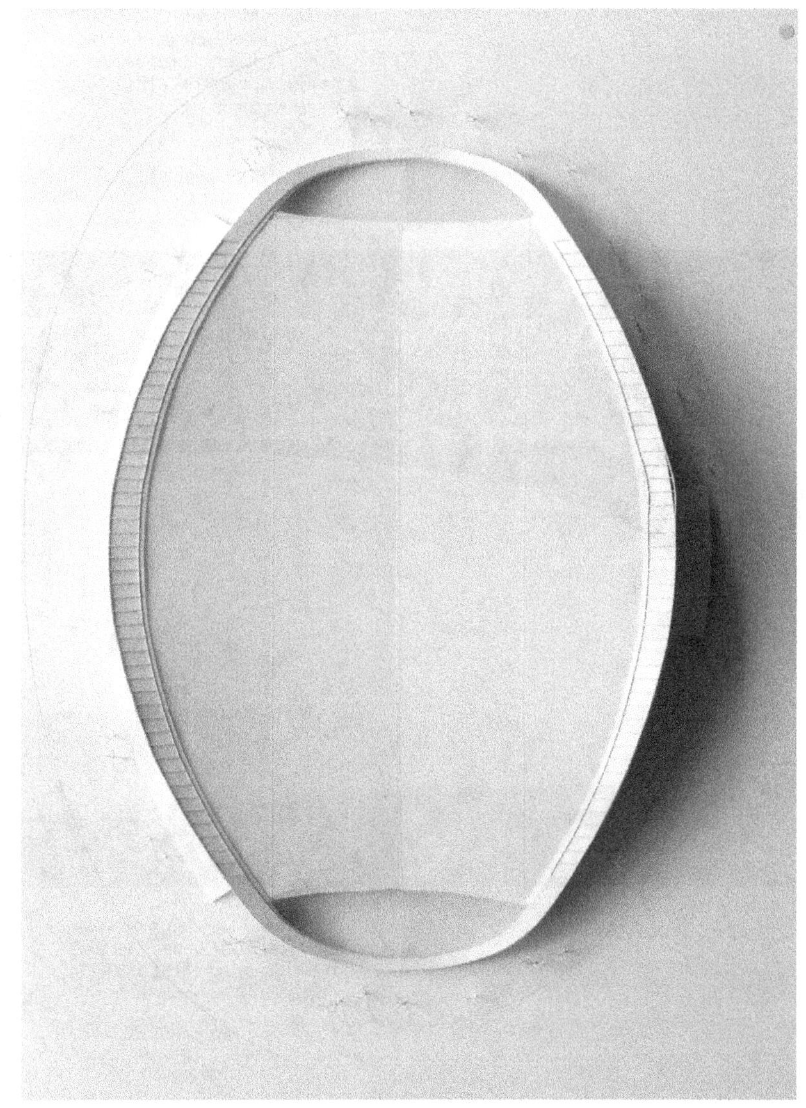

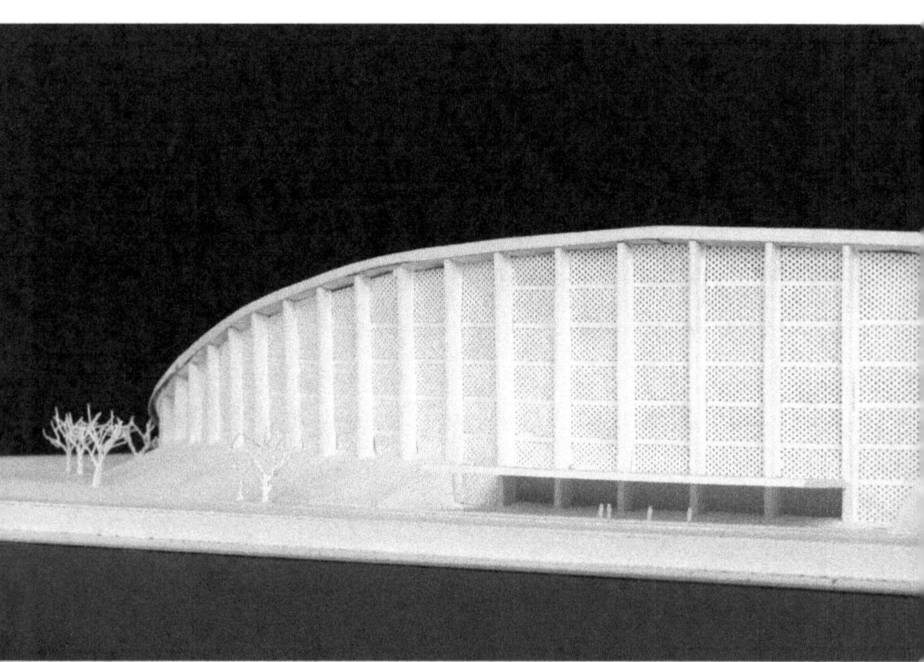

São Cristóvão Pavilion, model developed for Fausto Sombra's doctoral thesis, Rio de Janeiro RJ, 1957-1960. Photos by André Nazareth

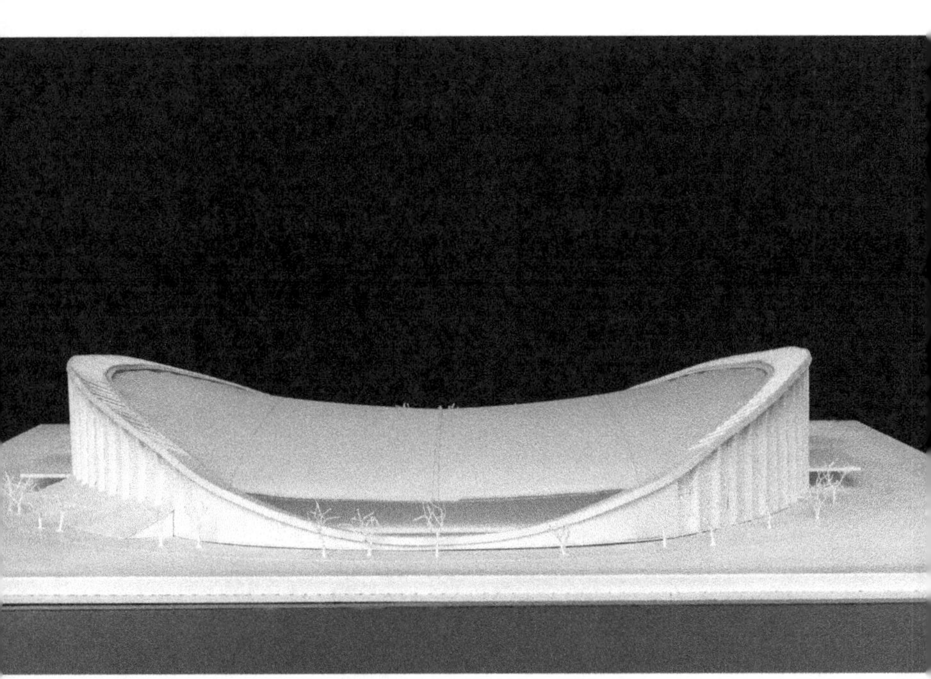

São Cristóvão Pavilion, structural
plan of the roof at a scale of 1:200,
redesign of the preliminary project on
January 24, 1984, Rio de Janeiro RJ,
1957-1960. Collection NPD FAU UFRJ
/ Sérgio Bernardes Fund

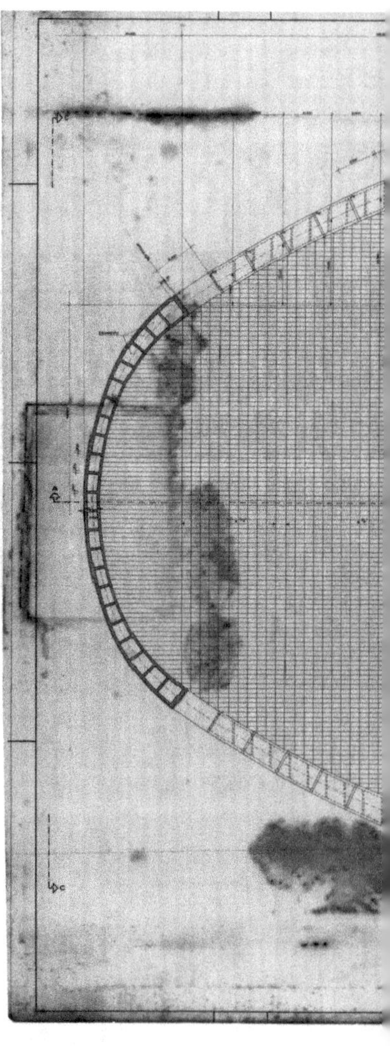

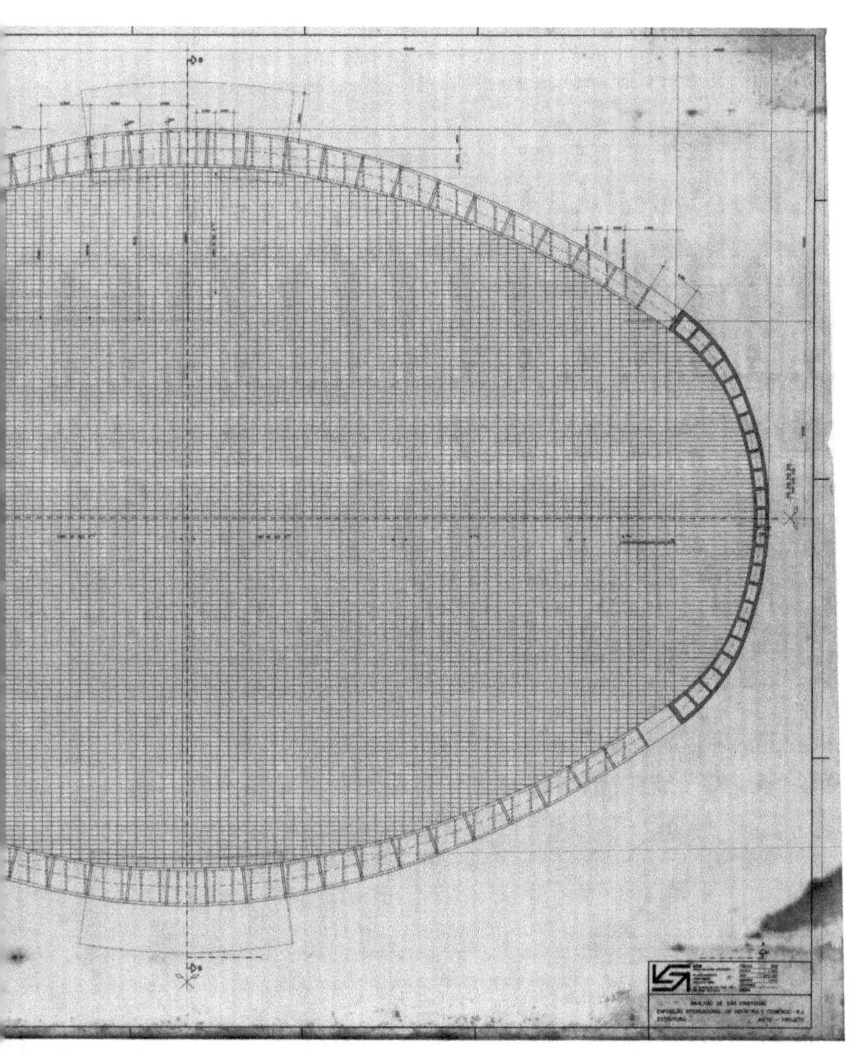

São Cristóvão Pavilion, elevations and sections at a scale of 1:200, redesign of the preliminary project on January 24, 1984, Rio de Janeiro RJ, 1957-1960. Collection NPD FAU UFRJ / Sérgio Bernardes Fund

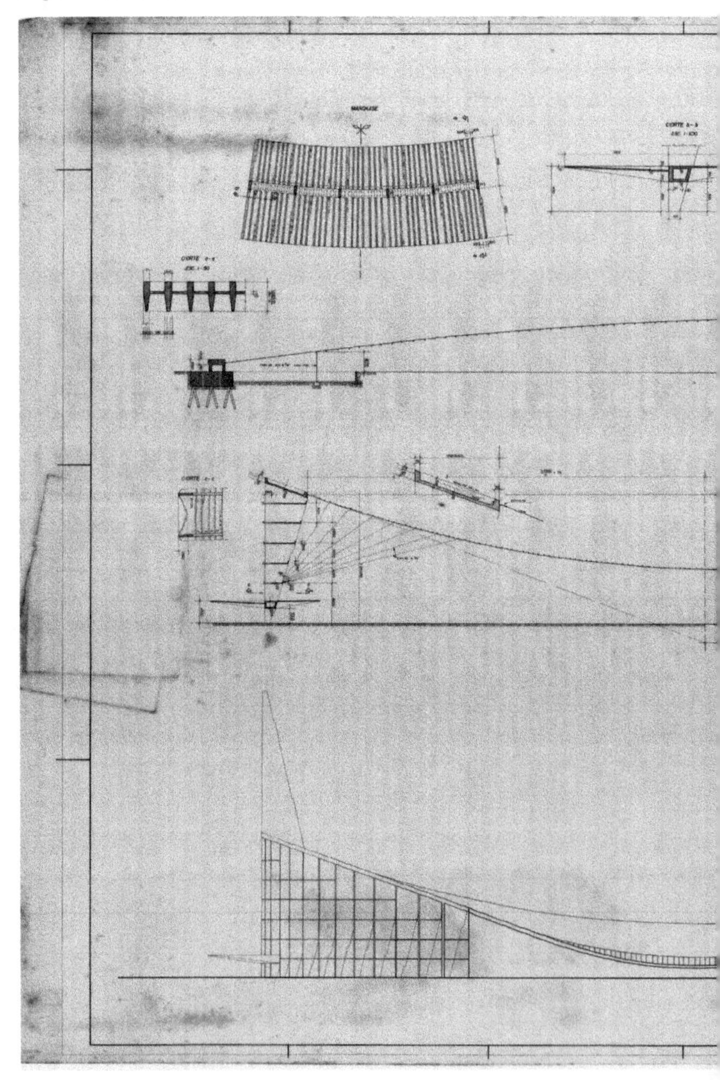

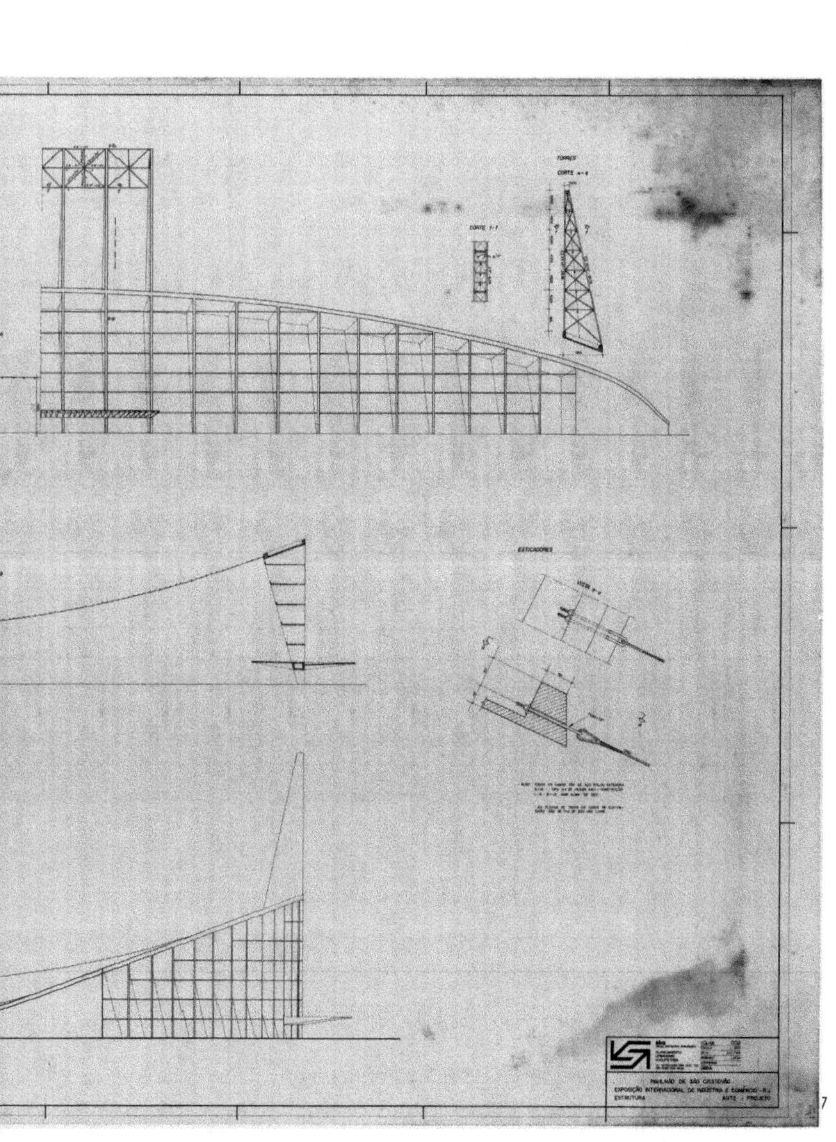

CORTE F-F
TORRES
CORTE A-A
ESTICADORES
VISTA A-A
PAVILHÃO DE SÃO CRISTOVÃO
EXPOSIÇÃO INTERNACIONAL DE INDÚSTRIA E COMÉRCIO - R.J.
ESTRUTURA
ANTE - PROJETO

São Cristóvão Pavilion, site plan at a scale of 1:500, redesign from March 5, 1965, Rio de Janeiro RJ, Public Works Department of the State of Guanabara, 1957–1960. Collection NPD FAU UFRJ / Sérgio Bernardes Fund

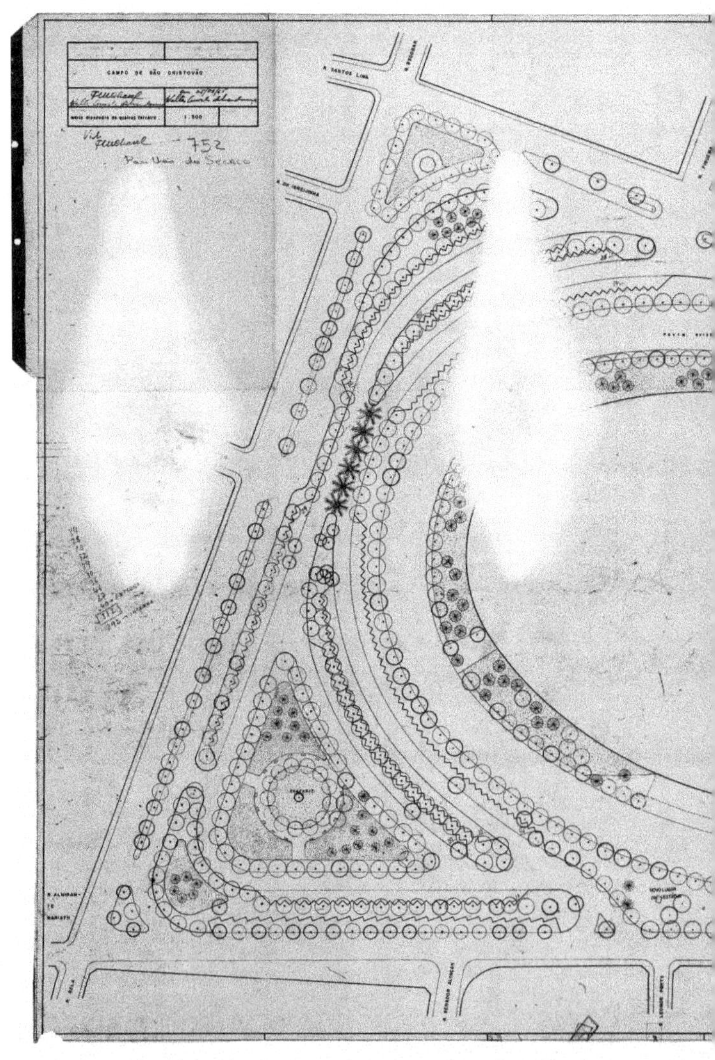

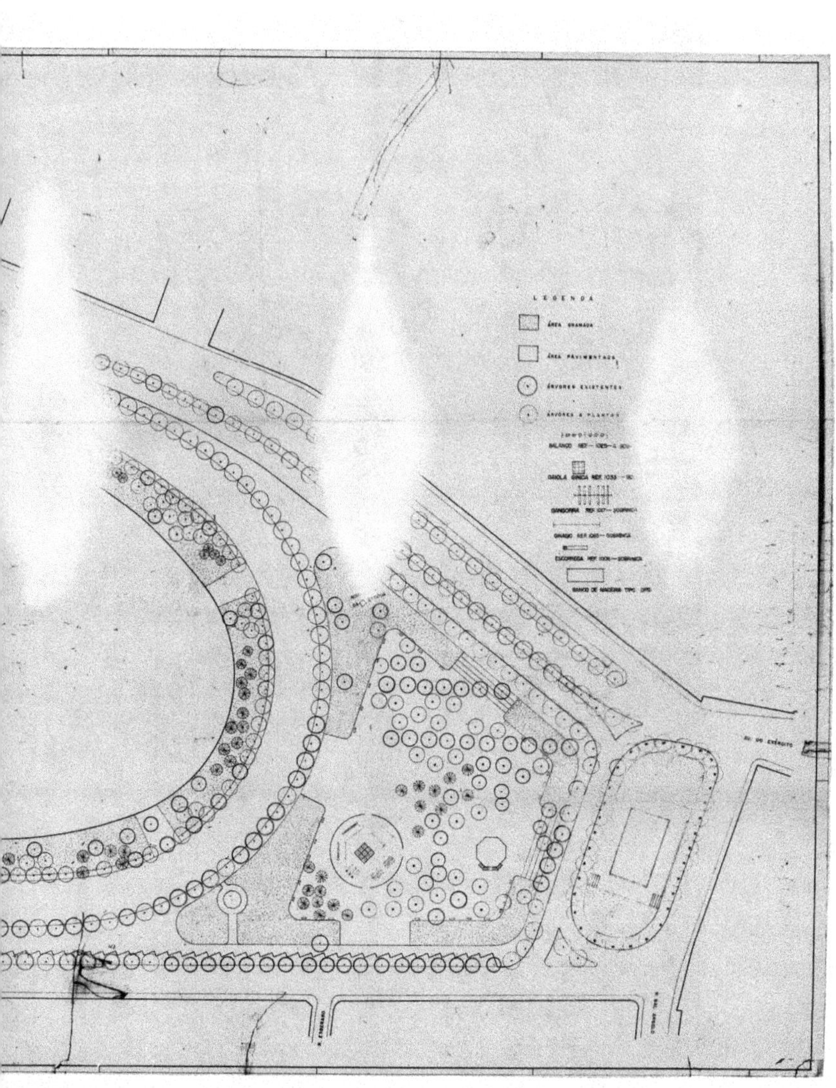
LEGENDA
ÁREA GRAMADA
ÁREA PAVIMENTADA
ÁRVORES EXISTENTES
ÁRVORES E PLANTAS
(IMPEDIDO)
BALANÇO REF. 1065—4 BOL.
GAIOLA GIRICA REF. 1053 — 1C
GANGORRA REF. 1017 — SEGURANÇA
GINÁSIO REF. 1065 — SEGURANÇA
ESCORREGA REF. 1006 — SEGURANÇA
BANCO DE MADEIRA TIPO 1975

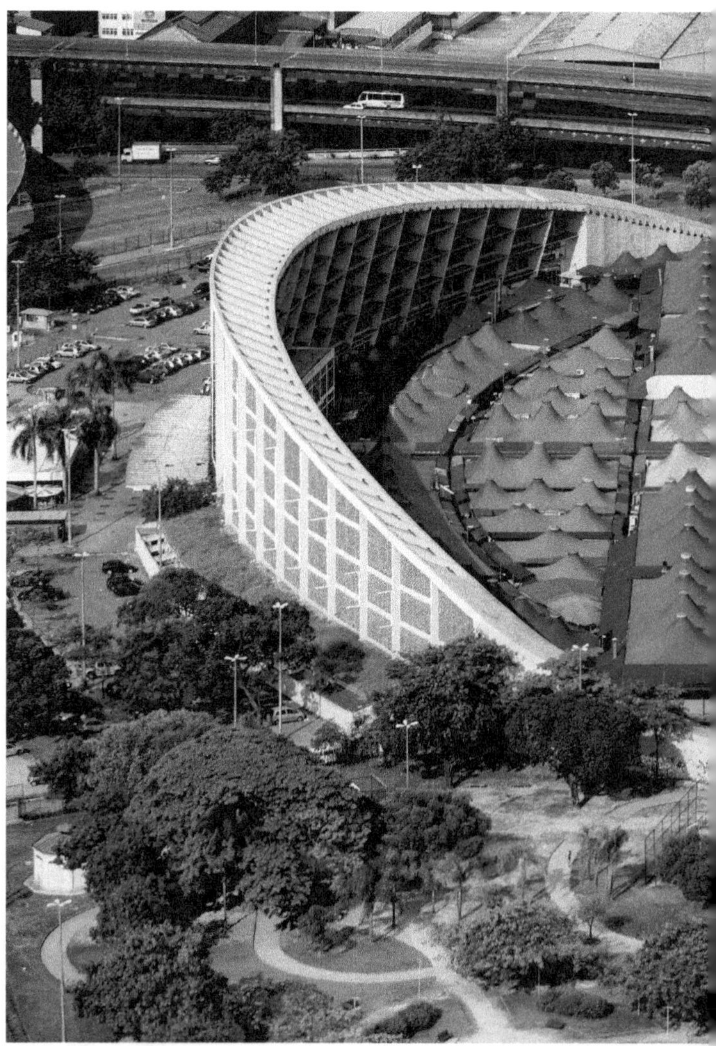

Brazilian Northeastern Fair currently
occupying the São Cristóvão Pavilion,
Rio de Janeiro RJ, 1957-1960. Photo
by Leonardo Finotti

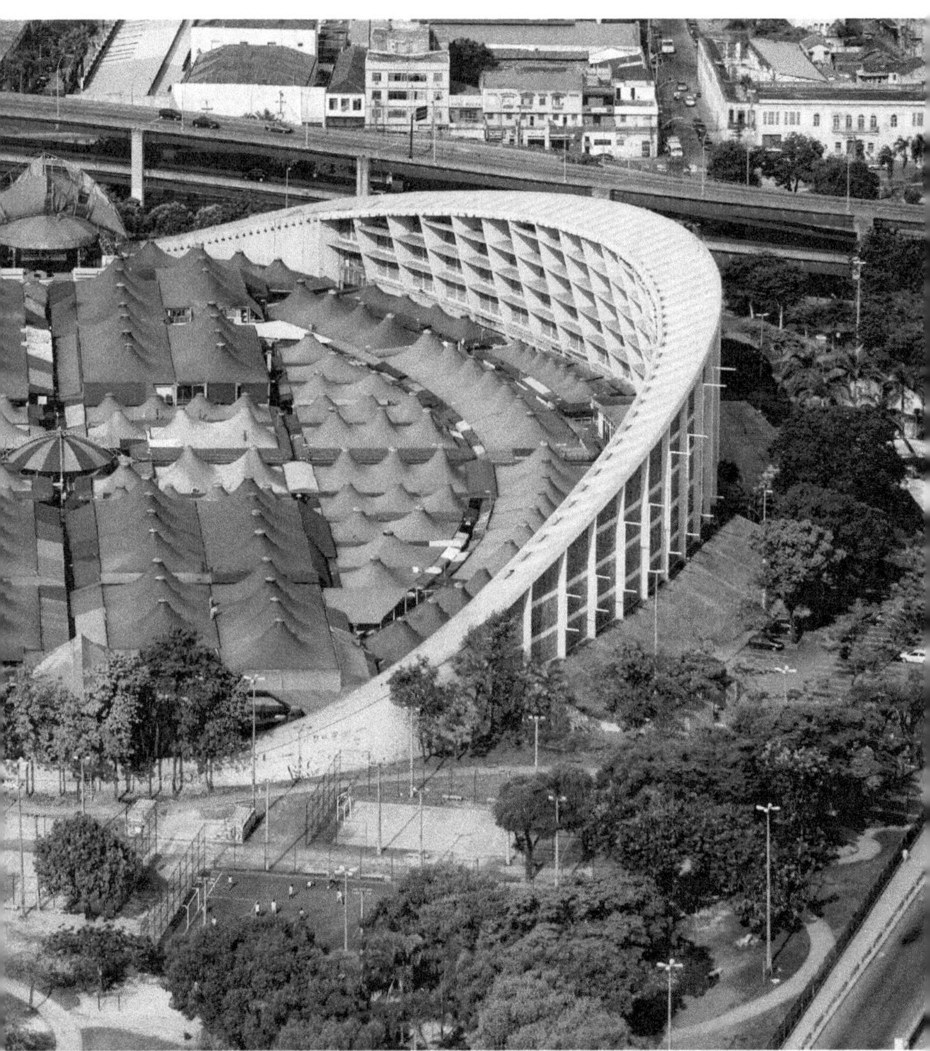

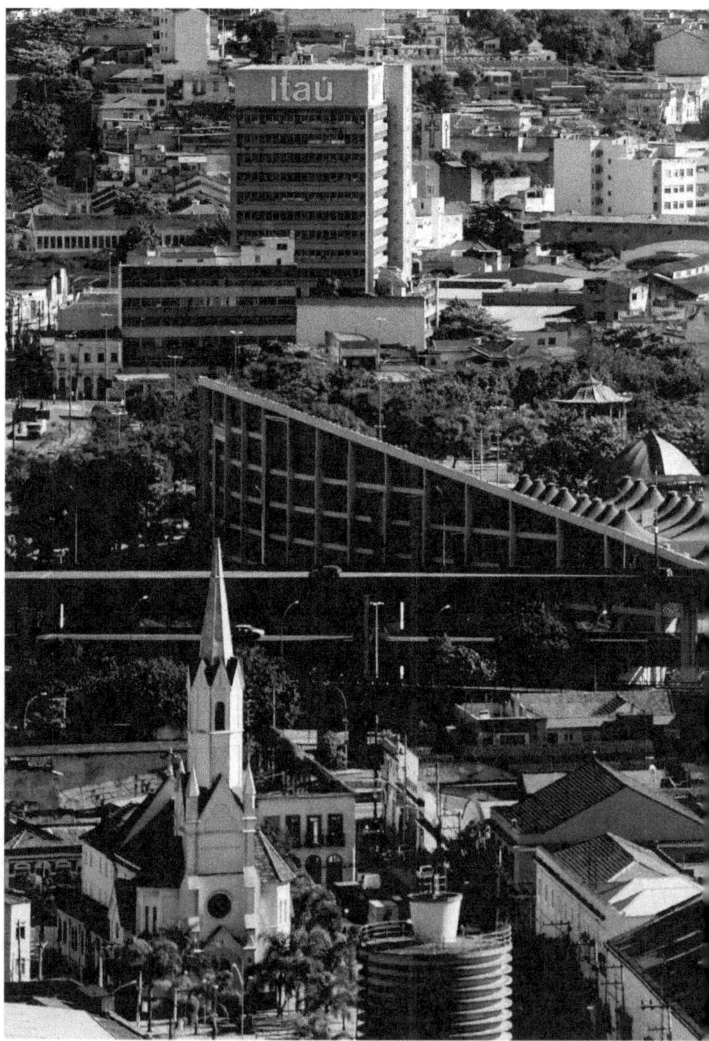

Brazilian Northeastern Fair currently
occupying the São Cristóvão Pavilion,
Rio de Janeiro RJ, 1957-1960. Photo
by Leonardo Finotti

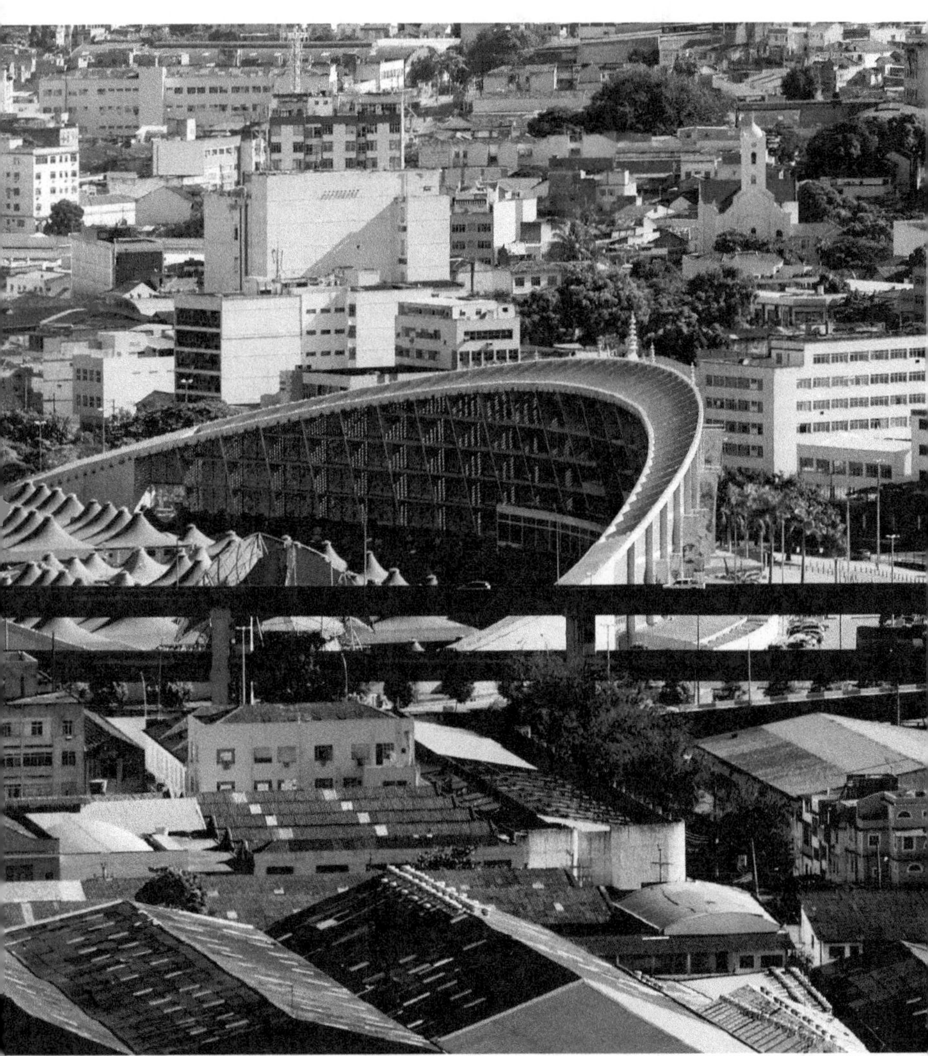

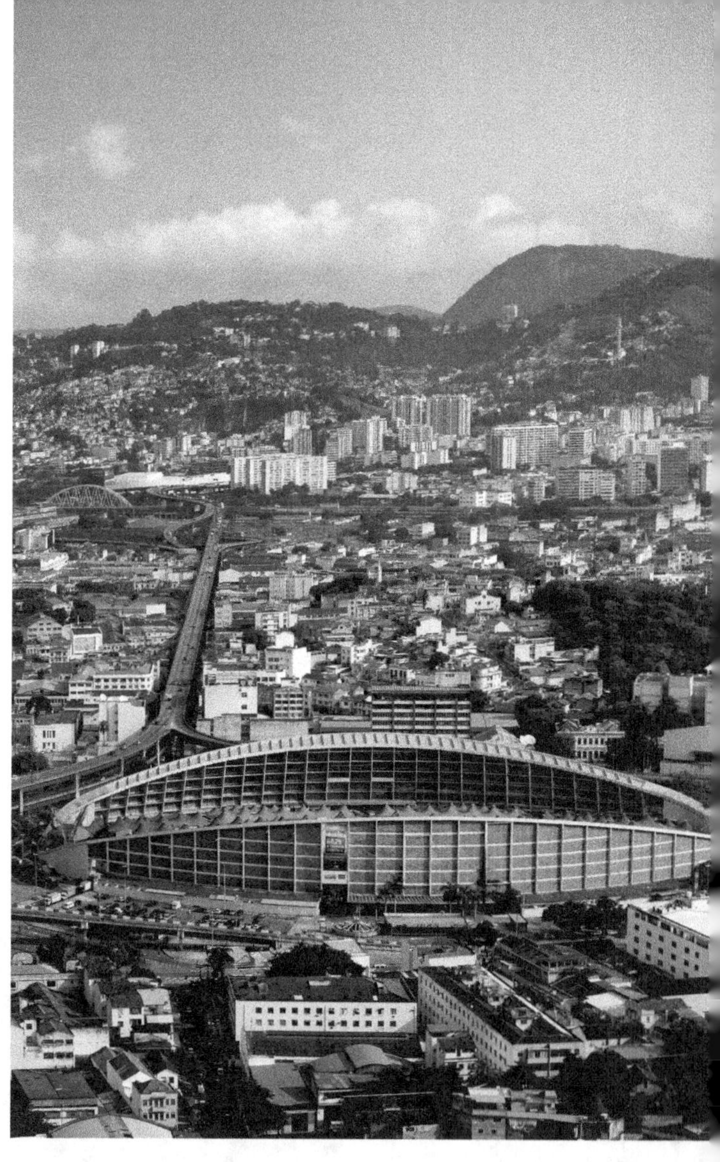

Brazilian Northeastern Fair currently
occupying the São Cristóvão Pavilion,
Rio de Janeiro RJ, 1957-1960. Photo
by Leonardo Finotti

Next page
Brazilian Northeastern Fair currently
occupying the São Cristóvão Pavilion,
Rio de Janeiro RJ, 1957-1960. Photo
by Leonardo Finotti

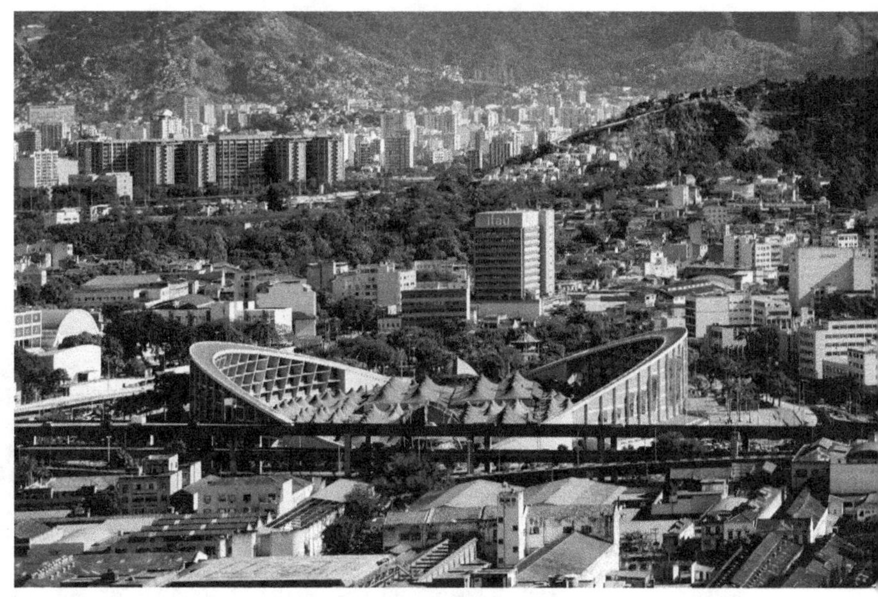

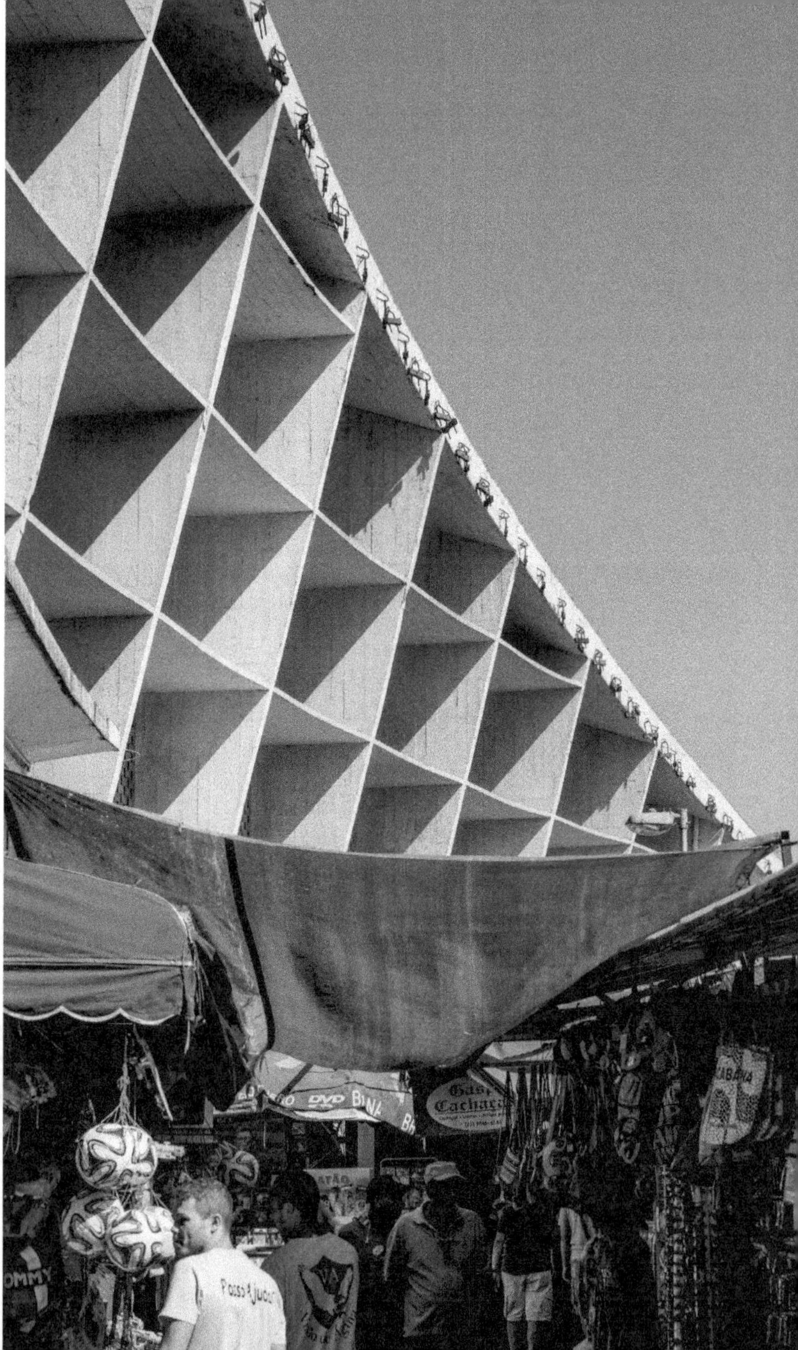

any transverse displacements due to the loss of tension in the system, a situation that, if materialized, would require the re-stretching of the cables:

"4. Conclusions
Examination of table 10 shows that, in three bands, the prevailing tension is superior to the design ($T/Tp >$ 1), however being inferior in the other five; in two of them (CD-84 to 93 and AB-64 to 73), the insufficiency is small (<2%). These results, combined with the observation of the stress evolution in the cables during the period 1960-1973 (table 10 and figure 13), suggest the convenience of proceeding to the re-stretching of the cables in opportune time. This need for re-stretching can be confirmed, or even denied, by analyzing the transverse displacements effectively suffered by the suspension structure over time. In order to record these transverse displacements, it is essential to install, repeatedly advised, the oscillometers provided by the LE-EESC in 1968, and not yet used. It is understood that the projected prestressing essentially aims to contain these transverse displacements within adequate limits, for this reason it is essential to obtain these displacements to judge the sufficiency of the current prestressing.

In addition, it is advisable to lubricate the cables properly in the interest of their good conservation. Note, however, that the LE-EESC cannot guarantee that the cables have not suffered any internal corrosion.

Furthermore, it is essential to provide adequate protection for the cable anchor bolts."[11]

Although without access to the original plans, on the other hand, Ana Luiza Nobre's dissertation makes available in its annexes a certain amount of reproduction of plans and drawings related to the pavilion's structure project. This material added to and compared with other documents, publications of articles in specialized magazines, and articles published in magazines of great circulation, allow the present publication to contribute punctually with new considerations about this emblematic and still little (re)known building of Brazilian modern architecture.

Manchete magazine, in April 1959, with the title "Desenhada contra o céu carioca uma prodigiosa teia de aranha", highlighted the pavilion during its construction. With photos by Vicent Giantar, the initial text exalted the building designed by Sérgio Bernardes, equating the project to a work of art:

> "Rio de Janeiro shall receive a truly monumental work of art and engineering: the International Trade and Industry Exhibition Pavilion. In the design, Sérgio Bernardes has demonstrated how far the audacity of world-famous Brazilian architecture could go, and would go."[12]

In the final part of the brief text, the article clarifies the form and functionality of the design, even by mentioning other places in Rio de Janeiro that would have been previously considered for its construction. The article also states that the inauguration of the building would take place within "a few months", though, as seen, it would only happen in the late 1960, twenty months later:

> "The Pavilion for the International Trade and Industry Exhibition. The Rio de Janeiro project designed by architect Sérgio Bernardes being built in Campo de São Cristóvão is the most audacious engineering work ever undertaken in Brazil and perhaps in the world.
> Among the technical specifications that make it cyclopean and shall certainly make its fame throughout the Earth, the Pavilion for the International Exhibition in Rio de Janeiro has the largest known free span, with

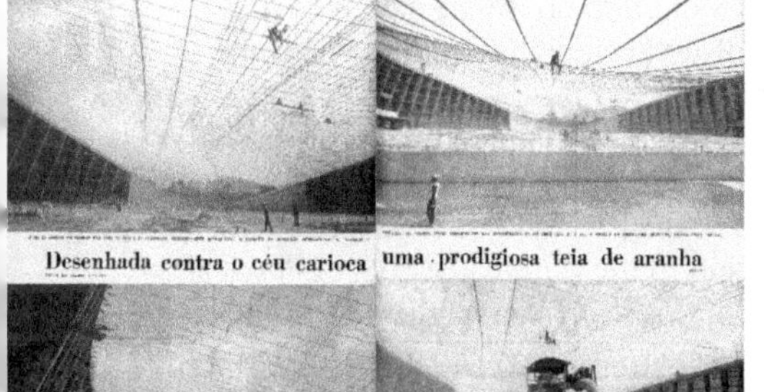

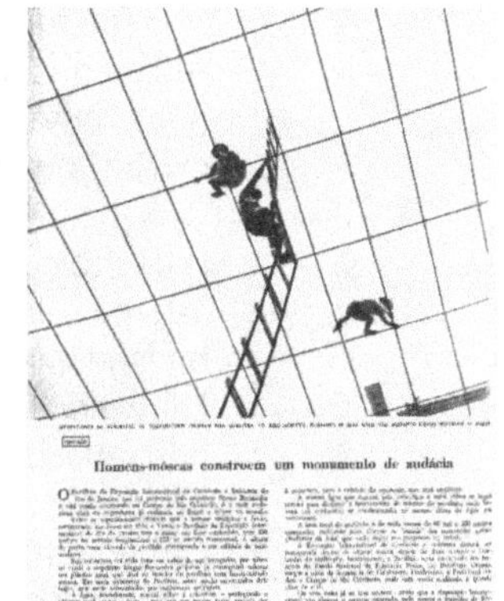

Article "Designed Against the Rio de Janeiro Sky, a Prodigious Spider's Web", published in the magazine *Manchete*, issue 363, on April 17, 1959. Fausto Sombra Collection

250 meters in the longitudinal direction and 175 in the transversal direction. The pavilion's highest point corresponds to an eleven-story building.

Its roof was entirely made of braided steel cables, over which architect Sérgio Bernardes designed (and managed to place) blue plastic, which shall give the pavilion's interior a pleasant light. At each extremity of the Pavilion, two lakes are being built, and shall be fed by artificial waterfalls.

The water shall initially run over the roof – protecting the blue plastic from fire – to fall into the four lakes via waterfalls. Powerful pumps shall then make the water return to the roof to restart the continuous operation.

The same water that shall run through the roof and fall over the lakes is going to reduce the temperature inside the pavilion, where there will be true air conditioning, in the same climate as the moving water.

The total area of the pavilion is no less than 68,550 square meters, enough to house the stands of the numerous countries (including Asia) that will come to exhibit their progress in Brazil.

The International Trade and Industry Exhibition is due to open within a few months after two failed attempts. Initially, the Pavilion was supposed to be built on land belonging to the National School of Physical Education, in Botafogo. Then came the idea of building it in Calabouço. Finally, the city hall granted Campo de São Cristóvão, where the great work of art is being carried out.

One thing is already certain: even if the International Exhibition shall not reach the expected success, at least the work by Sérgio Bernardes shall dignify Brazilian architecture even more.[13]

Even with discrepant information, also found in other documents on this project, the aforementioned publication seems to be of great value as it illustrates the architectural relevance attributed to the name of Sérgio Bernardes in that period, as well as clarifying the pretensions of the event that was idealized, the then international fair or exhibition, which ended up not taking place in the way originally expected, giving way to a show with a more national expression. In fact, the intended large exhibition would only gain international form and character more than a year later, with the opening of the Soviet Exhibition in May 1962.

It is also appropriate to point out that the aforementioned article, when describing the water course over the pavilion's roof "to fall into the four lakes", seems to be wrong, since according to the photos and plans handled, only two lakes are identified, one at each end, as will be discussed below in the brief description of the pavilion. The measurement defined for the building in the text also seems to be wrong, because according to the measurements carried out in the model and other documents handled, it is estimated that the covered exhibition area was approximately 28,000 square meters, very far from the mentioned 68,550 square meters.

It should also be clarified that, kept in the Sérgio Bernardes Fund at the NPD, only three sheets referring to the São Cristóvão Pavilion project were found. The two main ones illustrate the roof plan, sections and facades of the building, with the drawings mostly defined at 1:200 scale. These sheets, dated January 24, 1984, are stamped with the logo of Sérgio Bernardes Associados office and entitled "Structure, Preliminary Project." The third and last sheet refers to the distribution of streets and urban facilities around the Pavilion, which is not illustrated in the drawing however, leaving only a large empty elliptical space which is supposed to be occupied by the pavilion. It is also important to note that the stamp indicates that it is a project prepared by the Secretariat of Public Works of the State of Guanabara and the corresponding Department of Parks, with only the title "Campo de São Cristóvão." The sheet is dated March 5, 1965, and the design was drawn up in a 1:500 scale and authored by Mario de Alexandre Queiroz Ferreira.

The first two mentioned sheets are also illustrated in the book-catalog *Infinito Vão: 90 anos de arquitetura brasileira*, and it is possible to observe in the elevation and section sheet the proposed incorporation of two large central towers, formed by five structural modules and placed in the alignment of the two original marquees giving access to the pavilion. These new elements, which in the end did not get off the ground, possibly conceived by Sérgio Bernardes' office to house a lighting system, as if it were a large stadium, seem to suggest that, at that moment in 1984, the roof of the referred building would no longer be present. The fact lacks other supporting documents, not being duly equated and clarified by the present research and others cited. That is, it is unknown when the roof of the São Cristóvão Pavilion was definitively removed.[14]

The three aforementioned sheets of the São Cristóvão Pavilion, scanned in high resolution, allowed the redesign of the building to be carried out through digital models in three dimensions, an essential material for the elaboration of the physical model later executed, however not incorporating the lighting towers, as they were not original elements of the project.

In this sense and probing into the compositional characteristics of this exemplar, the following chapter is going to present a descriptive architectural synthesis, a work carried out by crossing the different sources and leaving for the subsequent and final chapter the chronological ordering of the facts that involved its constitution, a process carried out with the crossing of the facts present in the dissertation by researcher Ana Luiza Nobre, and the description made by the aforementioned researchers João Perdigão and Euler Corradi.

Pavilion for the International Trade and Industry Fair, São Cristóvão

The Pavilion for the International Trade and Industry Exhibition, located in a large oval-shaped lot of more than 120 thousand square meters in the geographic center of São Cristóvão neighborhood in Rio de Janeiro, a building designed by Sérgio Bernardes' team and again in partnership with engineer Paulo Fragoso, probably built between early 1958 and December 1960, after many setbacks, it has been considered – with its other two ephemeral predecessors, Volta Redonda and the Brussels Pavilion – as a building of great technical expression and refinement. Loaded with experimentation and great inventiveness, despite a certain formal simplicity, it has ended this fruitful and award-winning phase of Sérgio Bernardes' career.

Unlike its peers, however, the Pavilion for the International Trade and Industry Fair, despite partially disfigured by the absence of its hyperbolic paraboloid roof, destroyed by a fire according to Ana Luiza Nobre's dissertation,[15] is the only one that has survived full or almost complete dismantling after the end of the event for which it had been originally designed, gaining great relevance in this sense.

Being by far the largest pavilion of the three, with approximately 30 thousand square meters of total area and 28 thousand square meters of roof – at the time considered the largest covering in the world without intermediate supports –, it is a building characterized by an annular geometry formed by the joining of two pairs of mirrored elliptical segments, totaling 250 meters in length and 165 meters in width. In its central portion, its perimeter is formed by 52 inverted trapezoidal-shaped reinforced concrete pillars, with heights varying between approximately 30 and 13.5 meters, with bases of 1 meter long and inclined tops towards the center of the pavilion, reaching up to 8 meters in its largest portion. These supports are distributed in two sets of 26 pillars, defining fifty porticos that are connected at the ends of the pavilion through thick and continuous walls that vary between 13.5 and 2 meters high, closing and thus determining the exhibition space of the building.

Bracing the trapezoidal pillars, that is, positioned between the aforementioned porticos, there are a total of up to six rows of thin horizontal reinforced concrete slabs positioned at every four meters high, which also accommodate and structure the ceramic blocks laid in a interspersed way and with a certain distance from each other, thus contributing to the characterization of the facades, and allowing both the continuous exchange of air inside and the entry of filtered natural light during the day.

This system is crowned by a beam 90 centimeters high, internally composed of two groups of 48 small transverse

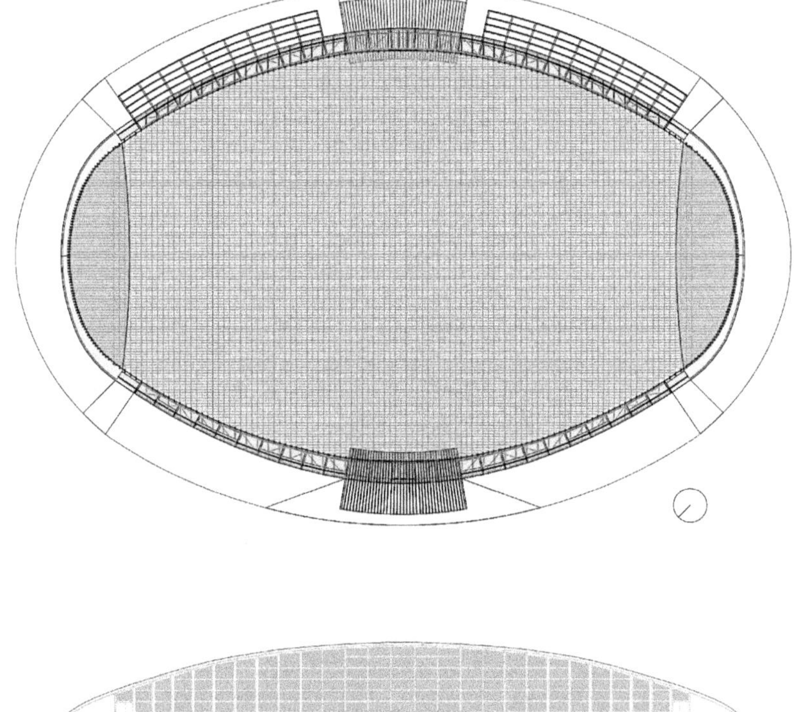

São Cristóvão Pavilion, plan and elevation, Rio de Janeiro RJ, 1957-1960. Redrawing by Fausto Sombra

beams each, referring to the shape of two large parallel grids, with a gentle curvature and concurrent to the length of the roof. The latter, in turn, presented at least two different applications of materials until its destruction and definitive removal, probably in the mid-1980s, but apparently, maintaining the original concept, that is, formed by a set of 106 transverse cables, positioned every two meters along the length of the building, and 148 longitudinal cables arranged at every meter, a conformation that generated inverted parabolas, providing a rich internal spatiality of curvilinear planes, with a height equal to 11 meters in the center of the pavilion and approximately 4.7 meters high at its ends. Over the cables – referring to the second and final version of the roof – there were trapezoidal aluminum tiles, Kingstrand model, 0.8 mm thick, with nine lines of longitudinal gutters, responsible for conducting rainwater to the ends of the

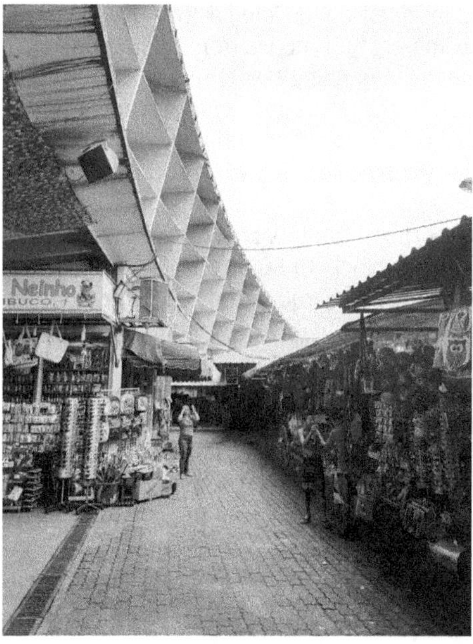

São Cristóvão Pavilion, market inside the building without roof, Rio de Janeiro RJ, 1957-1960. Photo by Fausto Sombra

pavilion, where originally two large water mirrors of approximately 1,250 square meters each were constituted. These,
like the water tank designed in the Brussels Pavilion, in addition to being responsible for receiving rainwater from the
interruption of the roof at these two ends of the building,
were also responsible for supplying the set of pumps that
released water on the roof, thus minimizing the intense
carioca heat inside the building, in addition to generating,
similarly to what was idealized for the Volta Redonda
Pavilion, the phenomenological effect of two waterfalls at
both inner ends of the pavilion.

With a simple and intelligent arrangement, the main
accesses, even today, happen through the longitudinal North
and South facades, marked and protected by two ribbed
marquees of slender reinforced concrete design. These
elements are structured and positioned on the five central
porticos on each of the aforementioned facades, projecting
into the outside and inside of the building as two horizontal
planes, raised approximately four meters from the floor, and
approximately 46 meters long and 22 meters wide. Both
marquees are opposed to the pillars and ceramic blocks of
the facades in their highest section, creating one of the few
interruption points of the long facade with a smooth convex
design.

Whereas the support and sanitary areas of the pavilion
would be restricted to two blocks of 80 meters long each,
positioned on each side of the marquee and South facade,
projecting uniformly out of the building by approximately
10 meters. Both blocks were protected by sloping reinforced
concrete roofs, starting from the pavilion at four meters high
towards the ground, a sensible design that minimized their
presence and interference in the cluster.[16] In addition, the
pavilion would have four more service accesses, positioned
at the meeting between the porticos of the facades and the
thick and continuous walls that occupy the longitudinal
ends of the building, next to the old water mirrors. These

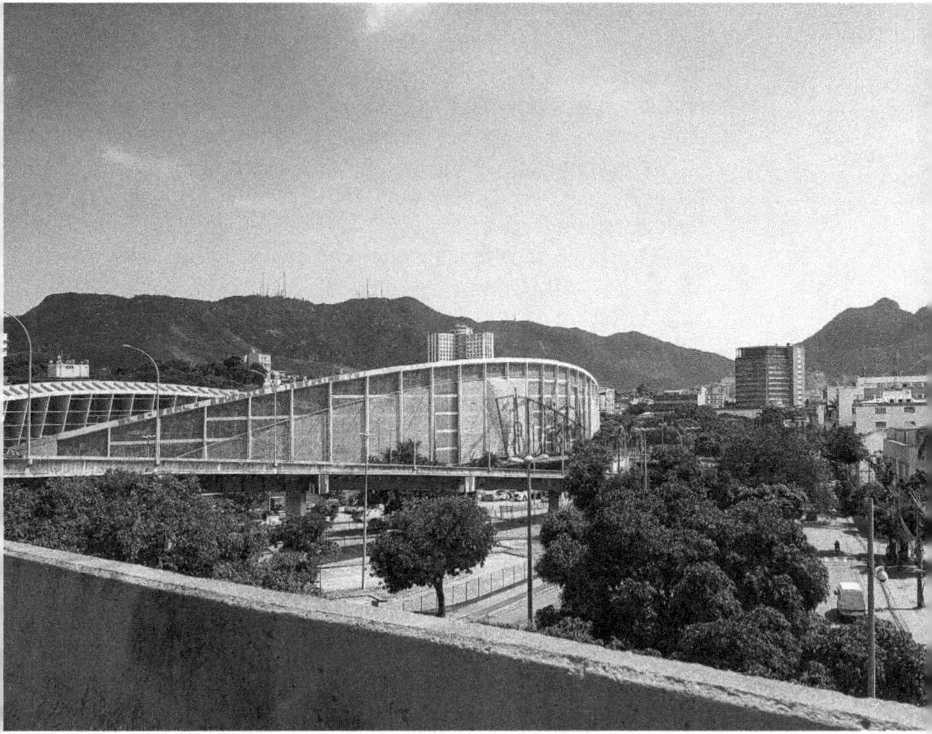

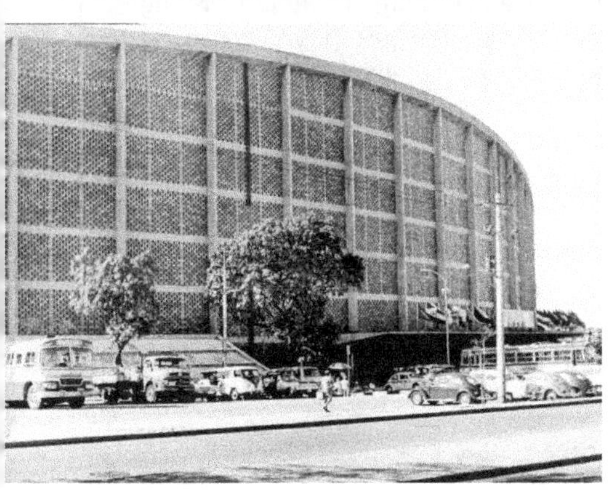

North facade (view from the Red Line) of the International Fair of Industry and Commerce Pavilion, São Cristóvão, Rio de Janeiro RJ. Sérgio Bernardes, 1957-1960. Photo by Fausto Sombra

São Cristóvão Pavilion, photo dated October 16, 1960, Rio de Janeiro RJ. Photo by Tania Bueno. Collection Correio da Manhã / Arquivo Nacional

secondary accesses, still existing today, and used as emergency exits, would be provided with high doors to allow access for heavy equipment to the interior of the pavilion, enabling the assembly of large-scale fairs and exhibition of larger-scale elements.

After numerous setbacks and cancellations of the event originally conceived by its organizers – entrepreneur Joaquim Rolla and then president Juscelino Kubitschek, who until 1960 tried to complete the works on the new capital –, the São Cristóvão Pavilion would receive its major exhibition with a truly international character, only on May 3, 1962 with the opening of the Soviet Exhibition. This great show, which lasted thirty days, ended up being the target of an unsuccessful bomb attempt involving again the ideological dispute between the United States and the former Soviet Union, a moment of great political polarization worldwide, even in Brazil, and only two years later, it would be used as a subterfuge for the military to seize power on May 1, 1964.

The aforementioned pavilion, which since 2003 has housed the Luiz Gonzaga Municipal Center for Northeastern Traditions – despite no longer enjoying its bold roof –, has been a testimony to the efforts made by its idealizers, and the innovative gaze that has characterized Sérgio Bernardes' work. Even today, while suffering from the lack of adequate maintenance by the State and its administrators, revisiting this paradigmatic exemplar is an opportunity to watch over its own existence, and its historical representativeness in the context of the carioca imaginary.

About the Chronology of Facts

A theme not often addressed in the articles and texts referring to the São Cristóvão Pavilion project, Joaquim Rolla from Minas Gerais – a businessman and entrepreneur behind the feasibility of this building in the former Campo de São Cristóvão – is a central figure in the biographical work of

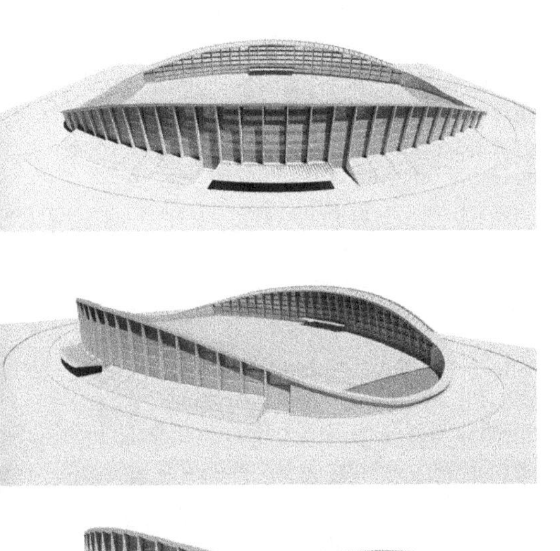

São Cristóvão Pavilion, 3D model perspectives, Rio de Janeiro RJ, 1957-1960. Drawings by Fausto Sombra

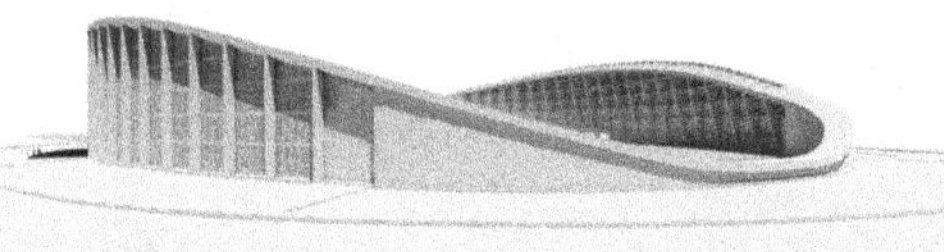

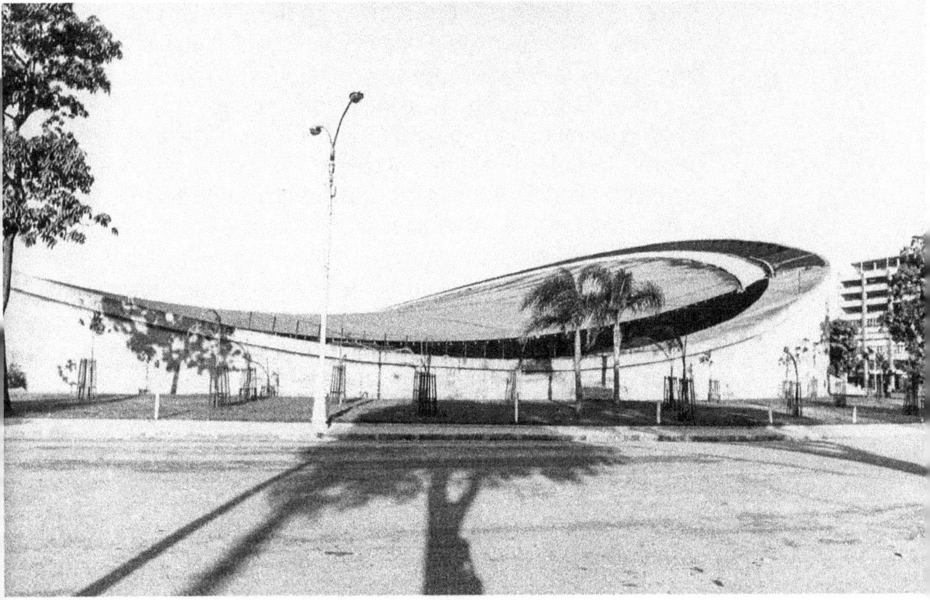

São Cristóvão Pavilion, photograph dated November 5, 1971, Rio de Janeiro RJ. Photo by Adalberto Diniz. Collection Correio da Manhã / Arquivo Nacional

researchers João Perdigão and Euler Corradi. Published in 2012, the book is entitled *O Rei da roleta, a incrível vida de Joaquim Rolla, o homem que inventou o Cassino da Urca e transformou a história do entretenimento no Brasil.*

A drover born in the district of Dom Silvério, a city in the interior of Minas Gerais, his commercial awareness and leadership skills conducted him to lead, at the request of then Governor Antônio Carlos Ribeiro de Andrada, a troop of soldiers in favor of the victorious coup that guaranteed Getúlio Vargas' rise to power in 1930. Two years later, alongside former president Artur Bernardes, Joaquim Rolla supported the paulistas in the Constitutionalist Revolution of 1932, a fact that led to his arrest and almost shooting.[17] After his political involvement in the early 1930s, Rolla focused his efforts on what would become one of the activities that most characterized him, the casinos. Through a group of businessmen, he was responsible for opening several gaming houses in different locations in Belo Horizonte, Pampulha, Niterói, Araxá, Poços de Caldas, Lambari and Petrópolis, relating to figures such as Assis Chateaubriand, Carmen Miranda and Grande Otelo. This phase lasted until 1946, with the prohibition of casinos throughout the country by then president Eurico Gaspar Dutra, and with the closing of its most important casino, the Quitandinha casino-hotel in the city of Petrópolis, Rio de Janeiro.

From that moment on, Joaquim Rolla, already recognized as an important figure linked to entertainment and tourism, began to invest in civil construction, commissioning architect Oscar Niemeyer in 1952 to design a large apartment building to be constructed in the capital of Minas Gerais, the JK Building consisted of two towers with 23 and 36 floors, totaling 1,086 apartments, currently housing five thousand residents.[18]

Five years later in 1957, Joaquim Rolla ventured into civil construction again, commissioning Sérgio Bernardes, at a time not precisely clarified, to design the São Cristóvão

Pavilion. This story, which gained several details in the aforementioned Rolla's biography, began to be reported by Perdigão and Corradi from the chapter "A mão de Deus atrasou (God's Hand Was Delayed)."[19] This title, referring to the various delays related to the completion of the São Cristóvão Pavilion, was an analogy to Sérgio Bernardes' supposed mention, when the carioca architect "questioned about the innovative roof" designed for the Brazil Pavilion in Brussels, replied that it was the "hand of God resting on Brazil".[20] The book, which at that moment justified the choice of Sérgio Bernardes as the appropriate professional for the elaboration of the São Cristóvão project, seems to be wrong in the order of facts, since according to the present research, it was possible to verify that the commission of both projects could have taken place almost simultaneously, that is, it was not the success of the Brazilian pavilion in Brussels – which only opened in May 1958 – that guaranteed the hiring of Bernardes for the São Cristóvão Pavilion. In fact, through an article in newspaper *O Estado de S. Paulo*, already transcribed in the previous chapter, on March 7, 1957, with the title "Participará o Brasil da Feira de Bruxelas (Will Brazil Participate in the Brussels Fair?)" – apparently for the first time – it was informed that architect Sérgio Bernardes had been commissioned the Brazil Pavilion in Brussels. At the end of this brief article, the text highlighted:

> "Rio, 6 ('Estado' – By phone)
> [...] The design of the Brazilian pavilion shall be presented briefly by architect Sérgio Bernardes, author of the national project for Trade and Industry, to be carried out in this Capital, during this year."[21]

Apparently, the article originated in Rio de Janeiro as highlighted above, referred to the São Cristóvão Pavilion project, also known as Trade and Industry. Another point that also seems to contribute to this hypothesis is the generous dimensions of the São Cristóvão Pavilion and the first scheduled opening date, September 7, 1959. This date pointed out by researchers Perdigão and Corradi at the beginning of that chapter,[22] was evidenced by an article published in the same newspaper *O Estado de S. Paulo*, of March 26, 1959 with the title "400 firmas nacionais e 60 do exterior na 1ª Exposição International do Rio (400 National Companies and 60 from Abroad at the 1st International Exhibition in Rio)":

> "The general attention of the trade and industry circles of São Paulo is turned to the 1st International Trade and Industry Exhibition to be inaugurated next September 7, in Campo de São Cristóvão, in Rio de Janeiro."[23]

In this sense, adopting March 1957 as the beginning of the conceiving process for the São Cristóvão Pavilion until September 7, 1959, the day scheduled for its inauguration, it would have taken a little more than two years to construct the building with the largest roof without intermediary support in the world, in addition to having time to promote the various invitations and procedures with interested companies and nations, a relevant factor to ensure the success of the planned event.

Still on the book about Joaquim Rolla, its authors, after mentioning the deadline for opening the pavilion – and including in their report the name of several figures such as engineer José Linhares, a friend of Rolla's, and general Olympio Mourão, appointed by Juscelino Kubitschek to supervise the work in progress[24] –, it was at this point that the reports of the problems involving the first roof idealized for the building began. According to Perdigão and Corradi, the North American roofing system suggested by Bernardes, a type of plastic structured over a cable mesh, was a type of material that required qualified technicians and adequate training, conditions not found here in Brazil at that time. According to the authors, the result after the roof was practically complete, during a storm "the wind had caused the roof to collapse".[25]

A different report was found in the dissertation by researcher Ana Luiza Nobre, because on the panels or "translucent plastic plates responsible for the original sealing system,"[26] the author describes that "shortly after the work was finished, there was a loss of resistance, under the action of the sun,"[27] not mentioning anything about a supposed gale. The author also did not mention anything about the panel system belonging to a North American company, leaving only for the photos, present in the final part of the work, the idea that the plastic tiles would have been supplied by a manufacturer named Goyana.[28]

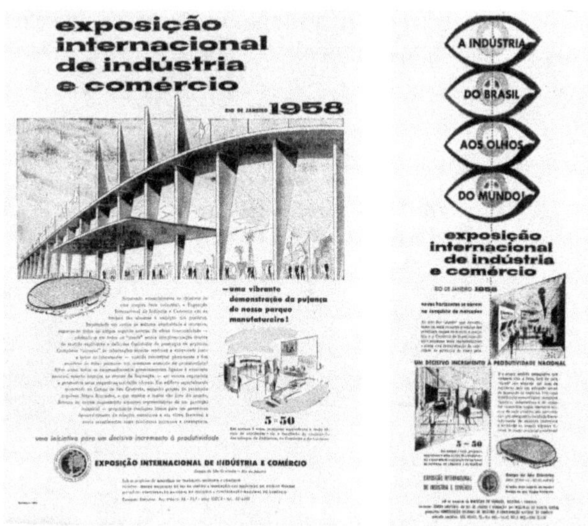

Advertisement for the International Exhibition of Industry and Commerce, published in the *Diário Carioca* newspaper on December 21, 1957. Hemeroteca Digital Brasileira / Fundação Biblioteca Nacional

Advertisement for the International Exhibition of Industry and Commerce, published in the *Correio da Manhã* newspaper in Rio de Janeiro on December 3, 1957. Hemeroteca Digital Brasileira / Fundação Biblioteca Nacional

Perdigão and Corradi told a different, longer and more detailed story, stating that the US system would have been acquired for a second time, but that due to financial problems of the aforementioned company – which was discovered to be "on the verge of bankruptcy"[29] – the order, after long six months, ended up being cancelled. At that moment, the system of the national manufacturer named Goyana was adopted. This, in turn, after carrying out the appropriate tests and after verifying its applicability, would end up delivering a product that did not technically correspond to the contracted one, and for this reason, Rolla "went to justice, returning all the material."[30]

During the process, more precisely after the collapse of the supposed North American roof – a fact that would have generated a strong disagreement between Joaquim and Sérgio Bernardes[31] – both authors revealed that Rolla,

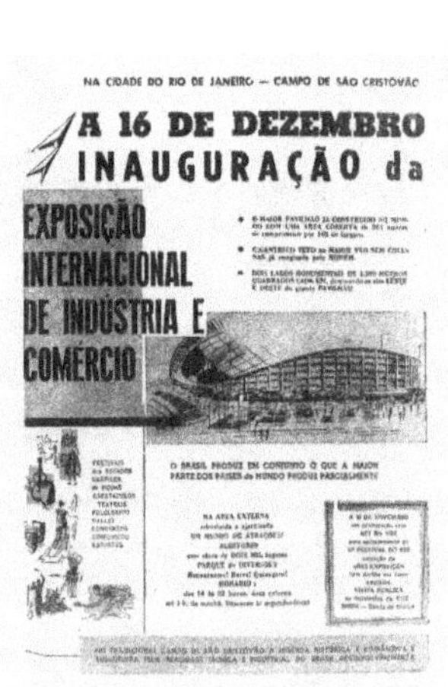

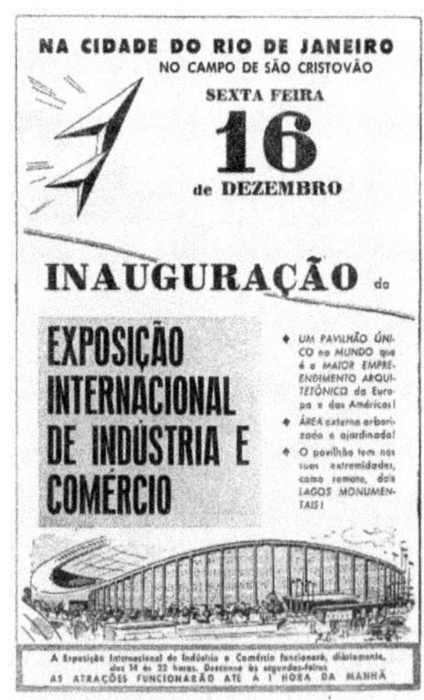

Advertisements for the inauguration of the International Exhibition of Industry and Commerce, published in the *Correio da Manhã* newspaper in Rio de Janeiro on November 15 and 30, 1960. Hemeroteca Digital Brasileira / Fundação Biblioteca Nacional

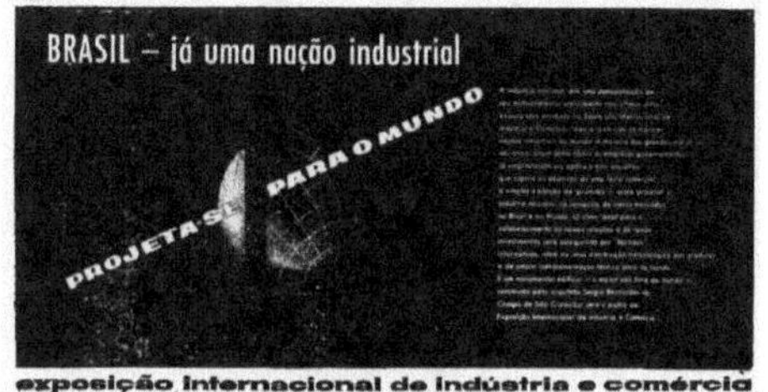

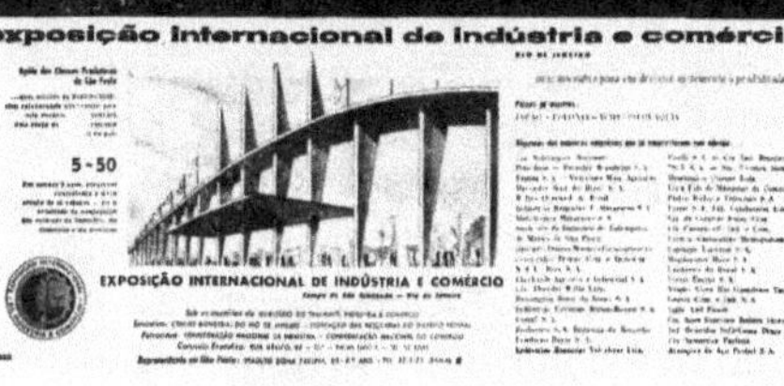

Advertisement for the International Exhibition of Industry and Commerce, published in the São Paulo newspaper *Correio Paulistano* on August 12, 1958. Hemeroteca Digital Brasileira / Fundação Biblioteca Nacional

desperate for the successive delays and cancellations of the event, came to suggest the possibility of covering the São Cristóvão Pavilion with canvas.[32] This statement, like all others reported in the book chapter, does not have sources or dates that allow attesting its veracity. However, a small note in *Manchete* magazine no. 407, dated February 6, 1960, has suggested that Perdigão and Corradi would have been correct on this point:

"Once confirmed that the plastic covering designed by Sérgio Bernardes for the Pavilion of the International Trade and Industry Exhibition in Rio de Janeiro will be impossible to operate, the concessionaire, Mr. Joaquim Rolla, wishing to open the fair until May 1960, is thinking about a temporary cover. If canvas is used, it will last the same two years and cost more than 30 million cruzeiros."[33]

As it seems that more research and documents are needed to prove one or the other version of what the first covering would actually have been, of North American or

Goyana origin, both discourses end up converging on the adoption of the final covering, the aluminum one. This one, as already briefly mentioned in the previous subchapter, defined by trapezoidal aluminum tiles 0.8 mm thick, with a fixation system and gutters developed by Austrian engineer Hans Eger, the same professional responsible for the geodesic design conceived by David Libeskind for Conjunto Nacional in 1955.

The publication of the project in the specialized magazine *Acrópole* – no. 265, of November 1960 –, seems to suggest that a supposed misunderstanding in the relationship between Sérgio Bernardes and Joaquim Rolla – as reported by Perdigão and Corradi in their book – in case it really had happened, at that moment of the work conclusion it might have been an overcome process. In fact, the

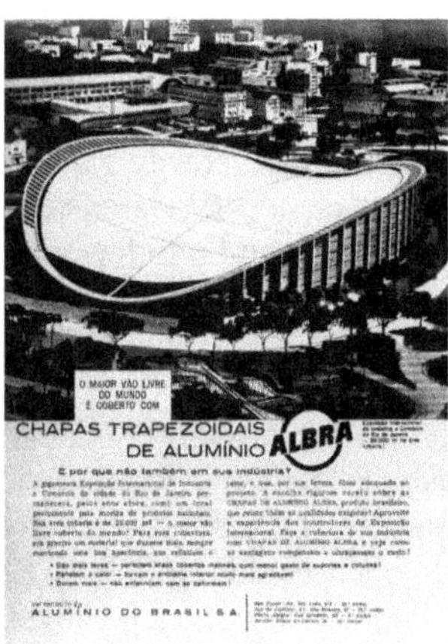

Advertisement for the Albra trapezoidal aluminum sheets used in the São Cristóvão Pavilion published in the Rio de Janeiro magazine *Módulo*, no. 23, in June 1961. Collection Romano Guerra Editora

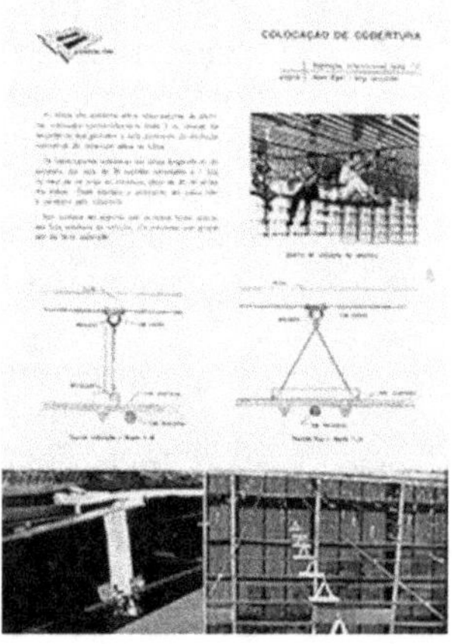

Technical article on the installation of the roof of the São Cristóvão Pavilion, a project by the engineer architect Hans Eger, published in the magazine *Acrópole*, no. 265, in November 1960. Collection FAU Mackenzie Library

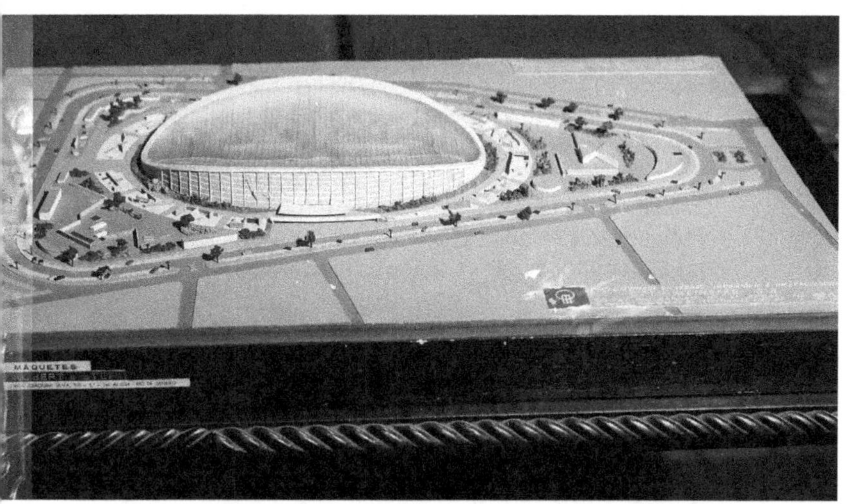

São Cristóvão Pavilion, model, Rio de Janeiro RJ, August 1960. Hemeroteca Digital Brasileira / Fundação Biblioteca Nacional

report described by researcher Ana Luiza Nobre diverges from the idea that Sérgio supposedly left the project after the problems that had occurred with the system originally designed for the pavilion's roof, and consequently, creating discomfort in the relationship with Joaquim Rolla, because the researcher states that "Edger studied, together with Bernardes, a specific solution for the covering of the São Cristóvão Pavilion,"[34] that is, suggesting that the architect would have remained in the process until the end.

It should be noted, however, and without any doubt, that the internal ambience provided by the aluminum tiles was completely different from the filtered light provided by the originally idealized translucent tiles, just as Frei Otto would achieve years later in the Munich Stadium in the early 1970s. Still, even with the withdrawal of numerous foreign companies and nations, the International Trade and Industry

Exhibition or Fair, according to figures that indicate the positive receptivity of the public presented in articles of the time, reached 100 thousand visitors on the first Saturday alone.

After more than a year, the foreign representation expected at the International Trade and Industry Fair happened with great expressiveness through the Soviet Exhibition, an event that had great exposure in the media, both because of curiosity about the aerospace equipment on display and the presence of the former Soviet Union in the country.[35]

An emblematic work that has composed and closed this design triad by architect Sérgio Bernardes, a moment of intense professional production, retains, as already pointed out, a great kinship with the North American pavilion built in Raleigh, North Carolina by architect Matthew Nowicki. However, a closer look at the details of the São Cristóvão

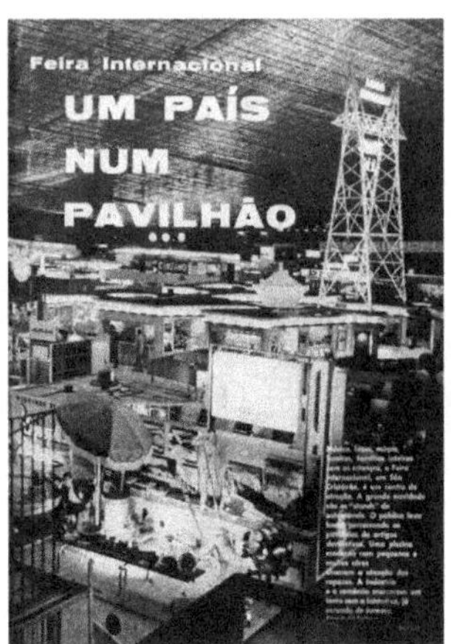

Article "A Country in a Pavilion" on the occasion of the inauguration of the São Cristóvão Pavilion, published in *Manchete* magazine, no. 455, on January 7, 1961. Collection Fausto Sombra

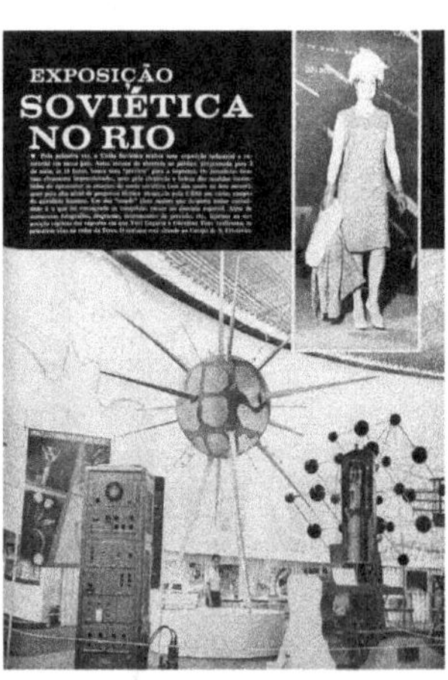

Article "Soviet Exhibition in Rio", about an exhibition at the São Cristóvão Pavilion, published in *Manchete* magazine, no. 525, on May 12, 1962. Collection Fausto Sombra

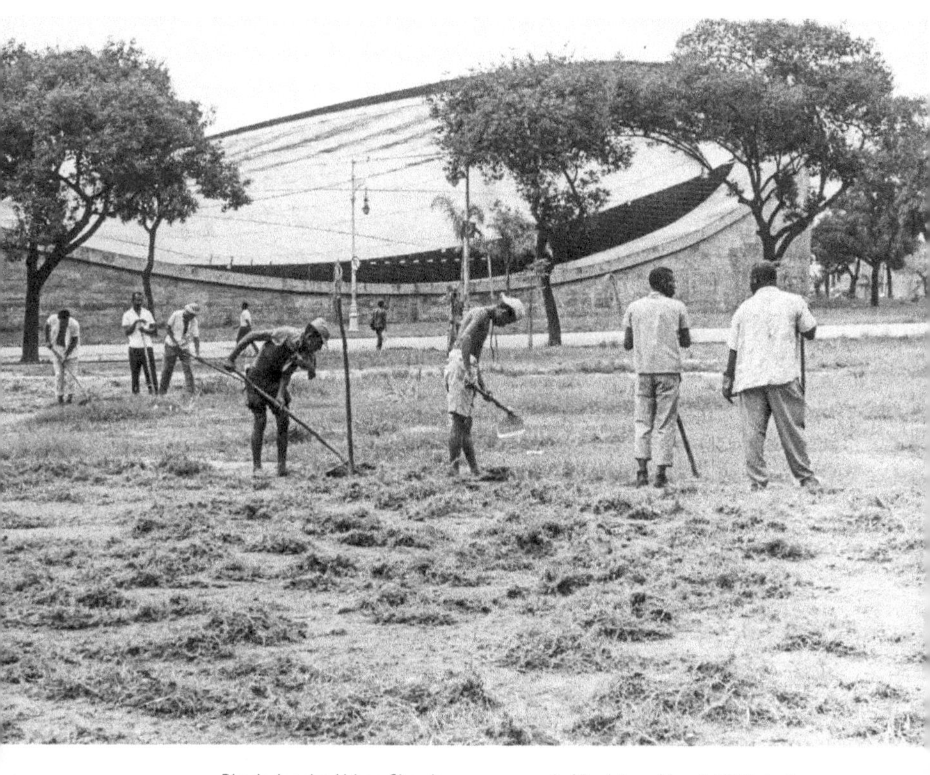

Rio de Janeiro Urban Cleaning workers clear land next to the São Cristóvão Pavilion. Photo published in the Rio de Janeiro newspaper *Correio da Manhã*, on May 4, 1966, in the Gerico column. Collection Correio da Manhã / Arquivo Nacional

Pavilion has suggested a great effort on the part of the carioca architect to adapt forms, techniques, climate and budget to the national reality, always seeking to contextualize and create a close dialogue between the work and the site to which it was conceived.

Notes

1. Sometimes, in articles and texts, the pavilion is portrayed with the name "International Trade and Industry Exhibition Pavilion"; in the present work, the adopted name is "International Trade and Industry Fair Pavilion", title also present in some publications.
2. Anelli, *Architettura contemporanea*, 22-23.
3. Fernando Serapião, "Escola carioca: arquitetura moderna no Rio de Janeiro", 132. In addition to the São Cristóvão Pavilion, the edition features a photo of the Justus Wallerstein Building, from 1953, on page 117.
4. Serapião, Wisnik, eds., *Infinito vão: 90 anos de arquitetura brasileira* (op. cit.), 92-95.
5. Of these images, the most famous is the aerial photo of the recently inaugurated building, taken by photographer Celso Brando, who explained the circumstances of the record in a statement. According to Brando, while carrying out another work, the helicopter passed over the pavilion and he improvised the photo. Great luck, considering the trajectory of this image, also published in this book. Celso Omena Brando, testimony to Fausto Sombra through phone call and electronic message, Rio de Janeiro, Jun. 27, 2019.
6. Nobre, "Fios cortantes", 146-154. It is also worth noting that the same researcher would be responsible, in 2010, for the conception and script of the short length film "Entre Morros e Mares", a documentary that addresses design of infrastructure, equipment and relevant buildings constructed in Rio in the beginning and middle of the last century, such as MAM-RJ, the Avenida Central Building, and the São Cristóvão Pavilion. In a brief statement, engineer Carlos Alberto Fragelli, who worked with engineer Paulo Fragoso, summarizes the structural design of the pavilion's roof. "Entre Morros e Mares", short-length documentary, 24'25", Rio de Janeiro, 2011. Conception and script Ana Luiza Nobre. Direction and photography Tiago Rios. Produced by Leticia Pires. Realized by PUC-Rio and Faperj <https://bit.ly/3xDqrTB>.
7. It is important to affirm the precedence of João Pedro Backhauser's monograph, "A obra de Sérgio Bernardes", by correctly attributing the name Goyana to the tiles that cover the São Cristóvão Pavilion.
8. In addition to the importance of his book for this research, João Perdigão also contributed with a statement. João Perdigão, testimony to Fausto Sombra through electronic message, Belo Horizonte, Apr. 10, 2019.
9. Nobre, "Fios cortantes", 148, footnote 113.

10. Ibid.

11. Dante A. O. Martinelli and Dauro Ribeiro da Silva, "Relatório LE/EXT-70/74 de Verificação da cobertura pênsil do Pavilhão de São Cristóvão", Oct. 1973. São Carlos, Escola de Engenharia de São Carlos, Departamento de Estruturas, Laboratório de Estruturas, Jul. 1974, 24-25.

12. Redação, "Desenhada contra o céu carioca uma prodigiosa teia de aranha", 74-75.

13. Ibid., 76.

14. On a visit to the São Cristóvão Pavilion in February 2020, a local visitor claimed to have seen the moment when the building's roof collapsed during a strong windstorm, a moment of great bang. According to the witness, who worked at the Rio de Janeiro headquarters of SBT, a TV station that still maintains its structure at 40 General José Cristino St in front of the pavilion, he did not remember the exact date, estimating only that the incident took place between the mid-1980s and early 1990s. The witness also stated that at that time the pavilion had been deactivated for some time.

15. Nobre, "Fios cortantes," 149.

16. It is believed that in order to comply with the norms and legislation in force, due to the large number of visitors to the Northeastern Fair, which currently occupies the afore-mentioned pavilion, including an appropriate place for medium-sized shows, the number of toilets and support areas was duplicated through the creation of two new blocks, similar to the originals, but with horizontal roofs, positioned on the opposite side of the pavilion, next to the north marquee.

17. Marco Rodrigo Almeida, "O dono da festa: o rei da roleta narra trajetória do mineiro Joaquim Rolla, que reformulou o Cassino da Urca, no Rio".

18. See Billy Brasil, "Joaquim Rolla" (entry).

19. João Perdigão, Euler Corradi, *O rei da roleta, a incrível história de Joaquim Rolla, o homem que inventou o Cassino da Urca e transformou a história do entretenimento no Brasil*, 392.

20. Ibid., 392.

21. Redação, "Participará o Brasil na Feira internacional de Bruxelas".

22. Perdigão and Corradi, *O rei da roleta , a incrível história de Joaquim Rolla, o homem que inventou o Cassino da Urca e transformou a história do entretenimento no Brasil*, 393.

23. Redação, "400 firmas nacionais e 60 do exterior na 1a Exposição Internacional do Rio", 9. See also Redação, "Exposição internacional de indústria e comércio da cidade do Rio de Janeiro".

24. Perdigão and Corradi, *O rei da roleta, a incrível história de Joaquim Rolla, o homem que inventou o Cassino da Urca e transformou a história do entretenimento no Brasil*, 393.
25. Ibid., 393.
26. Nobre, "Fios cortantes," 147.
27. Ibid.
28. Ibid., 299.
29. Perdigão and Corradi, *O rei da roleta, a incrível história de Joaquim Rolla, o homem que inventou o Cassino da Urca e transformou a história do entretenimento no Brasil*, 394.
30. Ibid., 394.
31. Ibid., 394.
32. Ibid., 394.
33. Redação, "Posto de escuta".
34. Nobre, "Fios cortantes," 148.
35. The main press agencies in Rio de Janeiro and São Paulo reported the event: Redação, "Exposição Soviética no Rio" (*Manchete* magazine); Redação, "Notícias dos Estados: será aberta dia 3 a amostra soviética" (*Folha de S.Paulo*); Redação, "Menezes Cortês atribui objetivos políticos à exposição soviética" (*O Estado de S. Paulo*); Redação, "Inaugurada ontem a exposição Russa no Rio; Lacerda falou" (*O Estado de S. Paulo*); Redação, "Exposição soviética vai mostrar trajes espaciais de Yuri Gagárin e Titov" (*Jornal do Brasil*).

Epilogue
Oscillation between Fame and Ostracism

Throughout this book, we sought to bring to light a small part of the vast work carried out by the carioca architect Sérgio Wladimir Bernardes.

A figure of great charisma for those who knew him and had the opportunity to coexist with him, he dedicated almost seven decades of his life to practice of architecture, urbanism, design, teaching, politics and many other actions related to knowledge and cultural milieu.

A professional who showed skills from a very young age, such as good treatment of wood, and owner of keen creativity and sensitivity, restless, he started working as a teenager, in internship with his uncle, the already renowned architect Paulo de Camargo e Almeida, a fact proven through *Manchete* magazine, relevant information unknown to most researchers so far.

In fact, the recent and complete digitization of the important weekly magazine collection – *Manchete* had great circulation in the country for many years, more precisely between 1952 and 2007 – and its availability through Hemeroteca Digital, a vehicle linked to National Digital Library, has provided access to information and actions by the carioca architect that were previously little – or even entirely – unknown, corroborating and reinforcing several reports – including a good number observed in the documentary *Bernardes*, from 2014 –, regarding the high degree of prestige that Sérgio Bernardes enjoyed, particularly during the 1950s and 1970s.

Throughout the present work, several reports from the aforementioned weekly magazine made it possible to illustrate adequately the different themes related to the actions of this professional, whose real work extension is still unknown to historiography, even to the researchers who have proposed to study his extensive design and theoretical production.

Through its initial pages and based on recognized bibli- ography about the conformation of the Brazilian modern movement, we have tried to ratify Sérgio Bernardes' participation in this milieu, whose guiding thought certainly came from the concepts and values developed by architect Lúcio Costa in the early 1930s. His ideals, developed in close dialogue with the built environment, topography, nature and the rescue of traditional elements that compose and in part define Brazilian colonial architecture, were brilliantly assimilated by Bernardes throughout the first years of his professional performance, being constantly improved and developed through the countless diversity of programs and projects, in which the carioca architect has participated in partnership with numerous and outstanding collaborators.

Within this universe of research, the chief archivist of Research and Documentation Nucleus – NPD, at FAU UFRJ, João Claudio Parucher da Silva, who passed away in 2021 and is here honored, presented, in the second half of 2019, supporting data that illustrate the great demand on the part of researchers on information, documents and projects conceived by architect Sérgio Bernardes, numbers that confirm the growing effort of countless professionals – even if reduced in terms of absolute numbers – committed to the dissemination and sharing of ideas and postulates by this professional.

In this sense, the role of NPD could be considered of paramount importance, because thanks to this collection, Sérgio Bernardes' work, little by little, has been gaining its due space in the main research nuclei in the country, becoming more and more, and gradually, the subject of articles in conferences and encounters of architecture and urbanism.

Of similar importance are the actions of Projeto Memória, maintained by Bernardes Arquitetura office – through Sérgio's grandson, architect Thiago Bernardes and his partners – with Kykah Bernardes, the last wife as one of the holders of the architect's estate, and its main representative. Its constant and growing efforts date back to the mid-1990s, when – with Sérgio Bernardes still alive, it had dedicated to the search for an adequate institution that could accommodate the infinity of documents, plans, reports, photos and other materials produced by the architect and his numerous collaborators throughout the years, also through the Laboratory of Conceptual Investigations – LIC, a non-profit entity inserted within the structure of the SBA office.

This relevant theme, undoubtedly worthy of further analysis, has been related in the present work only within a wide range of actions by architect Sérgio Bernardes, which are grouped in the final subchapter of Chapter 1 in order to give visibility to the reader about its extent. Defined as "The universe of Sérgio Bernardes: an overflight on his life and work" this more horizontal gaze – which can also be seen in Alexandre Bahia Vanderlei's dissertation – has allowed us to locate and position the constitution of the three studied pavilions within the whole of his work, as well as relating design elements and actions among the pavilions and the other works by the architect, building a broader and more adequate understanding base to advance the reader to the heart of the research: Volta Redonda Pavilion, 1954-1955; Brazil Pavilion in Brussels, 1957-1958; and São Cristóvão Pavilion, 1957-1960.

A design triad already briefly analyzed by French pale-ontologist Yves Bruand in his outstanding book *Arquitetura contemporânea no Brasil*, they are the objects that form the main question to be answered by the present work – Have the three pavilions by Sérgio Bernardes, conceived and built between 1954 and 1960, presented the minimum attributes needed to be defined as avant-garde exemplars of Brazilian modern architecture?

The vast documentation – largely primary – used during the analyzes and interpretations present in the three chapters corresponding to each of the distinct pavilions are intended to ratify the relevance of each of the referred exemplars in the Brazilian and even international modern architectural milieu, a process supported by the understanding of the architectural and/or artistic artifact capable of condensing and explaining relations of program, composition, technique, materiality, environment, etc., as well as the materialization of its own creative impetus, linked to aspects of the collective yearning in a given period.

Having established the objects, procedures and methods of study – the latter based on recognized scholars in architectural and cultural milieu – we have carried out a careful and detailed analysis of the set of design sheets and other documents found mainly in NPD, in Rio, but also in many other collections and institutions, allowing the creation of a framework of data and information that were gradually shared and presented to the reader in detail.

During this process, one can clearly see a certain detachment by Sérgio Bernardes from part of the ideals and defining characteristics of the carioca school, a fact already pointed out by the late researcher Roberto Segre in his article "Sérgio Bernardes (1919-2002). Entre o regionalism e o high tech", published in 2002. At this point, it is worth recollecting, the author has positioned Sérgio alongside masters Lúcio Costa and Oscar Niemeyer, however, stating that Sérgio would be the only one to point out new paths for a new crop of talented Brazilian architects.

Among the professionals who recognize interesting concepts and attributes in the works by Sérgio Bernardes, having them as inspiration for their work, is Paulo Mendes da Rocha, who, as reported, declared that he was inspired by the award-winning Brazil Pavilion in Brussels to design his also award-winning project for the Atlético Paulistano Club Gymnasium.

Originating from his experience at the Volta Redonda Pavilion, with its catenary roof conceived by the five cables that cut the Sapateiro stream in the heart of Ibirapuera Park, this small, ephemeral and paradigmatic bridge-building headed a list of Sérgio Bernardes' designs to adopt the steel cable as a key element, this topic was opportunely approached by Ana Luiza Nobre in her 2008 PhD dissertation, in which the carioca researcher has listed professionals – mostly foreigners – already familiarized with the applicability of this material to construction.

In this aspect, with no doubt, Sérgio Bernardes was part of a select group of Brazilian architects and professionals who took the risk of adopting steel as a structuring element for some of their projects, starting with his still timid – when compared to Volta Redonda Pavilion –, but rather essential experience in the residence of Lota de Macedo Soares, when he made use of lattice beams executed in-situ, with the use of rebars for structuring the large and slightly inclined covering panels.

It is interesting to note in this process that even while conceiving the three pavilions in a short space of time, in an interval of five years, Sérgio Bernardes had opted for considerably different architectural concepts and technical solutions in each of the pavilions. In fact, it is possible to state that the system developed for each of the distinct roofs is unique and designed precisely to serve completely different clients, uses and locations, that is, a small bridge-building; a medium-sized temporary building located on a considerable slope; and a building of monumental dimensions, of permanent character, to be built on a site with practically flat topography. This simple analysis has reinforced the idea that Sérgio Bernardes was constantly willing to review and improve the technical solutions designed for his projects, a behavior that has led him to conceive, on the proposal to rebuild the Volta Redonda Pavilion in the late 1990s, a considerably different building when compared to the original.

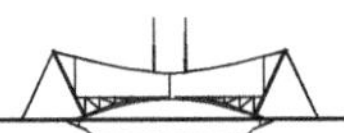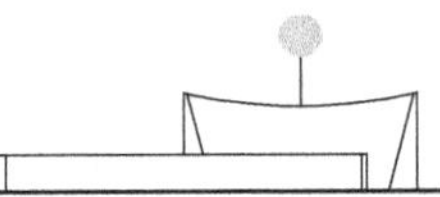

Scale comparison between the Volta Redonda Pavilion, the Brazil Pavilion in Brussels, and the São Cristóvão Pavilion, the three pavilions by Sérgio Bernardes. Drawing by Fausto Sombra

A theme deserving greater and deeper research, both for its connection with part of the conformation of the young urban and industrial Brazilian society, and for its relevance in the national and international architectural milieu, the three pavilions portrayed here, conceived and built together with a clear narrative by their idealizer – Sérgio Bernardes and his recognized team of collaborators – are objects that hold, according to this understanding, structuring elements common to the architect's work, namely: evolution and gradual improvement of technique, growth of complexity through experimentation, as well as a great leap in the adopted design scales. These qualities, synthesized throughout this text, also recognizable in the subsequent development of the architect's work from the 1960s onwards, mainly with the foundation of LIC, when his office began to work with considerably larger design scales and gradually more complex, led Sérgio Bernardes to develop, according to many researchers and critics, projects that were difficult to implement or even utopian ones. However, the outstanding carioca architect – a visionary for many others – was not carried away by such questions, a position that probably allowed him to conceive the inventive and award-winning buildings throughout his extensive career.

In this sense, and concluding these considerations, we have transcribed below an excerpt from the synthesis

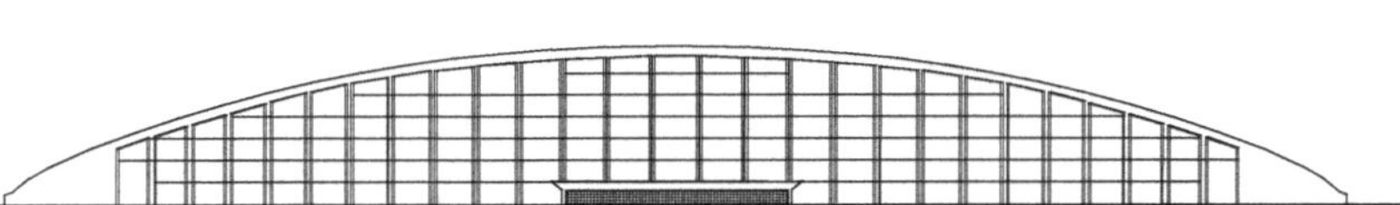

defined by Spanish architect Felix Candela, not about Sérgio Bernardes, but about his contemporary architect Frei Otto, because the words that so well defined the work of the award-winning German architect, recognized for the beautiful and diverse tensile roof structures that he developed, such as the one for the Olympic Stadium in Munich, from 1972, seem to perfectly suit the work developed by Sérgio Bernardes in the beautifully design exemplars that are portrayed here:

"In Frei Otto [or Sérgio Bernardes] several exceptional qualities are happily gathered, among them, it is worth mentioning that of being an indefatigable worker, which allows him to face all the difficulties that arise. He spares no effort to delve into the problems and acquire the necessary experience in fields that have not yet been tried and for which there is no precedent.

It would be interesting to know whether self-control, which reflects the continuous increase in dimensions, as well as the difficulties of the works according to their chronological order, is a deliberate objective or an unforeseen consequence caused by circumstantial conditions. Personally, I lean towards the former, since every intelligent and sensible person works cautiously, starting the experiments with small works, building on a

1:1 scale, and increasing the scale of the works, step by step, according to the knowledge he acquires."[1]

As defended in the Introduction to this work: "there is a long path to be followed before Sérgio Bernardes is able to regain his position alongside Lúcio Costa and Oscar Niemeyer in the history of Brazilian modern architecture. Perhaps a complete recovery is historically unfeasible, but little by little, gradually, the architect shall occupy a position more consistent with his trajectory in the constellation of great Brazilian architects.

Note

1.   Felix Candela, Prólogo, s/p.

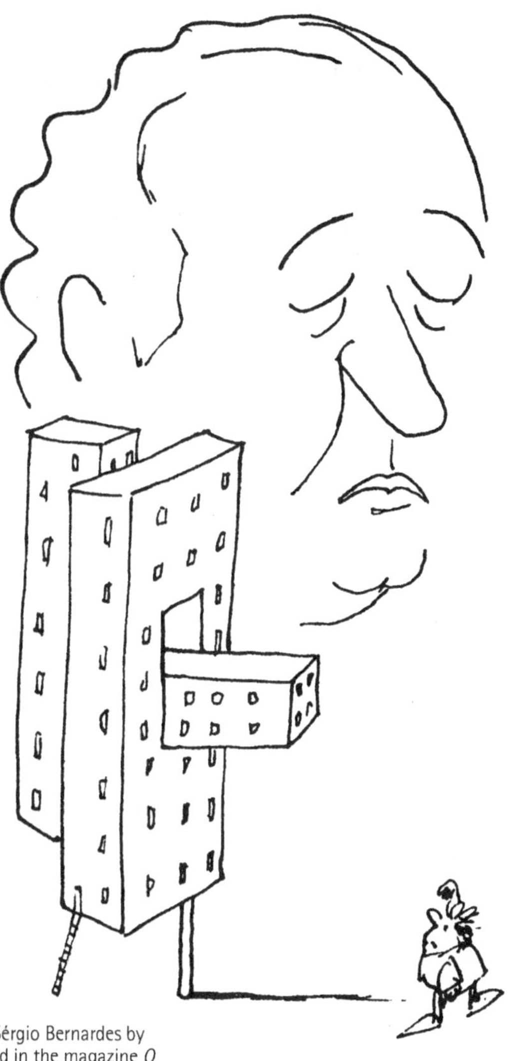

Caricature of Sérgio Bernardes by
APPE, published in the magazine *O
Cruzeiro*, issue 53, Rio de Janeiro,
September 30, 1967. Collection of
Fausto Sombra

My Friend Sérgio Bernardes

Gustavo Penna

It is typical of recent graduates wanting to get close to their idols.

I, at the age of 23, sought the great Sérgio Bernardes. I had already known almost all the work of this brilliant visionary. I had read about his always-grandiose ideas, his dreams, his projects. I insisted on following everything he created.

I found a way through a mutual friend, Marco Aurélio Moreira Leite, who was a typical carioca, ingenious and lots of fun. Our meeting was out there in Barra da Tijuca, on Sernambetiba Avenue, at the Laboratory of Conceptual Investigations, the LIC, created by him in the 1970's. The curious and solitary building on that wonderful beach was a three-story house with the aura of a spaceship. I arrived at the entrance and when asking for Sérgio, the secretary pointed out to me: "he is in the sea!".

When we arrived at the beach, still on the sand, I walked towards that giant sea, while Sérgio came out of the water accompanied by a friend. When he saw us, he immediately burst out laughing, adding the phrase: "We are here pushing through *The Third Wave*". I kept imagining that right there, considering Alvin Toffler, how many thousands of waves Sérgio had been able to push through.

When we entered his room, he sat at this big worktable where the world seemed small. We talked about an infinitude of subjects, as if we had always been friends. From that space, it was possible to look at the sea all around, and see the team working inside the office on drawings, models and prototypes. All breathing possibility, freedom to dream. That was another invention by Sérgio, in his utopia of helping the world.

He dealt with issues of permafrost, living in the ice of the Arctic and Antarctic regions, and thought about life in the Amazon, constructions using air convection and trees for environmental comfort. He imagined distributing housing in Rio de Janeiro, at quota 100, and articulating, in a single way, all the neighborhoods with the labor market. All without hurting forests and the harmony of nature. It was a powerhouse of inventions.

And because of all this connection with his ideas, we invited him to Belo Horizonte several times. He was always the best reason to have a party. In one of them, so as not to leave him at the hotel, I suggested: "come sleep with us at home!". And so, my daughter Laura, still a little girl at the time, gave in her little bed to the great Sérgio Bernardes. Perhaps today she is an architect due to this dreamlike influence of Sérgio's presence in her childhood. We often used to meet, also with Kykah, at our farm in Lagoa Santa, where he even missed his return flight after being distracted by our conversations.

Sérgio Bernardes has gone beyond the issue of architectural space to be a great inventor of everything, especially human relationships. He used to know, like no one else, how to treat simple people, grown-ups, students, young people. He had a desire to help everyone, to incorporate; he remembered the names, and remembered the stories of those who crossed his life. And he was, for me, this colloquial thinker, whose greatest merit was to speak of extremely profound things with very simple and captivating language.

The last time I saw Sérgio was at a lecture at PUC. Crowded auditorium, more than seven hundred people. He spoke for two hours with a single slide on the screen, the image of the globe: everyone cried. It was an emotional encounter, and is certainly part of the memory of those who lived the experience.

Now, every time I see the image of the Earth, I remember Sérgio Bernardes. He was a man who loved the planet, and demonstrated the world's dimension in his ideas and actions. Always inventing, from a chair, a glass, a spatial structure, ecstatic with the reflection of the moon on the wet rock, the wind passing through the house, the idea of the non-presence of architecture diluted in space.

I miss you, bold thinker, pilot and designer, discoverer of wonders.

A kiss from your friend,
Gustavo Penna

Bibliography

Books, Articles and Academic Papers

Almeida, Marcelo Jabor de Oliveira. "Vestígios de um futuro (ou o Hotel Tropical de Manaus de Sérgio Bernardes sob a óptica do redesenho)". Final graduation Project, advised by Adriana Caúla, Niterói, UFF, 2020.

Almeida, Marco Rodrigo. "O dono da festa: o rei da roleta narra trajetória do mineiro Joaquim Rolla, que reformulou o Cassino da Urca, no Rio". *Folha de S. Paulo*, São Paulo, Feb. 20, 2012 <https://bit.ly/3rBVhsi>.

Almeida, Moracy Amaral e. "Pilon, Heep, Korngold e Palanti: edifício de escritórios (1930-1960)". Masters thesis, advised by Helena Aparecida Ayoub Silva, São Paulo, FAU USP, 2015 <https://bityli.com/dAgtt>.

Amaral, Aracy. *Artes plásticas na Semana de 1922*. São Paulo: Editora 34, 1998.

Amarante, Leonor. *As Bienais de São Paulo: 1951-1987*. São Paulo: Projeto, 1989.

Amora, Ana Albano, Renato da Gama-Rosa Costa, and Thaysa Malaquias. "Sanatório de Curicica. Em perigo a obra exemplar do arquiteto Sérgio Bernardes". *Minha Cidade*, year 15, no. 173.02, São Paulo, Vitruvius, Dec. 2014 <https://bit.ly/38MUYUy>.

Amora, Ana. "Apresentação: muito além da arquitetura e urbanismo". *Cadernos Proarq*, no. 32, Rio de Janeiro, FAU UFRJ, Jul. 2019: XIV-XVI <https://bit.ly/34IokBo>.

Andrade, Mário de. "Brazil Builds". *Folha da Manhã*, São Paulo, Mar. 23, 1944: 7 <https://bit.ly/34OMyXb>.

Anelli, Renato. *Architettura contemporanea: Brasile*. Milão: Motta Architettura, 2008.

Araújo, Fábio Salgado. "A Companhia Siderúrgica Nacional e as políticas sociais de lazer para os trabalhadores: os clubes socio-rrecreativos". *Licere*, vol. 18, no. 3, Belo Horizonte, Sept. 2015 <https://bit.ly/3uye1Ll>.

Arruda, Maria Arminda do Nascimento. *Metrópole e cultura: São Paulo no meio século XX*. São Paulo: Edusp, 2015.

Arruda, Maria Arminda do Nascimento. "Metrópole e cultura: São Paulo no meio século XX". Full professorship diss., São Paulo, FFLCH USP, 2001.

Artigas, João Batista Vilanova. "A Bienal é contra os artistas brasileiros". *Fundamentos*, no. 23, São Paulo, Dec.1951: 10 <https://bit.ly/3OedBRP>.

Backhauser, João Pedro. "A obra de Sérgio Bernardes". Specialization monography, Recife, Department of Architecture at UFPE, 1997.

Backhauser, João Pedro. "Estruturas que se lançam no espaço". In *Sérgio Bernardes*, edited by Kykah Bernardes and Lauro Cavalcanti. Rio de Janeiro: Artviva, 2010, 64-73.

Backhauser, João Pedro. "Sérgio Bernardes: sob o signo da aventura e do humanismo". *Projeto Design*, no. 270, São Paulo, Aug. 2002: 24-26.

Barbosa, Marcelo Consiglio. "Adolph Franz Heep: um arquiteto moderno". PhD diss., advised by Abilio Guerra, São Paulo, FAU Mackenzie, 2012.

Barone, Ana Cláudia Castilho. *Ibirapuera: parque metropolitano (1926-1954)*. São Paulo: Intermeios/Fapesp, 2018.

Barone, Ana Cláudia Castilho. "Ibirapuera: parque metropolitano (1926-1954)". PhD dissertation advised by Maria Ruth Amaral de Sampaio, São Paulo, FAU USP, 2007 <https://bityli.com/AXMYP>.

Bastos, Maria Alice Junqueira, and Ruth Verde Zein. *Brasil: arquiteturas após 1950*. São Paulo: Perspectiva, 2010.

Berg, Marly, Lúcia Vasconcelos and Celso Arnaldo Araújo. "O que eles sonharam para os filhos. Para a escolha de uma profissão, a influência dos pais pode não ser um fator positivo". *Manchete*, no. 1583, Rio de Janeiro, Aug. 21, 1982: 50-53 <https://bit.ly/38ZT4QH>.

Bergdoll, Berry, Carlos Eduardo Comas, José Francisco Liernur, and Patricio del Real. *Latin American in Construction: 1955-1980*. Nova York: MoMA, 2015.

Bernardes, Kykah, and Lauro Cavalcanti, eds., *Sérgio Bernardes*. Rio de Janeiro: Artviva, 2010.

Bernardes, Kykah. "Memória da arquitetura moderna brasileira: sobre a conservação dos acervos de Sérgio Bernardes e outros arquitetos cariocas". *Drops*, year 19, no. 132.02, São Paulo, Vitruvius, Sep. 2018 <https://bit.ly/3LwOg63>.

Bernardes, Sérgio. *Cidade: a sobrevivência do poder*. Rio de Janeiro: Guavira, 1975.

Bernardes, Sérgio. "Sala Especial Sérgio Bernardes". *Acrópole*, no. 301, Dec. 1963: 1.

Bernardes, Sérgio. "Vanguarda: perspectiva e busca". *Revista Cultura*, no. 1, Rio de Janeiro, Jan./Feb. 1970: 30-31.

Bienal de São Paulo. "7ª Bienal de São Paulo" <https://bit.ly/3JUkF2q>.

Bloch, Pedro. "A humanização da arquitetura". *Manchete*, no. 584, Rio de Janeiro, Jun. 29, 1963: 98-101 <https://bit.ly/383BfzS>.

Boabaid, Murillo. "Pavilhões". In *Sérgio Bernardes*, edited by Kykah Bernardes and Lauro Cavalcanti. Rio de Janeiro: Artviva, 2010, 54-63.

Bondi, Mauro. "Se o nosso Land Rover falasse: os primeiros automóveis que trabalharam na preservação do patrimônio em São Paulo". *Arquitextos*, year 17, no. 193.08, São Paulo, Vitruvius, Jun. 2016 <https://bit.ly/3xLYk4P>.

Bopp, Raul. *Movimentos modernistas no Brasil (1922-1928)*. Coleção Ensaios. Rio de Janeiro: Livraria São José, 1966.

Bóscolo, Ronaldo. "Em Brasília, o aeroporto do século". *Manchete*, Rio de Janeiro, no. 428, Jul. 2, 1960: 64-66 <https://bit.ly/38RoGYx>.

Brasil, Billy. "Joaquim Rolla" (entry). *Recanto das Letras*, Sorocaba, May 22, 2014 <https://bit.ly/3uzAVlv>.

Britto, Alfredo. "Sérgio Bernardes e a invenção do espaço urbano". *Revista Urbana*, vol. 1, no. 1, Instituto Light, Feb. 20, 2005.

Britto, Alfredo. "Sérgio Bernardes e o Rio". In *Sérgio Bernardes*, edited by Kykah Bernardes and Lauro Cavalcanti. Rio de Janeiro: Artviva, 2010, 130-139.

Bruand, Yves. *Arquitetura contemporânea no Brasil*. São Paulo: Perspectiva, 2016.

Brugnera, Ana Carolina. "Meio ambiente cultural da Amazônia brasileira: dos modos de vida à moradia do caboclo ribeirinho". Masters thesis, advised by Abilio Guerra, São Paulo, FAU Mackenzie, 2015 <https://bit.ly/37LZJxv>.

Brugnera, Ana Carolina. "Rumo às comunidades criativas: as articulações entre natureza e cultura na gestão sustentável das paisagens culturais do Peruaçu, Brasil". PhD diss., advised by Abilio Guerra, São Paulo, FAU Mackenzie, 2020.

Cabral, Maria Cristina. "A multivalência de Sérgio Bernardes: da atualidade da obra de um raro arquiteto, um grande humanista". *Resenhas Online*, year 10, no. 117.03, São Paulo, Vitruvius, Sep. 2011 <https://bit.ly/3gzu6bf>.

Candela, Felix. Foreword to *Frei Otto: estructuras* by Conrad Roland, Barcelona: Gustavo Gili, 1965.

Casé, Geraldo. "Sérgio Bernardes". *Ventura*, no. 1, Rio de Janeiro, Sep./Nov. 1987: 124-135.

Caúla, Adriana, and Kykah Bernardes. "Exposição SB100: Sérgio Bernardes 100 anos". *Resenhas Online*, year 18, no. 208.06, São Paulo, Vitruvius, Apr. 2019 <https://bit.ly/3uAicGh>.

Caúla, Adriana. "Sérgio Bernardes e a utopia como plano de pensamento sobre a cidade". *Cadernos Proarq*, no. 32, Rio de Janeiro, FAU UFRJ, Jul. 2019: 145-161 <https://bit.ly/3LkqwQv>.

Cavalcanti, Lauro. "A importância de Sér(gio) Bernardes". *Arquitextos*, year 10, no. 111.00, São Paulo, Vitruvius, Aug. 2009 <https://bit.ly/3Ba29jH>.

Cavalcanti, Lauro. *Quando o Brasil era moderno: guia da arquitetura 1928-1960*. Rio de Janeiro: Aeroplano, 2001.

Cavalcanti, Lauro. *Sérgio Bernardes: herói de uma tragédia moderna*. Coleção Perfis do Rio. Rio de Janeiro: Relume Dumará, 2004.

Cerávalo, Ana Lúcia. "Paulo de Camargo e Almeida: arquitetura total na trajetória de um arquiteto brasileiro". Masters thesis, advised by Carlos Roberto Monteiro de Andrade, São Carlos, EESC USP, 2000.

Chataignier, Silvia Maciel Savio. "A imaginação arquitetônica em Sérgio Bernardes: projetos como esquemas". *Cadernos Proarq*, no. 32, Rio de Janeiro, FAU UFRJ, Jul. 2019: 13-144 <https://bit.ly/3uNR5r5>.

Claro, Marcel Alessandro. "Transcrição e reconstrução digital: utopias possíveis de Sérgio Bernardes". Masters thesis, advised by Patrícia Pimenta Azevedo Ribeiro, Uberlândia, FAUD UFU, 2017 <https://bit.ly/3xAH96e>.

Colin, Silvio. "A arquitetura na Semana de Arte Moderna de 1922". *Coisas da Arquitetura*, Rio de Janeiro, Jan. 28, 2011 <https://bit.ly/3LmTYVW>.

Colombo, Gabriel. "A questão agrária e a hegemonia do capital no campo". Brasília, Brazilian Communist Party, Jan. 28, 2022 <https://bityli.com/vhsJn>.

Costa, Juracy, and Muniz Sodré. "Favela cinco vezes inferno". *Manchete*, no. 720, Rio de Janeiro, Feb. 5, 1966: 27-32 <https://bit.ly/3uNZFWU>.

Costa, Lúcio (1936). "Razões da nova arquitetura". In *Registro de uma vivência*, by *Lúcio Costa*:108-116.

Costa, Lúcio (1936). "Vila Monlevade". In *Registro de uma vivência*, by Lúcio Costa:90-99.

Costa, Lúcio (1937). "Documentação necessária". In *Registro de uma vivência*, by Lúcio Costa:457-462.

Costa, Lúcio. *Registro de uma vivência*. São Paulo: Empresa das Artes, 1995.

Costa, Pedro Campos. "Blowing in the Wind. Sérgio Bernardes e o apagamento de um personagem histórico". *Resenhas Online*, year 14, no. 158.01, São Paulo, Vitruvius, Feb. 2015 <https://bit.ly/3vmt75u>.

Costa, Philipe Cunha, and Diego Nogueira Dias. "Uma vida em sistemas: rastros de uma escritura cibernética em Sérgio Bernardes". *Cadernos Proarq*, no. 32, Rio de Janeiro, FAU UFRJ, Jul. 2019: 113-129 <https://bit.ly/3uBqmhU>.

Costa, Renato da Gama-Rosa, Alexandre Pessoa, Estefânia Neiva de Mello, and Dilene Raimundo do Nascimento. "O sanatório de Curicica: uma obra pouco conhecida de Sérgio Bernardes". *Arquitextos*, year 03, no. 026.02, São Paulo, Vitruvius, Jul. 2002 <https://bit.ly/3B6nOcJ>.

Critelli, Fernanda. "Richard Neutra e o Brasil". Masters thesis, advised by Abilio Guerra, São Paulo, FAU Mackenzie, 2015 <https://bit.ly/3xDVqPo>.

Critelli, Fernanda. *Richard Neutra e o Brasil*. São Paulo/Austin: Romano Guerra/Nhamerica Platform, 2022.

Critelli, Fernanda. "Richard Neutra: conexões latino-americanas". PhD diss., advised by Abilio Guerra, São Paulo, FAU Mackenzie, 2020 <https://bit.ly/3OBjYOX>.

Cunha, Pedro. "A colônia que melhor contribuiu para as festas do IV Centenário". In *1554-1954. Os festejos do IV Centenário da Cidade de São Paulo*. Comissão colaboradora da colônia japonesa pró IV Centenário de São Paulo. (Book in Japanese)

Curi, Fernanda. "60 anos do Parque Ibirapuera". São Paulo, Bienal de São Paulo, Aug. 20, 2014 <https://bit.ly/35VhBEV>.

Davies, Colin. *A New History of Modern Architecture*. London: Laurance King Publishing, 2017.

Denison, Edward, ed. *30-Second Architecture: 50 estilos fundamentais explicados de forma clara e rápida*. São Paulo: Publifolha, 2016.

Devos, Rika, and Mil de Kooning. *L'Architecture Moderne à L'Expo 58: pour un monde plus humain*. Bruxelas: Fonds Mercator, 2006.

Dias, Luís Andrade de Mattos. *Edificações de aço no Brasil*. São Paulo: Zigurate, 1993.

Domin, Christopher, and Joseph King. *Paul Rudolph: the Florida Houses*. Nova York: Princeton Architectural Press, 2014.

Faria, Lina Rodrigues de. "Os primeiros anos da reforma sanitária no Brasil e a atuação da Fundação Rockefeller (1915-1920)". *Physis*, 1995, vol. 5, no. 1: 109-130 <https://bit.ly/3sqpk5F>.

Fausto, Boris. *História do Brasil*. São Paulo: Edusp, 2009.

Felicetti, Marcelo Augusto. "Rio-Zoo, 1978: Sérgio Bernardes nos jardins da ficção". In: *Anais do 5° Enanparq*, Salvador, UFBA, Oct. 13-19, 2018: 3809.

Felicetti, Marcelo Augusto. "Sérgio Bernardes e a biblioteca dos sentidos". *Cadernos Proarq*, no. 32, Rio de Janeiro, FAU UFRJ, Jul. 2019: 184-196 <https://bit.ly/3rABxW9>.

Felicetti, Marcelo Augusto. "Sérgio Bernardes e o Monumento ao Pavilhão Nacional, Brasília, 1972". *Arquitextos*, year 18, no. 216.05, São Paulo, Vitruvius, May 2018 <https://bit.ly/33719D7>.

Ferraz, Marcelo. "Arquitetura em vão?: sobre exposição da arquitetura brasileira em Matosinhos, Portugal". *Resenhas Online*, year 18, no. 205.04, São Paulo, Vitruvius, Jan. 2019 <https://bit.ly/3rywju0>.

Folgato, Marisa. "SP ganha no aniversário presente que havia sumido". *O Estado de S. Paulo*, São Paulo, Apr. 19, 2000: 26 <https://bit.ly/34IPat8>.

Fonseca, Antonio Claudio Pinto da. "Um breve olhar sobre o arquiteto Sérgio Bernardes". *Arquitextos*, year 03, no. 026.01, São Paulo, Vitruvius, Jul. 2002 < https://bit.ly/3snWW3T>.

Forty, Adrian. *Brazil's Modern Architecture*. Londres: Phaidon, 2010.

G1-PB. "Prefeitura de João Pessoa transforma Hotel Tambaú em bem de utilidade pública: em meio a disputas judiciais, Prefeitura quer manter a preservação do local. Próximo passo é tentar desapropriar o prédio". *G1 Paraíba*, João Pessoa, Dec. 21, 2021 <http://glo.bo/37ROCmt>.

Ginzburg, Carlo. *Mitos, emblemas e sinais: morfologia e história*. São Paulo: Companhia das Letras, 2016.

Goodwin, Philip L. *Brazil Builds: Architecture New and Old (1642-1942)*. New York: MoMA, 1943.

Gouthier, Hugo. *Presença: memórias*. Rio de Janeiro: Record, 1982.

Guanaes, Felipe. *Sérgio Bernardes: doutrina de uma civilização tropical*. Rio de Janeiro: Editora PUC-Rio, 2016.

Guerra, Abilio, and Fausto Sombra. "Avenida Paulista, 1951: cenário da 1ª Bienal de São Paulo". In *Bienal de São Paulo desde 1951*, compiled by Paulo Miyada. São Paulo: Fundação Bienal, 2022: 24-44.

Guerra, Abilio, and Fausto Sombra. "Três pavilhões de Sérgio Bernardes: exposição no Centro Histórico e Cultural Mackenzie". *Resenhas Online*, year 18, no. 215.05, São Paulo, Vitruvius, Nov. 2019 <https://bit.ly/3EQSOdS>.

Guerra, Abilio. *Arquitetura brasileira: viver na floresta*. São Paulo: Instituto Tomie Ohtake, 2010.

Guerra, Abilio. "Lúcio Costa, Gregori Warchavchik e Roberto Burle Marx: síntese entre arquitetura e natureza tropical". 2002. In *Textos fundamentais sobre a história da arquitetura moderna brasileira – parte 2*, compiled by Abilio Guerra. São Paulo: Romano Guerra, 2010: 299-325.

Guerra, Abilio. "Prêmio APCA 2014: Documentário Bernardes, direção de Gustavo Gama Rodrigues e Paulo de Barros. Categoria Difusão, modalidade Arquitetura e Urbanismo". *Drops*, year 15, no. 089.02, São Paulo, Vitruvius, Feb. 2015 <https://bit.ly/3GGFoVH>.

Guimaraens, Cêça. "Rodrigo Melo Franco de Andrade e a paisagem hiperreal do patrimônio". *Arquitextos*, year 13, no. 149.06, São Paulo, Vitruvius, Oct. 2012 <https://bit.ly/3EE8x4N>.

Guina, Romulo Augusto Pinto. "A casa de campo de Lota de Macedo Soares: por uma cronografia do ícone moderno projetado por Sérgio Bernardes". *Cadernos Proarq*, no. 32, Rio de Janeiro, FAU UFRJ, Jul. 2019: 17-36 <https://bit.ly/3oBbk7T>.

Herbst, Helio. *Pelos salões das bienais, a arquitetura ausente dos manuais: contribuições para a historiografia brasileira (1951-1959)*. São Paulo: Annablume, 2011.

Hitchcock, Henry-Russell. *Latin American Architecture Since 1945*. New York: MoMA, 1955.

Honorato, Rossana. "Sérgio Bernardes em João Pessoa: a paisagem recontada". *Minha Cidade*, São Paulo, year 08, no. 096.03, Vitruvius, Jul. 2008 <https://bit.ly/3KN78uO>.

Johnston, Daniel Merro. *La casa sobre el arroyo: Amancio Williams en Argentina*. Buenos Aires: 1:100 Ediciones, 2014.

Justino, Martins. "Talento, armado: Brasil em Bruxelas". *Manchete*, no. 339, Rio de Janeiro, Oct. 18, 1958: 102-105 <https://bit.ly/3voRuPY>.

Lambert, Pierre. "Bruxelas, capital do mundo por seis meses". *O Estado de S. Paulo*, São Paulo, Apr. 20, 1958: 96 <https://bit.ly/34IMLi8 >.

Lapouge, Gilles. "Inaugurado o pavilhão do Brasil em Bruxelas". *O Estado de S. Paulo*, São Paulo, May 4, 1958: 1 <https://bit.ly/3Gyne8F>.

Latteur, Francine. "Comissariado Permanente de Exposições e Feiras no Exterior: Exposição Universal e Internacional de Bruxelas". *Presence*, no. 21, Brussels, Apr./Sept. 1958: 2-3.

Leal, Carlos Eduardo. "Gazeta de Notícias" (entry). FGV CPDOC, Rio de Janeiro <https://bit.ly/3k1Wchh>.

Lemos, Carlos Alberto Cerqueira. *Trilogia do Copan: a história do edifício Copan*. São Paulo: Imprensa Oficial do Estado de São Paulo, 2014.

Levi, Rino. "A arquitetura e a estética das cidades: uma carta de um estudante brasileiro em Roma". *O Estado de S. Paulo*, São Paulo, Oct. 1925: 6 <https://bit.ly/3rvuiOW>.

Levi, Rino. "A arquitetura e a estética das cidades". In *Depoimento de uma geração: arquitetura moderna brasileira*, edited by Alberto Xavier, 38-39, São Paulo: Cosac Naify, 2003.

Lira, José. *Warchavchik: fraturas da vanguarda*. São Paulo: Cosac Naify, 2011.

Lores, Raul Juste. *São Paulo nas alturas*. São Paulo: Três Estrelas, 2017.

Ludemir, Bernardo. "O Rio caminha para o Sul". *Manchete*, no. 467, Rio de Janeiro, Apr. 1, 1961: 64 <https://bit.ly/3xE5liv>.

Malaquias, Thaysa. "A contribuição do arquiteto Sérgio Bernardes para a moderna arquitetura de saúde". Masters thesis, advised by Ana Maria Gadelha Albano Amora, Rio de Janeiro, FAU UFRJ, 2018.

Malaquias, Thaysa. "Sérgio Bernardes e o Sanatório de Curicica: herança da formação na FNA". *Cadernos Proarq*, no. 32, Rio de Janeiro, FAU UFRJ, Jul. 2019: 52-77 <https://bit.ly/3HF2Dkn>.

Mariano, Cássia. *Preservação e paisagismo em São Paulo: Otávio Augusto Teixeira Mendes.* São Paulo: Annablume, 2005.

Marinho, Teresinha. "Notícia biográfica". In *Rodrigo e seus tempos: coletânea de textos sobre artes e letras,* by Rodrigo Melo Franco de Andrade. Rio de Janeiro: MinC/Fundação Pró-Memória, 1986.

Marques, André Felipe Rocha. "A obra de João Filgueiras Lima, Lelé: projeto, técnica e racionalização". Masters thesis advised by Abilio Guerra, São Paulo, FAU Mackenzie, 2012 <https://bit.ly/3vdxBw9>.

Marques, André Felipe Rocha. "Aldary Toledo: entre arte e arquitetura". PhD diss., advised by Abilio Guerra, São Paulo, FAU Mackenzie, 2018 <https://bit.ly/3L9uSJP>.

Marques, André. *Lelé: diálogos com Neutra e Prouvé.* São Paulo/Austin: Romano Guerra/Nhamerica Platform, 2020.

Martínez, Ascensión Hernández. *La clonación arquitectónica.* Madri: Siruela, 2007.

Martins, Luis. "Coisas da cidade: o destino do Ibirapuera". *O Estado de S. Paulo,* São Paulo, Sep. 9, 1955: 11 <https://bit.ly/3GE7kK1>.

Mas, Vicente, Isabel Villac, Sergio García-Gasco, Isabel Oliver, Pedro Varella, and Caio Calafate. "Conversación con Paulo Mendes da Rocha". *En Blanco,* no. 15, Valência, TC Cuadernos, 2014: 115-117 <https://bit.ly/3rxEne9>.

Mason, Jayme. *Humanismo, ciência, engenharia: perspectivas, depoimentos, testemunhos.* Rio de Janeiro: Author's edition, 2001.

Mello Filho, Murilo. "Onde está o castelismo?" *Manchete,* no. 1059, Rio de Janeiro, Aug. 5, 1972: 22-23.

Meurs, Paul, Mil De Kooning, and Rony De Meyer. "Expo 58: the Brasil Pavilion of *Sérgio Bernardes*". In *4th São Paulo International Architecture Biennial.* Exibition Catalog (São Paulo, Nov. 19, 1999 to Jan. 25, 2000). Ghent: University of Ghent's, Department of Architecture and Urban Planning, 2000.

Meurs, Paul. "O pavilhão brasileiro na Expo de Bruxelas, 1958: arquiteto Sérgio Bernardes". *Arquitextos,* year 01, no. 007.07, São Paulo, Vitruvius, Dec. 2000 <https://bit.ly/34JUP25>.

Meyer, Regina. "Metrópole e urbanismo: São Paulo anos 50". PhD dissertation advised by Celso Monteiro Lamparelli, São Paulo, FAU USP, 1991.

Milazzo, Marco, Rômulo Almagro, and Suellen Trindade. "Hotel em Paquetá, de Sérgio Bernardes". *Projetos,* São Paulo, year 15, no. 178.04, Vitruvius, Oct. 2015 <https://bit.ly/3uPNAQT>.

Moreira, Regina da Luz, and Maurette Brandt. *CSN: um sonho feito de aço e ousadia.* Rio de Janeiro: Fundação CSN/Fundação Getúlio Vargas, 2005.

Morse, Richard. *Formação histórica de São Paulo: de comunidade a metrópole.* São Paulo: Difusão Europeia do Livro, 1970.

Mota, Carlos Guilherme, and Adriana Lopez. *História do Brasil: uma interpretação.* São Paulo: Editora 34, 2015.

Muro, Carles. Introduction to *Pabellones de exposición: 100 años* by Moisés Puente. Barcelona: Gustavo Gilli, 2000.

Neto, Lira. *Getúlio 1882-1930: dos anos de formação à conquista do poder*. São Paulo: Companhia das Letras, 2012.

Neto, Lira. *Getúlio 1930-1945: do governo provisório à ditadura do Estado Novo*. São Paulo: Companhia das Letras, 2013.

Neto, Lira. *Getúlio 1945-1954: de volta pela consagração popular ao suicídio*. São Paulo: Companhia das Letras, 2014.

Niemeyer, Oscar. "Mutilado o conjunto do Parque Ibirapuera". *Módulo*, no. 1, Rio de Janeiro, Mar. 1955: 18-31.

Nobre, Ana Luiza. "Fios cortantes: projeto e produto, arquitetura e design no Rio de Janeiro (1950-70)". PhD diss., advised by Ronaldo Brito Fernandes, Rio de Janeiro, History Department PUC-Rio, 2008 <https://bit.ly/3jI5oqH>.

Nobre, Ana Luiza. "Flor rara e banalíssima: Sérgio Bernardes e a casa de Lota de Macedo Soares". *Cadernos Proarq*, no. 32, Rio de Janeiro, FAU UFRJ, Jul. 2019: 1-9 <https://bit.ly/34IXG1J>.

Nobre, Ana Luiza. "Flor rara e banalíssima. Residência Lota de Macedo Soares, por Sérgio Bernardes". *Arquitetura.Crítica*, no. 015.01, São Paulo, Vitruvius, Feb. 2006.

Nobre, Ana Luiza. "Malhas, redes, cabos e triângulos". In *Sérgio Bernardes*, edited by Kykah Bernardes and Lauro Cavalcanti. Rio de Janeiro: Artviva, 2010, 28-45.

Nobre, Ana Luiza. "Sérgio Bernardes: a subversão do possível". *Arquitetura.Crítica*, no. 009.02. São Paulo, Vitruvius, Jun. 2002.

Oliveira, Fabiano Lemes de. "O Parque do Ibirapuera: projetos, modernidade e modernismo". In: *Anais do 5º Seminário Docomomo Brasil*, São Carlos, Oct. 27 to 30, 2003. São Carlos, EESC USP São Carlos, 2003 <https://bit.ly/3Je5Qrz>.

Oliveira, Fabiano Lemes de. "Os projetos para o Parque Ibirapuera: de Manequinho Lopes a Niemeyer (1926-1954)". Masters thesis advised by Carlos Roberto Monteiro de Andrade, São Carlos, EESC USP, 2003.

Pellegrini, Ana Carolina Santos. "Bolonha, Barcelona, Firminy: quando o projeto é patrimônio". *Arqtexto*, no. 12, Porto Alegre, Jan./Jun. 2008 <https://bit.ly/3B95SOP>.

Perdigão, João, and Euler Corradi. *O rei da roleta, a incrível história de Joaquim Rolla, o homem que inventou o Cassino da Urca e transformou a história do entretenimento no Brasil*. São Paulo: Casa da Palavra, 2012.

Pereira, Sabrina Souza Bom. "Rodolpho Ortenblad Filho: estudo sobre as residências". Masters thesis advised by Abilio Guerra, São Paulo, FAU Mackenzie, 2010 <https://bit.ly/3MuYwt5>.

Pinheiro, Maria Lucia Bressan. *Neocolonial, modernismo e preservação do patrimônio: debate cultural dos anos 1920 no Brasil*. São Paulo: Edusp, 2012.

Pisani, Daniele. *O Trianon do MAM ao MASP: arquitetura e política em São Paulo (1946-1968)*. São Paulo: Editora 34, 2019.

Pontes, Ana Paula. "Sérgio Bernardes e Eduardo de Almeida: arquitetura que ensina". *Arquitetura. Crítica*, no. 009.04, São Paulo, Vitruvius, Jun. 2002.

Prestes, Luiz Carlos. "Prestes dirige-se ao povo brasileiro". *Voz Operária*, Rio de Janeiro, Aug. 5, 1950: 1-2; 6-7 <https://bityli.com/XydFsi>.

Queiroz, Rodrigo. "Três pavilhões de Sérgio Bernardes: a geometria da tensão". *Resenhas Online*, year 18, no. 214.01, São Paulo, Vitruvius, Oct. 2019 <https://bit.ly/34IY7cn>.

Quetglas, Josep. *El horror cristalizado: imágenes del Pabellón de Alemania de Mies van der Rohe*. Barcelona: Actar, 2001.

Rebello, Yopanan Conrado Pereira. *A concepção estrutural e a arquitetura*. São Paulo: Zigurate, 2000.

Redação. "400 firmas nacionais e 60 do exterior na 1ª Exposição Internacional do Rio". *O Estado de S. Paulo*, São Paulo, Mar. 26, 1959: 9 <https://bit.ly/3HBL9p9>.

Redação. "A cidade que mais cresce no mundo". *Acrópole*, no. 157, São Paulo, May 1951, s/p. <https://bit.ly/3uO3ewk>.

Redação. "A expansão de São Paulo se fez explosivamente". *A Gazeta*, São Paulo, Jan. 8, 1954.

Redação. "Aberto o Pavilhão do Uruguai na 1ª Feira Internacional de São Paulo". *O Estado de S. Paulo*, São Paulo, Dec. 14, 1954: 16 <https://bit.ly/3soulpH>.

Redação. "Abertura dos festejos do IV Centenário: flutuarão sobre o Anhangabaú na manhã de hoje quatro grandes bandeiras nacionais". *O Estado de S. Paulo*, São Paulo, Jan. 23, 1954: 1 <https://bit.ly/3somMVG>.

Redação. "Aeroporto Intercontinental América do Sul-Brasília". *Módulo*, no. 19, Rio de Janeiro, Aug. 1960: 12.

Redação. "Brasília 50 anos". *Veja*, no. 2138, São Paulo, Nov. 2009: 122.

Redação. "Brésil". *L'Architecture d'Aujourd'hui*, no. 13-14, Paris, Sep. 1947.

Redação. "Bruxelles 58". *L'Architecture d'Aujourd'hui*, no. 78, Paris, Jun. 1958: 2-47.

Redação. "Ceará guarda as cinzas de Castelo". *O Estado de S. Paulo*, São Paulo, Jul. 19, 1972: 5 <https://bit.ly/3oAPbqb>.

Redação. "Centro de Convenções Ulysses Guimarães: neste icônico projeto, Sérgio Bernardes contemplou a vista de Brasília com uma grande construção horizontal". *Anual Design*, Goiânia <https://bit.ly/3jMfKWF>.

Redação. "Conjunto do Ibirapuera: clamorosamente mutilado o projeto inicial do grupo arquitetônico comemorativo do 4° Centenário de São Paulo". *Módulo*, no. 1, Rio de Janeiro, Mar. 1955: 18-21.

Redação. "Cultura é esquecida, mas tem novo projeto". *O Estado de S. Paulo*, São Paulo, Nov. 16, 1972: 18 <https://bit.ly/3GDIPg6>.

Redação. "Desenhada contra o céu carioca uma prodigiosa teia de aranha". *Manchete*, no. 363, Rio de Janeiro, Apr. 17, 1959: 74-76 <https://bit.ly/3vsJOw3>.

Redação. "Dois famosos arquitetos residem em autênticas obras de arte". *Manchete*, no. 686, Rio de Janeiro, Jun. 12, 1965: 58-62 <https://bit.ly/392zNOJ>.

Redação. "Eleições gerais no Brasil em 1958" (entry). Wikipedia <https://bit.ly/3sswGWe>.

Redação. "Expo Xangai 2010 termina como a mais visitada da história". *Terra*, São Paulo, Oct. 31, 2010. <https://bit.ly/38cQGFO>.

Redação. "Exposição de Bruxelas – 1958". *O Estado de S. Paulo*, São Paulo, Apr. 20, 1958: 97 <https://bit.ly/35NlgVd>.

Redação. "Exposição internacional de indústria e comércio da cidade do Rio de Janeiro". *Acrópole*, no. 265, São Paulo, Nov. 1960, cover, 18.

Redação. "Exposição Soviética no Rio". *Manchete*, no. 525, Rio de Janeiro, May 12, 1962: 93 <https://bit.ly/3uPpvJU>.

Redação. "Exposição soviética vai mostrar trajes espaciais de Yuri Gagárin e Titov". *Jornal do Brasil*, Rio de Janeiro, Mar.1, 1962: 5 <https://bit.ly/3jO13m5>.

Redação. "Homenagem da Bélgica à cidade de S. Paulo no seu IV Centenário". *O Estado de S. Paulo*, São Paulo, Dec.14, 1954: 16 <https://bit.ly/35T6uMJ>.

Redação. "Inaugura-se hoje, em São Paulo, a exposição do IV Centenário". *O Estado de S. Paulo*, São Paulo, Aug. 21, 1954: 9 <https://bit.ly/3vkPjwN>.

Redação. "Inaugurada ontem a exposição Russa no Rio; Lacerda falou". *O Estado de S. Paulo*, São Paulo, May 4, 1962: 5 <https://bit.ly/337LuRv>.

Redação. "Inaugurado na exposição do Ibirapuera o Pavilhão da Cia. Siderúrgica Nacional". Specialized Affairs Column. *Folha da Manhã*, São Paulo, Feb. 17, 1955: 10 <https://bit.ly/3LgcPSR>.

Redação. "Inaugurado ontem no Ibirapuera o Pavilhão da Companhia Siderúrgica". *O Estado de S. Paulo*, São Paulo, Feb. 16, 1955: 12 <https://bit.ly/3GvpXzO>.

Redação. "LIC – Laboratório de Investigações Conceituais". *Módulo*, special edition Sérgio Bernardes, compiled by Olínio Coelho and Lauro Cavalcanti, Rio de Janeiro, Oct./Nov.1983: 15-16.

Redação. "Menezes Cortês atribui objetivos políticos à exposição soviética". *O Estado de S. Paulo*, Jun. 12, 1962: 48 <https://bit.ly/3JMwNIV>.

Redação. "Movimento Concretista nas artes plásticas". *Arte Concretista* <https://bit.ly/3GxVQHW>.

Redação. "Notícias dos Estados: será aberta dia 3 a amostra soviética". *Folha de S. Paulo*, Apr. 20, 1962: 4 <https://bit.ly/3KNYgoP>.

Redação. "O monumento-mausoléu". *O Estado de S. Paulo*, São Paulo, Jul. 9, 1972: 5 <https://bit.ly/3oAPbqb>.

Redação. "O pavilhão da engenharia civil em Bruxelas". *Habitat*, no. 46, Jan./Feb. 1958: 16-17.

Redação. "Os festejos populares marcados para hoje e amanhã no Ibirapuera". *O Estado de S. Paulo*, São Paulo, Sept. 18, 1954: 10 <https://bit.ly/37YRFcl>.

Redação. "Participará o Brasil na Feira internacional de Bruxelas". *O Estado de S. Paulo*, São Paulo, Mar. 7, 1957: 26 <https://bit.ly/3rA68mw>.

Redação. "Pavilhão da Bélgica no Ibirapuera". *O Estado de S. Paulo*, São Paulo, Sep. 18, 1954: 10 <https://bit.ly/3oBsDWI>.

Redação. "Pavilhão da Companhia Siderúrgica Nacional". Specialized Affairs Column. *Folha da Manhã*, São Paulo, Aug. 4, 1954: 8 <https://bit.ly/3uzZui8>.

Redação. "Pavilhão de Volta Redonda, Parque Ibirapuera, São Paulo". *Arquitetura e Engenharia*, São Paulo, no. 36, Jul./Aug. 1955: 25-27.

Redação. "Pavilhão do Brasil na Exposição Internacional de Bruxelas". *Módulo*, no. 9, Feb. 1958: 22-24.

Redação. "Pavilhão do Brasil na Feira internacional de Bruxelas". *Arquitetura e Engenharia*, no. 48, Belo Horizonte, Jan./Feb. 1958: 22-23.

Redação. "Pavilhão do R. Grande do Sul no Ibirapuera". *O Estado de S. Paulo*, São Paulo, Jun. 15, 1957: 14 <https://bit.ly/3rDGMV7>.

Redação. "Posto de escuta". *Manchete*, no. 407, Rio de Janeiro, Feb. 6, 1960: 18 <https://bit.ly/3vifWIW>.

Redação. "Posto de escuta". *Manchete*, no. 657, Rio de Janeiro, Nov. 14, 1964: 102 <https://bit.ly/3uOwumn>.

Redação. "Quando os arquitetos projetam cadeiras". *Manchete*, no. 610, Rio de Janeiro, Dec. 28, 1963: 101 < https://bit.ly/3rx5LJk>.

Redação. "Rem Koolhaas" (entry). *Infopédia*, Porto, Porto Editora <https://bit.ly/3rFIV3O>

Redação. "Seminário e exposição SB100 – Sérgio Bernardes na FAU UFRJ". *Archdaily*, São Paulo, Aug. 14, 2019 <https://bit.ly/3Je40a9>.

Redação. "Será oficialmente instalada amanhã a grande exposição do IV Centenário". *O Estado de S. Paulo*, São Paulo, Aug. 20, 1954: 13 <https://bit.ly/3uxlYPB>.

Redação. "Sérgio Bernardes: Country Club e Petrópolis. *L'Architecture d'Aujourd'hui*, no. 13-14 (special edition Brésil), Paris, Set. 1947: 96.

Redação. "Sonho de arquiteto é liberdade de paulista. Tribuna da Imprensa, Rio de Janeiro, 20-21 Dec. 1958: 10 <http://bit.ly/3yNv8di>.

Redação. "Um dicionário hilariante". *Manchete*, no. 784, Rio de Janeiro, Apr. 29, 1967: 76-77 <https://bit.ly/3rx6FFC>.

Redação. "Um país num pavilhão". *Manchete*, no. 455, Rio de Janeiro, Jan. 7, 1961: 65-67 <https://bit.ly/3EkfM1z>.

Redação. "Un nuevo edificio conformará el paisaje de Puebla, México: Torre Helea". *ArchDaily* México, Sep. 2018 <https://bit.ly/3GF0qV1>.

Redação. "V. Redonda em Ibirapuera". *O Lingote*, Volta Redonda, CSN, Mar. 10, 1955: 12.

Retto Jr., Adalberto. "Entre arquitetura e política: a mostra Três pavilhões de Sérgio Bernardes". *Resenhas Online*, year 18, no. 214.02, São Paulo, Vitruvius, Oct. 2019 <https://bit.ly/34LqEYk>.

Ribeiro, Darcy. *Aos trancos e barrancos: como o Brasil deu no que deu*. Rio de Janeiro: Guanabara, 1985.

Rocha, Germana Costa. "O caráter tectônico do moderno brasileiro: Bernardes e Campello na Paraíba (1970-1980)". PhD diss., advised by Nelci Tinem, Natal, PPGAU UFRN, 2012.

Rocha, Germana, Nelci Tinem, and Marcio Cotrim. "Hotel Tambaú, de Sérgio Bernardes: diálogo entre poética construtiva e estrutura formal". *Arquitextos*, year 18, no. 206.00, São Paulo, Vitruvius, Jul. 2017 <https://bit.ly/3B74Mmm>.

Sander, Roberto. *O Brasil na mira de Hitler: a história do afundamento de navios brasileiros pelos nazistas*. Rio de Janeiro: Objetiva, 2007.

Santos, Cecília Rodrigues dos. "Teatro do Parque Ibirapuera: em nome de quem?" *Arquitextos*, year 04, no. 038.06, São Paulo, Vitruvius, Jul. 2003 <https://bit.ly/34uUMHL>.

Segre, Roberto. *Ministério da Educação e Saúde: ícone urbano da modernidade brasileira (1935-1945)*. São Paulo: Romano Guerra, 2013.

Segre, Roberto. "Sérgio Bernardes (1919-2002): entre o regionalismo e o *high tech*". *Arquitextos*, year 03, no. 026.00, São Paulo, Vitruvius, Jul. 2002 <https://bit.ly/3rzFEl6>.

Serapião, Fernando, and Guilherme Wisnik, eds. *Infinito vão: 90 anos de arquitetura brasileira*. São Paulo: Monolito, 2019.

Serapião, Fernando. "Escola carioca: arquitetura moderna no Rio de Janeiro". *Monolito*, no. 31, São Paulo, Feb./Mar. 2016: 14-149.

Silva, Claiton Márcio da. "Nelson Rockefeller e a atuação da American International Association for Economic and Social Development: debates sobre missão e imperialismo no Brasil, 1946-1961". *História, Ciências, Saúde-Manguinhos*, vol. 20, no. 4, Oct./Dec. 2013: 1695-1711 <https://bit.ly/3oyzgsH>.

Silva, João Claudio Parucher da. "Arquivo Sérgio Bernardes: a análise do seu significado cultural como justificativa para a sua preservação". *Cadernos Proarq*, no. 32, Rio de Janeiro, FAU UFRJ, Jul. 2019: 37-51 <https://bit.ly/3GD4qoX>.

Solà-Morales, Ignasi, Cristian Cirici, and Fernando Ramos. *Mies van der Rohe: el Pabellon de Barcelona*. Barcelona: Gustavo Gili, 1993.

Sombra, Fausto. "Luís Saia e Lúcio Costa: a parceria no Sítio Santo Antônio". *Arquitextos*, year 14, no. 161.03, São Paulo, Vitruvius, Oct. 2013 <https://bit.ly/3rOohwK>.

Sombra, Fausto. "Luís Saia e o restauro do sítio Santo Antônio: diálogos modernos na conformação arquitetônica paulista". Masters thesis advised by Abilio Guerra, São Paulo, FAU Mackenzie, 2015 <https://bit.ly/3OBGVBD>.

Sombra, Fausto. "O pavilhão da I Bienal do MAM SP: fatos, relatos, historiografia e correlações com o Masp e o antigo Belvedere Trianon". *Arquitextos*, year 17, no. 195.08, São Paulo, Vitruvius, Aug. 2016 <https://bit.ly/3JbC3Q9>.

Sombra, Fausto. "Os pavilhões de Sérgio Bernardes: Volta Redonda, Bruxelas e São Cristóvão. Contribuição à vanguarda arquitetônica moderna brasileira em meados do século 20". *Cadernos Proarq*, no. 32, Rio de Janeiro, Jul. 2019: 78-98 <https://bit.ly/3Kc4PAt>.

Sombra, Fausto. "Sérgio Bernardes e o pavilhão brasileiro na Exposição Universal e Internacional de Bruxelas, 1958: industrialização, inventividade e experimentação". *Anais do 5º Encontro da Associação Nacional de Pesquisa e Pós-Graduação em Arquitetura e Urbanismo – vol. 2*. Salvador, FAUFBA, 2018: 3886-3885.

Sombra, Fausto. "Sérgio Bernardes e o pavilhão brasileiro na Exposição Universal e Internacional de Bruxelas, 1958: industrialização, inventividade e experimentação". *Arquitextos*, year 20, no. 233.04, São Paulo, Vitruvius, Oct. 2019 <https://bit.ly/3B5weRl>.

Sombra, Fausto. "Três pavilhões de Sérgio Bernardes: Volta Redonda, Bruxelas e São Cristóvão. Contribuição à vanguarda arquitetônica moderna brasileira em meados do século 20". PhD diss., advised by Abilio Guerra, São Paulo, FAU Mackenzie, 2020 <https://bit.ly/3ElNcae>.

Sombra, Fausto. "Um breve olhar sobre a obra da família Bernardes". *Monolito*, no. 44-45, São Paulo, 2019: 290-293.

Souza, Lydio de. "Brasil potência arquitetônica". *Manchete*, no. 33, Rio de Janeiro, Dec. 6, 1952, cover, 18-25 <https://bit.ly/3OepSWp>.

Teixeira, Novais. "O Pavilhão do Brasil". *O Estado de S. Paulo*, São Paulo, Jun. 28, 1958: 7 <https://bit.ly/3B5VlUm>.

Toledo, Carolina Rossetti de. "A doação Nelson Rockefeller de 1946 no Acervo do Museu de Arte Contemporânea da USP". *Revista de História da Arte e Arqueologia*, no. 23, Jan./Jun. 2015: 149-173 <https://bit.ly/3xK1eXM>.

Tota, Antonio Pedro. "Como um Rockefeller sonhou em modernizar o Brasil". In *Anais do XI Encontro Internacional da ANPHLAC*, Jul. 29/Aug. 01, 2014. Niterói: UFF, 2014 <https://bit.ly/3Kddnai>.

Tota, Antônio Pedro. *O amigo americano: Nelson Rockefeller e o Brasil*. São Paulo: Companhia das Letras, 2014.

Tota, Antonio Pedro. *O imperialismo sedutor: a americanização do Brasil na época da Segunda Guerra*. São Paulo: Companhia das Letras, 2000.

Vanderlei, Alexandre Bahia. "Pabellón de Brasil – 1958: ampliación del desafío y perfeccionamiento del manifiesto". *Cadernos Proarq*, no. 32, Rio de Janeiro, FAU UFRJ, Jul. 2019: 99-112 <https://bit.ly/3KOukcb>.

Vanderlei, Alexandre Bahia. "Pavilhão da CSN 1954: recorrência técnica e manifesto da modernidade". In: *Anais do 11º Seminário Docomomo Brasil: o campo ampliado do movimento moderno*, Recife, UFPE, 2016 <https://bit.ly/3LcOVHE>.

Vanderlei, Alexandre Bahia. "Sérgio
  Bernardes: el desafio de la
  técnica". PhD diss., advised by
  Jaime José Ferrer Forés and
  Beatriz Santos de Oliveira,
  Barcelona, Universidade
  Politécnica da Catalunha, 2016.
Vieira, Monica Paciello. "A provocação
  sensorial na arquitetura de
  Sérgio Bernardes". *Arquitextos*,
  year 07, no. 084.05, São Paulo,
  Vitruvius, May 2007 <https://bit.
  ly/34s7F5t>.
Vieira, Monica Paciello. "O Parc La
  Villette na concepção de Sérgio
  Bernardes". *Cadernos Proarq*, no.
  32, Rio de Janeiro, FAU UFRJ,
  Jul. 2019: 162-183 <https://bit.
  ly/336eEQP>.
Vieira, Mônica Paciello. "Sérgio
  Bernardes: arquitetura como
  experimentação". Masters thesis,
  advised by Mauro César de
  Oliveira Santos, Rio de Janeiro,
  UFRJ, 2006.

Special Issues of Magazines

L'Architecture d'Aujourd'hui, no. 49
  (special edition Houses by
  Richard Neutra), Oct. 1953.
Acrópole, no. 301 (special room Sérgio
  Bernardes, 7th Biennial), São
  Paulo, Dec. 1963. <https://bit.
  ly/3v7p5Pu>.
Módulo (official catalog of Sérgio
  Bernardes exhibition), Rio de
  Janeiro, Oct./Nov.1983 <https://
  bit.ly/3OfLHER>.
Manchete (special edition 4th
  Centenary), Rio de Janeiro, 1954
  <https://bit.ly/36l0VHs>.
Manchete, no. 678 (special edition
  Rio do futuro), Rio de Janeiro,
  Apr. 17, 1965 <https://bit.
  ly/3KQTORt>.

Advertisement

Brazil's Industry in the Eyes of the
  World. International Exhibition
  of Industry and Commerce -
  Rio de Janeiro 1958. *Diário de
  Pernambuco*, Recife, December
  6, 1957, 8.
The Models of the Garden City
  Eldorado in Belo Horizonte are
  Still on Display for a Few More
  Days. *Diário Carioca*, Rio de
  Janeiro, April 10, 1954, 9.
Brazil - already an Industrial Nation.
  Projecting Itself to the World.
  International Exhibition of
  Industry and Commerce. *Correio
  Paulistano*, São Paulo, August
  12, 1958, 7.
Albra Trapezoidal Aluminum Sheets.
  Módulo, no. 23, June 1961.
Invitation - Garden City Eldorado
  in Belo Horizonte, S.Stockler-
  Compax-Imp. Exp. and Sales S/A.
  O Jornal, Rio de Janeiro, April 4,
  1954, 7.
Maragato Building - Luxury -
  Comfort - Beauty. Real Estate
  Supplement. *O Jornal*, Rio de
  Janeiro, February 10, 1952, 1.
Maragato Building - to Meet the Most
  Refined Taste in Luxury, Comfort,
  Beauty. *O Jornal*, Rio de Janeiro,
  March 13, 1952, 5.
They Have already Seen the New Ducal
  Clothing. *Tribuna da Imprensa*,
  Rio de Janeiro, April 27, 1956, 5.
I Bought this Lot for Cr$125 Monthly.
  Sombra, No. 139, Rio de Janeiro,
  April 1956, n/p.
Examine the Plan of this Apartment -
  Arati Building. *O Jornal*, Rio de
  Janeiro, April 15, 1952, 5.
International Exhibition of Industry
  and Commerce, Rio de Janeiro,
  1958. *Diário Carioca*, Rio de
  Janeiro, December 21, 1957, 9.

International Exhibition of Industry
and Commerce, Rio de Janeiro,
1958. *Diário de Pernambuco*,
Recife, November 21, 1957, 7.
International Hotel of Galeão. *Jornal
dos Sports*, Rio de Janeiro,
November 10, 1968, 7.
Constructions with Mauá Cement –
Jadir de Souza House. *Gazeta de
Notícias*, Rio de Janeiro, March
29, 1955, 8.
If Sérgio Bernardes' House was Painted
with Ypiranga paints, Why
Would You Paint Yours with
Another Brand? *Jóia*, No. 177,
Rio de Janeiro, May 1968, 123.
Are you Keeping Devalued Money?
– Lots in Enseada Azul in Cabo
Frio. *O Jornal*, Rio de Janeiro,
July 8, 1956, 8.

Primary Sources

Bernardes, Sérgio. Pavilhão da
Companhia Siderúrgica Nacional
no Parque Ibirapuera – SP. Rio
de Janeiro, n.d. Sérgio Bernardes
Collection.
Comissão do 4º Centenário da Cidade
de São Paulo. São Paulo em
números. Wanda Svevo Archive,
Biennial of São Paulo, Fundo
FMS_0441-06.
Companhia Imobiliária Kosmos.
Correspondência a Sérgio
Bernardes. Rio de Janeiro,
Jul. 3, 1956. Sérgio Bernardes
Collection.
Companhia Siderúrgica Nacional. CSN
assina convênio para reconstruir
um espaço cultural no Parque
Ibirapuera. Volta Redonda,
c.2000. Sérgio Bernardes
Collection.

Galeria Marco. A Galeria Marco, inau-
gurando sua exposição perma-
nente de arquitetura, engen-
haria, urbanismo e decoração,
patrocina a mostra do Pavilhão
Brasileiro na Exposição
Internacional de Bruxelas de
1958, de autoria do arquiteto
Sérgio W. Bernardes. Rio de
Janeiro, n.d. Sérgio Bernardes
Collection.
Gouthier, Hugo. Correspondência a
Olavo Falcão. Brussels, Jan. 31,
1957. NPD FAU UFRJ Collection.
Gouthier, Hugo. Correspondência
à Secretária de Estado das
Relações Exteriores. Brussels,
Feb. 7, 1957. NPD FAU UFRJ
Collection.
Kubitschek, Juscelino. Carta a Sérgio
Bernardes. Rio de Janeiro, Feb.
22, 1972. Sérgio Bernardes
Collection.
Martinelli, Dante A. O., and Dauro
Ribeiro da Silva. "Relatório LE/
EXT-70/74 de Verificação da
cobertura pênsil do Pavilhão
de São Cristóvão", Oct. 1973.
São Carlos, São Carlos School
of Engineering, Structure
Department, Structure
Laboratory, Jul. 1974.
Moens de Fernig, Georges. *Exposição
Universal e Internacional de
Bruxelas*. Translated by Luiz
Galvão Valle. Brussels, Kingdom
of Belgium: Permanent
Commissioner of Exhibitions and
Fairs Abroad, Apr. 24, 1957.
Suplan. Placa de inauguração do
Tambaú Hotel. João Pessoa,
Governo Estadual da Paraíba,
Sep.11, 1971.

Testimonies

Álvarez, Karla Lopez. Testimony to
Fausto Sombra. São Paulo,
Bernardes Arquitetura Office,
Jun. 7, 2018.
Aronis, Jacqueline. Testimony to Fausto
Sombra. São Paulo, artist's
atelier-residence, Sep. 21, 2019.
Arruda, Maria Arminda do Nascimento.
Testimony to Fausto Sombra,
Director's Office FFLCH USP, São
Paulo, Oct. 31, 2016.
Bernardes, Kykah. Testimonies to
Fausto Sombra. Rio de Janeiro,
Bernardes Arquitetura Office,
Jul. 31, 2018; Apr. 19, 2017; Apr.
15, 2022.
Boabaid, Murillo. Testimony to
Fausto Sombra. Rio de Janeiro,
Bernardes Arquitetura Office,
Apr. 19, 2017.
Boabaid, Murillo. Testimony to Fausto
Sombra. Rio de Janeiro, elec-
tronic message, Nov. 22, 2019.
Brando, Celso Omena. Testimony to
Fausto Sombra. Rio de Janeiro,
phone call and electronic
message, Jun. 27, 2019.
Cerávalo, Ana Lúcia. Testimony to
Fausto Sombra. São Carlos, elec-
tronic message, Jan. 29, 2019.
Figueroa, Mario. Testimony to
Fausto Sombra. São Paulo, CBI
Esplanada Building, Jun. 28,
2017.
Folgato, Marisa. Testimony to Fausto
Sombra. Rio de Janeiro, elec-
tronic message, Jun. 19, 2017.
Fonseca, Antônio Claudio Pinto da.
Testimony in lecture. São Paulo,
FAU Mackenzie, Oct. 9, 2018.
Katchuian, Rosa. Testimony to Fausto
Sombra, Kykah Bernardes,
Renata Bernardes, Adriana Caúla
and Mary Moda. São Paulo,
Casa Mansur (Cincinato Cajado
Braga), Sep. 19, 2019.
Malaquias, Thaysa. Testimony to
Fausto Sombra during visit.
Rio de Janeiro, Sanatório de
Curicica, Feb. 25, 2019.
Mello, Ennes Silveira de. Testimony to
Fausto Sombra. São Paulo, archi-
tect's residence, Feb. 6, 2018.
Mello, Ennes Silveira de. Testimony to
Fausto Sombra. São Paulo, elec-
tronic message, Nov. 22, 2019.
Nobre, Ana Luiza. Testimony to Fausto
Sombra. Salvador, V Enanparq,
Oct. 16, 2018.
Nobre, Ana Luiza. Testimony to Fausto
Sombra. Rio de Janeiro, elec-
tronic message, May 21, 2019.
Perdigão, João. Testimony to Fausto
Sombra. Belo Horizonte, elec-
tronic message, Apr. 10, 2019.
Rebello, Yopanan Conrado Pereira.
Testimony to Fausto Sombra.
São Paulo, engineer's office, Aug.
20, 2018.
Vieira, Monica Paciello. Testimony to
Fausto Sombra. Matosinhos,
Porto, electronic message, May
2, 2018.
Villà, Joan. Testimony in lecture. São
Paulo, FAU Mackenzie, Oct. 9,
2018.

Exhibitions

Amora, Ana, Claudio Brandão,
and Thaysa Malaquias(Cur.).
Exhibition *SB-100.* Rio de
Janeiro, FAU UFRJ, Aug. 19/Jun.
20, 2019.
Bernardes, Kykah, and Adriana
Caúla (Cur.). Exhibition *Sérgio
Bernardes 100 anos.* Rio de
Janeiro, Centro Carioca de
Design, Apr. 17/Jun. 01, 2019.
Bernardes, Kykah, and Adriana
Caúla (Cur.). Exhibition *Sérgio
Bernardes 100 anos.* Rio de
Janeiro, Museu Nacional Belas
Artes, Dec. 17, 2019/Mar. 14,
2020.
Guerra, Abilio, and Fausto Sombra
(Cur.) Exhibition *Três pavilhões
de Sérgio Bernardes.* São Paulo,
Centro Histórico e Cultural
Mackenzie, Sep. 18/Nov. 14,
2019.
Europalia Brasil (Cur.). Exhibition
*Sérgio Bernardes. Expo'58 –
Brazil Pavilion.* International
Arts Festival. Belgium, Atomium
Museum, Oct. 2011/Jan. 2012.
Serapião, Fernando, and Guilherme
Wisnik (Cur.). Exhibition *Infinito
vão: 90 anos de arquitetura
brasileira.* Matosinhos, Centro
Português de Arquitetura, Sep.
2018/Apr. 2019.
Serapião, Fernando, and Guilherme
Wisnik (Cur.). Exhibition *Infinito
vão: 90 anos de arquitetura
brasileira.* São Paulo, Sesc 24
de Maio, Nov. 25, 2020/Jun. 27,
2021.

Films and Videos

Bernardes, feature-lenght docu-
mentary, 1h31', Rio de Janeiro,
2014. Directed by Gustavo
Gama Rodrigues and Paulo de
Barros. Story line by Thiago
Bernardes. Produced by 6D
Filmes e Rinoceronte Produções.
Co-produced by GNT.
Entre Morros e Mares, short-length
documentary, 24'25", Rio de
Janeiro, 2011. Concept and
screenwriting by Ana Luiza
Nobre. Direction and photog-
raphy by Tiago Rios. Production
by Leticia Pires. Produced by
PUC-Rio and Faperj <https://bit.
ly/3xDqrTB>.
O vigilante rodoviário. Episode
34 – A repórter. TV Tupi, São
Paulo, 1961-1962 <https://bit.
ly/3gFe13K>.

Consulted Collections

Acervo Digital Estadão (digital) / news-
paper *O Estado de S. Paulo*
Gaston Schoukens Family Collection,
Atomium Museum, Heysel /
document and model
Acervo Família Sérgio Bernardes /
document and project
Acervo Folha (digital) / newspapers
Folha da Manhã and *Folha de
S. Paulo*
MoMA New York Collection (digital)
/ catalog
Acervo NPD FAU UFRJ / Fundo Sérgio
Bernardes
Arquivo Histórico Wanda Svevo,
Fundação Bienal de São Paulo /
document and photo
Biblioteca Faculdade de Arquitetura
e Urbanismo e Design,
Universidade Federal de
Uberlândia / thesis

Biblioteca Faculdade de Arquitetura e
Urbanismo, Universidade Federal
do Rio de Janeiro / dissertation
and thesis

Biblioteca Faculdade de Arquitetura
e Urbanismo, Universidade
Presbiteriana Mackenzie (physical and digital) / magazine,
book, dissertation and thesis

Biblioteca Nacional Digital,
Fundação Biblioteca Nacional /
Fundamentos, Manchete and *O Cruzeiro* magazines

Bibliotecas Faculdade de Arquitetura
e Urbanismo, Universidade de
São Paulo / (Physical and digital)
/ magazine, book, dissertation,
thesis and *Acrópole* magazine

Centro de Documentação Corporativo
– CEDOC / Companhia
Siderúrgica Nacional – CSN

Portal Vitruvius / *Arquitextos, Drops,
Minha Cidade, Projetos,
Resenhas Online* magazines

Visited Works and Dates

Aeroporto Castro Pinto, 1981, João
Pessoa, Paraíba, May 19-20,
2018.

Casa dos Passarinhos, 1960 (restored
by Estúdio América, 2014-2015),
Pacaembu, São Paulo, Sep. 21,
2019.

Casa Jayme Souza Dantas, 1960s,
Jardins, São Paulo, Dec. 5, 2019.

Casa Mansur, 1994 (originally
Cincinato Cajado Braga, 1952),
Jardim Guedala, São Paulo, Sep.
19, 2019.

Edifício Justus Wallerstein, 1953,
Copacabana, Rio de Janeiro, Nov.
8, 2021.

Espaço Cultural José Lins do Rêgo,
1980, João Pessoa, Paraíba, May
20, 2018.

Hotel Tambaú, 1966-1970, João
Pessoa, Paraíba, May 19-20,
2018.

Palácio da Abolição, 1960-70, and
Mausoléu Castelo Branco, 1972,
Meireles, Fortaleza, Nov. 14,
2020.

Pavilhão da Companhia Siderúrgica
Nacional (remaining bridge),
1954-1955, Parque Ibirapuera,
São Paulo, Oct. 12, 2016; Jul. 11,
2017; Feb. 3, 2019.

Brazil Pavilion at the Brussels Universal
and International Exhibition
(site where the building was
installed), 1957-1958, Heysel,
Parc de Laeken, Brussels, Aug.
6, 2019.

Pavilhão da Feira Internacional da
Indústria e Comércio, 1957-
1960, Campo de São Cristóvão,
Rio de Janeiro, Dec. 22, 2017;
Sep. 11, 2019.

Sanatório de Curicica, 1949-1951,
Jacarepaguá, Rio de Janeiro, Jan.
25, 2019.

About the author
Fausto Sombra is an architect and
urban planner (Belas Artes, 2002),
holds a master's degree (FAU
Mackenzie, 2015, with a Fapesp scholarship) and a PhD (FAU Mackenzie,
2020, with a Capes scholarship). He
attended the master's program "El
Proyecto: aproximaciones a la arqui-
tectura desde el medio ambiente
histórico y social" (UPC Barcelona,
2008). He participated in various
commemorative actions for the centenary of Sérgio Bernardes' birth and
co-curated, with Abilio Guerra, the
exhibition *Three Pavilions by Sérgio
Bernardes*, held at the Mackenzie
Historical and Cultural Center (São
Paulo, Sep./Nov. 2019). In partnership
with Abilio Guerra, he is the author
of the text "Avenida Paulista, 1951:
scenario of the 1st São Paulo Biennial,"
an article that opens the book *Bienal
de São Paulo since 1951*, organized by
Paulo Miyada. He is currently the coordinator of the buildings department at
Bernardes Arquitetura office (2021–).

Romano Guerra Editora
Rua General Jardim 645 cj 31
01223-011 São Paulo SP Brasil
rg@romanoguerra.com.br
www.romanoguerra.com.br

Nhamerica Platform
807 E 44th St
Austin, TX, 78751 USA
editors@nhamericaplatform.com
www.nhamericaplatform.com

Cover image
Brazilian Pavilion, sketch, Parc de
Laeken, Brussels Expo 1958. Sérgio
Bernardes Collection – Memory Project
/ Bernardes Architecture Office

Support

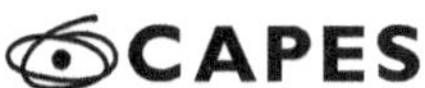

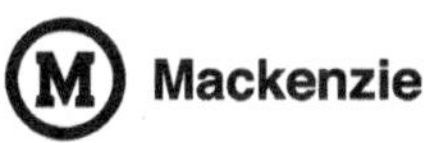

Acknowledgements
Bernardes Arquitetura (Antonia
and Thiago Bernardes, Nuno Costa
Nunes, Marcia Santoro, Camila
Tariki, Dante Furlan, Francisco
Abreu, Thiago Moretti e Rafael de
Oliveira), FEG Brasil Construções
Metálicas (Leonardo de Souza),
Arquivo Wanda Svevo (Ana Paula
Marques), Acervo Centro Cultural
Fundação CSN – Cedoc (Edna C. da
Silva), Practica Maquetes (Carina
Freitas de Oliveira e Carlos Henrique
de Oliveira), Núcleo de Pesquisa e
Documentação FAU UFRJ – NPD
(Andres Passaro e Claudio Parucher
da Silva, in memoriam), Projeto
Memória / Bernardes Arquitetura
(Kykah Bernardes), Centro Histórico e
Cultural Mackenzie (Luciene Aranha
Abrunhosa e Helen Yara Altimeyer)

Gustavo Penna, Adalberto Retto
Junior, Adriana Caúla, Alexandre
Bahia Vanderlei, Ana Amora, Ana
Lucia Cerávalo, Ana Luiza Nobre,
André Nazareth, Angélica Benatti
Alvim, Anthony Wilkinson, Antonio
Carlos Barossi, Antonio Claudio
Pinto da Fonseca, Camila Ripani,
Celso Brando, Charles Plaigin, Daniel
Vivona, Dina Uliana, Ennes Silveira de
Mello, Gabriel Falcade, Helena Ayoub,
Helio Herbst, Jacqueline Aronis,
Joan Villà, João Pedro Backhauser,
João Perdigão, Karla Lopez Álvarez,
Lauro Cavalcanti, Luiz Guilherme
Rivera de Castro, Marcelo Dall'Acqua,
Marcio Sartorelli, Maria Arminda do
Nascimento Arruda, Mario Figueroa,
Mil de Kooning, Monica Paciello
Vieira, Murillo Boiabad, Paul Meurs,
Rafael Perrone, Ricardo Mattos,
Rodrigo Queiroz, Rosa Katchuian,
Thaysa Malaquias, Yopanan Rabello

Edição impressa em português
Três pavilhões de Sérgio Bernardes
Fausto Sombra, 2023
ISBN 978-65-87205-21-2
(Romano Guerra)
ISBN 978-1-946070-51-7
(Nhamerica)

Edição impressa em inglês
Three Pavilions by Sérgio Bernardes
Fausto Sombra, 2023
ISBN 978-65-87205-25-0
(Romano Guerra)
ISBN 978-1-946070-53-1
(Nhamerica)

Edição ebook em português
Três pavilhões de Sérgio Bernardes
Fausto Sombra, 2023
ISBN 978-65-87205-22-9
(Romano Guerra)
ISBN 978-1-946070-52-4
(Nhamerica)

Edição ebook em inglês
Three Pavilions by Sérgio Bernardes
Fausto Sombra, 2023
ISBN 978-65-87205-24-3
(Romano Guerra)
ISBN 978-1-946070-54-8
(Nhamerica)

Sombra, Fausto
**Three Pavilions by Sérgio Bernardes
Contribution to the Brazilian
Modern Architectural Avant-Garde**
in the Mid-20th Century
Fausto Sombra
Foreword
Abilio Guerra
Afterword
Gustavo Penna

1ª edição   São Paulo, SP:
            Romano Guerra;
1st edition Austin, TX:
            Nhamerica Platform
            2023

352 p. il.
(Latin America: Thoughts: Brasil, 9)

ISBN 978-65-87205-25-0
Romano Guerra
ISBN 978-1-946070-53-1
Nhamerica

1. Bernardes, Sérgio 1919-2002
2. Pavilions for Exhibitions
3. Architects - Brazil - 20th Century
4. Modern Architecture - Rio de Janeiro - 20th Century

I   Guerra, Abilio
II Penna, Gustavo
III Title

CDD 725.91

Catalog sheet prepared by librarian
Dina Elisabete Uliana – CRB-8/3760